SPENSER STUDIES

XV

SPENSER STUDIES

A Renaissance Poetry Annual
XV

EDITED BY

Anne Lake Prescott   *Thomas P. Roche, Jr.*
William A. Oram

AMS PRESS
NEW YORK

SPENSER STUDIES
A RENAISSANCE POETRY ANNUAL

edited by

Anne Lake Prescott, Thomas P. Roche, Jr., and William A. Oram

is published annually by AMS Press, Inc. as a forum for Spenser scholarship and criticism and related Renaissance subjects. Manuscripts must be double-spaced, including notes, which should be grouped at the end and should be prepared according to *The Chicago Manual of Style*. Authors of essay-length manuscripts should include an abstract of 100-175 words and provide a Windows-Compatible disk version of the article. One copy of each manuscript should be sent to Thomas P. Roche, Jr., Department of English, Princeton University, Princeton, NJ 08544, one copy to Anne Lake Prescott, Department of English, Barnard College, Columbia University, 3009 Broadway, New York, NY 10027-6598, and one copy to William A. Oram, Department of English, Smith College, Northampton, Mass. 01063

ISSN 0195-9468
Volume XV, ISBN 0-404-19215-7

Contents

SUSANNE WOODS

Making Free with Poetry:
Spenser and the Rhetoric of Choice

Milton is generally credited as the champion of individual liberty, but his acknowledged master Spenser provided Milton with his first model for a poetry that values and seeks to extend human freedom. Spenser claims throughout his work that making true poetry is an exercise in freedom and an invitation to the free spirit. Despite the imperial ideal Spenser derives from Virgil and from Elizabethan colonial aspirations, ideas of freedom wash through key portions of his work, moving across intersections of social hierarchy, law, religion, love, and English identity. He employs traditional limited definitions of freedom as "not slavery" and "generosity of spirit," but extends them to include the poet's right to speak freely. In *Mother Hubberds Tale* and throughout *The Faerie Queene* Spenser can be found subverting stated assumptions about hierarchy and governance, and redefining freedom as knowledgeable choice and a condition for virtue. His rhetorical technique is to show and invite rather than tell and exhort, in keeping with the Protestant focus on the individual. This vision and technique culminate in Book VI, which presents the most direct encounter between poet and his courtly reader. Here, particularly in the Mt. Acidale episode, Spenser presents his vision of freedom most clearly as a paradox of revelation through disguise and invitation through instruction.

*I*N SPENSER'S *Teares of the Muses* lyric Euterpe is given eleven stanzas, as opposed to each of her sisters' ten, to lament the ignorance and barbarity of contemporary letters. Her case is particularly hard, it would seem, since she goes not only from joy to sorrow, summer to winter, but from freedom to oppression:

. . . we, that earst were wont in sweet accord
All places with our pleasant notes to fill,
Whilest favourable times did us afford
Free libertie to chaunt our charmes at will:
All comfortlesse upon the bared bow,
Like wofull Culvers doo sit wayling now.

(241–46)[1]

"Stonie coldnesse" (253), and "hellish horrour Ignorance" (259), we
are told, have overwhelmed the "free llibertie" of the true singers,
and have "trampled" (275) "The sacred springs of horsefoot *Helicon*"
(271). Pegasus by a sacred stream and a bird whose free voice offers
songs that are chants, carminas that are magic charms, bring free will
and sacred poesy together if only in laments of absence and oppression. Conventional as these ideas may seem, Spenser underscores
here, as he does variously throughout his work, that making true
poetry is an exercise in freedom and an invitation to the free spirit.

Milton is the poet we generally credit as the champion of individual liberty who led English-speaking culture to its rhetoric of freedom. Yet in the context of his greatest argument on behalf of a free
press, Milton praises "our sage and serious Poet Spencer," as in one
his earliest theological tracts he credits the *May* eclogue with anticipating "these reforming times."[2] Even the conservative Dryden insisted that "Milton was the Poetical Son of Spencer," adding the
personal testimony that "Milton has acknowledged to me, that Spencer was his Original."[3]

Critics occasionally pause over republican Milton's adulation of
imperialist Spenser, only to move on to agendas that focus on such
things as the two poets' common sources. More recently, however,
thoughtful critics such as John King, who has taught us the subtlety
and complexity of Spenser's Protestant poetics, Susanne Wofford,
who shows how the *Faerie Queene's* characters make uncompelled
moral choices, and Richard Hardin, who emphasizes Spenser's devotion to law over imperial pronouncement, have revealed strategies
and ideas in Spenser that make the earlier poet a much clearer "original" for the later.[4] If Milton, as I believe, succeeded in defining and
inviting a concept of freedom as knowledgeable choice that would
inform British Whig politics ultimately infusing Anglo-American
cultural self-definitions, Spenser provided him with his first model
for this ambitious and eventually successful enterprise.

Determined to establish an England worthy of Augustan Rome,
and model himself on Virgil, Spenser's laureate ambition led him to

serve his state and glorify his culture. But like Virgil and Chaucer before and Milton after him, to serve and glorify meant also to challenge and define. Despite the imperial ideal, ideas of freedom wash through key portions of his work, moving across intersections of social hierarchy, law, religion, love, and English identity. For the most part those ideas may be predictably arranged according to sixteenth-century definitions of freedom: a "free" person was neither a slave nor a prisoner, and was therefore physically unconfined and capable of personal agency. The Fox and the Ape in *Mother Hubberds Tale* want to walk about "like two free men," and "wander free/ Whereso us listeth" (ll. 161, 168–69). To be free is to be uncompelled, as in Hellenore's longing "to be free from hard restraint and gealous feares" (3.9.4). Freedom is also associated with generosity and liberality of spirit, as the heavens "favourable were and free" in the gifts of nature they bestowed on Britomart (3.6.2). In general, though, freedom is mainly conceived as the precondition for human agency, and therefore as the moral and efficient basis for all choices.

What does it mean, though, for Euterpe to claim the Muses once had "free libertie," or for Spenser to send his *Shepheardes Calendar* forth with a "free passeporte"? I want to examine particularly how Spenser presents the relationship between poetry and freedom, inviting his gentlemen and noble persons not only to virtuous and gentle discipline, but to a vision of personal freedom that incorporates and challenges the religious and political debates of his time.

Spenser did not envision John Milton, whatever Milton in a Bloomian moment may have thought, but he did read and draw from both classical and vernacular models. Among the latter was the popular complaint tradition, which he used early to show his sophistication by drawing from Petrarch and Du Bellay. Like some of us who cut our teeth on Sartre and Camus and were tempted by Derrida and Foucault, but loop back to simpler moralists like George Orwell and the English tradition that assumes language carries meaning and has consequences, Spenser returns from his flirtation with the continental Renaissance to pseudo-Chaucerian archaisms and an unacknowledged debt to the most popular narrative of his own youth, *The Mirror for Magistrates*.[5]

Spenser would need to seek no further than the *Mirror* to find traditional English attitudes toward the world's vanity and the ruins of time, of which his *Complaints* provides his own ample compendium. But the *Mirror* also glosses the quote with which I began. Its one tragic story about a poet, "Howe Collingbourne was cruelly executed for making a foolishe rime," claims free speech as an ancient privilege of poets. "The Poet Collingbourne," as it is usually called,

purports to be in the voice of a rhymer who penned a riddle that
enraged that favorite Tudor villain, Richard III:

> The Cat, the Rat, and Lovel our Dog,
> Do rule al England, under a Hog.

(69–70)

The doggerel rime, and the relative lowliness of the poet compared
with the aristocratic norm of the *Mirror's* other ghostly protagonists,
at first makes this tale seem like comic relief, but a poet who writes
about the execution of a poet is not apt to maintain the humor. And
the ghost's arguments turn out to be interesting. Although Collingbourne acknowledges that his rime *was* a criticism of Catesby, Rat-
cliffe, Lovel, and the king, he justifies himself by invoking intention
and tradition: he meant to show off his wit in the cause of warning
those at fault, he explains, and poets, in the tradition of Horace, have
a special right to exercise their wit freely:

> Theyr lawles dealynges al men dyd lament,
> And so dyd I, and therfore made the rymes
> To shewe my wyt, howe well I could invent,
> To warne withal the careles of theyr crymes,
> I thought the freedome of the auncient tymes
> Stoode styll in force. . . .
> Belyke no tyrantes were in Horace dayes,
> And therefore Poetes freely blamed vyce.

(92–100)

Further, since he names "no man outryght But ryddle wise" his
utterance cannot be taken as treasonous speaking. Even if it is not
legal to charge those in power directly with their tyrannies, the cloak
of riddle, indirect speech, and metaphorical discourse grant certain
long-acknowledged permissions. The poet clothes his criticism in
riddle and metaphor both to be safe from the charge of directly
criticizing those in power, and as a traditionally recognized vehicle
for precisely such criticism. He associates the rights of the poet with
the rights of a lawyer pleading the law against the arbitrary tyrannies
of rule by the monarch's fickle will:

> I thought the Poetes auncient liberties

Had bene allowed plea at any barre.
I had forgot howe newfound tyrannies
With ryght and freedome were at open warre,
That lust was lawe, that myght dyd make and mar.

(197–201)

The wise and learned, he goes on to explain, can tell the difference
between genuine argument, whether at law or in poetry, and can
dismiss the inept or outrageous for the nonsense it is. This is the
germ of Milton's argument for a free press in *Areopagitica*.

Collingbourne himself was viciously executed, as he reports, with
great pain and indignity. He complains that the suffering he endured
was excessive "for this trespas smal" (130) and that condemning a
writer's words without examining his intention is unfair. The "auncient freedome" of free exchange of ideas

   ought not be debarred
From any wyght that speaketh ought, or wryteth.
The authours meanyng should of ryght be heard,
He knoweth best to what ende he endyteth:
Wordes sometyme beare more than the hart behiteth.

(211–15)

All expression, but especially the poet's, is capable of multiple interpretation; the poet should at least be granted a fair hearing on his
true meaning and intention.

With the same balance between complaint and irony that infuses
the whole, the poem concludes with Collingbourne's ghostly admonition to other poets:

Warne poetes therfore not to passe the bankes
Of Hellicon, but kepe them in the streames,
So shall their freedome save them from extreames.

(278–80)

The wit here provides a moderately dense example of what it urges.
By staying inexplicit, in the literary and metaphorical streams of Helicon, poets will have the freedom to pursue their calling without
suffering *in extremis*, as Collingbourne himself did. So, too, will the

bounds of the literary occupation keep the poet in his right calling, and away from extreme raving or perhaps the extremes of inappropriate political involvement. Riddle and metaphor hide, reveal, contain, and liberate, all at the same time. The author of *The Shepheardes Calendar, Mother Hubberds Tale,* and *The Faerie Queene* understood very well disguise and revelation, entertainment and admonition.

But if poets ought to have "Free libertie to chaunt [their] charmes at will," what did that mean in the Protestant and imperial world in which Spenser lived and for which he wrote? Certainly political freedom in the modern sense was an alien concept, and free will was a centrally contested issue of the Reformation.

Order and obedience are the first foundations of freedom for the Elizabethans, as the Queen's homilists everywhere insisted.[6] Whatever the poet's perception of "auncient liberties" for fictive discourse, freedom for the Elizabethan was largely the citizen's right to participate, under the law, in affirming and maintaining public order.[7] As freemen, as the English almost universally asserted themselves to be in contrast to continental "villeins," Englishmen had agency, the ability to choose and act, with which they were encouraged to act magnanimously for the public good. Freedom becomes a presumed prerequisite to both personal and civic virtue. In *The Faerie Queene,* as throughout *Paradise Lost,* virtue is frequently depicted as right choice, particularly in the face of temptation. Choice depends first on autonomy, or sovereignty over the self, but since it also depends on knowledge, the acquired knowledge of a serious humanist allows more freedom than the sovereignty acquired by high birth alone.[8] The humanist meritocracy, beginning as early as Skelton and continuing through Milton (for whom "knowledge" and "merit" were loaded words) tended to subvert stated assumptions about hierarchy and governance, and reinforce the notion of freedom as knowledgeable choice and as a condition for virtue.

Reformation debates over the freedom of the will complicate the issue. Protestant theologians were virtually unanimous in their rejection of postlapsarian free will. In 1524 Erasmus presented free will as a condition for human choice and salvation, defining it as "the power of the human will whereby man can apply to or turn away from that which leads to eternal salvation."[9] Luther responded vigorously in 1525, insisting that free will was forever lost through original sin, and only God's gift of grace, mysteriously dispensed to the elect, allowed for salvation: While man may have movement and appear to have choice, Luther says, "with regard to God, and in all things pertaining to salvation and damnation, man has no free will, but is a captive, servant, and bondslave, either to the will of God, or to the will of Satan."[10] Where, then, is human agency and choice? Where is freedom? The simple answer is that it remains in the natural man even as it is no longer possible for the spiritual man. You can make any choice, that is, except your own salvation.

Of course salvation by faith alone was never intended to justify human inaction. As Elizabeth's early apologist, John Jewel (or rather, as his translator, Lady Anne Bacon) expressed it in 1563: "Now although we say we have no confidence in our workes and doynges, and doe grounde the whole course of our salvation in Christ onely, neverthelesse we say not therupon that we may live loosly and wantonly, as thoe it were inough for a Christian man to be dipped onely in the water and beleve, and that nothing els is to be looked for at his hande. Trew faith is lively and can not be idell."[11]

How this is possible comes perhaps most clearly from Spenser's contemporary William Perkins, a former Catholic and a Protestant apologist whom Milton much admired. Perkins distinguished between our physicial and ethical agency, which we retain, and our spiritual agency, which original sin has lost us absolutely: "Humane actions are such as are common to all men good and badd, as to speake and use reason, the practice of all mechanicall and liberall artes, and the outward performance of Civill and Ecclesiasticall duties, as to come to the Church, to speake and preach the word, to reach out the hand to receive the Sacrament, and to lend the eare to listen outwardly to that which is taught. And hither we may refer the outward actions of civill vertues: as namely Justice, temperaunce, gentlenes, and liberalitie. And in these also we join with Rome and say (as experience teacheth) that men have a naturall freedome of the will, to put them or not to put them in execution."[12]

The disagreement with the Catholics, Perkins goes on to claim, is whether a man (I use his term) has any power whatsoever to contribute to his own salvation. "The Church of Rome sets forth the estate of a sinner by the condition of a prisoner, and so doe we: marke then the difference. It supposeth the said prisoner to lie bound hand and foote with chaines and fetters, and withall to bee sicke and weake, yet not wholly dead but living in part: it supposeth also that being in this case, he stirreth not himself for any helpe, and yet hath abilitie and power to stirre. Hereupon if the keeper come and take away his bolts and fetters, and hold him by the hand, and helpe him up, hee can and will of himselfe stand and walke and goe out of prison. . . . We in like manner graunt, that a prisoner fitly resemb[l]eth a naturall man, but yet such a prisoner must he bee, as is not only sicke and weake, but even stark dead: which cannot stir though the keeper untie his boltes and chanes, nor heare though hee sound a trumpet in his eare: and if the said keeper would have him to moove and stirre, he must give him not onely his hand to helpe him, but even soule and life also."[13]

Spenser follows these assumptions in *The Faerie Queene*. Red Crosse Knight is very like the prisoner who can do nothing on behalf of his own salvation. The dramatic moments—the fights with Error and Despair, and the ultimate contest with the dragon Satan, in which the Knight is twice visibly dead, each require divine intercession. On his own, Red Cross Knight's decisions are disasters. Who would believe that Fidessa nonsense, anyway? Spenser's answer is that we all would—we cannot help ourselves.

But after we get *that* out of the way—after our gentleman or noble person is presumed, that is, to be saved by grace and destined for eternity after all—we may and do turn to those areas of our daily lives for which even Protestant discourse grants us judgment and agency, grants us, in fact, free will. But like the prisoner whose will is free only within the confines of his cell and the routine imposed on him, Spenser's agents still live in a fallen and limited world. If the poet has a special freedom, a right and responsibility to warn and interpret, a synesthetic vision of horse-footed Helicon and the free libertie to chaunt his charmes at will, what vision of freedom does he give us, and how does he entice us not only to accept it, but enact it?

Spenser negotiates two paradoxes to develop his idea of freedom. The first, which has long been understood as central to his method, is to reveal by hiding—whether it is under cover of pastoral, fable, allegory, or simple metaphor. The rhetorical and linguistic properties of these techniques are complex and fascinating, forming the core of literary interpretation from the Greeks to the post-Modernists. For simplicity, I will call all these techniques the language of disguise. Following the poet Collingbourne safely into the streams of Helicon, Spenser is a rich and avowed user of the language of disguise, famously with his "Allegory, or darke conceit," the "historicall fiction" by which he escapes the confinement, among other things, of the "envy, and suspition of present time" ("Letter," Smith ed., 2:485).

Disguise not only allows the poet freedom to venture heterodox ideas, it also insists upon interpretation, on the reader's exercise of judgment. This is the second paradox at the heart of Spenser's approach to freedom: language which requires systematic decrypting necessarily demands that the reader make choices. Spenser, and this is very like Milton after him, seeks to educate his readers into making their own knowledgeable choices, which in turn frees the reader from inevitably accepting the poet's (or any one else's) direction.

The Faerie Queene begins by warning the reader about the author's own methods. In Book I, richly allegorical though it is, disguise itself is always bad. Archimago's holy hermit and false Red Cross and Duessa's Fidessa are emblems of the impenetrability of evil in a wicked world. The grace of Arthur's revealing shield and Una's intervention at key moments invite the reader to recognize that Holiness cannot be earned, and human choices cannot contribute toward salvation. In this world, freedom is an illusion. The character described as most "free" in this context is the unhappily condemned Sir Terwin, whose freedom, like Arthur's "liberty," has been trumped by love (I.ix.10; I.ix.27). For Arthur, the result is a quest. For Sir Terwin, it is despair and death. Despair himself, while not disguised, is a hidden and hiding character. He lurks in a "darkesome cave," his long "griesie lockes" hide his face (I.ix.35). His language is rich with "suddeine wit," masterful rhetoric that invites Red Cross to interpret metaphor in Despair's terms: "Sleep after toyle, port after stormie seas,/Ease after warre, death after life does greatly please" (I.ix.40). If Una did not snatch the knife away from him, Red Cross would fall into the fatal mistake of interpreting wrongly. Where salvation is concerned mankind is enslaved and there are no choices.

In Book II the world changes from impenetrable evil to measurable deceptions. Guyon represents a temperance continually asked to interpret language, gestures, and the physical world. He is much more successful than Red Cross Knight, though not perfect. Accompanied by the Palmer, who we generally agree represents a God-given reason, though not salvation, he is able to adjust to changing circumstances, to bind Furor and Occasion (and resist them unbound), and to triumph over the irascible and concupiscible passions, represented by Pyrocles and Cymochles. Separated from the Palmer, he still resists the riches of the world in the Cave of Mammon, seeing past the temptations and deceptions to the end:

> . . . he was warie wise in all his way,
> And well perceived his [Mammon's] deceiptfull sleight,
> Ne suffred lust his safetie to betray,
> So goodly did beguile the Guyler of the prey.
>
> (II.vii.64)

Like Red Cross confronting Despair, Guyon survives the temptations and deceptions of a cave dweller, but unlike Red Cross, he is entirely his own agent. The result is not a near-escape from death and damnation, but exhaustion. It is possible for natural man to read the false world rightly, but not possible for him to survive its wickedness without a great natural toll, as Arthur's rescue and the Castle of Alma illustrate and explain. In Book II, Spenser invites his readers to become confident interpreters, only to underscore the limits of human nature. Aware of those limits, and again redeemed by grace, we go on to tell the false beauty from the true, and to resist the false art that changes our natures from human to bestial.

Books III and IV turn from impenetrable evil and resistable wrong desires to the distorting fantasies of love. Neither Satan nor the fallen world deceive us here, but only our own longing to create and form bonds. In Books I and II we must learn to see past outward deception and tame the wickedness around us; in Books III and IV we must learn to sift the fantasies and tame the monsters of our minds. Freedom comes not from reading past the disguise, but from becoming disguised. As Britomart hides her gender and Arthegall his courtly nature, they express deeper truths (of Britomart's armor of chastity, Arthegall's natural power). Britomart, especially, uses her disguise to rest in her world but not be of it, distracted in neither Book, for example, by beauty's chase.

Books II, III, and V may seem to have the most to say about freedom in conventional terms. Book II is about knowledgeable choice that can see and avoid the extremes, Book III about seeing and choosing rightly in the face of love's deceptions, and Book V would seem to have most to do with issues of civil liberty. However civil liberty, in Milton's terms, scarcely appears in Spenser's book of Justice, but the continuing contradictions of bondage and choice, disguise and revelation, permeate this book as much as the others. Arthegall sees past Radigund's armor to a physical beauty that disguises her real danger, a complex misreading that forces him into slavery, expressed through ignominious disguise as he languishes, captive, in women's clothes. There is much more about gender that might make us pause here and throughout Book V, but here I will simply underscore that Arthegall in drag loses his public agency, as Britomart in armor gains it.

If Books II, III, and V appear on the surface to be more about ideas of individual freedom (or their absence) in the wood of this world, Books I, IV, and VI are more about relationships and grace, and I turn to examples from each of these that show Spenser using poetry to illustrate and invite unexpected kinds of freedom.

The Protestant world of Book I shows a will in bondage, brought
to new life only through grace. If this were not clear enough from
Red Cross Knight's constant misjudgements about himself and everyone else, we see it even in his experience of grace in the house of
holiness. You recall that there Penaunce teaches him to see his sins,
and Mercie ("both gratious, and eke liberall" I.x.34) gives him the
tour of the holy Hospitall. The seven Bead-men demonstrate the
simple virtues of Christian behavior, concluding with ministrations
to widows and orphans, supplying their needs and giving to them
"ever free" (I.x.43) From these demonstrations Mercie hands our
hero over to Charissa who teaches him "godly worke of Almes and
charitee" (I.x.45). After all this he is brought to the height of Contemplation's holy hermitage, an acute contrast both to Archimego's
lowly false hermitage and Despair's cave. The Hermit gives Red
Cross an understanding of his election and destiny, and a vision of
the New Jerusalem. Surely, now he is saved, now he can know, now
he can be free, through this lavish outpouring of grace.

But no. The main thing the vision does for him is make him want
to quit life, right now:

O let me not (quoth he) then turne againe
Backe to the world, whose joyes so fruitlesse are;
But let me here for aye in peace remaine,
Or streight way on that last voyage fare.

(I.x.63)

The Hermit must again correct him and remind him of his responsibilities. In Canto 11 he must repeatedly die and be born again. In
Canto 12, all his quest accomplished, he must still confront the de-
ceivers of the world, Archimago and Duessa, and, betrothed to Una
as he may be, continue on his earthly quest.

Grace in Book I is a continuous process that upholds and gives
life to the dead prisoner, and by which the disguised world must
continually be interpreted for the blind, fallen soul. Una must explain
Error's cave, though Red Cross will still be prone to foolhardy assaults. The Hermit reveals the new Jerusalem, which Red Cross could
not otherwise see and in any case which he cannot quite read correctly even with his visionary guide. Freedom in Book I is a function
of grace, poetry, and interpretation, but all three are an ongoing
process. If any should fail—divine intervention, word, or revelation—life would fail, the will would be useless, and William Perkins's
prisoner would fall back to his deathlike swoon.

By contrast, grace and freedom in Book IV are functions of earthly relationships, however magically presented. Just as Triamond incorporates and then expends the power of his brothers in order to be free from danger and free to love, every character gains the power of choice from the bonds of relationship. Consider an instance in which a bond is broken, an example that also serves to illustrate how Spenser invites the reader to judge a complex situation, and then devises an image of poetic freedom to free both character and reader from an emotionally confining dilemma.

In Canto 7 Belphoebe discovers Timias, in whose keep she had left the wounded Amoret, all too eager to assuage the darling girl's pain.

> There she him found by that new lovely mate,
> Who lay the whiles in swoune, full sadly set,
> From her faire eyes wiping the deawy wet,
> Which softly stild, and kissing them atweene,
> And handling soft the hurts, which she did get.
>
> (IV.vii.35)

At this point it scarcely matters that Amoret is Belphoebe's long lost twin, or, as the earlier reference to tobacco (III.v.32) and Spenser's friendship with Ralegh invite us to assume, that this is an allegory of the Queen's displeasure with Ralegh, probably over his marriage in 1592 to Elizabeth Throckmorton. As readers we are invited to see the scene and invest our own judgment, exercise our own freedom of interpretation, on the characters' reactions. A love-starved Timias has encountered the more submissive twin, which has challenged his devotion to the virginal Belphoebe. Or is it all a misunderstanding? The moral weight seems initially with Belphoebe, given the value of constancy and all the fuss in Book III about Timias's willingness to serve Belphoebe, even though their only progeny will be good deeds. As in so many of the unglossed narratives of *The Faerie Queene*, the reader is forced to evaluate the evidence and choose the appropriate interpretation and its related moral stance.

Here, I would say, Timias has indeed let his affection stray, and Belphoebe's anger, if extreme, is at least partially justified. Like King David, though, Timias can repent magnificently. When Arthur happens upon his former squire, finding him filled with penitence, more than a little mad, and obsessed with the name Belphoebe, which he has carved "on every tree," the magnificent Prince is unable to reason with him. Deprived of the salvific role we have come to expect, Arthur leaves Timias to recover at his own pace.

The cure comes not through heroic action, but through a delicate image, not through physical but poetic agency. Timias finds himself accompanied by a sweetly singing turtle dove, whose "mournefull muse/ . . . much did ease his mourning and misfare" (IV.viii.5). Somewhat renewed, he begins to sift through his "miniments," and finds a gift he received from Belphoebe "whilst goodly grace she did him shew." It was

A ruby of right perfect hew
Shap'd like a heart, yet bleeding of the wound,
And with a little golden chaine about it bound.

(IV.viii.6)

When he ties this token on the dove, she flies away to the beloved and entices Belphoebe back to Timias. The bird, perpetual symbol of freedom and poetry, negotiates a rebonding that frees the abandoned spirit from the bondage of pain. We courtly sophisticates may see here a little allegory of Ralegh's mournful poetry inviting the queen to renew her favor, but the images of poetry and freedom resonate much more widely. Like the the holy spirit who creates and confirms the divine relationship, who announced God's pleasure in Jesus at his baptism and, for Milton, "dove-like sat'st brooding o'er the vast abyss/ And mad'st it pregnant," reconciliation and re-creation are disguised as a bird who evokes the agency of poetry.

Book VI presents the most direct encounter between poet and his courtly reader, where we can most easily see Spenser's doctrine of freedom as a paradox of revelation through disguise and invitation through instruction. Book VI is arguably the least disguised of all the books. While allegorical figures still abound, characters and figures are largely what they seem. Their situations, however, are not. Mirabella's captivity seems a ready opportunity for Arthur's saving power:

Now Lady sith your fortunes thus dispose,
That if ye list have liberty, ye may,
Unto your selfe I freely leave to chose,
Whether I shall you leave, or from these villains lose.

(VI.viii.29)

She uses this gift of free will to choose her continuing bondage. Too much liberty has led her to scorn love, and now she must endure disdain and scorn until a fully mature penitence will release her to appropriate bonds of love. Spenser makes much of Mirabella's lowly parentage, which typically signifies a baser nature than the gentlemen and noble persons who are the poet's presumed readers. Yet Arthur's gift of freedom and Mirabella's choice of penance suggest that low birth is no hinderance to free choice, nor to choosing morally. Courtesy itself, that flower on a lowly stalk, comes from virtue, and "vertues seat is deepe within the mynd,/And not in outward shows, but inward thoughts defynd" (VI.proem.5). Virtue, as in its masculinist Latin original, is power, and even the low-born has the power to choose and choose rightly.

Calidore's adventure on Mt. Acidale is above all the encounter of the courtly reader with the poet engaged in his craft. I once thought, and wrote, that this signature episode confirmed Spenser's intent to close his allegorical epic romance after six books. I now view it differently, as the poet handing his reader not only the basic tools for interpretation, but an invitation to interpret freely.

Attracted to pastoral otium, Calidore takes a break from his exhausting chase of the Blatant Beast and immerses himself in the freedom of the low born. He falls in love with Pastorella, gets a lesson in pastoral values from her putative father, Meliboe, insults Pastorella's suitor Coridon with condescending praise, and stumbles into, and ruins, Colin Clout's moment of inspiration. If Calidore had maintained his peep show posture, hiding in the woods, he might have looked at naked ladies and enjoyed Colin's playing indefinitely. But he is driven to understand the beauty that he sees, "Therefore resolving, what it was, to know,/Out of the wood he rose, and toward them did go" (VI.x.17). The vision vanishes and a furious Colin becomes the sixteenth-century version of Jimi Hendrix. If love and youth led Colin to break his pipe at the end of January, frustration with a courtier's bumbling intrusion does it at a more mature moment. In both cases, pastoral disguise invites the reader to interpret the feelings and values of a more sophisticated world, but here the stakes are much higher and the reader both a character in the story and his critic. We overhear, as we did in January, but we also overhear Calidore overhearing, and oversee what he sees, and are given the choice of whether to judge his intrusion as if it were our own.

Colin explains everything to Calidore, and this illusion of clarity is the greatest disguise of all. The Mt. Acidale episode functions almost as a parable. Here is the vision, and here is the courtier watching the vision, and when he invades the mysterious space of the poet the vision vanishes, and here's why. But the why—a story about graces and their origin and their service to Venus—tells us nothing, except that the poet may have reasons for his poetry beyond your personal edification. Jesus interprets the parable of the sower for his disciples, but the conclusion is as mysterious as the explanation—what does it mean for the righteous to shine like the sun, anyway (Mat. 13:43)? Without grace it will all be meaningless. Colin cannot explain grace; he can only describe its power and effects. The poet cannot, finally, force the fashioning of a gentleman or noble person; he can only draw a world and invite the reader to look. The reader makes choices in a world where the future is always disguised, and the Blatant Beast always runs wild.

In Book I, RCK represents the spiritual condition of the gentlemen and noble persons Spenser is seeking to fashion. He makes mistakes. His own choices are always blind and almost always bad. He cannot recover on his own, but the love of God, coming in the form of mercy and grace, saves him. In Books II-V, the various protagonists also make mistakes, but their choices are more visible and are often right. In Book VI Spenser's world of glass comes right up to our faces, even as we try to see through it, darkly. The poem seeks to stay within the banks of Helicon, Mt. Acidale's "gentle flud" by which the nimphs and fairies sit "tuning their accents fit." Like the "horsefooted Helicon" of Euterpe's nostalgia, this stream represents a world of freedom—*from* bondage, *to* action, *from* care, *to* love.

Spenser's poetry is his freedom, however exhausted with *The Faerie Queene* he reports himself to be in the *Amoretti*. His inventive verse forms are his freedom (to him blank verse was too bound by all those experiments with classical meters). His syncretic vision, unmediated by a single model or even a set of models, is his freedom. His various disguises, from metaphor to polyvalent allegories, are his freedom. He makes, and is, free with his poetry, which comes to us like Arthur's gift of choice to Mirabella. When, like Milton, Spenser creates a world whose value depends on the reader making knowledgeable choices, he also helps to create our freedom. The rest depends on grace.

Wheaton College

NOTES

1. Edmund Spenser, *Poetical Works*, ed. J. C. Smith and Ernest De Selincourt, (London and Oxford: Oxford University Press, 1912). All Spenser references are from this edition.

2. John Milton, *Complete Prose Works*, ed. Don M. Wolfe, Ernest Sirluck (New Haven: Yale University Press, 1959, 1953) 2:516, 1:722.

3. R. H. Cummings, ed. *Spenser: The Critical Heritage*, (New York: Barnes and Noble, 1971), 205.

4. John N. King, *Spenser's Poetry and the Reformation Tradition* (Princeton, Princeton University Press,: 1990); Susanne Lindgren Wofford, *The Choice of Achielles: The Ideology of Figure in the Epic* (Stanford: Stanford UP, 1992); Richard F. Hardin, *Civil Idolatry: Desacralizing and Monarchy in Spenser, Shakespeare, and Milton*, (Newark: University Delaware Press, 1992. See also Joseph Wittreich, *Interpreting Samson Agonistes*, (Princeton: Princeton UP, 1986), 257–58, and John Guillory, *Poetic Authority: Spenser, Milton, and Literary History*, (New York: Columbia University Press, 1983), 22, 73.

5. All citations are from Lily B. Campbell, ed. *The Mirror for Magistrates* (Cambridge: Cambridge University Press, 1938). This collection, ed. William Baldwin, originally appeared in 1559 and ran through seven additions by 1587. "The Poet Collingbourne," 347–58, first appeared in the second ed., 1563.

6. "An Exhortation concerning good Order and obedience, to rulers and Magistrates" was one of the standard sermons in the official book of Tudor sermons and homilies, originating in 1547 and added to in 1563 as *Certain Sermons appoynted by the Quenes Majesty, to be declared and read, by al Parsons, Vicars, and Curates, everi Sunday and holiday, in their Churches*, bound with *The seconde Tome of homelyes*. This quarto double volume was often reprinted until well into James I's reign, when it was published in folio as *Certaine Sermons or Homilies*, 1623. Most versions of *The second Tome* conclude with "An Homilie Against disobedience and wilfull rebellion," in five parts, first published separately around 1571. The first two parts of this extensive sermon show "the doctrine of the holye scriptures, as concerning obedience of true subjects to their princes, even as well to such as be evill, as unto the good." Parts 3 and 4 illustrate punishments rebels may expect from God, and part 5 warns against ambition and ignorance as the causes of rebellion.

7. See, e.g., Joel Hurstfield, *Freedom and Corruption in Elizabethan England* (London: Jonathan Cape, 1971), 11–76.

8. See, e.g., Sir Thomas Elyot's *Boke Named the Governour* (1531), where those with "understandynge" and "knowlege" "oughte to be set in a more highe place than the residue." A4–A4v, and *passim*.

9. Erasmus, *The Free Will*, in *Erasmus-Luther: Discourse on Free Will*. Tr. and ed. By Ernst F. Winter (New York: Continuum, 1999), 20.

10. Luther, *The Bondage of the Will*, in *Erasmus-Luther: Discourse on Free Will*, 113.

11. John Jewel. *An apologie, or aunswer in defence of the Church of England, concerning the state of religion used in the same*. London, 1563. "Newly set forth in Latin, and nowe translated into Englishe [by Ann Cooke, Lady Bacon], E2r.

12. William Perkins, *A Reformed Catholike* [1597] (1605 *Works*, Lll5r-Sss6v), Mmm2r.

13 Perkins, Mmm2v-Mmm3r.

KENNETH BORRIS

Flesh, Spirit, and the Glorified Body: Spenser's Anthropomorphic Houses of Pride, Holiness, and Temperance

Whereas Spenser's most extensive allegorical representation of the body, Alma's Castle, has been recently said to portray "the natural body" in contrast to "the mystical body" associated with Caelia's House of Holiness, Books I and II are profoundly interanimated. They share much the same conceptions of the body, soul, and human prospects, so that their heroes' exploits are fully complementary and the development of *The Faerie Queene* is cumulative. Anatomical, medical, and theological discourses and concerns are synthesized in both Books I and II, so that Spenser's representation of Lucifera's and Caelia's houses deals in part with the natural body, and his portrayal of Alma's domain depends on sanctification and related Pauline doctrines of the flesh, spirit, and glorified body. Although prior Spenser criticism affords little comment on the relevance of Elizabethan beliefs in bodily glorification, that is the ultimate physical ideal for humankind in *The Faerie Queene*. Alma's dominion not only constitutes a model for Temperance as it is to be pursued in life, but also Spenser's most full and detailed prefiguration of the finally transfigured somatic state, when the body would supposedly become spiritualized to the maximum extent possible, while yet remaining physical. Likewise, we should avoid imputing to *The Faerie Queene* sharp oppositions between nature, physicality, and the body on the one hand, and grace, spirit, and soul on the other; or between Books I and II, or Holiness and Temperance.

NOTIONS OF SHARP CONTRAST or contradiction between Books I and II of *The Faerie Queene* still largely spring from A. S. P.

Woodhouse's division of the poem according to two contrary orders, grace and nature: "Book I moves . . . on the religious level, or . . . with reference to the order of grace, and the remaining books . . . on the natural level only." Whereas "Redcrosse adheres to a spiritual ideal," James Nohrnberg similarly declares in his marvellous *Analogy of "The Faerie Queene,"* "Guyon adheres to a natural ideal—his is an earthly and physical excellence." Such views also appear in *The Spenser Encyclopedia* (1990), and Elizabeth Bieman's recent *Plato Baptized* urges "dismissal of Christian implication for purposes of Book 2." Yet for others, Spenser's Temperance is a Christian virtue pursued through the continuing process of sanctification, beyond the justification by faith treated in Book I. Hence *The Faerie Queene* is not a structurally and thematically broken-backed poem as in Woodhouse's kind of view, which opposes Book I to the rest, but rather a cumulative development. Moreover, Woodhouse's supposed disjunction between grace and nature in *The Faerie Queene* is illusory. As Darryl Gless explains, "grace constantly bridges the gap, causing a perpetual interaction between the two orders," which "enables human nature both to act naturally and, among the chosen, to participate in the order of grace." In the first canto of Book II, Guyon himself hails "The sacred badge of my Redeemers death" on Redcross's shield, and the Palmer tells Guyon, "God guide thee" (II.i.27, 32). Book II and its successors spring from Book I and the attainments of Holiness, so that Spenser's Temperance in particular is, as Gless states, "a subsidiary manifestation" of Redcross's primary virtue.[1]

Here I seek to clarify the long-standing debate about the relationship of Books I and II through several interrelated contributions that also have broader significance for interpretation of *The Faerie Queene*. Books I and II share much the same theological and medical conceptions of the body, soul, and human prospects, I argue, so that their heroes' exploits are fully complementary. Not only are Pauline doctrines of the flesh, spirit, and glorified body fundamental for Book I, as we would expect, but also for Book II. Moreover, the other half of the dichotomy deriving from Woodhouse, relegation of body and nature to Book II and its successors, does not work either, for Book I is also much concerned with the physiological state of the body. Medical and theological discourses are profoundly intertwined in both these books. As Michael Schoenfeldt differently argues in treating the belly, many writings of Spenser's time likewise evince a "remarkable nexus of spirituality and corporeality."[2] Numerous medical texts and guides to healthful living assumed that humanity was created in the image of God, treated the divine image as a jointly physical and spiritual model, and promoted temperate behavior as a means of conforming to it.

I focus on the anthropomorphic Houses of Pride, Holiness, and Temperance, since the latter two are commonly considered central, or allegorical cores, for their respective books, while Lucifera's distempered palace travesties both. Spenser's Temperance so complements his Holiness, we find, that Alma's house provides a main normative standard even for Book I. Hence I can also clarify the critically vexed relationship of Alma's and Caelia's households. Just as they are still often starkly contrasted in accord with Woodhouse's general claims, so *The Spenser Encyclopedia* tells us that Alma relates to "temporal virtues of the natural body" and Caelia to "the spiritual or mystical body," while Guyon's allegiances are "earthly" and his virtue "constructs a finite identity for man," the "castle or body," or "morally . . . the frame of ordinary human integrity."[3] But Alma significantly dresses like Fidelia and betrothed Una. Much as Peter says, "as livelie stones, be made a spiritual house" (1 Pet. 2:5),[4] Caelia's and Alma's households both express somatic edification whereby the body itself becomes divinely consecrated, and their edifices contrast with Lucifera's palace much as spirit does to flesh in Elizabethan Reformed discourse. The Alma allegory further expresses that basic contrast in Alma and Maleger's conflict. From the standpoints of both Spenser's Holiness and Temperance, the spirit should subdue the flesh, thus revivifying fallen human nature through grace and somewhat sanctifying the body itself, so that it comes to prefigure the spiritual or glorified body said to be assumed by each of the redeemed in the general resurrection.

Although prior criticism affords little comment on the relevance to *The Faerie Queene* of the body's supposedly ultimate glorification, that common Elizabethan belief was not only central for conceptions of the personal state of individuals after the general resurrection, but even had implications for earthly life as well, and the process of sanctification. Not only the dominion of Caelia evokes the glorified body, as we would expect according to previous commentary, but also that of Alma, I show, and Alma's is indeed its most full and detailed prefiguration. For Spenser, the "natural body" is properly to anticipate and finally become assimilated to its glorious fulfillment. And yet, by definition, that is not to be merely abstract, but consists in full physical recovery of the earthly body, even the same veins and sinews, in a spiritualized aspect.

As that somatic transfiguration is Spenser's ultimate physical ideal for humankind, so it is the final model and goal of his Temperance insofar as that virtue concerns the bodily state of individuals. David

Lee Miller observes that the allegory of *The Faerie Queene* is "organized with reference to the anticipated-but-deferred wholeness of the ideal body, which serves to structure the reading of the text in a manner comparable to the use of a vanishing point to organize spatial perspective in drawing. This 'body' is an ideological formation derived from the religious myth of the *corpus mysticum* and its imperial counterpart, the notion of the monarch as incarnating an ideal and unchanging political body." In this sense, "Spenser's art fantasizes its own perfection in terms of access to a spiritual body replete with truth."[5] Although Miller's definition of Spenser's projected ideal body is mystically ecclesiastical with a political counterpart, I would modify it to include another phase more specifically relevant to individuals: the glorified body that is supposedly to fulfill the physical potential of each of the redeemed. Pursuit of the glorified body is one of the anagogical dimensions of the poem's overarching quest for Gloriana, like incorporation into the *corpus mysticum*. The textually inward structural and hermeneutic focus or perspectival vanishing point of the Spenserian bodily ideal subsumes glorification of the physical body, which is thus to be rendered replete with presumed spiritual Truth, in the much-anticipated-but-deferred wholeness of its idealization.[6] Though the glorified body has this role for all the virtues in *The Faerie Queene* insofar as they constitute disciplines of particular subjectivities exercised by incarnate means, its relation to Book II is especially pregnant, so to speak, because Temperance most of all pertains to the general governance and potential of the body.

In assessing the representation and significance of the human body throughout *The Faerie Queene*, we should allow for the formerly expected eschatological glorification of the bodies of the redeemed: a conception which claimed to define the ultimate potential of humans as embodied beings. In the English Renaissance, as Debora Shuger observes, religion was "the cultural matrix for explorations of every topic," and constituted, in Claire McEachern's phrase, "the entelechy of identity, both corporate and individual," animating "imagined, staged, mystical, and material bodies."[7] On account of Spenser's strong theological and apocalyptic interests we should expect that concepts of bodily glorification would likely qualify negotiations between soul and body generally in the poem, and its representations not only of selfhood but affect. Taking cognizance of such early modern beliefs can help us avoid imputing to *The Faerie Queene* inappropriately sharp or schematic oppositions between nature, physicality, and the body on the one hand, and grace, spirit, and soul on the other. Although the supposedly "natural" virtue of Temperance has been most contrasted with Book I in Spenser studies to date, the poet's spiritualized temperate ideal indicates that sanctification, a state in which human will cooperates with grace according to Reformers, subsumes the whole series of virtues succeeding Holiness in *The Faerie Queene*, so that the poem's allegory of virtue is developmental.

FLESH AND SPIRIT

According to Paul, σάρξ (*sarx*, flesh) and πνεμα (*pneuma*, spirit) each refer to the whole person, both body and soul, under different aspects. Paul sharply distinguishes the body itself (σωμα, *soma*) from the pejorative flesh, for the body can be subsumed in the flesh or the spirit, and spiritually comes to constitute God's temple, to be restored and glorified in the general resurrection. In the *Decades* prescribed for weekly ministerial study by Archbishop Whitgift in 1586, the continental Reformer Heinrich Bullinger comments: "the old man is all that which we have of nature, or of our first parents [i.e., Adam and Eve], to wit, not the body only or the flesh, I mean the grosser and substantial part of the body; but even the very soul, with the strength, the power and faculties of the same. Therefore, whereas in some places of the holy scriptures the flesh is put for man, we must not only understand the massy substance and grosser part of the body; but the very flesh together with the soul and all the faculties thereof, that is, the whole man not yet regenerate. . . . The word 'flesh' therefore doth import the natural power and faculties of man." Whereas "the flesh is usually put for the old man, so is the spirit by an antithesis commonly used and taken for the new man," who is "regenerate by the Spirit of God in Christ, or is renewed according to the image of Christ, with all the gifts and virtues of the Holy Ghost." Or, as the prominent Reformer John Bradford explains, flesh "comprehendeth all and every of the natural powers, gifts, and qualities of man," and "all that ever is in man," excepting only "the 'sanctification of the Spirit.'" Conversely, "'spirit' . . . doth signify that which in man the Holy Ghost hath . . . sanctified to righteousness."[8]

Paul assumes that flesh and spirit must ever conflict during earthly life. Likewise, Bullinger declares "the renovation by the Spirit of Christ of the image of God" is "a continual observance of our whole life," or "a daily putting off and renewing," for "they that are regenerate . . . are never so purged that they feel no motions of the flesh, of sin, and of carnal affections." This ongoing struggle, he stresses,

involves "great watching, abstinence, constancy, fortitude, and patience," requires "the whole armour of God" according to Paul's
exposition in Ephesians 6, and ends only with death. This process
of personal renewal corresponds to sanctification, which Thomas
Wilson's *Christian Dictionary* defines as entry into "the liberty of ho-
lynesse, begun heere," through "renovation of Nature" and "alteration of qualities from evill to good," and "daily to be encreased till
we be perfect." That perfection is the glorification ascribed to afterlife, including assumption of the glorified body at the general resurrection. Paul is thus highly optimistic about the body, and even the
flesh is not inherently sinful, but passively neutral in itself, and prone
to infection by sin. Discourse incorporating Pauline perspectives,
especially complex poetry such as Spenser's, can thus use "flesh" and
its cognates and synonyms, such as "carnal," in several senses, including the broadly neutral meaning, "substance of the body." For clarity,
I will use "flesh" in its pejorative Pauline sense opposed to the spirit,
unless I contextually indicate otherwise.[9]

Paul's somatic theology is fundamental for Spenser's representation
of the body in *The Faerie Queene*, and as relevant to his treatment of
Temperance and the following virtues as to Holiness. Unfamiliarity
with Pauline doctrine leads some to assume that Spenserian deprecia-
tion of "the flesh," in Paul's spiritually adverse sense, entails contempt
for the body and flesh in general, dualistically opposes matter to spirit,
and condemns bodily pleasure and the body.[10] But, unlike many Renaissance writers who express loathing of the body, such as Pal-
ingenio, Spenser's often sensual verse revels in the body's wonder,
beauty, and erotic potential. Spenser's bodily optimism, including its
erotic aspects, is largely underwritten by Pauline notions of sanctification contrary to the flesh, so that flesh itself, in its general meaning,
becomes relatively purified.

EVACUATING THE HOUSE OF PRIDE

A main allegorical paradigm of sinful flesh in *The Faerie Queene* is
Lucifera's palace, which exalts pride and the other deadly sins in its
"fleshly might" (I.x.1). Contrary to the spirit, Thomas Becon declares, "the flesh . . . calleth unto pride, haughtiness of mind, envy,
malice, vengeance, discord, whoredom, avoutry, gluttony, drunk-
enship, & c."[11] Besides indicating adverse social implications of fleshly
values, Spenser's House of Pride also satirizes conditions of the flesh

through anthropomorphic allegory. Although critics have most commonly contrasted the Houses of Pride and Holiness, both Alma's and Caelia's households are positive norms underwriting the satire. As Alma's standards complement Caelia's, so Book II complements Book I in further expressing renewal of spirit. For Spenser, unregenerate flesh deforms human potential, spirit renews it, and Temperance, building on Holiness, is a main means of further regeneration. Many pointed contrasts and correspondences between Lucifera's and Alma's residences invite their analytic comparison, and I will only address some examples particularly revealing for the relations of flesh and spirit, Spenser's synthesis of medical and theological discourses, and the interanimation of Books I and II.

The poet bases his anthropomorphic House of Pride on the architectural figures and "mixed allegory" of the partially overlapping religious, moral, and medical discourses of his time. Philip Barrough's *Method of Phisick* evinces such intersections where he defines the bodily state of those whose lives are "inordinat" or "dissolute" in his medical context. Like a bad "tenant" who ruins the "faire dwelling house" of "his Land lord," so "they, when God hath bestowed their bodies upon them as gorgeous palaces," "by this evill demeanour . . . suffer them to run to destruction," and "at every little paine, do expect a final dissolution." Alluding to the motif of the Gospels in which the bad steward gets his comeuppance when his lord suddenly returns in judgment (e.g., Matt. 24:37–51; Luke 12:37–45), Barrough implies the body is a divine gift held in some trust. An implicit standard for various households in *The Faerie Queene*, this biblical model further applies to personal treatment of the body itself, as in Barrough, at least in Lucifera's and Alma's cases.[12]

Spenser's creationist view of appropriate humanity further depends on doctrines of the divine image and spiritual mastery of the flesh. Just as the introductory stanza for the canto presenting Alma's Castle contrasts the soberly governed human body, deemed God's most "faire and excellent" work in the world, with the "Monster" of the body "Distempred through misrule and passions bace" (II.ix.1), Alma's and Lucifera's contrasting houses, where the latter's counsellors are the personified monstrosities of the Sins, are mutually definitive. Alma's household partly measures the fleshly deformity of Lucifera's, and there are precise verbal parallels between Spenser's descriptions of them. Noting that Alma's Castle is built from matter like "*A Egyptian* slime," Spenser exclaims "O *great pitty*, that no lenger time/So *goodly workemanship* should not endure:/Soone it must turne to earth; no earthly thing is sure." Though Lucifera's "*goodly* heape" also declares "the *workmans* wit," its sandy "weake foundation" is a *"great pittie"* (II.ix.21, I.iv.5; my emphasis). While the supposed creation of the human body from earth or dust occasioned much emphasis on the transience of life, anticipation of afterlife, and impropriety of pride, earth also defined the prospects of living according to the flesh. Whereas "the first man is of the earth, earthlie," Paul declares, those spiritually renewed through Christ will "put on incorruption" so that "Death is swallowed up into victorie" (1 Cor. 15:47–55). These are implied conditions of both Alma's and Lucifera's ways of life, except spirited Alma has heavenly affinities (II.ix.18, 22, 47).[13]

Human powers were divided into several loosely corresponding Platonic and Aristotelian tripartite hierarchies that privileged mental functions, and the tours of Caelia's and Alma's houses culminate in the heights of Contemplation or mind, whereas Lucifera's house travesties that progression, remaining low, sub-rational, and, according to definitions of humanity based on rational powers, sub-human.[14] Spenser correlates Caelia's Mount with Alma's tower, and Lucifera travesties both. Featuring "mind . . . full of spirituall repast" and the personified mental capacity of Contemplation (I.x.48), Caelia's cephalic Mount appears "like that sacred hill, whose *head* full hie/*Adorned* with fruitfull Oliues" is "For euer with a flowring *girlond crownd*" (I.x.54; my emphasis). Arthur's head similarly sports a crest like "an Almond tree ymounted hye/On top of greene *Selinis*" (I.vii.32). From the Mount, a path leads to the heavenly city containing a "bright Angels towre" (I.x.55–58). Since Alma's turret-head is "likest . . . vnto that heauenly towre,/That God hath built for his own blessed bowre," it corresponds to the Mount of Contemplation in Book I, and likewise manifests, to some extent, the conditions of heaven, much as Spenser insists the world displays no "more faire and excellent" divine work than the well-governed human body. As Alma's tower positively rises "high aboue this earthly masse," it also prefigures the higher destiny of the spiritual or glorified body (II.ix.1, 45–47).[15] Caelia's and Alma's highly disciplined ways of life subdue the "flesh" to keep the body "low," as Spenser says of Contemplation (I.x.48), so that the functions of mind are set relatively apart and above (as they are physically also), within the allegorical settings. But Lucifera's anthropomorphic domain affords no exalted perspective other than herself proudly enthroned, supplanting the position of mind in Caelia's and Alma's establishments; Lucifera's "six sage Counsellours," the deadly sins other than pride, appear only at the level of earth in the pageant outside the palace, riding beasts that body forth their "bestiall beheasts" and natures (I.iv.18).

The House of Pride further travesties Alma's Castle in that Spenser satirically associates Lucifera's realm with excrement, gross disorders of basic physiological functions, and both physical and spiritual death. Spenser thus mixes anatomical, medical, and theological concerns and discourses in Book I; moreover, the main positive model on which this satire depends is not within Book I, but appears in Book II, so that these books are fully interrelated. Redcross exits the House of Pride on the level of excretion and interment, at the extreme bottom of the three-part human hierarchies positively manifested in Alma's house and evoked in Caelia's. Alma's houseplan features "two gates . . . placed seemly well": "The one before, by which all in did pas,/Did th'other far in workmanship excell" (II.ix.23). As the former figures the mouth, so the latter the anus, where Concoction's staff dump refuse:

> all the liquour, which was fowle and wast,
> Not good nor seruiceable else for ought,
> They in another great round vessell plast,
> Till by a conduit pipe it thence were brought:
> And all the rest, that noyous was, and nought,
> By secret wayes, that none might it espy,
> Was close conuaid, and to the backe-gate brought,
> That cleped was *Port Esquiline*, whereby
> It was auoided quite, and throwne out priuily.
>
> (II.ix.32)

Also constructed on such a two-gated plan, Lucifera's palace presents an impressive facade, but has "hinder parts, that few could spie" (I.iv.5). The *"fowle way"* or *"shamefull end"* of Lucifera's symbolically anal *"priuie Posterne,"* which opens onto a kind of *"donghill,"* finally realizes the anatomical possibilities of hinder parts (I.v.52–53; my emphasis). Redcross's itinerary in the Lucifera episode thus reproduces the brief initial description of her palace (I.iv.5): splendid first impression of the gorgeous facade, but final discovery of "hinder parts" satirically corresponding to the anus. His discovery of Duessa's soiled rump is likewise belated (I.viii.48).[16]

Much of Spenser's satire of the "shamefull end" of fleshly pride depends on his representation of the anus in Alma's castle, just as the Alma and Lucifera episodes are interpretively complementary. Spenser designates Alma's "backe-gate" the *"Port Esquiline"* (II.ix.32), and though not directly named in the Lucifera episode, corses . . ./ Of murdred men . . . therein strowed lay" "And came to *shamefull end*"; "A *donghill* of dead carkases he spide,/ The dreadfull spectacle of that sad house of Pride" (I.v.52–53; my emphasis). Unlike the body as temple, Lucifera's anthropomorphic home is a whited sepulchre, "beautiful outwarde, but . . . ful of dead mens bones, and of all filthines" (Matt. 23:27).

The disclosure of the necropolis behind the palace aptly concludes the satire of prideful flesh in one sense, for Spenser stresses the edifice's instability from the outset, and the episode ends with mortal reversion to dust. Outside the Esquiline gate, criminals were executed, and carcasses of slaves and paupers were cast into pits, much as, outside Lucifera's back gate, "many corses, like a great Lay-stall/ . . . therein strowed lay." In another sense, the satire concludes in revealing fleshy "hinder parts," and excremental functions furnished an exemplum against pride in the discourse of moralized anatomy. So the encyclopedist Pierre de la Primaudaye declares that "those goodly shoppes wee have in our bodies full of stinking drugges [i.e., dregs] . . . ought to take from us all matter of pride" and "put us in minde of our infirmities." Thomas Becon's "Prayer against Pride" insists the body is "a carcase and sack of dung." To rebuke the exaltation of self above others that pride entails, Spenser finally assimilates Lucifera's palace to bodily parts and processes ordinarily hidden by social convention. Having strayed into her domain, Redcross undergoes a humbling flight by the back door, and the symbolism anticipates his mortifying experiences in the House of Holiness (I.x.25–28).[18]

Although association of evil with excrement was conventional in medieval and Renaissance culture, the conclusion of the Lucifera episode further links "fowle" processes of the viscera with death to satirize the flesh and related excesses. Alma's and Caelia's households contrarily promote physical and spiritual health through discipline of fleshly appetites (II.ix.27; I.x.2, 25; I.x.48). But Lucifera's steward is Gluttony, and, as her pageant shows, she further entails the five further sins of Idleness, Lechery, Avarice, Envy, and Wrath, each of which could disturb the supposed humoural balance of the body, and produce decadent or corrupt humours. In Galenic theory, disease results from disturbance of the normal humoural order, and Spenser's representation of the Sins includes much admonitory medical discourse. The "lawlesse riotise" and "euill" behaviour of Idleness incur "grieuous malady," a continuous "shaking feuer." Perpetually vomiting, Gluttony is ironically "Full" only "of diseases." Lechery has "that fowle euill, . . ./ That rots the marrow, and consumes the braine"—either leprosy or syphilis. Avarice has "A grieuous gout" and Envy a "leprous mouth." As well as excess choler, Wrath has a "swelling Splene," and "where the splene flourishes," Phineas Fletcher advises, "all the body decayes, and withers" (I.iv.18–35).[19] The procession of these "sage Counsellours" tramples "Dead sculs and bones of men, whose life had gone astray." The few who escape Lucifera lie "Like loathsome lazars, by the hedges," and, behind its false front, the house finally discloses a spectacle of mass death (I.iv.18, 36, 3; v.53).

As Spenser's description of Lucifera's pageant of sins mixes both religious and medical discourses, there were no practically easy divisions between realms of grace and nature, or spirituality and corporeality. Spenser's association of Lucifera's domain with disease and death reflects current medical theory. According to Barrough's *Method of Phisick*, "untimely death" is "hastened" by "inordinate and heedlesse living," and Thomas Cogan's *Haven of Health* emphasizes that "intemperancie" can so corrupt even a sound humoural complexion as to cause untimely death or a "loathsome" old age. Elizabethan handbooks of healthful living used humoural theory to promote moderation in exercise, diet, and sex. Much like Cogan and Thomas Elyot, Levinus Lemnius advises "right orderly diet and good trade of life," for "superfluous abundance of ill humours . . . bring putrefaction and corruption to the whole body." By promoting rational control of passions, desires, and appetites in general, treatises on health condemned the whole range of Lucifera's vices, and the ecclesiastically prescribed Elizabethan homilies gave much the same advice: "all kind of excess offendeth . . . God," incurring "diseases and great mischiefs." Eating or drinking "unmeasurably" produces "unnatural heat" and "incurable diseases" that "diversely infect the whole body" and may bring "desperate death." Such homiletic counsel shaded into more specifically theological discourse, as in promotion of fasting "to chastise the flesh, that it be . . . brought in subjection to the spirit."[20]

Some common biblical and theological assumptions about sin, death, and the flesh complement the medical critique of Lucifera's deathly palace. Death supposedly originated from the primal sin of the Fall (Gen. 3:16–19), and thus signified human separation from God, as with the tempting "strange woman" or whore of Proverbs, analogous to Lucifera, who forgets God's covenant: "surely her house tendeth to death, and her paths unto the dead" (2:16–18; 7:27). In a related biblical theme, committing sin hastens death, so that "the wages of sinne is death" (Rom. 6:23), whereas righteous living extends life (e.g., Job 15:32, Ps. 55:22–23, Deut. 30:15–20, Prov. 10:2). Sin was conceived to deaden both body and soul, and Christian discourse distinguished three related types of mortality: physical, spiritual, and finally damning secondary or "second death." Physical death separates body from soul, Wilson explains, but spiritual death separates "soule and body from Gods favor in this world." "The spiritual death by sin in this life," he adds, "begetteth the first deth which is naturall in the end of our life; also the second Death which endureth eternally after this life ended," and constitutes "Eternall Death and damnation of soule and body in Hell." Sins themselves "come from persons spiritually Dead."[21] Paul expostulates against "the bodie of this death," the felt rule of sin in his members (Rom. 7:24). Much as the Geneva Bible glosses that phrase "this fleshlie lump of sinne and death," Spenser's association of Lucifera and her followers with mortality signifies a living death of the spirit, and prospect of incurring the second death. For Paul, the flesh gives death and the spirit life, anticipating glory of the resurrection that includes the body: "if ye live after the flesh, ye shal dye: but if ye mortifie the dedes of the bodie by the Spirit, ye shal live" (Rom. 8:6, 13).

CAELIA'S EXTIRPATION OF FLESH

Though Redcross's "soule-diseased" condition involves "grieued conscience," "Inward corruption, and infected sin" (I.x.23–25), his treatment in the House of Holiness administers fleshly mortification through mixed medical and religious discourses, again conflating nature and grace, corporeality and spirituality. The cure shares much with Alma's values and Renaissance guides to healthful living such as Cogan's, for Caelia's consulting specialist, Patience, immediately seeks to discipline Redcross's bodily appetites through "streight diet" and other austerities. However, much more drastic than Alma's regimen, this physician's program complements Christian "mortification," which aims to subdue the flesh by various inner and outward means, including "fastings, weeping, lamenting, neglecting and hatred of dainty diet, trimming of the body, and also of allowable pleasures." The good order and heavenly associations of Alma's anthropomorphic household, with all its cheerful friendliness, reflect much progress in such subjection, contrary to the state of Lucifera.[22]

As Spenser portrays Redcross's renewal within the House of Holiness, it involves a death that brings new life or rebirth, and life-saving surgical intervention. Redcross is "The man that would not liue, but earst lay at deathes dore," and the remedy requires putting him "priuily/Downe in a darkesome lowly place farre in," like a dungeon,

grave, or tomb, where his body appears a "daintie corse" (I.x.23–27).
Redcross is in a state of living or spiritual death entailing "infected
sin" that festers "sore . . . within" (I.x.25), and Wilson's *Christian
Dictionary* explains that amendment of such a condition requires
"mortification" or dying into new life, "to kill and to breake the
strength and rage of sinne, by the Spirit," and thus "by little and
little, to crucifie and destroy the Old man, with al his affections and
lusts which bee either in his Reason or Will, till they be wholly
abolished . . . at the time of our death." Redcross becomes "dead to
sin" in the biblical phrase: "one, in whom the Death of Christ hath
broken the force of sin," Wilson comments, so that "it cannot
reigne," but is "sore abated, and lessened daily." If the House of
Pride displays the flourishing of the Old Man, the House of Holiness
portrays the Old Man's demise that begets the New Man. When
Redcross is thus "recouer'd," Charissa "By this" (not only "by this
time" but also causally) gives birth, and comes to nurture Redcross
in charity (I.x.29–33). Hence he is delivered "from the bodie of this
death" and walks "in newnes of life" (Rom. 7:24, 6:4).[23]

Aside from using biblical metaphors of death and rebirth, the allegorical vehicle also involves mortification in a further sense from
Elizabethan pathology, "gangrene, necrosis." The treatment for Redcross's rankling "Inward corruption" employs the imagery and technical terminology of surgical intervention to arrest gangrene:
"extirpe," meaning surgical excision; "corrosiues," cauterizing caus-
tic chemicals; "humors"; and cauterization with a "whot" implement
(I.x.25–26). Just as extirpation was a medical last resort, the episode
represents theological mortification as a radical procedure to save a
desperate case of, in effect, fleshly necrosis. "Somtimes ther ensueth
such a *Gangraena*, or mortification," Jacques Guillemeau observes in
The Frenche Chirurgerye, "that ther is noe hope at all, of any health,
then onlye throughe the extirpatione of the same, fearinge least . . .
Gangraena, shoulde further infect and pollute all the circumjacent
partes." After excising the "corrupted, and mortified" part, "the
fluxion of bloode, must be . . . stopped, throughe the applicatione
of glowinge cauteryes." Amendment extirpates Redcross's rotting
"superfluous flesh" with cauterizing "pincers fierie whot," until
nothing "corrupted" remains (I.x.26).[24]

The surgical aspect of Redcross's cure evinces typically close Spenserian interconnection of bodily and spiritual states, or the purviews
of nature and grace. The mixture of vehicle and tenor in the allegory,
so that Patience, Amendment, and other personified moral qualities
administer physiological procedures, heightens this effect. Likewise,
for example, medical, physiological, moral, and theological senses

that gate of ancient Rome is nonetheless fundamental for its satire. Local hints in Canto Five of Book I are only clarified by a classical reference supplied in the Alma episode of Book II, and Spenser's initial account of Lucifera's palace offers a self-reflexive interpretive challenge: "all the hinder parts, *that few could spie,/*Were *ruinous and old, but painted cunningly*" (I.iv.5; emphasis mine).

Although prior commentators note the Roman porta Esquilina, located near a cemetary, was a main exit for human corpses, that does not explain Spenser's name for Alma's back door. Why identify the anus with that type of disposal? This Roman gate was not particularly associated with elimination of garbage. However, anthropomorphic topography was a literary convention dating from the ancients, and Spenser's allusion involves that type of conceit. Though Roman topography has now been much levelled, the Esquiline hill had definite twin peaks, the mons Oppius and mons Cispius, separated by the valley of the Subura; through this cleft proceeded the clivus Subur*anus*, which ran to the porta Esquilina, located about midway between the Oppian and Cispian elevations, in the Servian wall. Outside this aperture was the necropolis on the left. Phineas Fletcher's anatomical allegory in *The Purple Island* appreciatively repeats Spenser's term for the anus, "port *Esquiline*," and glosses the Roman topographical implications:

> This gate endow'd with many properties,
> Yet for his office sight and naming flies;
> Therefore *between two hills, in darkest valley lies.*

Possibly traditional rather than Spenserian, this joke had continued currency, as in *Fanny Hill.*[17]

So strongly is the Alma episode factored into Book I that, even though *The Faerie Queene* does not mention the Esquiline gate until we reach Alma's Castle, Spenser bases the satiric conclusion of Redcross's sojourn in the House of Pride on the linkage of that gate with carcasses and ignominious mass burials, and its topographical homology with the anus. Not only the general correspondence of Lucifera's house with Alma's (both have a chatelaine and two featured gates, front and back) but also the preponderance of Romans attending Lucifera's back gate evoke the Esquiline context explicitly associated with Alma's postern. Moreover, Spenser's account of Redcross's escape by Lucifera's "*priuie Posterne*" mixes discourses of death and excretion: "*Scarse could he footing find in that fowle way*"; "many complementarily converge in the phrase "proud humors." Redcross's treatment aims "to abate" these humours, mitigate "swelling of his wounds," and excise "superfluous flesh" (I.x.26). In organic applications, "proud" meant "overgrown, too luxuriant," and often referred, as in the expression "proud flesh," to swelling around a wound. In wounds where "appearethe anye swellinge, or tumefactione," Guillemeau observes, "the venomous humours" have "gatherede . . . aboute the wounde." Also, "proud humors" readily refers to "the state of pride" and "the swelling of concupiscence," A. C. Hamilton notes, just as "proud" could mean "sensually excited." Excessive passions and wrongful desires and actions were thought to imbalance and even corrupt bodily humours, and "proud" itself here implies and correlates variously adverse physiological, moral, and spiritual conditions.[25]

Redcross's revival also has an anagogical sense that anticipates ultimate repletion of the body with the spirit, and transcendence of the deathliness focused in Lucifera's household. On becoming "dead to sin," Paul insists that "if we be grafted" with Christ "to the similitude of his death, even so shal we be *to the similitude* of his resurrection," for "our olde man is crucified . . ., that the bodie of sinne might be destroyed" (Rom. 6:2–6). As Christ's death and resurrection provided a model for mortification and regeneration in earthly life, so also for the general resurrection. Hence regeneration itself could prefigure the latter, through which the "natural bodie," "sowen in corruption" of death, was supposedly to be "raised in glorie," reconstituted as "a spiritual bodie" "made partaker of the divine nature." Thus death and its "sting," sin, were finally to be vanquished (1 Cor. 15:42–55 and gloss). Parallel to the death, burial, descent into hell, and rising attributed to Christ, Redcross does not simply recover, but is "laid . . ./Downe in a darksome lowly place" at "deathes dore" and thus rises from the dead, as it were (I.x.25–27). Shortly afterward, Spenser evokes the general resurrection by referring to death and the grave as a "bridall bed" for meeting the "heauenly spouse," Christ (I.x.42); according to the Book of Revelation, the redeemed or Church are to encounter him like "a bride trimmed for her housband" (21:2, 9–10). Spenser celebrates the human body, "euen dead," by insisting upon "The wondrous workemanship of Gods owne mould,/Whose face he made" (I.x.42).

ALMA, BODILY SANCTITY, AND GLORIFICATION

Alma's Castle further anatomizes the conditions of spiritual liveliness into which Caelia ushers Redcross, but from the standpoint of

Temperance. Like Redcross's opponents, Alma's also seek "To bring the soule into captiuitie," imposing "sinfull vellenage" (II.xi.1). Despite assigning Book II to the sphere of nature, Woodhouse relates Alma's chief opponent, Maleger, to "original sin or human depravity, the result of the fall," and such interpretation of that character has become quite normative.[26] However, since Alma's Castle determinedly resists Maleger even before Arthur's and Guyon's entourage arrives, her edifice cannot simply allegorize "the natural man" as Woodhouse and his current followers maintain, for nature was supposedly fallen and thus Maleger's domain. If Alma's antagonist, whom she resists, relates to the Pauline flesh, then her own realm is relatively one of the spirit, like Caelia's. Alma's Castle figures forth a nature to some extent spiritually renovated, regenerated, and sanctified, or such potential, and defines the temperate ideal accordingly for both sexes in Book II, just as the Castle itself is somehow hermaphroditic (II.ix.22), and lacks any symbolic correlates for gender-specific genitals.[27]

As Peter Stambler observes, the flesh best sums up Maleger's theological significance, and his meaning thus "includes sin because the flesh inclines toward sin through original sin." In the *Booke of Christian Prayers* authorized and personally used by Queen Elizabeth, the "Prayer Against the Flesh" appropriated from Juan Luis Vives clarifies the basics of Spenser's allegory opposing Maleger to Alma:

> While man was in innocency, reason made the spirit a sovereign; but now the sinfulness, that we have received by inheritance from our first parents, hath matched the rebellious flesh against her superior and ruler, the mind. . . .
>
> But thou, O Lord Christ, . . . restore us . . . so as our flesh may be in subjection to the Spirit, and our affections be made obedient to right and uncorrupted reason; or, at least wise, that although the flesh rebel, and fight against the spirit, yet the power of the mind may be so strong, and the strength of our reason so mighty, through thy grace, as they may get the upper hand in all encounters, and finally overcome all assaults. . . .

To portray the primary exemplar of Temperance in Book II, Spenser places the assaults of "the rebellious flesh" outside Alma's fortifications, so that she has "the upper hand": allegorically, the affections are relatively "obedient to right and uncorrupted reason" here, and spirit withstands flesh. Nevertheless, Maleger's forces continue to threaten Alma's household, as befits the unremitting spiritual warfare attributed even to renovated human nature during life, as in Romans 7:22–24. In effect, Alma and her Castle figure forth a state of self-discipline that approaches recovery of original "innocency" by restoring some sovereignty of the spirit. However, such restoration remains contingent on grace just as Spenser's descriptions of Alma herself and Arthur's final defeat of Maleger use much Christian symbolism, and Spenser contextually deploys the Incarnation in *Briton Moniments* "To purge away the guilt of sinfull crime" in "fleshly slime" for all of "*Adams* line" (II.x.50). The fundamental threat to Alma's besieged situation is allegorically the same as Caelia addresses in Redcross's case. If Maleger's siege were successful, Alma's Castle would become, in effect, Lucifera's palace. While the Alma allegory focuses on temperate self-control, to counter "strong affections" and sensory temptations in keeping with the topic of Book II, Alma's idealized condition also follows from the previous disciplines of Holiness focused in Caelia.[28]

In the Pauline epistles, the main characteristics of the flesh, from which its power paradoxically derives, are "infirmitie" or weakness, mortality or deathliness, and death in life, as the "bodie of this death" (Rom. 6:19, 7:23). Spenser develops much of Maleger's characterization accordingly: "pale and wan," "leane and meagre," and "withered," seeming "to tremble euermore," Maleger is a "dead-liuing swaine," "like a ghost" with "graue-clothes . . . vnbound," and "a dead mans skull" as helmet (II.xi.20, 22, 44). Spenser strongly hints at the flesh in his riddling account of Maleger's identity: "*Flesh* without bloud, a person *without spright*" or spirit, "That could not die, yet seem'd a *mortall* wight,/That was *most strong in most infirmitee*" (II.xi.40; my emphasis). Much as Paul stresses that subduing the flesh requires continuous spiritual struggle ended only by death, Arthur finds Maleger a most elusive and difficult opponent and must be sustained by "grace":

So feeble is mans state, and life vnsound,
That in assurance it may neuer stand,
Till it dissolued be from earthly band.

(II.xi.30)

Much of the psychomachia involves Arthur and Maleger falling to the earth, exchanging places there, and rising from it; Maleger ever rises "freshly . . ./From th'earth," his "mother" (II.xi.42–45). "The first man," the man of flesh, Paul advises, "is of the earth, earthlie"; "mortifie therefore your members which are on the earth," or "extinguish all the strength of the corrupt nature which resisteth against the Spirit, that ye may live in the Spirit, and not in the flesh" (1 Cor. 15:47; Col. 3:5 and gloss). Maleger's refreshment by the earth mythologically relates him to Antaeus, and Arthur to Hercules; since at least Fulgentius, mythographers had traditionally associated earthy Antaeus with the flesh, thus turning this Herculean exploit into allegorized spiritual warfare. Arthur's setbacks and suffering express fleshly recidivism and theological mortification.[29]

The conflict ends when Arthur tosses Maleger into a "standing lake" symbolizing baptism, as Woodhouse observes (II.xi.46). Though "standing" has often been glossed as "stagnant," which makes no sense in a baptismal context, it much more likely means "still, not ebbing" here, and plays on the senses "constant, permanent," and "authoritatively . . . set up," just as this sacrament was ascribed enduring effects, readiness, and authority. According to the Elizabethan *Book of Common Prayer* on baptism, God sanctified "all . . . waters to the mystical washing away of sin," and "none can enter into the kingdom of God, except he be . . . born anew of water." Moreover, "the ancient custome of baptising," Perkins observes, was submersion of "all the bodie."[30]

Maleger's fate does not specifically baptise Alma or her supporters for their condition already implies baptism's effects. Already much renovated, she and her Castle have long successfully resisted Maleger; upon arriving, Arthur and Guyon fight his forces without succumbing (II.ix.13–17). Likewise, when Spenser first introduces Alma, before Maleger's defeat, one of her main attributes is a white robe (II.ix.19), and although the authorized Elizabethan baptismal rite did not include that garment, it had been associated with baptized inclusion in Christ since at least the fourth century. The 1549 *Book of Common Prayer*, the first Edwardian prayer-book, designates "white vesture . . . a token of the innocencie, which by . . . this holy sacramente of Baptisme, is given unto the [i.e., thee]," to be worn figuratively throughout life. Rather than baptising Alma and her party, then, Maleger's end allegorizes the baptismal basis of resisting what he represents, and anticipates its ultimate defeat. Baptism is inherently proleptic, Calvin explains, for "at what time soever we be Baptised, we are at once washed and cleansed for all our life," and this sacrament is a divine "earnest" or "promise" of regeneration (4.15.3, 12; 4.16.2). Article 27 of the Thirty Nine Articles and the Elizabethan *Book of Common Prayer* similarly emphasize that baptism betokens divine *"promises"* of release from sins, salvation, and fulfillment (emphasis mine).[31]

Maleger's allegorical demise seems especially inspired by a main type of baptismal mortification and purification noted in the Elizabethan liturgy, the drowning of Pharaoh and his army in the Red Sea to save the Israelites (Ex. 14). "Baptisme . . . promiseth us that our *Pharao* is drowned, and the mortification of sin," says Calvin; not that sin is thus "no more, or may no more trouble us, but onely that it may not overcome us." God thus "promiseth to us in baptisme, . . . that we are by his power brought forth . . . out of the bondage of sinne" (4.15.11, 9). Perkins notes the water specifically "seales unto us remission of sinnes and sanctification," and Calvin stresses "we are baptised into the mortifying of our flesh, which is begon by baptisme in us" (4.15.11). In the Elizabethan baptismal rite, the priest prays "that all carnall affections may die" in those baptized, "and that all things belonging to the Spirit may live and grow."[32]

The baptismal conclusion of the Maleger allegory further clarifies Spenser's riddle about Maleger's identity: "Flesh *without bloud*, a person without spright"—or spirit (II.xi.40; my emphasis). Baptismal water signifies "the blood of Christ," Calvin notes, "our true and onely washing" for "the clensing of sins" (4.15.2, 16.2). Maleger signifies flesh without blood in that sense, and fleshes out the perceived threat of graceless nature. Alma's need for Arthur's intervention against Maleger's forces allegorizes human need for grace and the intercession of Christ as redeemer in continuing spiritual struggles of life, in accord with basic soteriology of the English church (II.xi.15–17). While we should not equate Maleger with the flesh, it is a main component of his complex meaning and subsumes or contextualizes diverse other implications such as, in A. C. Hamilton's partial inventory, "the passions, sensuality, deadly sin, physical disease."[33]

Spenser represents Alma herself as a bride of Christ in waiting, in effect, and her character as such is diffused throughout her Castle, so that her anthropomorphic edifice expresses some sanctification contrary to urgencies of the flesh. Just as "alma" means "the soule of man" in Italian, and the introductory stanzas of Canto Eleven comment on "the fort of reason" and "the soul," she signifies the soul or, more particularly, the rational soul itself, which were commonly imagined as feminine: "in a body, which doth freely yeeld/His partes to reasons rule obedient," "There *Alma* like a virgin Queene most bright,/Doth flourish in all beautie excellent" (II.xi.1–2). Spenser introduces Alma as "a virgin bright" who has declined many suitors for marriage, and her dress here is highly significant:

In robe of lilly white she was arayd,
That from her shoulder to her heele downe raught,
The traine whereof loose far behind her strayd,
Braunched with gold and pearle, most richly wrought. . . .

                                                    (II.ix.18–19)

Alma's dress, I have noted, implies she shares in the state of baptized incorporation in Christ. Moreover, as Anthea Hume observes, Alma's clothing alludes to various passages in Revelation that associate the redeemed with white robes, implying that Alma "is clothed in Christ's righteousness" (e.g., 3:4–5, 18; 7: 9–17; 19:7–8). Those whom "the Lambe . . . shal governe," in "eternal felicitie" according to the Geneva gloss, "are *araied in long white robes*" that have been "washed . . . white in the blood of the Lambe" (Rev. 7:9–17; emphasis mine). Spenser describes Alma with much the same sartorial imagery and diction, Hume points out, for "white," "robe," and "arayd" reappear, while Alma's garment, stretching from shoulder to heel with a "traine . . . far behind," is emphatically "long." This sartorial symbolism of the Book of Revelation, I would add, underwrote the significance of the baptismal white robe, which was, according to Luther and others, to be worn before Christ's judgment seat to obtain eternal bliss. Implying that Alma is "full of grace" theologically as well as otherwise, just as "heauen" itself rejoices to see her (II.ix.18), the doubly liturgical and biblical allusion of her dress strongly invests Alma, her castle, and Spenser's Temperance with Christian sanction.[34]

Hume's brief account of Alma's costume can be supplemented much beyond the further baptismal resonance I have proposed. According to Bullinger on the white robes in Revelation, wearing such a garment "is the greatest prayse and most certaine signe of perfit godlynes." It signifies having indeed "put on the new man, . . . even Christ," our "weddyng garment," through whom we are "apparrelled with righteousnes, temperaunce, and all goodnes." The gold and pearl of Alma's train may partly correspond to those of the heavenly Jerusalem, or the "golde tryed by the fyre" of those whom Christ clothes with "white raiment" (Rev. 21:21, 3:18). She is "crowned with a garland of sweete Rosiere," and since Alma promotes Temperance, not virginity, I would not, as Hume does, dissociate Alma from roseate Venus and love. Alma's "crowned" head might further relate to the "crowne of life" or "crowne of righteousnes" to be obtained by the redeemed, who are biblically to "reigne" in the loving kingdom of heaven (Rev. 2:10, 22:5; 2 Tim.

4:8). Her "lilly white" and roses may evoke the betrothed in the Song of Songs, whose relationship with Solomon was conventionally allegorized as that of the Church or faithful soul to Christ: "I am the rose of the field, and the lilie of the valleis," Solomon says, and "Like a lilie . . ., so *is* my love among the daughters" (2:1–2).[35]

Most conclusively for the Christian import of Alma and Temperance, her "robe of lilly white" corresponds to Fidelia's "all in lilly white," and Una's, "All lilly white," when Una's father betroths her to dragonslaying Redcross after the liberation of Eden (II.ix.19; I.x.13, xii.20–22). Although previous critics seem not to have noticed, or been willing to press, these correspondences, Spenser integrates Alma into a pattern of symbolism initiated in Book I, based mostly on the sartorial imagery of Christian redemption in the Book of Revelation, just as Books I and II are fully complementary. The lily whiteness of Alma's, Una's, and Fidelia's robes may evoke Solomon's comment on his betrothed in the Song, just quoted. While Hume helpfully relates Alma's rejection of many marital suitors to the Christian topos of the heart's many suitors, of whom only Christ is worthy,[36] the Lamb's "wife" is "readie" for marriage to him when "araied with pure fyne linen and shining, for the fine linen is the righteousnes of Sainctes" (Rev. 19:7–8). As Spenser assigns Alma this long white robe while stressing her virginity and rejection of many marital suits, so her state, like Fidelia's and Una's, allegorizes spiritual readiness for Christ, and in biblical Hebrew, 'almâ means a marriageable or maritally ready young woman or virgin. In effect, Alma awaits the "heauenly spouse" who saves the soul from death, rendering the grave a "bridall bed," as Spenser says in treating the House of Holiness, much as in *Daphnaida* (I.x.42; lines 267–69). Unlike Lucifera, Alma correlates with the virgins who keep themselves ever "readie" for the "bridegrome" in the Parable of the Wise and Foolish Virgins: all are thus to "watche, . . . for ye knowe nether the day, nor the houre, when the Sonne of man wil come," and Alma posts a watch with "goodly Beacons" that flame "continually" (Matt. 25:1–13; II.ix.11, 46).

Clearly insisting on the spiritual role of Temperance, Spenser's depiction of Alma attributes potential for sanctification even to the body in earthly life. Though some Reformers would deny that, such as Bullinger, Pietro Martire Vermigli observes that "regeneration . . . hath his first originall from the mind, from whence it is derived unto all the parts of man," considered as "the whole man." For Perkins, sanctification includes gaining "sanctitie of bodie," whereby "all the members" are "preserved from being meanes to execute any sinne" and become "the instruments of righteousnes and holiness," so that the body itself comes to constitute "a fit instrument for the soule to accomplish that which is good." Likewise William Ames, who stresses, as Vermigli, that sanctity of soul in turn sanctifies the body. Alma's own physical perfection as a character may well imply some bodily sanctification (II.ix.18–19). Moreover, even if we consider her only as a symbol of the soul, her anthropomorphic household is so well and happily ordered that her relative sanctification allegorically includes the body. Truly in her case "the soule doth rule the earthly masse,/And all the seruice of the bodie frame" (IV.ix.2).[37]

The train of Alma's richly symbolic white robe is indeed "borne of two faire Damsels, which were taught/That seruice well," and A. C. Hamilton notes that they signify "the irascible and concupiscible faculties which attend the temperate soul," and thus, in Alma's exceptional case, serve it dependably (II.ix.19). This image, I would add, significantly reconfigures Plato's famous tripartite allegory of the soul in the *Phaedrus*, the charioteer who drives two horses: one noble, good, and "a friend of . . . temperance and modesty," the other the opposite, so that his task of controlling them, and hence self-control, is difficult. As in Plato's psychic theory in the *Republic*, these three agencies correspond to reason, its proper ally irascible *thumos*, and rebellious desires situated in the groin; the latter two components were conventionally correlated with or subsumed in later notions of the irascible and concupiscible appetites. Spenser's psychic triad pointedly redevelops the Platonic model so that the appetites in Alma's realm are not only both domesticated and subservient but fully humanized, becoming handmaidens who follow her movements and directives, rather than constituting unmatched, potentially restive and unruly beasts that precede and in a sense lead the directing agency, and could readily resist or violate its commands. Instead of interrelating the three psychic agencies with Plato's symbolic medium of the chariot and reins, Spenser substitutes the white robe, so that the appetites themselves in Alma's exemplary case have come to serve Christian spiritual values and ends, yet with latitude or *sprezzatura* rather than rigidity, just as Alma's splendid gold- and pearl-embroidered "traine" strays "loose far behind her" as tended by her well-taught helpers (II.ix.19).[38]

By harmoniously tempering the relations of soul and body, Alma's realm recurs to the legendary prelapsarian state of humanity and somewhat approximates the original divine image. Representing Temperance as an embattled state of resistance to temptations, Spenser bases his portrayal of the temperate body on the motif of the anthropomorphic castle, rather than the biblical metaphor of the body

as God's temple. Nevertheless, Spenser evokes the latter perspective
by repeatedly insisting that well-tempered human bodies are most
wondrous divine works (II.ix.1, 22, 33, 45, 47). The poet assumes
people are "The images of God in earthly clay" (I.x.39), and Alma's
temperate fidelity to that model allegorically ensures the rejoicing of
"heauen" to see "her sweete face," in which "sweete" involves its
former meaning "pure" (II.ix.18). As beholding God's face in the
beatific vision was considered the soul's supreme joy, so heaven rejoices to contemplate the faithful soul, Spenser implies, in which
God's image would be especially reflected. By focusing on Alma's
"face" and "faire" aspect, the wording also valorizes the well-tempered body as a locus of spiritual significance and revelation.

Moreover, Spenser's account of Alma and her Castle anagogically
prefigures attainment of the glorified or spiritual body, which is thus
to consummate the personal discipline of Temperance. Since "glory
in scripture is taken for light, brightness, and shine," as Otho Wermullerus stresses in his treatise on bodily glorification, "clarity" or
radiance was considered its most obviously definitive characteristic.
So Bullinger declares, "glory in this sense is used for a lightsomeness
and shining brightness," and "a glorious body is a bright and shining
body." The transfiguration of Christ on Mount Tabor, where "his
face did shine as the sunne, and his clothes were as white as the
light," was the standard exemplar of such physical glory (Matt. 17:2).
White-clothed Alma is specifically "a virgin *bright*" or "*most bright*"
(II.ix.18, xi.2; emphasis mine). That is not simply the light attributed
to beauty in Platonic and Neoplatonic aesthetics, for Alma has further
characteristics of the glorified body. The white clothes of the blessed
in Revelation further symbolized glorification through Christ, including being "clothed . . . with the incorruption of their bodyes"
on the last day, and also the glorious state of heaven. These meanings
complement baptismal symbolism, for the white robe of baptism had
been anciently said to symbolize union with the risen Christ, in
anticipation of the general resurrection, and glorification through his
glorious body.[39]

As Alma is "in the flowre now of her freshest age" (II.ix.18), so
resurrected bodies of the blessed were to be, as Vermigli affirms, "of
full growing, . . . ripe and strong," "a perfect age," "perfect in their
kind," like Adam's and Eve's upon creation. Gold was a traditional
symbol for the qualities of the glorified state, and Spenser aurifies
Alma with "golden heare" and "traine . . ./Braunched with gold"
(II.ix.19). Also, despite Alma's relative maturity, she has "not yet felt
Cupides wanton rage" (II.ix.18), and the allegorical anatomy of her
Castle displaces, elides, or omits specific genitals. While that may

reflect the threat of erotic desire to Temperance, stress the importance
of sexual self-control for this virtue, befit the relevance of the allegory
to persons of both sexes, and imply approximation to a hermaphroditic ideal such as concludes the 1590 Book III and would arise
from Arthur and Gloriana's union, Spenser's distancing of Alma from
active sexuality further befits the glorified body. Though endued
with genitals, it was conventionally said to lack use of sex. Also,
though endued with the whole digestive tract, it was to lack use of
food and drink. Although Alma's Castle includes allegorized viscera
and exemplary digestion, she and her household do not represent but
to some extent prefigure ultimate physical glorification, which by
definition could only happen after death and the general resurrection,
so that total correspondence here would be inappropriate. Through
rational sovereignty of "soule," Spenser declares, Alma "to her
guestes doth bounteous banket dight,/Attempred goodly well"
(II.xi.1–2). In one sense, then, the banqueting in the Castle signifies
a physicality that fully assimilates the soul's provisions, as it were, and
physical glory was to involve such harmony.[40]

The qualities of the glorified body termed "impassibility" and
"subtlety," which imply perfection of temperament, constitution,
and apprehension, are most relevant to Temperance and the significance of Alma and her Castle. On impassibility, Bullinger explains
that "this body of ours in the resurrection shall be set free from all
evil affections and passions," or from, in Wermullerus' phrases,
"bodily frail lusts and temptations" of the "stained and defiled flesh."
Vermigli maintains that the body will only retain capacities for passions that "helpe nature, and make it perfect." Subtlety, John Woolton observes, is to be understood as "perfect power of the senses,"
and according to Vermigli, they and the affects will thus "not be
grosse and full of impediments; neither shall they trouble the mind."
Hence, while remaining fully corporeal, "the humane bodie" will
"as much as may be, drawe unto the propertie of a spirit, as touching
knowledge and affects." The glorified body would thus correspond,
in effect, to Alma and her Castle freed from all pressures of Maleger,
without need for defences. While resisting him, the temperate state
of Alma and her household anticipates the condition of the glorified
body, but most nearly approaches it, allegorically, upon Arthur's final
defeat of Maleger. Then Spenser exclaims:

Now gins this goodly frame of Temperance
Fairely to rise, and her adorned hed
To pricke of highest praise forth to aduance. . . .

                                                      (II.xii.1)

The highest and most temperate condition for humanity was glorification, and Spenser's portrayal of Alma and her Castle anagogically
points to that as the most full human realization of temperate ideals.[41]

Since successful spiritual struggle against the flesh during life was
to be fulfilled in attainment of the glorified body "fashioned like unto
the glorious body of Christ," in John Hooper's phrase, Spenser's
relation of Alma to such bodily glory defines her ends and those
of Temperance accordingly. Physical glorification would mark the
maximum humanly possible assimilation to the spirit; flesh, in a generally neutral sense, "material of the body," would then be fully
purged of "flesh," in the pejorative Pauline sense. A basic text for
the theology of the general resurrection is "flesh and blood can not
inherit the kingdome of God, nether doeth corruption inherit incorruption" (1 Cor. 15:50). Paul's phrase "flesh and bloud," Vermigli
explains, means "corruption, unto . . . which flesh and bloud in this
life are subject," and corresponds to flesh as opposed to spirit. Accordingly, when Wermullerus insists "our own very true flesh shall
rise again" with "true . . . blood, bones, sinews, joints, members,"
he uses "flesh" in its broad neutral meaning, and adds the body will
then be "clean, perfect, . . . purified," fully "subject and obedient
unto the spirit," or purged of the flesh in its adverse sense. "Glorious
bodies," Bullinger writes, are "very flesh indeed" in the general sense,
yet drained of "all corruption . . . and infirmities"; they are to be
had "of Christ, . . . made to the likeness of the body of Christ," and
"quickened and preserved by the Spirit of Christ." Whereas the
earthly or natural body lives by the soul, Bullinger and Wermullerus
emphasize, the glorified body lives by Christ. However, on account
of the doctrine of fleshly antagonism to the spirit during earthly life,
so that rational faculties have imperfect control, the glorified state of
repletion with Christ also ensures the final bodily supremacy of the
soul. The special attributes of the spiritual body partly result from
that, Vermigli declares, "for the bodie and members shalbe wholie
subjected unto the soule," and "neither contend nor strive against
it," so that "the soule shall perfectlie governe the bodie." Insofar as
the Alma allegory relates to rule of the body by "the soule" in "sure
establishment" (II.xi.1–2), its ultimate ideal and goal is the glorified body.[42]

However, as often in Spenserian theological allegory, the relationship between Alma and bodily glorification is not simply anticipatory
and anagogically figurative but to some extent synechdochal. Insofar
as Alma and her household prefigure the state of the glorified body,
they also somewhat share in and manifest its qualities as I have shown,
and so, then, would other temperate persons. Some Renaissance

theologians appear to imply such partial manifestation of the glorified body in earthly life. As later cited favorably by the Puritan Henry Jeanes, Estius or Van Est, an eminent sixteenth-century Roman Catholic commentator on the Pauline epistles, thus explains the clarity or radiance ascribed to physical glorification: "the joy of the soule hath even here in this life an unperfect impression upon the body, making the countenance serene, and cheerefull," so that "glory and happinesse" redound "from the soule unto the body. The spirituall glory of . . . soules shall be conspicuous by the bodily brightnesse of their [resurrected] countenances." For Van Est and Jeanes, as the earthly body reflects a good spiritual state, so will the resurrected body superlatively. But if so, any such current earthly reflection would indicate something of the body's ultimate glorification. Likewise, to explain glorified clarity, Vermigli states, "neither is it unknowen to anie, that the mind and spirit doth exhilerat the countenance, and make the bodie chearefull." The change of old man to new man said to begin and continue in earthly life through the conflict of spirit with flesh, and which sanctified the body according to some, could be considered a synechdoche of full bodily glorification, since that was held to follow from repletion with Christ.[43]

Whereas Reformers would tend to avoid positing some earthly proto-glorification because that could seem to allow too much to fallen humanity and earthly life, thus encouraging human pride, enhancing valuation of works, and undercutting emphasis on continuous spiritual struggle, Spenser's poetic program of celebrating heroic virtue somewhat contrarily promotes insistence on the wondrous extent of divinely aided human potential and on its ultimate fulfillment. Hence Spenser's representation of human virtue more readily accommodates present physical expression of some bodily glory of the resurrection, as in Alma's case. Some biblical passages could appear supportive, such as "your bodie is the temple of the holie Gost," "glorifie God in your bodie, and in your spirit" (1 Cor. 6:19–20). And some Protestant theologians, such as Ames, assumed that glorification begins in this life, to be perfected on the "last Day." In this century, John Robinson, among others, has argued for some earthly physical sharing in glorification. Darryl Gless finds Redcross incipiently glorified at the end of Book I. Spenser's ardent Christian Platonism, which assumes that body readily manifests soul, could well encourage belief in the present significance of ultimate human glory. Since the soul is the formal principle of the body, a soul that most resembles "heauenly light," Spenser writes in his "Hymne of Beavtie," frames its "fleshly bowre" "most beautifull and braue," and "the grosse matter by a soueraine might/Tempers so trim, that it may well be seene,/A pallace fit for such a virgin Queene" (lines 120–26). The relative Christ-likeness of anyone could thus, in Spenser's view, have physical consequences even in life, and the logic of the Alma allegory depends on that. While she and her retainers anagogically prefigure bodily glorification, Alma especially evinces some of its traits, so that her very capacity to signify such a potential depends on her present approximation to it.[44]

To be purged of the Pauline flesh, the Spenserian body is ideally to be subsumed in the spirit. Though that state was supposed only partially attainable in earthly life, it was to be fully realized in the general resurrection, when the human body, in Vermigli's phrasing, would become glorified and have "the propertie of a spirit" "as much as may be," yet with no alteration of "substance," for "the same bodie and the same flesh" would be "raised up" and "restored." Each, Hooper affirms, shall thus rise in the flesh originated in the "mother's womb," but likened to Christ's "glorious body," as an embodied being replete with the spirit. For Spenser that is not simply a condition of afterlife but has some earthly relevance, and he depicts his virtuous, exemplary, or inspirational characters such as Alma accordingly.[45]

Not merely abstract or theoretical, Spenser's highly spiritual way of understanding the proper nature and prospects of the body has a paradoxically strong physicality. Donne's "Valediction: Forbidding Mourning," A. C. Chambers argues, attributes glorification to the living lovers' bodies,[46] and Spenser's notions of the body's potential for sanctity seem to produce his own Protestant erotics. In the Temple of Venus, Spenser's description of Amoret, his very type of nubile womanhood, intratextually reproduces his prior accounts of Faith, betrothed Una, and Alma. Like them, Amoret is "all in lilly white arayd" and "Shyning" both "with beauties light, and heauenly vertues grace." She appears "Like to the Morne, when first her shyning face/Hath to the gloomy world it selfe bewray'd," and her description thus evokes the white raiment and sun-like face of the incarnate Son first appearing transfigured to the world, the prototype of the glorified body for humanity (Matt. 17:2). As "soone" as Scudamour sees her in this state, his "hart gan throb," and he wonders if, by acting as "Cupids man" with her, he would commit "sacrilege" to the "Church," but proceeds anyway (IV.x.52–54). On account of Amoret's appearance here, "Church" not only refers to the Temple of Venus but allegorically suggests Amoret's espousal and ecclesiastical incorporation by Christ, and the further Pauline correspondence between matrimonial and ecclesiastical unions that would help resolve her suitor's quandary (Eph. 5:22–33). Earlier, Sansloy reacts to Una's similar appearance with "lustfull heat" (I.vi.3–5). Again imagery of sanctity, anticipating bodily glorification, conjoins with powerful sexual desire in the *Epithalamion* about the poet's own marriage to another erotically pneumatic virgin "Clad all in white" with "sunshyny face" like Una or transfigured Christ, before the annually "shortest night, when longest fitter weare" (lines 151, 119, 271–72). These passages not only seem to reflect the common ethical association of virtue with powerful attractiveness, but also linkage of Christian bodily and spiritual purity with authorization of erotic pleasure and desirability.

PLEASURE, GRACE, AND SPENSER'S TEMPERANCE

Contrary to Woodhouse's long-influential claims that Book II involves "no significant reference to the Bible at all" and operates solely in the order of nature, apart from grace, Spenser emphasizes sanctification and related Pauline somatic theology in his portrayal of Alma's anthropomorphic domain, his central exemplar of Temperance. Whereas Alma has been recently identified with "the natural body" contrary to Caelia's inclusion in the mystical body of Christ, many details, such as Alma's symbolic white garment, show that she and her Castle constitute Spenser's primary model for the assimilation of the natural body into the mystical body. Whereas another recent critic assumes Spenser's Temperance "constructs a finite identity for man," the "castle or body," according to "ordinary human integrity," Alma's Castle shows that neither human identity nor the body are finite from the standpoint of Temperance, and this virtue's mode of integrity depends upon the extraordinary Christian transformation from old man to new man, or flesh to spirit. The virtue aims to sanctify human nature to restore, as far as possible, its supposedly prelapsarian condition, yet also to anticipate heavenly glorification of body and soul. Just as both Caelia's and Alma's ways of life allusively counter the House of Pride in Book I, with its endemic disorders of the Pauline flesh, Alma and her Castle represent substantial transformation into the new man according to the spirit.[47]

Spenser's Christian definition of Alma and Temperance is only to be expected. As Protestant-Pauline doctrine of sin and salvation was "a fundamental ground" and "major influence, thematic and structural," for the religious lyrics of Donne and others, so too it broadly underwrites *The Faerie Queene*, in accord with the poem's focus on the possibilities and limits of human effort to pursue and maintain virtue, while addressing the Reformed cultural context. After the access of faith in Book I, especially sanctification shapes both the structure and content of Spenser's allegory. As Darryl Gless explains, the successive titular virtues thus "act explicitly in nature but originate in and are persistently enabled by grace"; each "represents a particular manifestation of the comprehensive Christian virtue of holiness."[48]

The Alma episode confirms that Spenser's Temperance follows that paradigm. The Elizabethan "Homily against Gluttony and Drunkenness" urges "eschew . . . all intemperancy," for then "the mind of man is more lift up to God, more ready to all godly exercises." The "Homily of Repentance" enjoins, "live soberly and modestly . . . by using abstinence and temperance in word and in deed in 'mortifying our earthly members here upon earth'" (Col. 3:5). The latter comment assumes temperance is a part of sanctification, to subdue the flesh, exalt the spirit, and advance regeneration or "the renewing of the man," in Bullinger's phrase. This constitutes "a new creature," he affirms, "repaired now according to the image of God, and endued with a new nature or disposition." Reformers considered postlapsarian human nature a deformity of created nature, or a naturalization of sin in humanity, so that the original prelapsarian nature could only be regained through radical renewal. "Sanctification," Ames declares, "is a reall change of a man from the filthinesse of sin, to the purity of God's Image." Throughout the Alma episode Spenser posits divine creation of humanity, and human creation in the divine image (II.ix.1, 18, 22, 33, 46, 47): exemplary Alma and her Castle allegorize significant renewal on that model. Spenser's Temperance aims to bring good governance to "mans body" conceived as God's handiwork and the vehicle for his image; otherwise, he claims, the human frame becomes a "Distempred" "Monster" (II.ix.1). Alma's white dress, Arthur's saving intervention, and the baptismal symbolism of Maleger's demise all indicate that restoration of the divine image occurs through Christ, and so Christ's body allegorically subsumes Alma, her Castle, and those who avoid becoming "Distempred," like Guyon and Arthur.[49]

Complementing Spenser's Holiness, his Temperance is a means of advancing incorporation in Christ, but focuses on the mode of spiritual discipline that was supposed to govern the body, thought ultimately inseparable from the destiny of the soul. Even the bodies of the damned, Reformers emphasized, were to be resurrected, but in corruption. So powerful was the theological ideology of the body

that it shaped many medical texts of the period, so that Cogan introduces his medical injunctions for health by advocating conformity
to the proper human nature, as he conceives it, of the divine image.
God created "man . . . after his owne likenesse, and endued with
reason, wherby he differs from beasts," and so man should not "be
yet beastlike, to be moved by sense to serve his belly, to follow his
appetite." Hence "by the very order of nature, reason ought to rule,
and al appetites are to be bridled and subdued. . . . Wherefore, in a
moderate and temperate man, . . . the seate of affections, must yeeld
to reason," and thus "true delight is best perceived." From such a
viewpoint, fidelity to the divine image is a physiological and psychological necessity of human well-being, and temperance a main practice
for maintaining that condition. Since human physical nature conventionally bore a supernatural imprint from its origin, temperance could
readily have spiritual significance on that account, even aside from
its role in sanctification. To define "the temperate state . . . that is
in each respect perfect and absolute," the sixteenth-century physician
Levinus Lemnius assumes we could "chuse no better paterne
. . . either for the body or the minde" than "Christ himselfe."[50]

Although Book II may seem austere on account of its disciplinary
impetus, Spenser thus frames it as the book to liberate pleasure by
harmonizing the whole person. Cogan thinks "true delight" arises
from temperate fidelity to the divine image, and Spenser likewise.
So replete with "gracious delight," "drapets festiuall," amorous play,
and feasting is Alma's home, that Robert Reid assumes she caters
to "fleshly appetites," with Pauline resonance, contrary to Caelia's
spirituality (II.ix.20, 27, 34; x.77). However, white-clothed Alma's
household, in which there is significantly general good will and harmony, unlike Lucifera's, has evolved far beyond Redcross's need for
ascetic shock treatment, extirpating the flesh, in Caelia's house.
Spenser assumes that spiritual revivification through Temperance restores some Edenic capacity for the fullest savoring of pleasure at
best, just as Cupid gambols in Alma's Castle, but harmlessly. Perkins
comparably declares that sanctification affects both soul and body, and
produces "sanctified affections," which are "inclined to that which is
good, to imbrace it," and "not commonly . . . stirred with that
which is euill, unlesse . . . to eschew it." Rendering discipline a
means to pursue the fullest delight in Book II, Spenser's Temperance
might somewhat evoke prospects of Christian hedonism, and the
critical controversies produced by the Bower's destruction attest to
the ambivalences inherent in such a program. In any case, on account
of its particular perspective on virtue, Book II introduces, or yields
to, the books of authorized eros.[51]

McGill University

Notes

1. Sharply dividing Book I from Books II to VI, Woodhouse states a Spenserian synthesis would have to conclude *The Faerie Queene*; hence the poem, being unfinished, is, in his view, profoundly incoherent. "Nature and Grace in *The Faerie Queene*," *ELH*, 16 (1949): 194–228 (quoting 198). Nohrnberg, *The Analogy of "The Faerie Queene"* (Princeton: Princeton University Press, 1976), p. 73. In *The Spenser Encyclopedia*, ed. A. C. Hamilton *et al.* (Toronto: University of Toronto Press, 1990), cf. Robert L. Reid, "Holiness, house of," and James Carscallen, "temperance," pp. 373–74, 680–82. Bieman, *Plato Baptized: Towards the Interpretation of Spenser's Mimetic Fictions* (Toronto: University of Toronto Press, 1988), p. 218. Gless, "Nature and Grace," in *The Spenser Encyclopedia*, pp. 505–07 (quoting p. 506), with bibliography; his *Interpretation and Theology in Spenser* (Cambridge: Cambridge University Press, 1994), p. 192. Cf. Harold Weatherby, *Mirrors of Celestial Grace: Patristic Theology in Spenser's Allegory* (Toronto: University of Toronto Press, 1994), chs. 5–7, 9. On the stages of Elizabethan Protestant spiritual life, cf. Barbara Kiefer Lewalski, *Protestant Poetics and the Seventeenth-Century Religious Lyric* (Princeton: Princeton University Press, 1979), pp. 13–25. For Spenser, I use *The Works of Edmund Spenser: A Variorum Edition*, ed. Edwin Greenlaw et al., 11 vols. (Baltimore: Johns Hopkins University Press, 1932–57). Except in archaistic Spenser's case, I silently expand contractions and normalize usage of u, v, i, and j when quoting Renaissance sources.

2. Schoenfeldt, "Fables of the Belly in Early Modern England," in David Hillman and Carla Mazzio, eds., *The Body in Parts: Fantasies of Corporeality in Early Modern Europe* (New York and London: Routledge, 1997), pp. 243–61.

3. Quoting Reid, "Holiness, house of," and Carscallen, pp. 373–74, 680–82. Likewise Reid's "Spenserian Psychology and the Structure of Allegory in Books 1 and 2 of *The Faerie Queene*," *Modern Philology*, 79 (1981–82): 361–68; and "Alma's Castle and the Symbolization of Reason in *The Faerie Queene*," *JEGP*, 80 (1981): 527.

4. For biblical citations, I use *The Geneva Bible: A Facsimile of the 1560 Edition*, introd. Lloyd E. Berry (Geneva, 1560; facsim. rpt. Madison: University of Wisconsin Press, 1969).

5. Miller, *The Poem's Two Bodies: The Poetics of the 1590 "Faerie Queene"* (Princeton, N. J.: Princeton University Press, 1988), pp. 4, 71.

6. On the general anagogy of questing for Gloriana, cf. Kenneth Borris, *Allegory and Epic in English Renaissance Literature: Heroic Form in Sidney, Spenser, and Milton* (Cambridge, U. K.: Cambridge University Press, 2000?), ch. 3, Section Two, "Allegorization of Heroic and Civic Ideals," and ch. 7; Jeffrey P. Fruen, "'True Glorious Type': The Place of Gloriana in *The Faerie Queene*," *Spenser Studies*, 7 (1986): 147–73, his "The Faery Queen Unveiled? Five Glimpses of Gloriana," *Spenser Studies*, 11 (1990): 53–88; and Miller, pp. 4, 67–72, 111, 116–17, 119, 127–30, 138–40, 163.

7. Quoting Shuger, *Habits of Thought in the English Renaissance: Religion, Politics, and the Dominant Culture* (Berkeley and Los Angeles: University of California Press, 1990), p. 6; Claire McEachern, "Introduction," in Claire McEachern and Debora

Shuger, eds., *Religion and Culture in Renaissance England* (Cambridge, U.K.: Cambridge University Press, 1997), p. 4.

8. Bullinger, "Of Repentance," Fourth Decade, in his *Decades*, ed. Rev. Thomas Harding, trans. H. I., Parker Society, 4 vols. (Cambridge, 1849–52), III, 98. Bradford, "The Flesh and the Spirit," in his *Writings*, ed. Aubrey Townsend, Parker Society, 2 vols. (Cambridge, 1848–53), I, 301. In Paul's complex vocabulary, Bradford observes, the spirit corresponds to the "mind," "inward man," "new man," and "new nature"; and "flesh" to the "body," "outward man," and "old man." Yet "in these terms and in every of them is comprehended whole man, both soul and body, to be considered either according to regeneration and to the sanctifying of God's Spirit, or else according to all that ever he is or hath by nature, . . . by any means, inwardly or outwardly." Compare Jean Calvin, *The Institution of Christian Religion*, trans. Thomas Norton (London, 1599), 2.3.1; within my text, further references to this work will appear parenthetically. Also compare William Perkins, *The Combat of the Flesh and Spirit*, in his *Two Treatises* (London, 1595), pp. 41–55. Cf. Robert H. Gundry, *Soma in Biblical Theology with Emphasis on Pauline Anthropology* (Cambridge: Cambridge University Press, 1976), ch. 15; John A. T. Robinson, *The Body: A Study in Pauline Theology* (London: SCM Press, 1952), ch. 1; and W. David Stacey, *The Pauline View of Man in Relation to its Judaic and Hellenistic Background* (London: MacMillan, 1956), chs. 11–13.

9. Bullinger, "Of Repentance," in *Decades*, III, 107–08. "So much as we are regenerate and endued with God's Spirit," Bradford similarly affirms, we seek to bring our "natural and corrupt affections . . . as much as may be into obedience to the Spirit; at the least to bridle them, that they bear not dominion or rule in us" (I, 302). Wilson, *A Christian Dictionary* (London, 1616), s.v. "Sanctification."

10. Madelon S. Gohlke, e.g., considers Spenser dualistic in "Embattled Allegory: Book II of *The Faerie Queene*," *English Literary Renaissance*, 8 (1978): 130, 138–40.

11. Becon, *A Fruitfull Treatise of Fasting*, in his *Catechism*, ed. Rev. John Ayre, Parker Society (Cambridge, 1844), p. 543.

12. Quoting Barrough, *The Method of Phisick* (London, 1601), sigs. A6[b]-A7[a]. On anthropomorphic edifices, cf. Leonard Barkan, *Nature's Work of Art: The Human Body as Image of the World* (New Haven: Yale University Press, 1975), pp. 151–74; Roberta D. Cornelius, *The Figurative Castle: A Study in the Mediaeval Allegory of the Edifice* (Bryn Mawr: Bryn Mawr College Press, 1930); G. R. Owst, *Literature and Pulpit in Medieval England*, 2nd, rev. ed. (Oxford: Basil Blackwell, 1961), ch. 2; and C. L. Powell, "The Castle of the Body," *Studies in Philology*, 16 (1919): 197–205.

13. In Genesis, God creates Adam from earth (2:7). "Adam" was commonly taken to mean "earthlie," as in the Geneva Bible's interpretive table of proper names.

14. Though the Platonic and Aristotelian tripartite hierarchies of human powers were not fully correspondent, since Aristotle did not, for example, assign reason to the brain, and though Spenser tends to privilege Plato's, they are jointly relevant to Alma's and Caelia's houses, as Reid shows, and also, I add, underwrite much satire of the House of Pride. Cf. Reid, "Spenserian Psychology," and "Holiness, house of"; also Walter R. Davis, "The Houses of Mortality in Book II of *The Faerie Queene*," *Spenser Studies*, 2 (1981), p. 123; and Nohrnberg, p. 350.

15. On traditions of figuring intellectual and devotional presence of mind as a tower, cf. Don Cameron Allen, *The Harmonious Vision: Studies in Milton's Poetry*, 2nd, rev. ed. (Baltimore: Johns Hopkins Press, 1970), pp. 17–18.

16.   The anus was "readily likened to a door" in Greek and Latin, and studies of Elizabethan dramatic bawdy have documented the anal possibilities of back doors, gates, and posterns. Quoting J. N. Adams, "*Culus, Clunes* and their Synonyms in Latin," *Glotta*, 59 (1981): 244–45. Cf. James T. Henke, *Courtesans and Cuckolds: A Glossary of Renaissance Dramatic Bawdy (Excluding Shakespeare)* (New York: Garland, 1979), s.v. "Back-door'd," "Door"; Frankie Rubinstein, *A Dictionary of Shakespeare's Sexual Puns and Their Significance*, 2nd, rev. ed. (London: Macmillan, 1989), s.v. "gate," "postern," "privily." Cf. *OED*, 2nd ed., s.v. "postern," sb. 1, 3; "private" B sb. II 7 (plural); "privy" A adj. III 8d, B sb. II 3; and "stern" sb.[3] 3. In *A Generall Practise of Physicke*, Christopher Wirtzung's chapter "Of the Arsegut or Fundament in generall" refers to its features as "privie places." Trans. Jacob Mosan (London, 1598), p. 302.

17.   As the Variorum notes, Upton and Wickham gloss Spenser's Esquiline gate according to disposal of carcasses (II, 293), and Douglas Brooks-Davies follows suit in *Spenser's "Faerie Queene": A Critical Commentary on Books I and II* (Manchester: Manchester University Press, 1977), p. 165. But a major latrine or sewer, such as the Roman Cloaca Maxima, would thus seem a much more appropriate choice for Spenser to make, architecturally and otherwise, for this anatomical homology. In A. C. Hamilton, ed., *The Faerie Queene* (London: Longman, 1977), the "*Port Esquiline*" is "a gate in ancient Rome, its anus as it gave passage to the common dump" (p. 253*n*). But this gate gave onto a necropolis, not a general dump. Cf. Samuel Bell Platner, *A Topographical Dictionary of Ancient Rome*, rev. ed. (London, Oxford University Press, 1929), s.v. "Campus Esquilinus," "Cispius Mons," "Esquiliae," "Horti Maecenatis," "Murus Servii Tullii," "Oppius Mons," "Porta Esquilina," and "Puticuli." On Roman topographical representations of the buttocks and anus, cf. Adams, 253–55. Fletcher, *The Purple Island*, ii.43, my emphasis; in Giles and Phineas Fletcher, *Poetical Works*, ed. Frederick S. Boas, 2 vols. (Cambridge: Cambridge University Press, 1908), II, 35. *Fanny Hill* clearly uses this motif to associate Rome, whether classical, contemporary, or possibly Roman Catholic, with anal sex between males: "he showed to the open air those globular, fleshy eminences that compose the mount-pleasants of Rome, and which now, with all the narrow vale that intersects them, stood displayed and exposed to his attack." John Cleland, *Fanny Hill*, ed. Peter Wagner (Harmondsworth: Penguin, 1985), p. 195.

18.   La Primaudaye, *The French Academie*, trans. T. B. (London, 1594), p. 352. Becon, *The Flower of Godly Prayers*, in his *Prayers and Other Pieces*, ed. Rev. John Ayre, Parker Society (Cambridge, 1844), pp. 57–58.

19.   Fletcher, *Purple Island*, iii.19 (II, 41).

20.   Barrough, sig. A6[b]. Cogan, *The Haven of Health* (London, 1612), sig. ¶4[a], p. 169. Elyot, *The Castel of Helth* (London, 1541; facs. rpt. New York: Scholars', 1936), fol. 57[a]. Lemnius, *The Touchstone of Complexions*, trans. T. Newton (London, 1633), pp. 73, 169, 58. Excessive eating . . . bringeth sudden death oftentimes, as *Galen* sheweth"; according to Galen and Avicenna, "such as use immoderate *Venus*, be short lived," for "*bloud and sede*" are "the very . . . foundation of our life," and must be aptly conserved (Cogan, pp. 169, 242). "An Homily of Good Works: And First of Fasting," and "An Homily Against Gluttony and Drunkenness," in *Certain Sermons or Homilies Appointed to be Read in Churches in the Time of Queen Elizabeth* (London, 1864), pp. 311, 318, 300. Cf. Schoenfeldt, pp. 253–54.

21. Wilson, *A Christian Dictionary*, s.v. "Death," "Second Death," and "Dead workes."

22. Quoting Bullinger on mortification, "Of Repentance," in *Decades*, III, 108. On fasting and control of diet in subjection of the flesh, see, e.g., Becon, *Treatise of Fasting*, pp. 543–45. For general discussion of Caelia's house, cf. Reid, "Holiness, house of," pp. 373–74.

23. Wilson, *Christian Dictionary*, s.v. "To Mortifie," "Dead to sin," "Man, Inner Man, and new Man," and "Man, Old Man." Cf. John Norden, "Prayer for Mortification," in *A Progress of Piety*, Parker Society (Cambridge, 1847), p. 74; Bullinger, "Of Repentance," in *Decades*, III, 97–108; and "A Prayer for True Mortification" and "A Meditation for the Exercise of True Mortification," in Henry Bull, comp., *Christian Prayers*, Parker Society (Cambridge, 1842), pp. 92–98. The prayer also appears in the *Booke of Christian Prayers* used by Queen Elizabeth (London, 1578).

24. *OED*, 2nd ed., s.v. "mortification" sb. 2. Guillemeau, *The French Chirurgerye*, trans. A. M. (Dort, 1597), fols. 37ª, 38ª.

25. *OED* s.v. "proud" adj. B II 7d, 8a. Guillemeau, fol. 2ᵇ. Citing Hamilton, ed., *The Faerie Queene*, p. 135n.

26. Woodhouse 221.

27. On the relations of gender to the Alma episode, which is beyond the practical scope of my topic here, cf. Miller, Ch. 4, and Dorothy Stephens, "'Newes of devils': Feminine Sprights in Masculine Minds in *The Faerie Queene*," *English Literary Renaissance*, 23 (1993): 363–81. Focusing on the lack of sexual organs at Alma's Castle and interpreting that as a symbolic castration, Miller argues that the Castle's representation of the temperate body is masculine because the penis is reinscribed as the head, so that Spenser appropriates femininity for definition of masculinity and service of empire. Stephens objects that "although masculine desires to reappropriate the feminine doubtless inform Alma's story, the text also makes way for the reverse action," and "Alma's genitals are in a sense displaced rather than entirely lacking" (378, 379n12). It could also be questioned whether the head was necessarily and simply gendered masculine in Renaissance culture. Representations of the soul were commonly feminine, as were many of the virtues. Spenser's Sapience is feminine.

28. Stambler, "The Development of Guyon's Christian Temperance," *English Literary Renaissance*, 7 (1977): 86–88. "Prayer against the Flesh" in *A Booke of Christian Prayers*, in *Private Prayers Put forth by Authority During the Reign of Queen Elizabeth*, ed. Rev. William Keatinge Clay, Parker Society (Cambridge, 1851), pp. 542–43. Compare Calvin, 3.3.14: "we are so cleansed by [Christ's] sanctification, that we are still besieged with many vices and much weaknesse, so long as we are inclosed in . . . our body," and "must watch with heedefull mindes, that we be not compassed unware with the snares of our flesh." Also Becon, *Treatise of Fasting*, p. 543.

29. Robinson summarizes characteristics of the Pauline flesh, pp. 19–21. For Fulgentius, Antaeus specifically signifies *libido*, and his earthy context the flesh, so that he means, in effect, the lusts of the flesh. *Mythologiae*, 2.4, in *Fulgentius the Mythographer*, trans. Leslie George Whitbread (Columbus: Ohio State University Press, 1971), pp. 69–70. On the currency of this allegory, cf. Phillip Rollinson, "Arthur, Maleger, and the Interpretation of *The Faerie Queene*," *Spenser Studies*, 7 (1986), p. 118n6.

30. Woodhouse, 221–22. For "standing," the glosses "stagnant" and "still, not ebbing" are both from the same *OED* category; its historical examples show that

"standing" water need not be stagnant (e.g., due to submerged springs). Cf. *OED*, 2nd ed., s.v. "standing" ppl. a. II 7a, 11a; III 13a, 17a. *The Book of Common Prayer, 1559: The Elizabethan Prayer Book*, ed. John E. Booty (Charlottesville: Folger-University Press of Virginia, 1976), pp. 270–71. Perkins, *A Golden Chaine, or the Description of Theologie* (London, 1595), p. 177.

31.   *Book of Common Prayer* of 1549, in *The First and Second Prayer Books of Edward VI*, introd. Rev. E. C. S. Gibson (London: Dent, 1910), pp. 240–41. The baptismal rite in the 1552 and 1559 versions excised the white robe. On controversies over its inclusion in Reformed liturgies, cf. J. D. C. Fisher, *Christian Initiation: The Reformation Period* (London: SPCK, 1970), Index, s.v. "white robe." It was retained by Zwingli and others. In the early church, baptized adults wore white robes for a week during Easter. Cf. G. R. Beasley-Murray, *Baptism in the New Testament* (London: MacMillan, 1963), pp. 148–49; and E. C. Whitaker, *The Baptismal Liturgy*, 2nd ed. (London: SPCK, 1981), pp. 50, 56–57. Oliver O'Donovan, *On the Thirty Nine Articles: A Conversation with Tudor Christianity* (Exeter, U.K.: Paternoster-Latimer House, 1986), p. 148. *Book of Common Prayer* (1559), p. 273.

32.   *Book of Common Prayer* (1559), pp. 270, 274. Perkins, *Foundation of Christian Religion* (London, 1595), sig. C4^b.

33.   Hamilton, ed., *The Faerie Queene*, p. 167*n*. For additional possibilities, cf. Nohrnberg, Index, s.v. "Maleger"; Rollinson, "Arthur, Maleger"; and his "Maleger" in *Spenser Encyclopedia*, pp. 449–50.

34.   Cf. John Florio, *A Worlde of Wordes* (London, 1598), s.v. "Alma." Compare the Latin adjectival "alma," "providing nurture, kindly." Anthea Hume, *Edmund Spenser: Protestant Poet* (Cambridge: Cambridge University Press, 1984), pp. 122–24. On Reformed interpretation of the baptismal white robe, cf. Fisher, Index, s.v. "white robe." It has clear eschatological connections in, e.g., the 1549 *Book of Common Prayer*, where the innocence of "white vesture" is to gain "lyfe everlasting" after "this transitorye lyfe" (*Prayer Books of Edward VI*, p. 241).

35.   Bullinger, *A Hundred Sermons upon the Apocalypse*, trans. J. Daus (London, 1573), fols. 49^b, 60^b. Cf. Calvin, 3.11.23; and Wilson, *A Dictionary, for that Mysticall Booke, called the Revelation*, in his *Christian Dictionary*, s.v. "White Robe," and "Pure fine linnen, and shining."

36.   Hume, pp. 122–23.

37.   Cf. Bullinger, "Of Repentance," in *Decades*, III, 101. Vermigli, *The Common Places*, trans. Anthony Marten (London, 1582), Part Two, p. 564. Perkins, *A Treatise Tending vnto a Declaration* (London, 1595), p. 46; *A Golden Chaine*, p. 208. Ames, *The Marrow of Sacred Divinity* (London, 1643), p. 126. The possibility and extent of earthly physical regeneration are still theologically controversial; cf., e.g., Gundry, pp. 228–43. Regeneration remains incomplete during life, for all these writers.

38.   Quoting Hamilton, ed., *The Faerie Queene*, p. 250*n*. Plato's correlative tripartite allegory of the charioteer appears in Plato's *Phaedrus*, 246A–48B, 253C–56E (quoting 253D–E, trans. H. N. Fowler). Unless otherwise noted, I use the Loeb series for all citations of classical texts. On representation of the appetites in heroic poetry, cf. Borris, ch. 3, section three, "Allegorism and the General Epic Repertoire."

39.   Wermullerus, *The Hope of the Faythful*, trans. Miles Coverdale, in Coverdale's *Remains*, ed. Rev. George Pearson, Parker Society (Cambridge, 1846), p. 179. Bullinger, "Of the First Articles of the Christian Faith," First Decade, in *Decades*, I,

174. Also quoting Bullinger on sartorially symbolic glory, *Sermons upon the Apocalypse*, fol. 92ᵃ; cf. fols. 49ᵇ-50ᵃ, 103ᵃ-05ᵇ, 257ᵇ. See further Wilson, *Dictionary, for . . . Revelation*, in his *Christian Dictionary*, s.v. "White array." Vermigli, Part Three, pp. 359–60. On symbolic connections of the baptismal white robe with eschatology, cf. Fisher, *Index*, s.v. "white robe," and Hugh M. Riley, *Christian Initiation: A Comparative Study of the Interpretation of the Baptismal Liturgy* (Washington, D.C.: Catholic University of America-Consortium Press, 1974), pp. 349–57, 413–51. On the glorified body in Donne's poetry, cf. A. C. Chambers, "Glorified Bodies and the 'Valediction: Forbidding Mourning,'" *John Donne Journal*, 1 (1982): 1–20.

40. On gold and glorification, cf. Chambers 9–12, and Bullinger, *Sermons upon the Apocalypse*, fols. 59ᵃ-61ᵃ. On sex and resurrected genitals, Vermigli declares "God . . . will take awaie from them that be raised up, the use and action of these parts: but not the substance and nature of them" (Part Three, p. 360; cf. pp. 357–58). On resurrected viscera, cf. Vermigli, Part Three, pp. 357–58, 360. For differing analyses of the Alma episode and its relations to gender issues and sexual organs, cf. Miller, Ch. 4, and Stephens.

41. Bullinger, "First Articles," in *Decades*, I, 173; Wermullerus, p. 182; Vermigli, Part Three, p. 359; Woolton, *A New Anatomie of Whole Man* (London, 1576), fol. 44ᵃ.

42. Hooper, *A Briefe and Clear Confession of the Christian Faith*, in his *Later Writings*, ed. Rev. Charles Nevinson, Parker Society (Cambridge, 1852), p. 61; Vermigli, Part Three, pp. 357, 359; Wermullerus, pp. 171, 175, 177, 181; Bullinger, "First Articles," in *Decades*, I, 175–76.

43. Jeanes, citing Van Est, in *A Treatise Concerning the Fulnesse of Christ* (Oxford, 1656), p. 371. Vermigli, part three, p. 359.

44. Bullinger would reject any earthly proto-glorification of the body, or even prefiguration of it, because he denies that regeneration includes the body, unlike Vermigli, Perkins, and Ames. Cf. "Of the Gospel" and "Of Repentance," in *Decades*, III, 35–38, 101. Though both Perkins and Ames assume that sanctification includes the body, glorification begins after death for Perkins (*Golden Chaine*, p. 231), but during life for Ames, who does not indicate whether that affects the body, nor how much (pp. 129–33). For recent discussion of this theological issue, cf., e.g., Gundry's critique of Robinson, pp. 228–43. Gless, *Theology in Spenser*, pp. 175–76.

45. Vermigli, Part Three, pp. 359–60; Hooper, p. 62.

46. Cf. Chambers, 16–17.

47. Woodhouse, 208; Reid, "Holiness, house of," p. 374; and Carscallen, p. 681.

48. Quoting Lewalski, pp. 13–14, 24; Gless, "Nature and Grace," pp. 506–07.

49. Homilies, *Certain Sermons*, pp. 322, 582. Bullinger, "Of Repentance," in *Decades*, III, 101. Ames, p. 125. On sin and created nature, cf. Calvin, 2.1.10–11: "man is corrupted with faultinesse naturall, but such as proceeded not from nature [i.e., as created]," of which God is "author."

50. Cogan, sig. ¶3ᵃ⁻ᵇ; Lemnius, pp. 52, 59.

51. Gohlke, e.g., finds Book II extremely austere: she assumes "the temperate body," as Alma's Castle, excludes "the pleasures of the senses" in general, and has "virtually no positive functions" (130). Reid, "Spenserian Psychology," 368. Perkins, *Declaration*, p. 43.

JOSEPH D. PARRY

Phaedria and Guyon: Traveling Alone in *The Faerie Queene*, Book II[1]

Guyon's progress through and past obstacles and diversions is a conspicuous feature of Book II's allegory in Spenser's *The Faerie Queene*. The whimsical, erratically mobile Phaedria, however, occupies a singular place among the female temptresses that accost Guyon in Book II. Consequently, Guyon must move temperately within Faeryland when he encounters Phaedria in a manner that is not exactly progress. In fact, Phaedria presents Guyon with the opportunity to learn that continual "progress" toward the sources and origins of desire—in the world or in the self—in order fully to comprehend and master our appetites is not necessarily a desirable thing. Spenser suggests in the Phaedria episodes an alternate way of configuring the motions of rational activity that complicates the allegory of self-knowing that seems to drive Book II: Guyon must move away from Phaedria, not by her. Phaedria's world is a concentrated and, perhaps, an exaggerated instance of the broader sense of mutability that predominates Faeryland, which, therefore, Guyon must learn to negotiate in order to get through it. Yet rather than getting through it, Phaedria delights in this semantically fluid world, and relishes traveling deeper into it. Guyon must travel like her to get past her, but in such motions the text demonstrates that Guyon's progress toward greater self-awareness leads him deeper and deeper into more troubling dimensions of the self. Guyon in motion reveals that motion and mobility in Book II become problematic ways of signifying progress, though they remain the only available signifiers that can perform this work.

ON THEIR FINAL approach to the Bower of Bliss in Canto xii of Edmund Spenser's *The Faerie Queene*, Guyon and the Palmer once

again encounter Phaedria on the shore of "one of those same Islands,
which doe fleet/In the wide sea, they needes must passen by,/Which
seemd so sweet and pleasant to the eye,/That it would tempt a man
to touchen there."[2] Phaedria seems to reappear briefly in the text for
Guyon once again to pass by her in his trek towards Acrasia and
the final temptation that will presumably prove him fully temperate.
Guyon's forward motion in Book II, and especially in Canto xii, is
a conspicuously important feature of the allegory that tracks Guyon's
moral progress; the text's language at the beginning of Canto xii is
particularly intent on representing Guyon's forward progress through
and beyond the obstacles that would prevent his arrival at the Bowre
of Blisse. In the context of Guyon's final voyage to the Bowre of
Blisse, Phaedria seems to be one of many temptations that prepare
him for his final encounter with Acrasia—the final, originary, and
culminating embodiment of the many lesser, preparatory representations of intemperance that Guyon must learn to negotiate on his
journey to the Bowre. When we finally see Acrasia herself, we feel
that we have already seen her, or at least that we have seen the danger
she poses previewed and unveiled many times over: the trip through
Book II, and particularly through Canto xii, is a process of establish-
ing patterns by which readers will comprehend Acrasia when they
finally see her.

While Phaedria is a part of this preparatory process for Guyon, she
is not a temptation that Guyon exactly passes by, or, in other words,
she is not precisely a vice that he fully comprehends and brings under
rational control. For that matter, Phaedria is not exactly a precursor
to, much less an avatar of, Acrasia. Spenser does not write her as the
kind of allegorical figure that we gaze at, throw a net over, nor
simply stride past to proceed on the journey of self-discovery and
self-mastery. Phaedria does not occupy a particular space, nor stand
still long enough to allow Guyon or Spenser's readers to arrest her
motion, to place her as a danger which we understand, recognize,
and successfully control. I wish to argue in this essay that Spenser
does not allow us fully to locate Phaeadria, that is, read her with the
interpretive stability our moral discourses tend to impute both to the
representations of virtue and vice, and also, perhaps more importantly, to the sense of knowledge those discourses make available concerning the *status* of what we know or recognize about others or,
especially, ourselves. Phaedria is not a piece of knowledge that Guyon
masters. She lives and moves right on the boundaries of what Guyon
can and perhaps should know and be able to control. Indeed, Phaedria
functions as an image of the persistently unstable, mobile, shape-
shifting character of the knowledge that Guyon seeks on his journey,

and she provides opportunities for Spenser's allegory to interrogate
the moral assumptions and the structural character that the narrative
itself relies on to render Guyon's "progress" towards complete rational self-knowledge.

Phaedria functions somewhat differently than the other figures Guyon meets in Book II, especially in Canto xii, who would impede,
divert, or altogether stop his progress. When Guyon encounters
Phaedria in Canto xii—his second time in Book II (no other figure
from the text reappears in Guyon's boat trip to the Bowre)—he gets
by her and her floating island, or, at least, away from her, and he
appears to do so more easily than he did the first time: he does not
need to visit her island, board her boat, or get involved in an ugly,
inconclusive scrape with someone like Cymochles. Yet once again,
Guyon's encounter with Phaedria is marked by a kind of incompleteness. Guyon turns from Phaedria to proceed on his journey,
but before Guyon "keeps on [his] gate," Phaedria first leaves them
"scornefully." After Phaedria's "merry," "wanton," and "immodest"
advances to Guyon, and after the Palmer rebukes her "for being loose
and light" (6), Phaedria does not "abide" the rebuke, "but more
scornefully/Scoffing at him, that did her iustly wite,/She turnd her
bote about, and from them rowed quite" (7–9). However, the next
stanza will tell us that it is the Palmer and Guyon who leave Phaedria,
(finally naming her here as Phaedria), "nought regarding, they kept
on their gate,/And all her vaine allurements did forsake" (17. 1–4).
Phaedria and Guyon leave each other here. Whereas Guyon can
negotiate the topographical perils on the water under the Palmer's
guidance (which, again, includes Phaedria's island), and whereas Guyon can move past the weeping Maiden (27–29) and the Sirens
(30–34. 3) after hearkening to the Palmer's counsel and reproof, he
does not encounter in Phaedria herself a static figure he can simply
pass by. Phaedria's freedom of mobility and her agency to act in
Faeryland allows her even in Canto xii to choose to pass by Guyon
as much as he can choose to pass by her. Unlike the evil female
figures that Sheila T. Cavanagh examines (which includes Phaedria),
who "generally either evaporate like the Snowy Florimell or fall
back under male domination" like Acrasia throughout Spenser's text,[3]
Phaedria withdraws from Guyon under her own power. She approaches them, rather than being approached by them, as they seem
to do with all of the other obstacles to their path towards the Bowre.
Nor is Phaedria one of the landmarks or figures that the Palmer
explicates to Guyon as they travel by the phenomena "they needes
must passen by": the Palmer does not chide or advise Guyon when
they meet Phaedria, as he does both when Guyon begins to steer

toward "the dolefull Mayd" to render her assistance (28. 2–29. 4), and also when his "senses [are] softly tickeled" by the Sirens flattering song (33. 7– 34. 1–2). Instead, when Guyon encounters Phaedria, the Palmer "rebukes" her directly, responding to her as a being capable of choosing her behavior. She is not on show as, say, the bathers in Canto xii's fountain are, and her relation to Acrasia is ambiguous. When Phaedria, for example, first meets and dallies with Cymochles in Canto vi, Cymochles does not recognize her, whereupon Phaedria chides Cymochles:

> Vaine man (said she) that wouldest be reckoned
> A straunger in thy home, and ignoraunt
> Of Phaedria (for so my name is red)
> Of Phaedria, thine owne fellow seruaunt;
> For thou to serue Acrasia thy selfe doest vaunt.
>
> (9. 5–9)

A. C. Hamilton understands line 8 to translate as " 'since you serve Acrasia, I serve you,'" rather than the weaker, " 'I am a servant of Acrasia even as you are.' "[4] Phaedria endangers Guyon's temperance, but not exactly as the servant of Acrasia, nor can Guyon deal with her as a danger in the same way he can, under Reason's direction. with Acrasia.

Phaedria's ability to move freely and unpredictably in Faeryland distinguishes her from all other female allegorical temptations in Book II, and especially in Canto xii. Even Acrasia hardly moves at all. She is the allegorization most deeply invested in immobility. Acrasia is, of course, the chief immobilizing force in Faeryland that stops knights from questing, moving, towards their righteous goals. In the logic of the allegory, then, she is herself to be rendered immobile, which the Palmer and Guyon do first with their "subtile net" (81. 4), then with "chaines of admant" (82. 6). Yet also, when we first (and finally) see her in Canto xii, Acrasia is conspicuously immobile; that is, she is rendered so that the narrative may linger over her with the same "hungry eies" (78. 2) it imputes to its onlooking characters and readers in order to convey the immobilizing effect she has on us. Though immobilizing Acrasia is the aim of Guyon's quest to the Bowre, Acrasia will never actually move in Spenser's text (until she fights within the restraints of the net), and therefore, will never herself act out before our readerly eyes her allegorical being as a destructively lustful figure. Her destructiveness lies in our lusting after her; she is in the text more lusted after than lusting. The narrative conveys her allegorical meaning in its very act of rendering her waiting and "bare to readie spoyle" (78. 1). She is, consequently, easily moralized, labeled, by the text.

Phaedria moves easily, erratically, and is, in the allegorical logic of the text, defined by her ability to move according to the whims of her intemperate fancy. In fact, Phaedria occupies and moves in a kind of spatial, topographical construct of the unrestrained imagination, in the manner of traditional faculty psychology; she enacts for Guyon the capriciousness of the fantasy that would divert his will away from the rule of reason. Consequently, her characterization is not constrained by rationally derived categories—her looseness of behavior and of motion, hence the looseness of her meaning in the allegory, make her a difficult figure to trace, follow, or, for that matter, rationally apprehend. Guyon (and we) will have some difficulty perceiving what kind of threat she poses, which itself is a serious threat to Book II's investments in the discourse of rational self-control. Initially, Spenser's narrative seems to imagine Guyon's inability fully to control or comprehend neither her nor the space within which she moves in erotic terms, and thereby casts her looseness as a sexual danger to Guyon—Guyon, as the argument to Canto vi states, "is of immodest Merth/led into loose desire." Indeed, Guyon's erotic appetite throughout Book II complicates his ability to negotiate the spheres of uncontrollable divergence, irresistible confusion, and/or encroaching self-forgetfulness he encounters because virtue in the Legend of Temperance exists and moves squarely in the world of self-reflexive, self-conscious control. By the time Guyon finds himself alone in Phaedria's boat, we have already seen the dire places Phaedria leads knights. As Phaedria dallies with Cymochles a few stanzas earlier, we seem, in fact, to have been primed to see her as a lesser version of Acrasia herself. When Phaedria ferries Cymochles to her island she is a "wanton Damzell" who offers him "loose dalliaunce . . . to quench his flamed mind/With one sweet drop of sensuall delight" (8.1,6–7). Like Acrasia after her, she is a Venus to this Mars (she herself invokes the Mars/Venus image when she attempts to persuade Guyon and Cymochles to stop their fight (35)). Phaedria will lead Cymochles to lay "his head disarm'd/In her loose lap" (14.6–7), just as Acrasia has Verdant's head in her lap (76.8–9). Cavanagh reads Phaedria as one of the many female figures Spenser gives us who seduces knights "away from the field and from virtue, using sex as the primary weapon."[5]

However, the danger Phaedria poses to Guyon is fundamentally more interpretive than sexual. Trapping Guyon within Phaedria's free, whimsical, "loose," mode of travel, Spenser will prevent Guyon, in the absence of the Palmer (not to mention, his horse), from pursuing a controlled, careful style of progress, initiating him instead into a kind of quixotic, confusing foreplay to the loose, dissolute world to which Phaedria leads Guyon. The cognitive difficulties Guyon experiences in Phaedria's world are first figured in the muddy quality of the lake they travel on to arrive at Phaedria's island: "Through the dull billowes thicke as troubled mire,/Whom neither wind out of their seat could forse,/Nor timely tides did driue out of their sluggish sourse" (20.7–9). Hamilton suggests that this lake is comprised of "a mixture of earth and water to which Phaedria reduces man's nature."[6] Such a gloss to the text ultimately accords with our sense of how Phaedria's island itself threatens Guyon. The pleasures and "dissolute delights" that lull knights asleep, overpowering the "natural" forces that spur them on to keep moving and progressing, represent limitations to Guyon's ability to be conscious of, to think adequately about, what he should do. Indeed, Phaedria's movements and actions are dangerous to Guyon because they perplex the faculties upon which he relies first to apprehend and then to comprehend his world, even before his appetites assert themselves.

Registering Phaedria's effect on the befuddled Guyon, the text renders everything about Phaedria's bearing, including her eroticism, more vaguely than it did her preceding scene with Cymochles, though the text also refers back to that scene:

> And by the way, as was her wonted guize,
>   Her merry fit she freshly gan to reare,
>   And did of ioy and iollitie deuize,
>   Her selfe to cherish, and her guest to cheare:
>   The knight was courteous, and did not forbeare
>   Her honest merth and pleasaunce to partake;
>   But when he saw her toy, and gibe, and geare,
>   And passe the bonds of modest merimake,
> Her dalliance he despisd, and follies did forsake.
>
>   (21.1–9)

The reader has seen her "wonted guize" with Cymochles, and when the text says she "freshly" begins it again, the reader is invited to turn back a few stanzas to refresh our memories. Yet Phaedria's "merry fit" and her attempts to "cheare" her guest walk a line for a time in this stanza between "honest merth and pleasaunce" and behavior that "passe[s] the bonds of modest merimake." Though the

stanza concludes with a condemnation of her "dalliance" and "fol-
lies," Spenser here is not as quick to label Phaedria with the same,
obvious, sexual tags as he did in the Cymochles episode. For a time
here the narrative sorts through her actions which are not immediately named as evil or intemperate. Spenser is careful to reproduce
the process by which Guyon comes to realize Phaedria's danger to
him. Without the Palmer to tell Guyon what he is experiencing,
Guyon is left to sort through his experience.[7] Four stanzas later Phaedria is finally revealed as a figure who would quell Guyon's "desire
of knightly exercize":

> So did she all, that might his constant hart
> Withdraw from thoughts of warlike enterprize,
> And drowne in dissolute delights apart,
> Where noyse of armes, or vew of martiall guize
> Might not revive desire cf knightly exercize.
>
> (25.5–9)

Yet again, Guyon did not immediately recognize her as a temptress.
As he is whirled about in Phaedria's world, Guyon is literally "at
sea" concerning her.

When Guyon first steps into Phaedria's boat, he finds himself irresistibly propelled towards a world meant to enmesh him in ignorance
and uncontrollability. Phaedria's "flit barke, obaying to her mind/
Forth launched quickly, as she did desire" (20.3–4), which seems to
indicate that the narrative's greatest anxiety at this moment is Guyon's
loss of control and understanding (suggested by his separation from
the Palmer). Movement (and, for that matter, stasis) is suspect, once
we are inside Phaedria's world. Already knowing that the Palmer
refuses to go, Spenser tells us that

> Guyon was loath to leaue his guide behind,
>   Yet being entred, might not backe retyre;
> . . . .
> Ne gaue him leaue to bid that aged sire
> Adieu, but nimbly ran her wonted course . . . .
>
> (II.vi.20.1,2,5,6)

Guyon wishes to go with Phaedria, but he is "loath"[8] to leave the
Palmer. The narrative has suggested that Guyon first steps into the

boat and expects the Palmer to follow, but the Palmer refuses, nor
does Phaedria wish him to go, even when Guyon importunes her:

> . . . himselfe [Guyon] she tooke a boord,
> But the Blacke Palmer suffred still to stond,
> Ne would for price, or prayers once affoord,
> To ferry that old man ouer the perlous foord.

$$(19.6-9)$$

Both Phaedria and the Palmer can be the subject of "suffred." In
fact, both should be the subject of the verb, because Phaedria refuses
to let him come, and the Palmer, as the allegorical figure of Reason,
refuses himself to go. The Palmer's refusal to go is represented by
his insistence on standing on the shore and not moving toward or
into the boat. The Palmer's standing here is, of course, opposed to
the motion of Phaedria's boat. Reason is a guide, not a passenger on
this journey through Faeryland; the boat will "obay . . . [Phaedria's]
mind," not the Palmer's nor Guyon's, for that matter. Reason directs
Guyon's progress by pointing out both right and wrong directions.
Reason wishes, however, only to move in right directions and avoid
taking the wrong paths. But Canto vi is a canto dedicated apparently
to a path Guyon should not have taken.

Of course, one can read this path as one that Guyon should take.
One could read Guyon taking this way in order to learn from mistakes, to experience a moment when he overestimates his own capacity to control the unsteadiness of his own soul, battling irrational
appetites on one side and the unruly powers of his own imagination
on the other, therefore, to demonstrate to himself and to us why he
should not have taken it. Along a similar, but a less moralistic, line
of logic, perhaps Guyon encounters the power of the repressions
which the ideologies of temperance rightly or wrongly cause in Guyon, but which, nevertheless, must be successfully negotiated for
well-adjusted living in human society. In other words, one can read
Guyon's journey in the narrative of Canto vi as wandering, as a
diversion from an appointed path which, however, when framed
within larger ethical and psychological courses we envision for Guyon, can also be read as a necessary part of the allegorical path Guyon
is to follow—that is, one is able completely to follow, for instance,
"the path of moral rectitude" or "the path of psychological wholeness," not only after, but also by, leaving it temporarily to follow "the
path of confronting one's mortality, spiritual inadequacies, repressed

anxieties, etc." "Wandering" and "not-really-wandering" both become interpretive categories necessary to our attempts to follow Guyon's motions here.[9] Though Guyon's path, like Redcrosse's before him, seems populated by ideologically static images that one contends with, learns how to read, and finally passes to keep progressing morally, Spenser scholarship has found that in Books I and II the allegorical and romance impulses of the text render divergence, slowness, etc., as a kind of necessary counterpoint to the quality of motion prescribed by the text's manifest ideology. Guillory, for example, finds that narrative "wandering" in Book I is a sign of inevitable conflict between what Spenser reads to write (Revelation) and how Spenser chooses to write (Romance allegory)—the narrative of Book I "wander[s] . . . farther and farther away from the redaction of the Book of Revelation (which is the 'origin' of Book I)," which suggests "an approach (albeit reluctant) to the truer and more dangerous origin of romance." The play and *dilatio*[10] that inheres in romance structures asserts itself over the desires of the text to push its "redaction" of Revelation to its appointed end. This is for Guillory "the inevitable displacement of sacred origin," which signals the beginning of the end of Spenser's endings as repeated "completions"(27)[11]. Teskey, on the other hand, finds Spenser consciously encouraging his narrative to wander, as part of its moral project, because the narrative has a stake in enmeshing its readers in error: "the openness of allegory to hermeneutic play is a consequence of the disorder that is generated by trying to make narrative and truth coincide: allegory can only teach by entangling." Readers of Spenser are supposed to wander through "a variety of adventures" that occupy a "space" between good and evil so that they can interpret through the "changes" Spenser's allegorical figures undergo in which direction (good or evil) they are headed.[12]

In both of these readings, "wandering" is the crucial signifier. For Guillory it signifies the unraveling of Spenser's intended moral structures; for Teskey "wandering" is the structure which invites the reader to discover the text's moral underpinnings. Wandering, of course, derives much of its meaning from whatever resistances the text applies to it; it is only visible as wandering if one can perceive the text trying to delineate straight, narrow paths that one should take. And though Guyon is, on the one hand, the rational individual who must pursue an unswerving path towards virtuous self-control, he is, on the other hand, a servant to a God who expects his knights, as he did his apostles, to wander through the world effecting the good by word and deed. Nevertheless, wandering will always suggest danger even if, and especially if, it is the text's approved mode of travel, for the wanderer necessarily, even willingly, encounters the dangers of traveling in a fallen world, vulnerable to evil's enticements and deceptions and never certain to what risks one must submit oneself for the sake of private and public virtue. But Phaedria's dangerousness derives, at least in part, from how comfortable she is with digressiveness, and how little she cares about the ends of chivalric quests. Our sense of the poem's posited narrative and ideological ends, and the way in which those posited ends influence our sense of how the text structures itself to produce those ends, configure, in turn, our understanding of how and where one travels in Faeryland.

Discerning the character of Faeryland is, as all readers of Spenser know, not an easy thing to do. In addition to the text's intertextual investments, the past progressive tense of Spenser's very first verbal construction in *The Faerie Queene*, I.i.—"A Gentle Knight was pricking on the plaine"—introduces the reader to a world of almost perpetual motion.[13] Spenser's allegorical figures are always on the go, and the phenomenal world itself in which these figures travel is always moving, shifting, reshaping itself according to the changing rhetorical demands of the narrative. Yet the particular challenge readers of Spenser face is flexibly to structure their own critical responses to the poetry, but not too flexibly. For while Spenser certainly inscribes into the fluidity of Faeryland his own desires for rhetorical mobility, he, like Guyon, must not completely lo(o)se himself on his journey precisely because his authority comes from his ability to manipulate his materials as he chooses. Guyon, Spenser knows, as the hero of Temperance needs to become a little more mobile, able to negotiate the vagaries of life and experience, in order to be temperate. Phaedria's world is a concentrated and, perhaps, an exaggerated instance of the broader sense of mutability that predominates Faeryland, which, therefore, Guyon must learn to negotiate in order to get through it. Phaedria already negotiates this world very well: her "flit barke . . . nimbly r[uns] her wonted course/Through the dull billowes thicke as troubled mire,/Whom neither wind out of their seat could forse,/Nor timely tides did driue out of their sluggish sourse" (20.3, 6–9). Yet rather than getting through it, she delights in traveling deeper into it. Phaedria thrives in this sematically fluid world, travels in it too easily, and enjoys for its own sake. She is, therefore, dangerous, but neither is she, as I wish to demonstrate in this essay, entirely wrong about how one travels in Faeryland where one wishes to go.

As Guyon gets through Phaedria's world, the narrative illustrates that each step taken in sequence carries a reading forward into Guyon's experience; each step in the narrative (forward, backward, or both) signifies a kind of progress in *our* sense of Guyon's experience with the challenges, obstacles, and surprises of Faeryland. Yet Guyon in motion in Canto vi reveals that motion and mobility in Book II become problematic ways of signifying progress, though they remain the only available signifiers that can perform this work. Motion and mobility will become even more problematic signifiers when the text reconfigures its selfhood-centered discourse of morality/rationality to fit the couple and communal consciousness of Book III and, more especially, Book IV. Books I and II, however, still invite us to descry in Redcrosse's fight on foot with the dragon in I.xii, or Guyon's foot-travel through nearly all of his adventures an expression of deliberate, self-reliant moral agency. Phaedria's mode of travel, therefore, is a challenge to the deliberateness and, more especially, the necessary self-consciousness of Guyon's mobility. The text notes that Phaedria's boat will move to her will so quickly that Guyon does not even have the chance to retrace his steps back out of the boat. Retracing steps is not an issue, it would seem, when Guyon travels in the right direction. Yet motion in manifestly wrong directions, or "straying," as Guyon will call it a few lines later (22.9), is a matter of concern to Guyon when that motion produces immediate, irreversible consequences because he does not know where they are going. Guyon is immediately swept away in a craft that "nimbly" negotiates the "slouthfull" and "sluggish" body of water (18.7, 20.6–9). While Guyon's disdain for Phaedria's intemperate cavorting in the boat gives us a preview of his reaction to Phaedria's island playground, he does not, however, seem to question the nature of their progress—the way the boat moves or the character of the Idle lake itself—but rather the correctness of their destination. Phaedria, on the other hand, responds with commentary on the nature of the boat trip:

> Faire Sir (quoth she) be not displeasd at all;
>> Who fares on sea, may not commaund his way,
>> Ne wind and weather at his pleasure call:
>> The sea is wide, and easie for to stray;
>> The wind vnstable, and doth neuer stay.
>> But here a while ye may in safety rest,
>> Till season serue new passage to assay;
>> Better safe port, then be in seas distrest.
> Therewith she laught, and did her earnest end in iest.
>
> (23)

Phaedria suggests that Guyon cannot insist, when he travels on water, that his journey will end where he intends it to end. In Phaedria's boat Guyon enters a realm wholly foreign to his experience thus far.

Clearly, Spenser wishes us to mistrust the quick, irresistible quality of motion of Phaedria's boat, as well as the quick, capricious movements of Phaedria herself, for her quick motions both convey the moral instability she represents for Guyon, and also make her an effervescent and, therefore, a difficult figure for Guyon to interpret in the first place. Quick motions themselves throughout *The Faerie Queene* reveal the power, and therefore, the reckless and uncontrollable qualities, that inhabit our passions, our appetites, but also potentially our own minds. The fervent, rapid motions of the explicitly evil or threatening figures, for instance, that pursue Florimell through Book III—the foster or the Hyena—convey the tremendous power and intensity of unleashed animal lust, yet Arthur's rapid, fervent pursuit of Florimell to save her is a striking and disturbing imitation of the very phenomenon Arthur would oppose.[14] For that matter, Linda Gregerson finds Florimell's fearful flight from Arthur, the witch's son, and the rest of her pursuers, as "a kind of promiscuity," as she, for instance "like fearful Malbecco . . . looks over her shoulder as she flees, the better to see her wake fill up with the figures of her fearful imagining."[15] Indeed, Spenser's figures act out in their rapid action the erratic motions of the imagination when reason and judgment are either absent or impaired, which implicates the mind in the moral ambiguities and dangers that the soul would otherwise shun. In their recklessness—inability to "reckon" the danger or evil that faces them—Arthur and Florimell unwittingly imitate the character, the intensity, therefore, the unleashed, "animal" nature of the very phenomenon they would resist. But the text distrusts such emotional intensity, not only for the ways in which our responses to perceived evils configure themselves according to the character of the evil itself, thus implicating us in that evil, but also because in such a state the mind experiences the power that the imagination possesses to reconfigure, recombine, or reinterpret images from the world, a power which competes with, challenges, and potentially can supervene reason's control. Quickness and recklessness for Spenser reveals too much about the innate unruliness of the fallen mind and, therefore, our capacity for evil.

Spenser boards Phaedria's craft to suggest a kind of motion that it mistrusts not because it moves mortals against their will, but it reveals to oneself the multiple directions the will is capable of pursuing and the contradictory, quickly-shifting motions of one's own desire. Again, perhaps his straying is a necessary part of the course he must follow towards righteousness. Certainly, the shape and character of the path, replete with strayings and encounters with unknown items, are not so surprising here. Readers learned fairly quickly in Book I that the Protestant subtext of human moral insufficiency would be an important structural principle throughout the text, and in that vein, Guyon's detour to Phaedria's island might still be structured as part of his progress towards full temperance. However, Guyon's will is still subjected to uncomfortable kinds of motion, and he is led to even more uncomfortable places through which the will moves when subject to the whims of desire. The motions of the will, of desire, are less traceable. The narrative first introduced us to this body of water—"The Idle lake"—and Phaedria's "wandring ship" when she carries Cymochles over (he is travelling from the Bowre of Blisse in search of Guyon to avenge himself on Guyon for Pyrochles' death):

> In this wide Inland sea, that hight by name
>   The Idle lake, my wandring ship I row,
>   That knowes her port, and thither sailes by ayme,
>   Ne care, ne feare I, how the wind do blow,
>   Or whether swift I wend, or whether slow:
>   Both slow and swift a like do serue my tourne,
>   Ne swelling Neptune, ne loud thundring Ioue
>   Can chaunge my cheare, or make me euer mourne;
> My litle boat can safely passe this perilous bourne.
>
> (10)

"Slow" or "swift," Phaedria's boat will reach its "ayme." The danger to errant knights that her boat represents is not in its slow or fast motion per se, but in its ability to change its character quickly and irresistibly and in its ability to proceed to Phaedria's, not the knight's, destination irresistibly. Guyon, who seems simply to end up in Phaedria's boat without explanation, can only retrospectively regret his decision once he realizes the Palmer refuses to follow and once he begins to experience his own powerlessness as merely a passenger.

Yet Guyon will end up in this episode on an island that apparently in itself is not all bad. When Guyon first sees it from the boat,

> He wist himself amisse, and angry said;
>   Ah Dame, perdie ye haue not doen me right,
>   Thus to mislead me, whiles I you obaid:
> Me litle needed from my right way to haue straid.
>
> (22.6–9)

But when the reader learns later that Guyon is only "halfe discontent" and that he encounters "ioyes," "happie fruitfulnesse," and "pleasant" things, the reader begins to realize that Guyon finds attractions here which do not necessarily derive from impure desires (24). In fact, the island itself would be "pleasant" for Guyon, but for Phaedria's intemperate competition with singing birds and laughing fields. The narrative does not frame its birds, trees, and fields to be temptations within themselves; they become one of the many ways by which Phaedria plies her "skillful art" to tempt Guyon's "constant hart" away from "warlike enterprize" (25). Guyon seems mostly troubled by Phaedria herself, that is, her intemperate jollity and her carelessness with regard to things Guyon cares very much about. She would use her island as a place that halts knights' forward progress and makes them forget what they are progressing towards. And because Phaedria cares nothing for Guyon's final destination, Guyon wishes to leave: "But fairely tempring fond desire subdewd, / And euer her desired to depart" (26.6–7). Guyon feels "desire" here, but what the qualities of that desire are is difficult to discern. It is "desire subdewd," but also "tempring fond desire." What is being tempered in this scene, what has been subdued, what is done first, what is done next, is certainly not clear. The line might read "tempring [himself] he subdued fond desire," or it might read "tempring his fond desire, he subdued [it] or [her]." The structure of temperance eludes causal sequentiality. It is the will already having the upper hand in its battles with the appetites and with the imagination, and it is the will that nevertheless must constantly fight those battles again. Guyon wanders in this episode and he progresses; he "shewes goodly maisteries" by "tempring" an appetite that is already "subdewd." The reader has left the moral oppositions that she/he began with to guide the journey through this episode (standing on the shore vs. being ferried) on the shore with the Palmer.[16]

Though Guyon comes through this experience as a "constant" knight, Spenser suggests that his susceptibility to the fluctuations of desire puts him in precarious situations precisely because these situations exploit his ignorance about the nature of his desires. Guyon finds himself at the end of this adventure in an indecisive fight with Cymochles (meaning "one who constantly fluctuates" in the Greek). That Guyon cannot completely overcome Cymochles implies not only that Guyon himself must fight the fluctuations of his mind, but that such fights will always be inconclusive. In Canto vi, Phaedria's island becomes a place where Guyon's ability to think, to process intellectually the world he encounters, and to act according to the dictates of reason, is impaired. Guyon will struggle to read this world rationally, and consequently, he does not necessarily act unvirtuously here. In fact, he will eventually exercise his choice to leave the island: "fairely tempring fond desire subdewd,/And ever [from Phaedria] desired to depart" (26.6–7). But one moves in Phaedria's world, even if it is to depart, on Phaedria's terms. Motion itself, whether slow or quick, rationally willed or not, is conducive to Phaedria's project. Movement in the world Phaedria controls leads to the end she wishes: the final cessation of "knightly exercize" (25.9), the end of the progress in which Book II is so deeply invested. The uncontrollability of motion itself that risks becoming finally a kind of mental, moral immobility, or at least a moral instability, seems to be what the text fears here. For Cymochles will awake from his "slouthfull sleepe" (27.5) to lash out at Guyon after he summons his rational faculties to "temper fond desire" and "desire to depart." Guyon lashes back, and they fight with equal success (or failure) until Phaedria comes "atweene them" and argues, not unpersuasively, for the "louely peace, and gentle amitie" that *Amour* offers them (32–35). In Cymochles and, to a lesser extent, in Guyon we might see in operation the Thomistic notion that "all irascible passions arise out of concupiscible passions" ["omnes passiones irascibiles incipiunt a passionibus concupiscibiles."[17]] However, such a formulation of the problems that Guyon faces at this moment seems inadequate here, for Phaedria's words are called "pleasing," at least to a certain extent without moral irony. Her loyalty to love here and her admonition to warlike knights to follow Mars' example in being "Cupidoes frend,/And is for Venus loues renowmed more,/Then all his wars and spoiles, the which he did of yore" (35.7–9), produces a desirable result. Borrowing Derrida's term, Phaedria is for Guyon a *pharamakon*—she is "poison and/or medicine," that is, her effect is generally poisonous, but can, at the same time, also be occasionally medicinal.[18] To be sure, Cymochles is the aggressor, and he is the figure that inextricably links self-indulgent slothfulness with the explosive destruction of vengeance. Yet as Guyon wields his "angry blade" (31.5), one sees in Guyon, as has been seen throughout this episode, a figure whose actions are reactive because he is forced to stumble his way through this episode, never quite comprehending what he is resisting.

In showing us Guyon's propensity to react to the assaults on his capacity for self-control, Spenser perhaps means to show us an attribute that needs a more comprehensive sort of rational control. This control would seem ultimately to be produced by acquiring more rational self-knowledge which, in turn, would produce Guyon's respect for his own susceptibilities to desire based on experience with those desires, as Cavanagh argues.[19] However, Guyon's progress toward greater self-awareness leads him deeper and deeper into more troubling dimensions of the self. Here and elsewhere in Book II there are places in the self the allegorical narrative is "loath" to discover. Spenser's poem is reluctant here, and again in Canto vii, to discover the destructive extent to which Guyon's anger can reach: when Disdayne prepares to attack Guyon, Mammon himself must restrain Guyon's "hasty hand" (vii.42.6–7), for as Hamilton points out, "to disdain Disdain, that is, to become angry with him, only increases his power."[20] Yet the narrative also seems reluctant to explore too deeply the nature of Guyon's desires. In fact, in the Cave of Mammon, the narrative will refuse Guyon any amount of desire for the things Mammon shows him, for if Guyon were to show the least amount of desire, he would be destroyed by the "feend" who guards Mammon's hoard from "other couetous feends" (32.1–5)—when Guyon declares that he has no desire for Mammon's "offred grace" (his riches), the narrative explains:

Thereat the feend his gnashing teeth did grate,
And grieu'd, so long to lacke his greedy pray;
For well he weened, that so glorious bayte
Would tempt his guest, to take thereof assay:
Had he so doen, he had him snatcht away,
More light that Culuer in the Faulcons fist.

(34.1–6)

Throughout Book II Guyon's own desires bring him terribly close to unleashing forces of aggression and annihilation to himself and others. Some of these desires are ones that the text specifically mentions Guyon feels anger (at Disdain, Cymochles, Atin) and lust (the two fountain bathers in Canto xii). Some of these desires (cupidity, for example, in Canto vii) are potentially his as an allegorical figure who represents a human subject whose total focus in this text is on the control of the impressive variety of human desires Spenser wishes to discuss. By rendering him all but impervious to indulging these desires, or by providing an intervening, pacifying figure (who is frequently an "evil" figure—Phaedria and Mammon), the text repeatedly keeps Guyon safe from dangerous and destructive desires within himself.

Consequently, while Spenser's temperate course for Guyon marks as dangerous the places which harbor figures who threaten his moral well-being, the course is perhaps even more particularly designed to alert Guyon to the places where he himself becomes his own worst enemy. Thus, the narrative will simply convey Guyon out of danger in Canto vi as Atin, the inciter of vengeance, "railes" at him: "Though somewhat moued in his mightie hart,/Yet with strong reason maistred passion fraile,/And passed fairely forth" (40.2–5). Reason, though not allegorized in the presence of the Palmer here, directs Guyon away because Guyon's armed response to armed aggression is of no virtuous effect in Phaedria's world. As with his "courteous" (26.4) deportment towards Phaedria, his use of arms more tightly enmeshes him in a world that negates his moral force. His abilities with sword and shield, signifiers of his capacity for moral action, only mimic the unstable, destructive antagonism of Cymochles. In fact, Cymochles's actions, like Phaedria's, shape to a certain extent the character and course of Guyon's actions. The speed and unpredictability of Cymochles's and Phaedria's moral instability give no room for reasonable action based on reasonable interpretation. Guyon, the temperate hero, is not equipped, at least at this point, to read and, therefore, act reasonably *and* suddenly. No one reads Phaedria's world and controls it—"Who fares on sea, may not commaund his way," she tells Guyon. Phaedria herself does not control her world; she "nimbly" moves through the "perlous" sea leading to her island. While her "disports" (etymologically "carryings away" in the Latin) take Guyon away from his temperate course through Faeryland, her devotion to fun and ease produces the most temperate response on this island when the fight erupts: her "pleasing words" "calme the sea of [Guyon's and Cymochles's] tempestuous spight" (36.4–5). She allows desire to be contradictory and happily goes along for the ride.

Spenser certainly does not recommend Phaedria's way of sailing laughingly through the storms of desire. But Guyon's experience with Phaedria has revealed that his aggressive defense against these storms only increases the intensity of their fury. The Phaedria episode suggests that temperance is not fully a rational confrontation with, and subduing of, the irrational. Confrontation, as a way of figuring the fight between good and evil, styled as rational and irrational, is deeply problematized in this episode. The rational and, by extension, the good cannot fully know the irrational and the evil. Reason discovers its own fundamental limitations in its very attempt to comprehend and control not only our senses and our appetites, but also the mind's own faculties, upon which reason depends for its own ability to perceive and interpret experience in and with the phenomenal world. Even more importantly, reason cannot beat its antagonists in a game in which the terms of the game are determined by those

antagonists. Clearly, Canto vi shows us, as earlier episodes have before
in Book II, and will again, Guyon's as yet incomplete temperance,
or continence (see 15n). Guyon's need for protection and assistance
from Arthur and his need for the moral and cultural education he
receives in Cantos ix and x underscores this incompleteness, as does
his vulnerability to Pyrochles and Cymochles, egged on by Atin and
Archimago, in Canto viii. Yet this is not the only dimension to
Guyon's incompleteness. What these episodes emphasize is Guyon's
ignorance and his need for guides and protectors in order to negotiate
the world in which he travels. He does not know, and perhaps can
never fully know, what capacities, abilities, and knowledge comprise
the virtue he both represents and more fully seeks to attain. The text
continues to claim that Guyon is the knight of temperance—he is
"shamefast," for example, though he does not recognize Shamefastness when he sees her: "why wonder yee/Faire Sir at that, which
ye so much embrace?/She is the fountaine of your modestee; You
shamefast are, but Shamefastnesse it selfe is shee" (ix. 43. 6–9). Yet
Guyon seems unable, without Alma's coaching, not only to read the
academic allegory Spenser indulges in here, but also to read himself—the parts that make up the whole of Guyon as Temperance.
Similarly, in Canto x Guyon must learn how to read himself by means
of his cultural identity. The canto spends far more time on Arthur's
heritage and conspicuously shortens the summary of the text that
Guyon reads. Guyon reads this text "greedily" (ix. 60. 3) and with
"delight" and "naturall desire" (x. 77. 1–2), which communicates
Guyon's need and his response to this education, but his encounter
with this text, unlike the more fully developed, allegorized scenes in
Book II, does not read him very deeply. Again, what seems emphasized here is how much Guyon does not know about himself.

Moreover, the form that the allegory takes here, despite the tour
it offers Guyon and us through the knowledge Guyon lacks, is unable
to show us finally a changed or improved Guyon. We come to Canto
xii perhaps expecting completion, but the text, especially after Guyon's sojourn in the House of Temperance, has set us up to expect
Guyon to know more about temperance and about himself, and
therefore, to be able to become fully temperate. Yet the House of
Temperance, as has the rest of Book II, also gives us a Guyon who
is perpetually the student of temperance, in constant need of a knowledgeable companion instructing him about the right, temperate action. Guyon is always in trouble when he is alone. Guyon's
fundamental need to be accompanied and led continues into Canto
xii as Reason guides him to the Bower. This final leg of the journey
through the "perlous" waters seems to cover a great portion of Book

II's parcel of Faeryland, as if it were a review of where we have been. Canto xii is structured so that we will review, under Reason's interpretive tutelage, where Guyon has been as we read Guyon's progress through the canto. By taking a quick look back at Phaedria before we get to Acrasia, Spenser invites us to read Phaedria as a pre-Acrasia figure; Phaedria's temptations to male knights certainly resemble Acrasia's. They both want knights to take off their armor and indulge their "looser" desires. The volatile aggressivity that sets into Cymochles and, to a lesser degree, into Guyon appears to fore-shadow the irrational animalism of the beast-men that range around outside the walls of Acrasia's Bower. Yet Phaedria is not the cause of this aggressivity, as Acrasia is for the beast-men, her former "louers," whom she has so "transformed" (85). While Phaedria, like Acrasia, leads knights astray from virtuous quests, it is only Acrasia who brutalizes and even kills such knights. Phaedria does not appear, at least deliberately, to wreak such havoc in Faeryland. In fact, she appears to abhor such destructiveness when she intercedes in the battle between Cymochles and Guyon. She indeed wishes to disarm both Cymochles and Guyon when she first encounters each of them, but there is no blood on her hands for her actions, nor is there a pen full of enslaved lovers on the fringes of her island.

Acrasia, on the other hand, seems to take delight in destruction and dehumanization. Before readers see her "snowy brest" (78.1) and "alabaster skin" (77.5) and before they see Verdant sleeping beside her, readers have seen the death of Mordant, Amavia's despairing suicide, Cymochles's irascibility, and the animalism of the beast-men that live outside the walls of Acrasia's dwelling. Even when readers see Cymochles in Acrasia's bower, they see nothing of Acrasia—Cymochles is busy "mingling" with "loose Ladies and lasciuious boyes" (v.28.9) when Atin comes to taunt him into seeking revenge on Guyon for Pyrochles death. Until Canto xii Acrasia exists primarily in the actions and character of her servants and in the conspicuously destructive effects her actions and influence cause to her victims. Acrasia exists in narratives about her throughout Book II. These narratives have rendered obviously and extremely Acrasia's capacity to destroy life and humanity. Based on the Acrasia narratives Guyon has heard from, for instance, the Palmer and from Amavia, Guyon reads Acrasia's world in Canto xii as a threatening one, a world that will entice him to the same, terrible results he has been told about. The approach to Acrasia's bower, full of "thousand thousands" of monsters (25.1) does nothing to alter Guyon's way of reading Acrasia, despite the fact that they are only "fearefull shapes."

When Guyon finally reaches Acrasia's Bower, she will not become
a monster for Guyon, but she is no less obvious or threatening than
she has been before in her extreme, destructive significations. The
threat, of course, derives from his own desire. When the narrative
pans over Acrasia, we have already seen him slow his progress to
watch the "naked Damzelles"; we know he feels the same desire "to
approch more neare" to see "many sights, that courage cold could
reare" (68.8–9). We see his desire emerge in the passively constructed
language that describes Acrasia "layd"

> Vpon a bed of Roses . . .
> As faint through heat, or dight to pleasant sin,
> And was arayd, or rather disarayd,
> All in a vele of silke and siluer thin,
> That hid no whit her alabaster skin,
> But rather shewd more white, if more might bee.
>
> (77.1–6)

She first appears "faint through heat," then "dight to pleasant sin"
to Guyon's eye. She appears asleep because of the heat; then he seems
to perceive what kind of heat produced this sleep; then she becomes
"dight to," or prepared for, "pleasant sin." He first sees her as "arayd," then "disarayd." He first sees the "vele" that covers her, then
sees her skin amplified by the veil. She is, in fact, apparently unaware
of a male, erotic gaze, though her unawareness and her luxurious
pose heightens the eroticism of the male gaze. Additionally, he first
sees Acrasia lying with the sleeping Verdant after their "sweet toyle"
(78.3), then as he and the Palmer draw close to cast their net, Acrasia
and Verdant seem awake again, reengaged in lovemaking, but unaware of their danger, "minding nought, but lustfull game" (81.2).
With Verdant Guyon first sees his "goodliness" and "nobilitie," then
proceeds to discern his "lewdness" and "wastfullness."

Spenser's narrative creates Acrasia in the articulated space of Guyon's desire for and horror at Acrasia; she exists in the language that
enacts Guyon's ambivalence. In amplifying Acrasia's effect on Guyon,
Spenser also implicates us in the desire for her, and as we review
Guyon's persistent difficulties with his sexual appeties, we become
implicated as well in the desire to eradicate the dangers of our own
desires permanently. The binding of Acrasia perhaps answers our
desires permanently to close down the textual space within which
Guyon's ambivalence emerges—we wish no longer to have to read

her while struggling with the difficulties that our appetites create for
our rational faculties. Phaedria, however, seems to occupy a textual
space situated more in the mental faculties themselves than in the
appetites. She will be labeled as "wanton" and "lewd," but we never
know, for instance, what Phaedria is or is not wearing. The narrative
will never pan over her slowly; we are not really invited to desire
her, nor are we invited to desire her destruction. Hers is the textual
space of the erratic, the unpredictable, and the not clearly discernible.
When we first meet her, we are told that in a boat

> sate a Ladie fresh and faire,
> Making sweet solace to her selfe alone;
> Sometimes she sung, as loud as a larke in aire,
> Sometimes she laught, that nigh her breth was gone,
> Yet was there not with her else any one,
> That might to her moue cause of merriment.
>
> (vi.3.1–6)

There is no discernible cause to her actions or her responses to Faeryland. Guyon in turn will respond to the ignorance and confusion
she evokes in him with confused, erratic violence. He irrationally
seeks to protect his rationality. And Guyon will always respond to a
threat, be it one of ignorance or of ambivalence, with violence. The
more calculated, organized, and also thorough destruction Guyon
commits in Canto xii, under the direction of the Palmer, displays a
volition for violence that is as persistent as are the sensual appetites
he wishes permanently to bring under rational control. His attempt
permanently to protect his rational capacities by destroying the Bowre, though it means to be rationally conducted, imitates the irrational he is fighting too closely.

Spenser is trying to tell us that temperance cannot fully initiate
Guyon into the radical change in the way he thinks about the world
in which he moves and acts that would enable him to become completely moral. The tradition in Spenser scholarship that finally situates
Guyon within a Christian sense of the limits of human progress—the
need for grace and redemption—points us in the direction of this
radical revision of temperance and of thought processes. Harry Berger, Jr., for instance, argues that "the quest for temperance is by its
very nature inconclusive. For once we see the world sustained by
God rather than Fortune, by the persuasion of Love rather than the
forces of Indifference, the temperance so highly valued by the ancients

begins to give way."[21] Guyon's morality depends on self-control, but morality itself must also rely on "the persuasion of Love," the ability to think for and incline towards the benefit of another. As the Knight of Temperance, Guyon is only equipped to take care of himself, and everything and everyone else is a means to that end. Consequently, Book II cannot establish the capacity to control the self without denying that capacity to another, or worse, violently imposing control on another. The discourse on temperance is deeply invested in notions of dominion, and Spenser will only further trouble the discursive marriage of virtue and domination in the couples he examines in the remainder of *The Faerie Queene*.

Yet within this fundamental limitation to temperance's ability to initiate Guyon into complete, moral action, the final lesson the Palmer will try to teach Guyon is the one he needed the most throughout his quest. Guyon, after he again has confronted his own mortal insufficiency, therefore his own need for salvation, wishes to release the beast-men from the spell Acrasia cast over them. The Palmer indulges him only to show him that their power to effect such a change is impossible. Whether Guyon actually learns here to "let Grille be Grille" (87.8) seems doubtful, given his automatic inclination to charge Britomart at first sight in the beginning of Book III, but again Guyon can follow directions and, at the Palmer's behest "depart, whilest wether serues and wind" (87.8–9). Guyon should indeed set out on adventures of protection, service, and relief in Faeryland, as Redcrosse also does, after his great quest is over. Like Redcrosse, as a mortal himself among other mortals, he is not done serving his turn in Gloriana's wide realm. But Book II has taught us that his acts of self-purification do not produce a similar end in others. He must learn only for himself how to read the wind and the weather in order to negotiate (with the Palmer) the perils of the sea that brought him and the Palmer to Acrasia's bower.

Acrasia, however, is still permanently removed from Faeryland as a danger both to Guyon and to others. Phaedria, on the other hand, is not bound up, packed off, and left behind, nor is she chased out of Acrasia's Bowre with Cissie and Flossie. She whisks away from Guyon as quickly and effervescently in Canto xii as she did before. Phaedria ends as she began—alone. Cymochles first found her "Making sweet solace to her selfe alone" (vi.3.2); she is first and finally a loner in Faeryland. Spenser's narrative does not take care of the threat she poses in Faeryland; it does not, at least completely, inscribe Phaedria within the bounds of its moral commentary. In the air of Book II lingers her laughter. It is difficult to know how seriously to take her laughter; that is, how far one might allegorize it. To be sure, in

her laughter is the sound of her intemperance, the cautionary sound
to Guyon's ears of the whimsical fluctuations to which his own mind
is susceptible, but also perhaps a sound of the power the mind is able
to exercise over its reception and response to the world, a power to
which Spenser himself is attracted. But perhaps there are less morally
urgent features to her laughter—a sign of the unruly energies of
youth-though perhaps one could read in her immature, buoyant behavior something of the foolishness that smirking, ambitious courtiers and ladies-in-waiting can insinuate into the courts of rulers who
themselves wish to defer or deny the degenerative progress of time.
But perhaps her laughter at the very stern and serious Guyon and
Palmer provides a subtle, social critique in another direction: laughter
that counters or, at least, counterbalances the diffusing comedy Maureen Quilligan discerns Spenser sprinkling around his female figures
(Belphoebe and Britomart) who represent "the doubled erotic and
political power" that Elizabeth held in Tudor England, transgressing
the age's patriarchal notions of women and power.[22] Phaedria may
not get the last laugh, but it is a laugh that Guyon at least cannot
silence or muffle. Whatever its allegorical possibilities and problems,
however, Phaedria, laughing and moving as she will, shares with
the sober, forward-moving Guyon, the most completely temperate
moment of Book II, as they each choose to leave the other alone.
Phaedria "scorns" Guyon, and Guyon scowls disdainfully at Phaedria,
but neither figure can control the behavior of the other, much less
comprehend it. They each have only their own agency to exercise
as they move how and where they will in Faeryland.

Brigham Young University

NOTES

1. I wish to thank Michael Rudick and Barry Weller for their guidance in the
early stages of this essay and, in the later stages, the editors of *Spenser Studies* and the
anonymous readers they chose to review this essay for the many insightful suggestions
and queries they offered me.

2. Edmund Spenser, *The Works of Edmund Spenser*, ed. Edwin Greenlaw et al.
(Baltimore: Johns Hopkins University Press, 1932–57), II. xii. 14. 3–6. I will cite the
Variorum edition for all Spenser quotations, acknowledging them parenthetically.

3. "Nightmares of Desire: Evil Women in *The Faerie Queene*," *Studies in Philology*
91(1994): 338. Cavanagh is interested in the way that Spenser's male characters, and
Spenser himself, negotiate their fear of, and complicit desire for, the threatening

female figures that populate Faeryland—most extremely, but not exclusively represented in Spenser's hags, succubi, and witches. Nightmares expose for Cavanagh the structures by which Spenser wishes to express and ultimately diffuse the power of his fears and desires, as the dreams and their females fade away. An Acrasia, however, does not simply fade away, but must be mastered in the narrative itself (322–24).

4. A.C. Hamilton, *The Faerie Queene*, by Edmund Spenser (London and New York: Longman, 1977), p. 215, 9.8n.

5. "Nightmares," 317.

6. *The Faerie Queene*, p. 18, 7n.

7. As Cavanagh begins to examine Guyon in Acrasia's Bowre, she argues that not only do Spenser's knights, when guideless, "frequently fail to understand the dangers they face," they also don't come to an understanding "until they have already committed an unvirtuous sexual act," "Nightmares," 322. Cavanagh's "committed" here occludes what I will argue is Spenser's particular interest with Phaedria: describing the cognitive difficulties that Guyon experiences, once the appetite for "unvirtuous sexual acts" is aroused and the Palmer is not around, whether or not "acts" are "committed." And I will argue that this scene provides a sneak preview of the problems Guyon will still have with Acrasia, even with the Palmer present.

8. "Reluctant" seems the best option the OED gives us for this context. As the cititation points out, the word is frequently used in situations of perceived danger.

9. Frances McNeely Leonard, in her *Laughter in the Courts of Love: Comedy in Allegory, from Chaucer to Spenser* (Norman, OK: Pilgrim, 1989), is interested in the way that virtue at first seems abnormal in Phaedria's world: Guyon "seems ludicrous" in the contrast between his apparel and bearing to Phaedria's playful world. Yet as readers realize that "it is the world and not the knight that is in error," they recognize their "own erroneous tendency to accept the world as the norm and to make pragmatism [their] own standard for conduct" (136).

10. See Patricia Parker, *Inescapable Romance: Studies in the Poetics of a Mode* (Princeton, 1979).

11. Guillory, *Poetic Authority: Spenser, Milton, and Literary History* (New York, 1983), p. 27.

12. Teskey, "From Allegory to Dialectic: Imagining Error in Spenser and Milton," *PMLA* 101 (1986), p. 13.

13. As Richard McCabe words it, "everything [Spenser] depicts exists in a whorl of flux. The element of permanence and stability so important to the Medieval and Renaissance mind is nowhere to be found," *The Pillars of Eternity: Time and Providence in The Faerie Queene* (Dublin, 1989), p. 56. This is overstated, since there are places of a sort of "permanence and stability" to be found imaginatively in a place like Mt. Acidale.

14. For Sheila T. Cavanagh, in her *Wanton Eyes and Chaste Desire* (Bloomington: Indiana University Press, 1994), Arthur's intense pursuit of Florimell is part of what prompts her to see in this pursuit a "lustful chase" (22–23).

15. Gregerson, *The Reformation of the Subject* (Cambridge: Cambridge University Press, 1995), 134–35.

16. Prominently among the oppositions that Spenser plays with and complicates is the Aristotelian-Thomistic tradition of distinguishing between temperance and continence. As Aristotle sets it forth,

both the continent man and the temperate man are such as to do nothing
contrary to the rule for the sake of bodily pleasures, but the former has and
the latter has not bad appetites, and the latter is such as not to feel pleasure
contrary to the rule, while the former is such as to feel pleasure but not to
be led by it.

Nicomachean Ethics, trans. David Ross (London: Oxford Univ. Press, 1984), 1151b–
1152a. Aquinas makes the same distinction that Aristotle does, but includes continence as one of the seven "potential parts" of temperance, or behaviors which
in themselves are incomplete expressions of temperance (continence, gentleness,
clemency, and four types of modesty—humility, studiousness, modesty of manners,
and modesty of dress). *Summa Theologiae*, Blackfriars Edition, trans. and ed., Thomas
O. Gilby, S. J., et al. (London: Eyre and Spottiswoode, 1968), 2a2ae, 143. "Continence," St. Thomas declares, "is to temperance as the unripe to the fully mature"
(q. 155, a. 4). For an overview of Spenser scholarship on this subject see F.M.
Padelford, "The Virtue of Temperance in *The Faerie Queene*," *Studies in Philology*
13 (1921): 334–46; Ernest L. Sirluck, "*The Faerie Queene*, Book II and the *Nicomachean Ethics*," *Modern Philology* 49 (1951): 73–100; and, most helpfully, Gerald Mor-
gan, "The Idea of Temperance in the Second Book of *The Faerie Queene*," *Review
of English Studies* 145 (1986): 11–39.

17.   *Summa Theologiae*, 1a, 81, 2. On this subject, see Zailig Pollock, "Concupiscence and Intemperance in the Bower of Bliss," *Studies in English Literature* 20 (1980):
43–58. Pollock attempts to demonstrate throughout his article (especially 58) how
Spenser uses this idea throughout Canto xii to show that in the physical and emotional setting of the Bower the irascible defends the concupiscible.

18.   "Plato's Pharmacy," *Dissemination*, trans. Barbara Johnson (Chicago: Chicago
University Press), 1981, 70. Both meanings—poison and medicine—are available to
the Greek term, *pharamakon*, but, of course, Derrida is interested in the play and the
logic of "supplementarity" that attaches itself to Socrates' use of the term in Plato's
Phaedrus for the activity of writing and, by extension, to the entire structure of
platonic essences. See 61–172. Phaedria playfulness accords quite nicely to Derrida's.

19.   Cavanagh, "Nightmares," 322.

20.   *The Faerie Queene*, p. 42, 6–9n.

21.   Berger, *The Allegorical Temper* (New Haven, 1957), p. 63. See also, for example,
Peter D. Stambler, "The Development of Guyon's Christian Temperance," *ELR* 7
(1977): 51–89.

22.   Quilligan, in her "The Comedy of Authority in *The Faerie Queene*," *ELR* 17
(1987): 156–71, especially 159–63, notices that Spenser sets around Belphoebe and
Britomart a kind of physical comedy (reminiscent of *commedia del'arte*) in the Bragga-
doccio scenes that both diffuses the kind of power that Belphoebe and Britomart
attempt to excercise in Spenser's text, and that Elizabeth wielded in actuality, and
"recuperates" in the text the right power relations of patriarchy.

KYONG-KAHN KIM

The Nationalist Drive of Spenserian Hermaphrodism in *The Faerie Queene*

Hermaphrodism in *The Faerie Queen* (1590, 1596) is one of Spenser's poetic designs to solve the succession problem, which is the most practical issue through the entirety of Elizabeth's reign. Many scholars have discussed the hermaphroditic imagery in the poem largely with a focus on the idea of the queen's two bodies, but they have disregarded the literally physical dimension of the image: it is simply a way of giving birth without marriage. The poem is full of Spenserian hermaphrodite figures, including Britomart, who strongly imply a self-sufficient way of procreation without the aid of a male partner and whose experience has also a dynastic effect. This manner of procreation justifies the queen's unmarried chastity without destroying her established cult of chastity and at the same time perpetuates the dynastic succession.

*A*MONG THE POETIC designs in *The Faerie Queen* (1590, 1596) that concern the national interests of Edmund Spenser's day is the image of the hermaphrodite or androgyne. In Ovid's *Metamorphoses*, known as the source of images of androgyny, Hermaphroditus and Salmacis are metamorphosed into a single being who has both male and female sexual characteristics.[1] *The Faerie Queen* is teeming with such hermaphroditic images. Venus in the Temple of Venus, for instance, is an androgynous figure. She wears a veil, because "she hath both kinds in one,/Both male and female" (IV.x.41).[2] In the 1590 edition, Spenser finalized both Book Three and the whole poem with the hermaphroditic union of Amoret and Scudamour, "that faire Hermaphrodite" (III.xii.46.2). Similar images are also seen in the marriage of the Medway and the Thames (IV.xi.8–53), in the description of Nature (7.7.5), and in the cross-dressing of the couple Britomart (III.iii.53) and Artegall (V.vii.37).

The hermaphroditic imagery in the poem has drawn the attention of many scholars. Thomas Roche thinks it symbolic of the mystical union of souls,[3] and Donald Cheney finds in the embrace of Amoret and Scudamour of the 1590 version a perfection or an ideal of marriage as indicated in Genesis 2.24, where man and woman become "one flesh" through marriage.[4] Challenging these views, Gary Grund argues that the hermaphrodite Britomart is not "merely the champion of married love" but also an expression of martial puissance, as the paradoxical epithet, "martiall Mayd," signifies. She is a reflection of the author's effort to reconcile the dual aspects of the queen's two bodies, public and private, masculine and feminine, martial puissance and chaste love, so as to "balance private fulfillment as a woman with public responsibility as a monarch."[5] Elizabeth Bellamy, on the other hand, develops a theory of "unresolved androgyny" against the theme of "discordia concors," the harmonious androgyny, because Britomart ultimately cancels her warrior image by overthrowing the Amazon Radigund—hence no unity, no resolution.[6] Constance Jordan goes further with a feminist slant, arguing for "political androgyny" that functions to authorize the female ruler to exercise male power under male-dominated society, Elizabeth being a man in political terms.[7]

To make a sweeping generalization, these views are all concerned largely with the queen's representation in a theoretical dimension based on the idea of the queen's two bodies, either individual or political. They disregard the literally physical dimension of the image: it is simply a way of giving birth without marriage. Bruce Boehrer touched on the marriage motif in Book Three in a somewhat different context—he did not discuss it in light of hermaphrodites, arguing that the praise of (wedded) chastity is a displacement of the barren queen; in other words, the celebration is calculated to transpose the reproductive problem. The problem is presented in such forms as the concern with Britomart's lineage, with the birth of Belphoebe and Amoret, and with the union of Amoret and Scudamour.[8] This paper argues, however, that as to the marriage problem, what Spenser is doing is to be sensed in a more extended and significant way than merely as transposed wedded chastity. He is offering a more immediate way of procreating issue by means of a hermaphrodite, which is more closely related to the matter of succession than that of chastity. The focus of the matter, then, should be centered on Britomart instead of Belphoebe or Amoret, for only Britomart among them most likely undergoes the hermaphroditic experience in the poem.[9]

We need to be reminded of the most immediate practical problem through the entirety of Elizabeth's reign from its foundation:

namely, the queen remained unmarried without an heir to the throne, and this dilemma loomed large enough to be a national obsession. As a loyal subject, Spenser must have been haunted by the dynastic problem as well. Intimately relevant to this problem is his use of the image of a hermaphrodite who meets the dynastic needs as well as displays the queen's private or public person theatrically. The biform image had been employed in many marriage rituals as a symbol of sexual intercourse and therefore fertility. The image of the hermaphrodite strongly implies a self-sufficient way of procreation, a capacity of giving birth without the aid of a male partner. Very suggestive is the self-generation story of Chrysogone in Book Three, "who by race/ A Faerie was, yborne of high degree" (III.vi.4.2–3) and who conceived the twins Belphoebe and Amoret simply by exposure to the sun's beams and delivered them unconsciously.

> Vnwares she them conceiu'd, vnwares she bore:
> She bore withouten paine, that she conceiued
> Withouten pleasure.
>
>   (3.6.27.1–3)

Venus is also seen as capable of conceiving and generating issue by herself: "She syre and mother is her selfe alone,/ Begets and eke conceiues, ne needeth other none" (IV.x.41.8–9). Spenser praises the goddess as an inspiration to procreation and the preserver of the world.[10]

Theatrical devices like cross-dressing, female warriors (Amazons), and hermaphrodites—these mechanisms embody masculine power, social and physical, in a female body, thereby blurring the typical distinction of the sexes—were actually widely practiced in the English Renaissance. Transvestism was "a social reality" of the period in Simon Shepherd's terms.[11] Linda Woodbridge states that women's fashion appropriating masculine attire was in real life "a recurrent phenomenon in Elizabethan times and a fairly permanent feature of the Jacobean landscape."[12] Therefore, she continues, a steady interest in female manliness or male effeminacy was reflected in the current literature including Spenser's *Faerie Queene* and Sir Thomas Elyot's *The Book Named the Governor*.[13] Drama is a notable case: consider the transvestite disguise of many Elizabethan heroines. Viola's disguise as Cesario is the central dynamic of William Shakespeare's *Twelfth Night,* as is Rosalind's cross-dressing as Ganymede in *As You Like It.*

It should be noted that Renaissance society, however, still remained one where the principles of order and degree in notions of state, society, family, and gender were strictly observed. Despite the well-meant attempt at achieving perfection by the union of both sexes, transvestism was basically considered a cultural trespass on sex roles, a challenge to the very foundation of Renaissance society. According to Woodbridge, transvestism had been a social issue since the 1570s. George Gascoigne wrote a formal satire of "the new fashion" of feminine attire in *The Steele Glas* in 1576. Later, Philip Stubbes (*Anatomy of Abuses,* 1583) and William Averell (*A Mervailous Combat of Contrarieties,* 1588) identified the man-clothed woman respectively as "Hermaphrodita" and "Androgini," both calling them "monsters."[14] The deeply rooted abhorrence and fear of masculine women extends to dismissing them as unnatural subversive monstrosities.

The official reaction to the first edition of *The Faerie Queen* (1590) that ends with the hermaphroditic union of Scudamour with Amoret as Spenser's view of ideal love, spiritual and physical oneness between man and woman, can be understood in this sense. Apparently the criticism was made by a senior statesman, probably William Cecil, Lord Burleigh, the queen's chief minister, who charged Spenser with being too much preoccupied with love.[15] The censure might be responsible for the deferring of the union of Scudamour and Amoret in the second edition of 1596, even though Spenser sticks to the hermaphroditic image in different ways through the whole poem.[16]

The fact that the practices had prevailed despite the official criticism and that many Elizabethan writers implicitly or explicitly had employed the androgynous image warrant our critical attention here. These practices have something to do with the unique situation of the time. Investing Elizabeth with the authority of a religious symbol in this way seems to have been required at the time for some immediate reasons.

An incipient form of nationalism had been established since Henry's decisive break with Rome. England had to be independent of Rome and construct its own church, one that would endorse the sovereign as its head. After experiencing a temporary setback under "Bloody Mary" (1553–58), Tudor nationalism was considerably intensified by the unprecedented conditions of Elizabeth's reign, in which national unity around the queen was the priority. Richard Helgerson sees the significant role of nationalism in Spenser's literary undertaking, but from a different viewpoint. As indicated in Spenser's claim to "have the kingdom of our own language," he argues, the poet recognizes a tension between the two competing claims of the state and poetry, between the duty to deal with the exigencies of monarchy and the humanist self-representation to emulate the greatness of antiquity. The result, he contends, is a poetry that articulates "a national community whose existence and eminence would then justify [his] desire to become its literary [spokesman]." This process, he continues, projects a shift of the nature of nationalism "from an essentially dynastic conception of communal identity ('the kingdom') to an assertion of what we recognize as one of the bases of postdynastic nationalism ('our own language')," from the dynastic sense of pre-modern nationalism to the democratic ("humanistic" in his terms) sense of modern nationalism. Obviously, Helgerson situates Renaissance humanism in terms of conflict or competition with sovereign authority, seeing humanism as a way to construct the individual self against the overwhelming force led by monarchy, thereby identifying Renaissance humanism as a primary force leading to modern popular nationalism.[17]

It would be misleading, however, to characterize Tudor nationalism using the modern sense of popular nationalism. The nation was principally identified with the monarch and his/her dynasty rather than the people because the nation was still viewed as the monarch's private realm or kingdom. The monarch's private matters or interests were themselves grave interests of the nation, shaping national consciousness as Henry VIII's example demonstrates; his private or dynastic matter motivated the development of English national consciousness itself. The situation of the Elizabethan period rearticulated Tudor nationalism as dynastic at its foundation. Queen Elizabeth's unique condition—she remained a virgin queen without an heir to the throne—haunted the nation through her entire reign. This issue directly involved national security, for it was a matter that could lead to civil war and that was related directly or indirectly to Catholic threats and war with Spain. Absolutely required for England to survive the dangers of the time, was the unity of the nation, that to a large extent depended on the monarch.

From the start, the Elizabethans were well aware of the devastating power of civil war in undermining social order, taking this knowledge both from the French and Dutch religious and civil wars and from their own in the previous century. Elizabeth's accession passage—Elizabeth's royal entry from the Tower of London to Westminister the day before her coronation in 1559—eloquently reveals the theme of unity as the nation's primary concern. The first pageant, for instance, recalled to the queen the sense of "unitie" or "concorde" with reference to the Wars of the Roses:

And all emptie places thereof were furnished with sentences concerning unitie. And the hole pageant garnished with redde

roses and white and in the forefront of the same pageant in a
faire wreathe was written the name, and title of the same, which
was *The uniting of the two houses of Lancastre and Yorke.* This
pageant was grounded upon the Queene's majestie's name. For
like as the long warre betwene the two houses of Yorke and
Lancastre then ended, when Elizabeth daughter to Edwarde the
fourthe matched in marriage wyth Henry the seventhe heyre
to the howse of Launcaster, so synce that the Queene's majestie's name was Elizabeth, and forsomuch as she is the onelye
heire of Henrie the eyght, which came of bothe houses as the
knitting up of concorde, it was devised that like as Elizabeth
was the first occasion of concorde, so she another Elizabeth
might maintaine the same among her subjectes, so that unitie
was the ende wherat the whole devise shotte, as the Queene's
majestie's names moved the firste grounde.[18]

If Elizabeth were to leave no issue, the crown could pass to either
of two principal heirs presumptive, Mary Stuart, Queen of Scots, or
Lady Catherine Grey of Suffolk. From the start, this was not merely
a legal controversy but directly involved national security, for it was
a question of whether the nation should follow Catholicism (Mary
Stuart) or Protestantism (Catherine Grey), a question that would
surely lead either to civil war or to national consolidation. Thus, the
issue, Mortimer Levine says, became the key concern of Elizabethan
writings. For example, the issue was centrally treated and performed
before Elizabeth in the form of a tragedy, *Gorboduc* (1561/2), "the
first Elizabethan succession tract," by the lawyers and gentlemen of
the Inns of Court.[19] Her typical indecisiveness about marriage and
the succession resulted in a persistent national apprehension about
the future.

The nation's desire for unity and security, however, in turn accel-
erated the growth of nationalism around the queen. Elizabeth was
often equated with the nation as a unifying center. Writing for the
nation meant writing for the queen, a national symbol that could
settle all social, religious, and political discords. The government
consciously used and controlled writings to create beliefs and to secure the allegiance of their subjects through state apparatuses, such
as spectacles, patronage, censorship, imprisonment, execution, and
so on.[20] The task of writers, including Spenser, was to provide a
theoretical model to perpetuate the nation and the authority of the
queen, who stayed heirless without marraige. Elizabeth served as a
cultural constant in framing the Elizabethan cultural paradigm.

It is not known precisely when Elizabeth determined to remain a virgin. We can speculate that it was at least by the time the last opportunity to create a dynasty turned out to be hopeless around 1582. A marriage proposal had been made by the duke of Alençon, the younger brother of the French King Henry III, in 1572. Elizabeth's desire to accept it, however, met with persistent opposition from the earl of Leicester and Sir Francis Walsingham, who opposed the match because of the chance of Catholic reinstatement. It is well known that Sidney, Leicester's nephew, lost Elizabeth's favor for writing her a letter of objection. The failure seemed to shift the focal point of writing from marriage advice to a praise of Elizabeth's unmarried chastity, devising the theatrical backdrops of the mystique of such a monarch. Every writer was engrossed in these matters. Around 1582, when it became clear that Elizabeth's marriage was not a possibility, the Inns of Court revelers stopped lecturing Elizabeth in the person of Juno and began to mirror images of Astraea and Diana (Cynthia) mainly to represent Elizabeth's chastity. Sir Walter Ralegh and John Lyly are probably two of the earliest writers who associate Elizabeth with chastity. Ralegh's poem, "The Ocean to Cynthia," was being written sometime in the 1580s, and Lyly's play Endimion, in which Cynthia represents Queen Elizabeth[21], was performed at court in 1586.

Since the late Elizabethans accepted as a fact the impossibility of the queen's marriage, it would be inconceivable that any advice on love and marriage was intended in The Faerie Queen. We need to see the theme of love and marriage from a different angle, which might account for the real significance of Spenserian hermaphrodism and thus why the proposed marriages in the poem are deferred without good reason.

Indeed, several marriages related to the queen directly or indirectly are expected in the poem—of Gloriana to Arthur, of Una to Redcrosse, of Britomart to Artegall, and so on. Yet it is not clear whether any union is consummated in the end. Instead, we can only witness it in other forms, in the androgynous form of a mythical union of the queen with the nation that is almost always detected in all types of marriage in the poem. Marriage might be unnecessary if the queen figures themselves are self-sufficient in terms of procreation.

For this reason, rather than describe the adventures directly related to love and marriage, Spenser is intent on tracing the genealogy of England and Elizabeth. A genealogical device was an epic convention in the Renaissance for the dynastic mythmaking of a nation that Ariosto and Tasso used after Virgil.[22] The act of reviewing the past expresses a wish ultimately to foresee the future, a hope for the permanence of the nation. This device is especially apt when dealing with a dynastic theme. Spenser's serves to justify the English nation and the Queen's legitimate ancestry by connecting the past with the present, projecting a vision of the nation's glorious future and assuring its continuous succession.

The theme of androgynous marriage of the queen to the nation is established in the poem by way of the genealogical method in the promised union of Gloriana with Arthur. Arthur reads his "Briton Moniments" in Canto X, Book ii, where his lineage traces back to the line of the Trojan Brutus who was grandson to Aeneas, founder of Rome, and established Britain (II.x.69). British history, on the other side, involves a fusion of another line of faerie ancestry, the Welsh lineage. This is read subsequently by Guyon under the title of "Antiquitie of Faery Lond." Faery Land in this way is lifted to an ideal level despite its essentially pagan nature. Arthur's visit to the Faerie Queene, the mythical merging of two chronicles, therefore, is meant to unite England with Faery Land, the old British kings with the new Tudor monarchy, and by implication, becomes the marriage of England to Elizabeth.

The figurative use of the kingdom or the people as a spouse, in fact, was a metaphorical commonplace that the queen employed to justify her virgin authority. Elizabeth demonstrably stated in response to the persistent marriage request: "To conclude, I am already bound unto an Husband, which is the Kingdome of England, and that may suffice you."[23]

In this regard, the androgynous symbolism of the wedding of the two rivers dissolving into one in Book Four is also very significant. Following Alastair Fowler's interpretation, it is purely allegorical, intimating the nation's marriage to Elizabeth, for the Medway is at the center of the naval operations of England.[24]

This marriage theme is most clearly represented by the promised union of Britomart and Artegall. Etymologically, Artegall means Art-egall, namely, "equal to Arthur," and also "[thou] art equal" as befits a knight of justice. These senses are historically confirmed: Artegall proves to be a maternal half-brother to Arthur (III.iii.27)[25] Yet, in practice, it is Britomart who plays Arthur's role in many ways. Both are identified as noble Britons in search of their partners. Like "that most noble Briton Prince" (I. proem 2.6), "this Briton Mayd" (III.ii.4.5) is seeking her spouse Artegall whom she saw in a vision similar to Arthur's. The British chronicle read by Arthur, in fact, is completed by Merlin's prophecy to Britomart (III.iii.25–50). Merlin confirms that the Tudors were the descendants of Arthur and predicts that from Britomart will descend the line of Briton kings down to Queen Elizabeth.

Britomart's union with Artegall is not realized in the poem as well, but suggested instead by her androgynous vision, in which her dynastic destiny, predicted in Book Three by Merlin, is materialized. In her mysterious vision Britomart sees the "moon-like Mitre" of Isis' priest on her head transformed to "a Crowne of gold" and herself dressed in the royal "robe of scarlet red" (V.vii.13). Given that the moon goddess Cynthia plays the role of Spenser's poetic substitute for the queen in the poem, Isis' association with the moon imagery (V.vii.4.6–8) is closely linked to royal symbolism, strengthening the dynastic import of Britomart's generation story. Britomart's dream in the Temple of Isis culminates in a hermaphroditic fusion of both sexes in her single body. It is an experience of sexual intercourse and procreation, where the phallic crocodile curls around her in a sexual embrace that gives birth to a mighty lion (V.vii.16). Isis' priest reads her mysterious dream in an allegory of dynasty. The crocodile is Osyris, symbolic of justice, an Artegall figure, while Isis stands for clemency, figuring Britomart. Out of their union a lion-like son will be born as a successor to the throne:

> . . . that same Crocodile doth represent
> The righteous Knight, that is thy faithull louer,
> Like to Osyris in all iust endeuer
> For that same Crocodile Osyris is,
> That vnder Isis feete doth sleepe for euer:
> To shew that clemence oft in things amis,
> Restraines those sterne behests, and cruell doomes of his.
>
> That Knight shall all the troublous stormes asswage,
>   And raging flames, that many foes shall reare,
>   To hinder thee from the just heritage
>   Of thy sires Crowne, and from thy countrey deare.
>   Then shalt thou take him to thy loued fere,
>   And ioyne in equall portion of thy realme.
>   And afterwards a sonne to him shalt beare,
>   That Lion-like shall shew his powre extreme.
> So blesse thee God, and giue thee ioyance of thy dreams.
>   (V.vii.22–23)

As a concluding statement, Spenser seems to foresee the nation's future in permanence through embodying another hermaphrodite figure, Nature, in the Mutabilitie Cantos. The argument of Canto 6 indicates that permanence is the principle of the moon and the heaven above and all that the earth beneath the moon is under the control of Mutabilitie, who rules the earth by changing "all which Nature had establisht first/ In good estate, and in meet order ranged" (VII.vi.5.2–3). The bold Mutabilitie climbs up to the moon "[w]here Cynthia raignes in euerlasting glory" (VII.vi.8.2) and claims her "throne," arguing that change rather than perpetuity is the governing law of the universe. Yet, as a judge, Nature sees through the cycle of the seasons and months that reveal continuity in variation, and rules over change.[26] This explains why Spenser sets up Nature, not Mutabilitie, as a hermaphrodite figure. Nature is self-sufficient, not affected by time, the greatest enemy to the permanence of generation. She veils herself like Venus, because she is man and woman, young and old, moving and unmoved, seen and unseen (VII.vii.5.5–9, VII. vii.13.1–4), and is responsible for procreation and fertility, growing trees out of her bosom (VII.vii.8). Even Mutabilitie recognizes Nature as Mother: "Sith of them all thou art the quall mother/ And knittest each to each, as brother vnto brother" (VII.vii.14.8–9). Like other androgynous figures, Nature reveals her dynastic significance. Similar to the description of the visionary son of Britomart and Artegall, Nature is depicted as looking like a lion (VII.vii.6.1–4), and the lion image in the poem is a consistent image of British ancestry, like Artegall's ancestor, as Merlin's chronicle shows (III.iii.30).

Spenserian hermaphrodite figures are self-sufficiently procreative, and especially Britomart's androgynous experience has a dynastic effect, representing a Spenserian vision for or answer to the succession problem. As a way of generation without marriage, the hermaphroditic procreation justifies the queen's unmarried chastity and at the same time perpetuates the dynastic succession. Hermaphrodism is understood as Spenser's way of representing Elizabeth's authority, coping with the dynastic matter.

The apparent violation of gender codes, the device implies, does not necessarily confuse sex roles, or praise the feminine in a feminist way, or express uneasiness about gynecocracy as some scholars argue.[27] The exception is confined only to the queen as the ruler, and the device is much more a means to cope with the national and dynastic situations of her day. Spenser intends to establish and praise the mystique of his queen, not of the feminine per se.

Despite her man-like power, Britomart is depicted as far from threatening to the old order founded on patriarchy. Arguably, she could reverse the normal order because she has such magical power as to play both man's and woman's parts, yet she does not make everything confused. Despite Britomart's rescue, Amoret as a virgin wife of another still feels insecure in the presence of a man (disguised Britomart) after all. At this point, Britomart reveals her gender and removes Amoret's fear by taking off her helmet after overthrowing a knight, who claims Amoret for his love (IV.i.13–15). Even the masculine attire does not hide a woman's nature. Disturbed by Redcrosse's question about the reasons that brought her to Faery Land, Britomart begins to cry and laments her life of hardship since babyhood. She expresses her wish to lead a womanly life:

> I haue beene trained vp in warlike stowre,
> To tossen speare and shield, and to affrap
> The warlike ryder to his most mishap;
> Sithence I loathed haue my life to lead,
> As Ladies wont, in pleasures wanton lap,
> To finger the fine needle and nyce thread.
>
> (III.ii.6.3–8)

The male principle in Britomart reaches a climax in the Radigund episode, where Britomart herself reaffirms women's subjection to men's rule.[18] Spenser's aversion to the Amazon Radigund is obvious, who uses her masculine strength for lustful ends turning the order of the commonweal upside down.

> Such is the crueltie of womenkynd,
>   When they haue shaken off the shamefast band,
>   With which wise Nature did them strongly bynd,
>   T'obay the heasts of mans well ruling hand,
>   That then all rule and reason they withstand,
>   To purchase a licentious libertie.
>   But vertuous women wisely vnderstand,
>   That they were borne to base humilitie,
> Vnlesse the heauens them lift to lawfull soueraintie.
>
> (V.v.25)

As the last line indicates, Spenser is conceding only the queen as an exception to men's rule because she is ordained by divine law. By implication, Britomart is intimately identified as the exceptional ruler, who should be more of a divine than feminine figure in the poem. As an instrument of divine justice Britomart subdues Radigund, the dark side of herself as a warrior woman, and rules the city of Radigund as "Princess" restoring its laws to the original male supremacy (V.vii.42.3–7). The transvestite disguise is simply a strategy to perform her task, and it is not intended to skew gender distinctions. Britomart is content to assume her womanly nature.

Between the Protestant reluctance to admit a cultural trespass and the demand for national security, Spenserian hermaphrodism was licensed to provide the queen with magical power to work out the national and dynastic problems. The queen remained an unmarried virgin ruler throughout times of national crisis. Hermaphrodism suggests a solution to the succession problem, which replaces a marriage that would not likely happen during her reign, and therefore the succession issue, without destroying the established cult of chastity. Hermaphrodism in *The Faerie Queen* is Spenser's inscription of the nationalist cause on the Queen over Protestant principles.

Seoul National University Seoul

NOTES

1.   See Lauren Silberman, "Mythographic Transformations of Ovid's Hermaphrodite," *Sixteenth Century Journal* 19 (1988): 643–55.

2.   Edmund Spenser, *The Faerie Queene,* ed. A. C. Hamilton (N.Y.: Longman, 1977). All references to the text are to this edition.

3.   Thomas P. Roche, Jr., *The Kindly Flame: A Study of the Third and Fourth Books of Spenser's Faerie Queene* (Princeton: Princeton University Press, 1964) 134–36.

4.   Donald Cheney, "Spenser's Hermaphrodite and the 1590 *Faerie Queene,"* *PMLA* 88 (1972): 193–95.

5.   Gary R. Grund, "The Queen's Two Bodies: Britomart and Spenser's *Faerie Queene,* Book III," *Cahiers Elisabethains* 20 (Oct. 1981): 11–13. It seems a critical convention to refer to the doctrine of the king's two bodies when discussing the queen's self-representation in the poem. On the evolution of the concept of kingship in western Europe during the Middle Ages and early sixteenth century, see Ernst H. Kantorowicz, *The King's Two Bodies: A Study in Medieval Political Theology* (Princeton: Princeton University Press, 1957). Around the late eleventh century, Kantorowicz claims, an idea arose that the king is two persons—a body natural, which is subject to death, and a body politic, which is an eternal principle. When a monarch dies, the body politic passes to a new monarch and so never changes (15–58). Marie Axton, applying the doctrine to the reign of Elizabeth I, claims that Elizabeth embodied the same monarch in her body natural—see her *The Queen's Two Bodies: Drama*

and the Elizabethan Succession (London: Royal Historical Soiciety, 1977). She finds the debate of the queen's two bodies in the early succession question raised by the lawyers of the Inns of Court as in *Gorboduc* and in its later development of secular plays and poetry, where the queen's two bodies were represented in various heightened forms. Related to them, for instance, were "double plots and the use of twinned characters" (x). In her estimate, Elizabeth well recognized the theory as indicated in one of her first speeches to the council: "I am but one bodye naturallye considered though by his [God's] permission a bodye politique to governe" (38).

6. Elizabeth J. Bellamy, "Androgyny and the Epic Quest: The Female Warrior in Ariosto and Spenser," *Postscript 2* (1985): 32, 34–35.

7. Constance Jordan, "Representing Political Androgyny: More on the Siena Portrait of Queen Elizabeth I," *The Renaissance Englishwoman in Print,* ed. Anne M. Haselkorn and Betty S. Travitsky (Amherst University of Massachusetts Press, 1990), 157, 160–61.

8. Bruce Thomas Boehrer, " 'Careless Modestee': Chastity as Politics in Book 3 of *The Faerie Queene,*" *ELH* 55 (1988): 557–66.

9. Britomart comes closest to the multiple representation of the queen in Spenserian theater. Like an actor on the stage, she sometimes plays a chaste goddess, other times a man-like warrior, and still other times, a merciful ruler. She has both male strength and female virtue as a composite of the queen's multi-mirrors: "Wise, warlike, personable, curteous, and kind" (III.iv.5.9). This image recalls Guyon's description of his "Queene of Faerie" on his shield, revealing the queen's various virtues:

> She is the mighty Queene of Faerie,
>> Whose faire retrait I in my shield do beare;
>> She is the flowre of grace and chastitie,
>> Throughout the world renowned far and neare,
>> My liefe, my liege, my Soueraigne, my deare,
>> Whose glory shineth as the morning starre,
>> And with her light the earth enlumines cleare;
>> Far reach her mercies, and her prayses farre,
> As well in state of peace, as puissaunce in warre.

(II.ix.4)

In Proem 5 to Book Three, Spenser clearly states that he will mirror the queen's body in multiplicity: "Ne let his [Sir Walter Ralegh's] fairest Cynthia refuse,/ In mirrours more then one her selfe to see." In theory, Gloriana and Belphoebe are the figures personifying the queen, representing her body politic and the body natural respectively/He pronounces this explicitly in both the same proem and the *Letter to Ralegh.* In practice, however, neither of these types seems to be fully realized in the poem. The theory of the so-called queen's two bodies, in fact, is further expanded in Spenser's poem. Spenser celebrates the power of the queen in almost unlimited ways through Britomart, who combines the masculine and feminine virtues as of Elizabeth. As a female knight, only she is invested with both qualities of man and woman, unlike other figures who stand for feminine virtues alone. As suggested in her name, Britomart amalgamates "Brito" with "Mars," signifying "the Britonesse" (III.i.58.5) and at the same time "Faire martiall Mayd" (III.ii.9.4). Also, the name is associated with the nymph Britomartis from Virgil, *Ciris*, who is linked to the chastity of Diana—see Hamilton's note to III.i.8.6. Therefore, Britomart can be marked by Gloriana's divine glory and grace, Belphoebe's chastity and beauty, Mercilla's justice and mercy, and above all, it is foretold that as a royal maid her issue will be related to Elizabeth (III.iv.3).

10.   See John Manning, "Venus," *The Spenser Encyclopedia*, ed. A. C. Hamilton et al. (London: Routledge, 1990), 708.

11.   See Simon Shepherd, *Amazons and Warrior Women: Varieties of Feminism in Seventeenth-Century Drama* (Brighton: The Harvester Press, 1981), 67.

12.   Linda Woodbridge, *Women and the English Renaissance: Literature and the Nature of Womankind, 1540–1620* (Urbana: University of Illinois Press, 1984), 153.

13.   See Woodbridge 140–41, 153–55.

14.   See Woodbridge 139–40, and Shepherd 67–68. See also, Laura Levine, *Men in Women's Clothing: Anti-theatricality, 1579–1642*. (Cambridge: Cambridge University Press, 1994).

15.   See Hamilton's note to IV., proem 1.

16.   Spenser's spirited defense of love ensued in the 1596 edition, attacking "[t]he rugged forhead that with graue foresight/ Welds kingdomes causes, and affaires of state" (4. proem 1.1–2) for his lack of perception of the true sense of love he intended (4. proem 2).

17.   See Richard Helgerson, *Forms of Nationhood: The Elizabethan Writing of England* (Chicago: The University of Chicago Press, 1992), 1–3.

18.   Arthur F. Kinney, ed., "The Queene's Majestie's Passage," *Elizabethan Backgrounds: Historical Documents of the Age of Elizabeth I* (Hamden: Archon Books, 1975), 19.

19.   See Mortimer Levine, *The Early Elizabethan Succession Question: 1558–1568* (Stanford: Stanford University Press, 1966), 1, 30, 39–40. To summarize, the play draws on the story of Gorboduc, king of Britain, pointing up the tragic end of a kingdom left without a recognized successor. The breaking up of the kingdom originates in a doting father who disregards the principle of primogeniture and divides the realm between his sons. The younger kills the elder for greed and the queen takes her revenge on the younger but finally is killed with the king by the people in rebellion. The country falls into civil war.

20.   See Roy Strong, *Splendor at Court: Renaissance Spectacle and the Theater of Power* (Boston: Houghton Mifflin, 1973), 19–21, and Galler Waller, *Edmund Spenser: A Literary Life* (N.Y.: St. Martin's Press, 1994), 43–44.

21.   I have learned much of this information from *Ficino*, an Internet discussion group—see Peter C. Herman's query and the responses following about Elizabeth's moon imagery in the Oct. to Nov. logs of 1996. As to the transition of Elizabeth's praise, Cain's categorization of the cults of Elizabeth is very useful. According to him, they fall in four stages: 1. The earliest identifications of Elizabeth with national heroines from the Old Testament—Judith, Esther, and the righteous judge Deborah; 2. the transposition of the medieval cult of the Virgin Mary to that of the Virgin Queen after 1570, who rules the realm successfully unmarried; 3. a more secular

devotion patterned after Petrarchan courtly love as in the sonnet sequence or after the more otherworldly fairy queen; 4. the tendency to mythologize Elizabeth as Greek and Roman goddesses like Diana, Venus, and Astraea. See Thomas H. Cain, "Images of Elizabeth" in Hamilton 236. See also John N. King, "Queen Elizabeth I: Representation of the Virgin Queen," *Renaissance Quarterly* 43:1 (Spring 1990): 30–74. King notes the shift of emphasis in encomia to Elizabeth from the earlier marriageable virgin to the late perpetual virgin.

22.   See Jane Hedley, "Lineage" in Hamilton 436–38.

23.   Axton 38.

24.   See Hamilton's note to IV.xi.8.

25.   See Judith H. Anderson, "Artegall" in Hamilton 62–63.

26.   See Hamilton's note to VII.vii.28–46.

27.   In order of appearance, David Norbrook, *Poetry and Politics in the Englilsh Renaissance* (London: Routledge & Kegan Paul, 1984), 114; Stevie Davies, *The Feminine Reclaimed: The Idea of Woman in Spenser, Shakespeare and Milton* (Lexington: University Press of Kentucky, 1986), 1; and Mary Villeponteaux, "Displacing Feminine Authority in the *Faerie Queen*," *Studies in English Literature, 1500–1900* 35:1 (Winter 1995): 58.

28.   Camille Paglia, on the other hand, differentiates Britomart from Radigund, employing Nietzsche's Apollonian and Dionysian concepts. According to her scheme, the "light-scattering" Apollonian androgyne is considered positive in *The Faerie Queene*, while the Dionysian androgyne "with its perpetual metamorphoses" exist only on the dark side (61–62). Therefore, Belphoebe and Britomart of the radiant light, "glittering chastity" represent the Apollonian androgyne, and Radigund is the Dionysian androgyne of "darkness and sensuality," which is "abhorrent to Spenser" (42). See Camille A. Paglia, "The Apollonian Androgyne and *the Faerie Queene*," *ELR* 9:42–63.

DONALD STUMP

Fashioning Gender: Cross-Dressing in Spenser's Legend of Britomart and Artegall

Close parallels between Britomart's experiences as a knight in the House of Malacasta and those of Artegall as a serving maid in the city of the House of Radigund suggest that Spenser regarded the crossing of traditional boundaries between the genders as a formative stage in the process by which each attains its own perfection. Britomart's tendency to excessive "frowardness" is gradually tempered by her adventures among men in Books III-V, much as Artegall's tendency to "forwardness" is moderated by his encounters with women. Though the poet generally portrays his idealized female characters as less forward by nature than the men they love, he follows humanists such as Sir Thomas Elyot in arguing that both genders are perfected in "virtuous and gentle discipline" by drawing toward the same Aristotelian mean. Although Spenser shares with other male writers of his age several of the attitudes toward gender-crossing noted in recent scholarship on Elizabethan medical treatises, marriage manuals, and stage plays, he also calls into question traditional distinctions between masculine and feminine in ways that deserve more scholarly attention than they have so far received.

D ESPITE THE RECENT FLURRY of scholarship on gender in *The Faerie Queene*, little attention has been paid to the delicate interplay between episodes of cross-dressing in the poem.[1] Critics have, of course, discussed the mingling of the masculine with the feminine in the armed Britomart of Books III-V and in the disarmed Artegall of the Radigund episode.[2] Several have also examined the tension between the independent and dominant Britomart of Books III and IV and the more submissive Britomart who places herself and the

95

city of the Amazons under Artegall's rule in Book V. Historical scholars have explored the implications of cross-dressing in Britomart's connections with Queen Elizabeth and in Artegall's connections with her male subjects (including Spenser himself),[4] and psychoanalytic critics have traced the effect of gender-crossing on Britomart's development as an idealized woman.[5] Yet the transvestism of Britomart has not been adequately related to that of Artegall, and neither has been satisfactorily integrated into the larger aims of the moral allegory. These relations are, moreover, precisely the ones that seem most puzzling.

If, as Spenser's *Letter to Ralegh* suggests, the overriding purpose of the poem is to "fashion a gentleman or noble person in vertuous and gentle discipline," what exactly does transvestism contribute to the project? Clearly, Spenser is not advocating cross-dressing per se. Yet he assigns it a conspicuous role in two major allegorical quests that are designed to instill such "discipline" in the Knights of Chastity and Justice—and, through them, in the readers of the poem. The question, then, is exactly what role gender-crossing plays in the process. Because Spenser gives mixed signals about the kinds of traditionally "masculine" activities he admires in women, the answer has proved elusive.

Britomart's experiences as a knight errant bring out virtues in her that were not commonly advocated for Elizabethan women, even those of the aristocracy. These include independence and self-reliance, courage, prowess in battle, and judicial equity in matters of social policy and governance. None of these are evident before she sets out on her quest, but all emerge by its climactic episode, when she conquers the Amazons. In her case, cross-dressing might be interpreted, then, as an imaginative first step in drawing noble women to the same ideal of "virtuous and gentle discipline" that Spenser looked for in a gentleman. That he intended something of the sort is suggested by passages in Book III, where he laments the loss of women's ancient skills in arms, the arts, and "pollicy" and where he calls for women to "awake" (ii.1–3, iv.1–3).[6] Yet after Britomart rescues Artegall from the tyrant Radigund in Book V, the poet confuses the issue by having her return to a more traditional and submissive posture toward men, enforcing it on the rebellious women of Radigone as well. The reversal lends credence to rather cynical assessments of Britomart's intentions such as that of Louis Montrose, who observes that "the woman who has the prerogative of a goddess, who is authorized to be out of place, can best justify her authority by putting women in their places."[7]

Since Spenser gives such mixed signals about the proper place that traditionally "masculine" virtues might hold in the ideal makeup of women, it is not surprising that critics have not been able to agree on the significance of Britomart's arming as a knight. Some see it as vital to the moral allegory. Harry Berger, for example, discusses the "ambiguous climate of early experience" and its effect in forcing Britomart to "abjure feminine behavior and play the game a man's way," and Benjamin Lockerd sees her quest as an opportunity to discover her "masculine side."[8] Others, such as Pamela Joseph Benson, reject such interpretations. According to Benson, Books III-V explore two strategies by which women can break free from traditional social constraints and develop their own potential: that of Angela and the Amazons, who expand their opportunities by emulating the violence and aggressiveness of men, and that of Britomart, who asserts herself without becoming man-like and without rebelling against the established social order. Although the Knight of Chastity begins her quest by appropriating Angela's armor, she ultimately renounces the rebelliousness that it represents and restores the city of the Amazons to the rule of men. Benson's conclusion, then, is that Britomart remains throughout her quest "an emblematic representation of the mystery of the power of the feminine."[9] Other commentators have simply given up on the problem, concluding that the submissive Britomart of the Radigund episode cannot be reconciled with the aggressive Britomart of former passages and signals the poet's retreat from his earlier views.[10]

Similarly difficult to sort out is the relation between cross-dressing and the ethical education of Artegall. Doing household chores and suffering unwanted sexual advances may be an appropriate corrective to his submissiveness toward Radigund, but any unpleasant and demeaning experience—from grooming her horses to plowing her fields —might have had a similar effect. It is not immediately apparent that playing a part traditionally reserved for women contributes anything special to his character. If anything, the experience gives him cause to repent the softening of his harsh masculine ethos that led him to pity Radigund and yield to her in the first place. In a book that moves from harsh retribution in Cantos i-iv to more refined judgments tempered by clemency and mercy in Cantos v-ix, it seems odd to treat Artegall's pity for Radigund, not just as unwise or imprudent, but as altogether shameful and emasculating.

One wonders, then, whether cross-dressing per se has any special value in the education of Britomart and Artegall. I believe that it does, though its importance is difficult to assess so long as we continue to consider Britomart's transvestite experiences in isolation from those of her future husband. To tease out the larger patterns in gender formation and ethics that Spenser is weaving, it is helpful to begin with two incidents that are rarely compared: Britomart's encounter with Malecasta and Artegall's enforced service to Radigund. These make a closely matched pair, the one beginning the most important love-story in the poem and the other ending it (at least in so far as Spenser lived to complete his design). On the basis of these episodes and their effects on the lovers, I would argue that Artegall's cross-dressing is at least as important in his ethical development as the arming of Britomart is in hers. As a comparison of their experiences with those of other couples in Books III-V reveals, Spenser sees the crossing of traditional boundaries between the genders as a formative stage in the process by which each attains its own perfection.

I

Artegall's humiliation at the house of Radigund is, in many respects, a reenactment of Britomart's earlier adventure at the house of Malecasta. At Castle Joyous, Britomart had rescued a beleaguered man (the Red Crosse Knight) from the servants of a domineering woman. At Radigund's castle, Artegall likewise rescues a hapless knight (Sir Terpine) from the forces of a female tyrant. In both cases, the despot demands that knights who enter her domain accept the same sort of compact: they are to do battle against her (or her knights), and if they lose, they are to become her servants. Both Britomart and Artegall accept these conditions, and both prevail in the battle that follows. Afterwards, however, they let down their guards, allowing themselves to be brought into the woman's castle and subjected to unwanted sexual advances. In Book III, when Britomart first encounters Malecasta's love-play over dinner, she pities the lady and so fails to take the sort of decisive action that might have avoided trouble later on. In Book V, the cause of Artegall's abuse is likewise his pity for the lady of the castle. Having knocked Radigund unconscious in the lists, he beholds her beauty and is "Empierced . . . with pittifull regard" (V.v.13), which prompts him to cast away his sword and yield to her. The difficulty in both episodes lies in knowing when to display the ruthlessness required on the battlefield and when the pity and restraint valued in domestic life. Britomart learns her lesson faster than Artegall, of course. In her encounter with Malacasta later in the evening, she draws her sword and defends herself, whereas

Artegall remains remarkably passive in the face of Radigund's abuse. The question of the proper limits of pity is, however, the same in both incidents.

Finally, and most significantly for our purposes, the two episodes are linked by their central concern with cross-dressing. Britomart enters Malecasta's court in full armor and resolutely refuses to reveal her sex, going only so far during dinner as to raise her visor. Absurd as this is, when all the others around her are feasting and dancing, it is also imprudent because it misleads Malecasta. Overpowered with desire for the unidentified knight, the mistress of the house remains blind to her guest's gender until their *fabliaux* confrontation in Britomart's bedroom later that evening. In the episode in Book V, similar confusions of gender occur. Once Artegall has put on women's clothing, he too is accosted by the lady of the castle, who has suddenly fallen in love with him.

To grasp the significance of these carefully crafted parallels for Spenser's theory of gender and ethics, it is helpful to look closely at the dispositions that Britomart and Artegall display before they are forced to put on the trappings of the opposite sex. In recounting her past to the Red Crosse Knight, Britomart claims that, from earliest childhood, she was "trained up in warlike stowre,/To tossen speare and shield, and to affrap/The warlike ryder to his most mishap" (III.ii.6–8). The truth, however, is that she has only recently taken up arms for the first time (iii.53). The outgoing and aggressive qualities that she displays later develop only gradually, as the demands of her quest press upon her. Before her nurse Glauce persuades her to disguise herself as a knight, she seems surprisingly timid and passive.

The best evidence of Britomart's initial disposition lies in her reaction to the vision of Artegall in Merlin's glass. In describing the love-sickness that follows, Spenser stresses her "feeble spright" (47), her vulnerability to nightmares and "ghastly feares" (29, 31), and her tendency to lapse into despair, which shows itself rather melodramatically when she exclaims to her nurse, "nought for me but death there doth remaine" (35). Rather than responding to love with a desire for action, as men such as Scudamour and Artegall do, she is inclined to be "sad, solemne, sowre, and full of fancies fraile" (27). Her nurse is also concerned that she may prove frigid or prudish. Noting that the young woman's limbs are "frosen cold" (34), Glauce reproaches her for repressing her natural desires and avoiding the company of men, saying "Thou in dull corners doest thy selfe inclose,/Ne tastest Princes pleasures, ne doest spred/Abroad thy fresh youthes fairest flowre, but lose/Both leafe and fruit" (31). At this point, of course, Glauce does not understand the situation fully, since she has not yet learned that Britomart has fallen in love with a disembodied image. Even after this fact emerges, however, the nurse continues to lecture her charge about the naturalness of sexual desire, stressing that to feel it is not, as Britomart fears, a "crime" (37) and involves "No guilt" (40). Clearly, Glauce is not so much concerned with the onset of adolescent sexuality as with Britomart's reaction to it, which is to treat it as "filthy lust" and draw back.

Now, it might be argued that such reactions tell us little about Britomart's native disposition. She is, of course, very young and very much in love, and in her first excessive responses to desire, she is clearly not herself. Yet I would argue that the peculiar nature of her reactions is revealing all the same. Not everyone who falls in love in *The Faerie Queene* withdraws from contact with others, pining and struggling with fear, shame, and despair in this way—not even those whose cases seem equally hopeless. On this point, it is instructive to compare the Princess with her closest analogue, Prince Arthur. Like her, he has fallen in love with a vision of someone whom he has never met. In consequence, he too must "feed on shadowes, whiles [he] die[s] for food" (III.ii.44). Spenser calls attention to the similarity in their predicaments by having both complain against destiny and the natural elements in lovelorn soliloquies in the same canto (iv.6–11 and 54–61). Yet Arthur's initial response to falling in love is altogether different from Britomart's. Whereas she becomes more and more passive and withdrawn, he becomes more outgoing and aggressive. In recounting his dream of Gloriana in Book I, he says, "From that day forth I cast in carefull mind/To seeke her out with labour, and long tyne,/And never vow to rest, till her I find" (ix.15). Britomart eventually bestirs herself in much the same way, but only after receiving an elaborate vision of her destiny from Merlin and after being scolded, comforted, urged, instructed, and encouraged by her nurse. Unless moved by the concerted efforts of others, she reacts—at least initially—in ways that mark her as what Spenser elsewhere calls a "froward" personality.

If we think back to the representation of psychological types at the House of Medina in Book II, we see that Britomart inclines toward the extreme represented by Elissa, or "deficiency." Though Elissa has made "frowardness" a vice in a way that Britomart has not, their reactions reveal similar impulses. In responding to her sister Medina's suggestion that their guests be invited to "prepare/Their minds to pleasure, and their mouthes to dainty fare," Elissa

> . . . did deeme
> Such entertainment base, ne ought would eat,
> Ne ought would speake, but evermore did seeme
> As discontent for want of merth or meat;
> No solace could her Paramour intreat
> Her once to show, ne court, nor dalliance,
> But with bent lowring browes, as she would threat,
> She scould, and frownd with froward countenaunce. . . .
>
> (II.ii.35)

She and Britomart share the same inclination to draw back from natural desires for food and sex, the same impulse to be "sowre" and depressed. For Elissa, as for her suitor Huddibras, excessive sternness and concern with honor lead to withdrawal from the pleasures of the senses. This, in turn, leads to gloominess, discontent, and belligerence. In Elissa, the aggression is of a passive sort, characterized by scolding and dark looks, whereas in Huddibras it takes the form of "rash adventures" in which reason is "with foole-hardize over ran" and courage is surpassed by "Sterne melancholy" (17). Though the youthful Britomart is neither so confirmed nor so extreme in her "frowardness," she displays many of the same tendencies.

When, for example, everyone else—including the Knight of Holiness—sits down to the banquet at Malecasta's castle, the Knight of Chastity refuses to participate or even to disarm. As the narrator remarks, she "sdeigned such lascivious disport/And loath'd the loose demeanure of that wanton sort" (III.i.40). There is nobility in her reaction, of course, but also a good deal of silliness and prudery. In the next episode, having fallen into despondency at her inability to find Artegall, she behaves very much like Sir Huddibras, emerging from her melancholy reveries to explode in a rash act of violence. When the hapless Marinell challenges her right to pass over his beach, she lashes out in "fierce furie," brutally lancing him and leaving him "transfixed" and "wallow[ing] in his gore." At pains to distance himself from this act, the narrator compares Marinell to a sacred ox struck down on "holy grownd" and remarks on the fact that she "stayd not him to lament" but went directly on, "despising" the things of worldly value on the beach (iv.13–18). Once again, her persistence and lack of worldliness are noble, but also cold and inhuman.

If, initially, Britomart is "froward," then her intended mate can only be termed "forward." When we first encounter Artegall in Book

IV, he is the most imposing of the knights who challenge the defend-
ers of Maidenhead—a list that includes such erotically aggressive figures as Bruncheval, Blandamour, and Paridell. Bruncheval's name,
which means "dark horse," calls to mind Plato's image of fleshly
appetite.[11] The company does Artegall little credit. His noblest ally
is Triamond, a man so fierce and possessive that he has expended
two of his three miraculously allotted lives to wrest a woman from her
equally possessive brother. Like others in this crew, Artegall refuses to
restrain his desires within the bounds of civilized conduct, proudly
announcing on his shield the motto "*Salvagesse sans finesse.*" As early
as Book III, Merlin had alluded to Artegall's "dreaded name" (iii.28),
and in Book V, we learn more about his youthful ferocity in the
descriptions of his tutelage under the goddess Astraea: "Ne any liv'd
on ground, that durst withstand/His dreadfull heast, much lesse him
match in fight,/Or bide the horror of his wreakfull hand" (i.8). The
priests of Isis warn Britomart that, even in later life, his "cruell
doomes" will require her moderating influence (vii.22). The ferocity
of Artegall—at once his glory as a defender of justice and his defect
as a prospective husband and peace-time ruler—is modeled on that
of Achilles and Hercules, whose furies, rages, and inordinate desires
were legendary.[12]

The dispositions represented in the opposing sides at Satyrane's
tournament are captured nicely in the heroic simile describing Britomart's victory over Artegall in the lists:

    Like as in sommers day when raging heat
      Doth burne the earth, and boyled rivers drie,
      That all brute beasts forst to refraine fro meat,
      Doe hunt for shade, where shrowded they may lie,
      And missing it, faine from themselves to flie;
      All travellers tormented are with paine:
      A watry cloud doth overcast the skie,
      And poureth forth a sudden shoure of raine,
    That all the wretched world recomforteth againe.

    So did the warlike *Britomart* restore
      The prize, to knights of Maydenhead that day. . . .

                                (IV.iv.47–48)

Imagery of opposite extremes—here "raging" heat mollified by cool rain descending from heaven—is used of Britomart and Artegall throughout the poem. In the episode at Isis Church and elsewhere, Britomart is represented by the moderate and beautiful (but cool) light of the Moon, whereas Artegall is compared with the intense and life-engendering (but scorching) light of the sun (V.vii.4).[13]

More than we might suppose, then, Artegall is like Medina's other sister, Perissa, whose name means "excess." In one respect, her disposition may seem different, since she loves extravagant clothing and spends her time in idle pleasure:

> No measure in her mood, no rule of right,
> But poured out in pleasure and delight;
> In wine and meats she flowd above the bancke,
> And in excesse exceeded her owne might;
> In sumptuous tire she joyd her selfe to prancke,
> But of her love too lavish. . . .
>
> (II.ii.36)

If we think of Artegall only as a stern figure who metes out justice in Book V, however, we are likely to misunderstand his character on this point. Earlier in the action, he shows himself exceptionally proud of his appearance, both when he makes his entrance in Satyrane's lists in the fantastic garb of the Salvage Knight and when he first appears in Merlin's glass tricked out in a helmet "covered with a couchant Hound," a shield depicting "a crowned litle Ermilin," and arms boasting "with cyphers old,/Achilles armes, which Arthegall did win" (III.ii.25). As the image of him as a crocodile in Britomart's dream at Isis Church suggests, moreover, he is as much inclined to sensuality as he is to aggression and self-display. In the dream, the crocodile devours a tempest of fire, and "swolne with pride of his owne peerelesse powre," proceeds to threaten Britomart. When she beats him back with her rod, he meekly seeks for "grace and love," but only as part of what the narrator describes as "his game." Before she can resist, he draws her to him and impregnates her (V.vii.14–16).

In Artegall's dealings with Radigund, we see further instances of his preoccupation with pleasure and "game." To bring him to accept her conditions for combat, the Queen of the Amazons sends enticing messengers tricked out in "best array," who come to his tent by night bearing gifts of "wine and juncates." Though we can imagine how Britomart might receive such an embassy from a usurper whose servants have just attempted to hang an innocent man, Artegall receives them "with curt'sies meete" and sends them back with "gifts and things of deare delight" (V.iv.49–51). In the morning, he allows himself to be overcome by Radigund's beauty, revealed seductively in the "Camis light of purple silke," which she wears "short tucked for light motion" (v.2). When he strikes off her helmet and beholds her beauty, he yields just as he had yielded earlier to Britomart. In doing so, he reveals the same vulnerability that he had displayed at Satyrane's tournament, where he fought fiercely to possess the beauty of the false Florimell.

As the romance progresses, the extreme dispositions of Britomart and Artegall are gradually thwarted, corrected, and refashioned. Though Spenser shows a healthy respect for the difficulties involved in molding moral character, his conviction that extremes of temperament can be moderated is apparent in the process by which the Knights of Chastity and of Justice draw toward a more satisfactory mean. It is as a stage in this process, I think, that their cross-dressing is best understood.

II

In the course of Britomart's quest, her tendency to "frowardness" is gradually tempered by her need to act like a knight. In traveling from castle to castle, she meets many kinds of people and becomes less standoffish.[14] In doing battle, she masters her timidity. The process begins at the House of Malecasta, where Britomart finds it easier to appear "forward" in the battles outside the castle than in the social intercourse within. Her tendency to be censorious and prudish is nowhere more apparent. In taking the edge off her contempt for those less "froward" than she, the most important incidents are her discovery that even the Knight of Holiness has difficulty with Malecasta's six knights and her own subsequent wounding by one of them, Gardante. Representing the first of the stages by which Courtly Love leads from the initial sight of the beloved to erotic consummation, Gardante calls to mind at least two kinds of "seeing." When Britomart wakes up to find Malecasta in her bed, she sees at last the "malengine and fine forgerie" of her hostess (53), who had earlier aroused her pity. If Hamilton and others are right, she also relives the time when she first beheld Artegall in Merlin's "mirror" and was overpowered by desires similar to those that drive Malecasta.[15] Both experiences are salutary, not only because they acclimate her to the fallen world in which she must work out her destiny but also because they show her that she is not immune to the lust that she sees around her.

In her subsequent forays into society in Book III, Britomart shows the effects of her initiation at Castle Joyous. More at ease in a world that falls short of her own standards, she is less cautious and withdrawn. At the house of Malbecco, she disarms completely, letting down her hair and joining in the socializing after dinner. Despite the evident crudeness and discourtesy of her host and the "hungry vew" cast her way by Satyrane and Paridell as she disarms (ix.24), she enjoys herself. For all his faults, Paridell deserves much of the credit. Having knocked some of the prissiness out of her by downing her with his lance in the mud outside the castle,[16] he so "empassions" her with pity for Troy in his epic stories over dinner that she offers the company an account of her own Trojan lineage and a prophecy of the coming glory of Troynovant (38ff.). That the Knight of Chastity should meet her match in a sophisticated womanizer like Paridell and should turn on him the "gracious regard of her faire eye" (25) suggests that she has begun to take a new and healthy delight in "amorous play."

The easing of Britomart's tendency to self-repression continues in her rescue of the even more "froward" Amoret. Just as she had seen the face of her own desire reflected in Malecasta, she now sees the image of her own prudery mirrored in the unhappy and unwilling bride. Amoret's reaction to the bawdy entertainment staged on her wedding-night recalls Britomart's own feelings during her first bout of love-sickness. Fearing that her desire for Artegall will end in degradation, she talks with her nurse about mythical figures of lust such as Myrrhe, Biblis, and Pasiphae (ii.38–41). Seeing "sinfull lust" in the wedding-masque, Amoret, too, is overpowered by images of lewdness and rape drawn from mythology and the arts (III.xi.28–52, IV.i.1–4). Though Britomart has reason to sympathize with the bride's feelings here, she chooses to side with the groom by offering to free Amoret from the spells of the magician.

The first episode of Book IV includes a series of jests that reveal just how much Britomart has changed. In traveling with Amoret, she continues to conceal her gender, taking a perverse delight in swaggering like a man and in making suggestive remarks to her frightened charge. This curious impulse to enact masculine "lustfulness" —which Spenser attributes partly to Britomart's desire to match her actions to her disguise and partly to her own "wounded mind" (IV.i.7) —suggests that Britomart is beginning to experiment with thinking as well as acting like a man. Although she reveals her sex to Amoret when they stop for the night, an element of gender-crossing remains. In a comic (and perhaps therapeutic) act of bedroom fantasy, she and

Amoret enact the traditional "bedding of the bride" that Amoret had earlier refused to Scudamour. As Spenser remarks, Amoret "to [Britomart's] bed, which she was wont forbeare,/Now freely drew, and found right safe assurance theare" (IV.i.15). Though homoerotic attraction doubtless plays a part in this scene,[17] it is subsumed in a parody of the wedding night that allows both women to play at intimacy and yet remain "safe."

Such indirect and incremental approaches to eroticism are not, however, altogether sufficient to prepare Britomart for marriage. At the Tournament of Satyrane, she continues to champion Maidenhead. When Artegall later waylays her to avenge his loss in the tournament, however, further signs of change emerge. The allegorical description of their struggle is tinged with desire. Unhorsed by her magic spear, he "Did leape to her, as doth an eger hound/Thrust to an Hynd within some covert glade,/Whom without perill he cannot invade" (IV.vi.12). The erotic suggestiveness is heightened by allusions to her horse, which carries its traditional Platonic significance as a symbol of the passions. To deprive her of the primary defense of her chastity, the lance, Artegall drives his sword down upon the horse's "hinder parts" (13), yet even when forced to fight on foot, the martial maid continues to thwart his advances. When at last he shears away her ventail and kneels in wonder at her beauty, she stands over him with sword raised in the traditional masculine posture of dominance. At this point, she has become nearly as fierce and aggressive as he.

The final stage in Britomart's transformation comes in her confrontation with Radigund. Driven by jealousy and by "sodaine stounds of wrath and griefe," she sets out in "The felnesse of her heart, right fully bent/To fierce avengement of that womans pride" (V.vi.17–18). Committing the most extreme act of man-like aggression of her quest, she defeats, kills, and seizes political power from her opponent. No sooner has she done so, however, than she experiences a change of heart. Seeing Artegall stripped of his trappings as the Salvage Knight and confined in "womens weeds," she misses the very qualities in him that, as recently as the Tournament of Satyrane, she had resisted:

> . . . when she saw that lothly uncouth sight,
>
> Of men disguiz'd in womanishe attire,
>
> Her heart gan grudge, for very deepe despight
>
> Of so unmanly maske, in misery misdight.

(V.vii.37)

To restore him to his former station, she offers him rule of the city that she has just conquered, subordinating herself and the rest of the women of Radigone to her future husband.

This last act is unexpected. Having put "frowardness" behind her to achieve her greatest triumph, Britomart reverts to her former tendency to submit and withdraw. I shall return to this point after discussing the changes brought about by the cross-dressing of Artegall. For the moment, I would only stress the larger pattern that makes the decision surprising, namely that, until this moment, the entire course of Britomart's ethical development has depended on tempering her native disposition by driving it to the opposite extreme.

III

A similar process takes place in Artegall. Just as victorious knighthood counters the deficiencies in Britomart's nature, so defeated chivalry moderates the excesses in his. The humiliation that he suffers among the Amazons is only the most obvious incident in this transformation, which begins with his reverses in Book IV.

Raised alone among beasts by the goddess Astraea, the Salvage Knight represents manliness in its raw and uncultivated state. He is not accustomed to defeat such as that which he suffers against the forces defending Maidenhead. When the similarly crude and passionate lover Scudamour later beholds Artegall kneeling in wonder at Britomart's beauty, he twits him for becoming "a Ladies thrall,/That whylome in your minde wont to despise them all" (IV.vi.28). Yet thralldom is precisely, I think, what Artegall needs to refine and humanize his character. Beginning with the "ruth" or pity that he feels when he first beholds Britomart's countenance, he rapidly progresses through a series of milder emotions from "obedience," humility, and "wonder" to devotion and love (21–22).

As if to press Artegall still further to the opposite extreme, Spenser designs his next adventure as a parody of this moment of infatuation. When he strikes off Radigund's helmet, the sight of her beauty robs him of his characteristic sternness. As the narrator observes, "No hand so cruell, nor no hart so hard,/But ruth of beautie will it mollifie" (V.v.13). Yielding, as he had earlier done with Britomart, he allows humility to lapse into self-humiliation and submissiveness to become servility. The contrast between the two incidents brings home to him, not only the difference between proper and improper

reverence for women but also that between true and false clemency.
In submitting to Radigund, he mirrors her tendency to escape the
confines of her gender by swinging suddenly and erratically to the
opposite extreme. As with Britomart in her encounter with Malecasta, Artegall learns from his experiences with Radigund partly by
discovering her guile and partly by seeing in her the image of his
own ambivalence about gender.

Better ways to temper Artegall's harshness and arrogance are revealed in the episodes that follow. In killing Radigund but sparing
her subjects, Britomart offers him an illustration of the principle of
classical equity, "Which from just verdict will for nothing start,/But
to preserve inviolated right,/Oft spilles the principall, to save the
part" (V.x.2). In judging Duessa two cantos later, Mercilla illustrates
such equity and also the higher virtue of Christian mercy, offering
Artegall and his companion Arthur "Royall examples of her mercies
rare,/And worthie paterns of her clemencies" (V.x.5).[18] Whereas Artegall's former way of ruling has consisted mainly in imposing retribu-
tive justice through the violence of his servant Talus, Mercilla
exercises her authority mostly through acts of love, only occasionally
nailing poets' tongues to pillars or drawing the sword of justice that
has grown rusty at her feet. The hallmarks of her rule—which mingles
"awe" and "order" with "peace and clemencie" (ix.23, 30)—stand
in contrast both to Artegall's earlier harshness and to his more recent
excesses of pity. As Mercilla's execution of the obdurate and unre-
pentant Duessa suggests, in a fallen world of the sort lamented in the
proem to Book V, stern legal justice has its place. When the situation
allows, however, it is better "to save the subject of [the ruler's] skill"
and "to reforme, then to cut off the ill" (x.2).

Although, at first glance, the process of Artegall's reformation
seems to involve only a single experience of gender-crossing, all the
incidents that I have discussed are, in fact, part of a larger strategy to
moderate the extremes of his masculinity. In each, he encounters a
dominant woman who changes him for the better. Just as, in his
youth, he had learned from Astraea the rough justice required in a
corrupt and violent age, he now learns from Britomart the more
refined virtue of judicial equity or clemency and from Mercilla that
of Christian mercy. Although, in his "zeale of Justice," he does not
initially share Mercilla's desire to save Duessa if at all possible, he
later changes his mind and acknowledges its wisdom (ix.49, x.4).

In his dealings with Grantorto at the climax of his quest, we see
the effects that these women have had in shaping his character.
Though earlier he had made no attempt to restrain Talus's violence
against the populace of Radigone, he reigns in his iron servant now,

sending a messenger to inform the tyrant that "not for such slaughters sake/He thether came" (V.xii.8). Though he had allowed himself to be taken in by a pleasant embassy from Radigund, he refuses to receive ambassadors now (10). Though he was unmanned by shame when he yielded to the Queen of the Amazons, he regards it as "No shame to stoupe" in fighting Grantorto so long as it furthers the cause of justice (19). His victory entails, then, a judicious mingling of the "froward" virtues of clemency, restraint, and humility with his usual courage and boldness.

As with Britomart, however, the process of tempering Artegall's excesses ends with a surprising reversal. After restoring Irena, the Knight of Justice refuses to extend clemency to her rebellious subjects as Britomart had previously extended it to the Amazons. Instead, he unleashes Talus to exact "grievous punishment" until "Not one was left, that durst [Irena] once have disobayd" (25–26). This extraordinary act of vengeance brings his recall to the Faerie Court and his savaging by the Blatant Beast and its handler Detraction, who charges the Knight of Justice with "reprochfull crueltie" (40). Artegall's unrestrained aggression in Ireland is, if anything, more baffling than Britomart's withdrawal after her conquest of the Amazons. At least in her case, there are plausible reasons for her to go against the general course of her ethical and political development. Her future husband needs to be put back on his feet, and she seems to accept Spenser's own position that women "were borne to base humilitie,/Unlesse the heavens them lift to lawfull soveraintie" (V.v.25).

In her case as well as his, however, Spenser may also have had in mind a basic tenet of Aristotle's theory of temperance. According to the *Nicomachean Ethics*, once we recognize the vices to which we are most inclined, "We should then drag ourselves towards the contrary extreme, for by drawing ourselves well away from our disposition to error, we shall be more likely to arrive at the mean, like those who straighten warped sticks by bending them in the contrary direction."[19] As we have seen, Artegall's sustained development as a man depends on "dragging himself" to virtues that Spenser regards as more natural to women, just as Britomart's depends on incorporating those that he saw as more natural to men. In the end, however, like Aristotle's warped sticks, both characters inevitably retain some of the tendencies of their original natures. For Spenser, "frowardness" in women and "forwardness" in men may be moderated but not entirely eradicated—nor should they be, for the tension between them is vital to his conception of the ideal social order. In Artegall's case, the poet muddies the issue of vengeance on the Irish. On the one hand, he treats the attacks of the Blatant Beast and Detraction

as malicious and unfair. On the other, he has the highest arbiter of
ethics in the poem, Gloriana herself, recall Artegall to court because
of his actions. In this way, Spenser opens up the possibility that, like
the Red Cross Knight and other heroes in the poem who suffer lapses
at some point after their finest hours, the Knight of Justice undergoes
his education in ethics without ever fully mastering either himself or
the virtue that he represents.

IV

Some might argue that the contrasting extremes represented by
Britomart and Artegall cannot be regarded as an allegory of the genders per se.[20] As the poem's chief exemplars of heterosexual love,
however, these characters embody tendencies that Spenser elsewhere
treats as altogether characteristic of their genders. Such tendencies
appear not only in the allegory of "forwardness" and "frowardness"
at the House of Medina but also in descriptions of pairs of idealized
lovers throughout the poem.

Although, in the allegory of classical temperance in Book II, Elissa
and Perissa embody opposite extremes, they also share traits common
to their gender, notably a tendency to be less violent and more retir-
ing than their male counterparts. Their suitors, Sir Huddibras and
Sansloy, are more hot-headed and assertive. Even the Knight of Temperance, who attempts to make peace between them, is characterized
as overly aggressive and "bold." All three males are quick to flaunt
their manliness and to envy one another, becoming "furious" and
"cruel" when roused. In Spenser's remark that they waged "A triple
warre with triple enmitee, / All for their Ladies froward love to gaine"
(II.ii.26), the word "froward" is revealing. Though Elissa and Perissa
are quick to display hostility of their own, they and their sister remain
on the sidelines, egging the combatants on or, in the case of Medina,
awaiting an opportunity to make peace. The entire passage, then,
reflects Spenser's belief in certain inborn tendencies in the genders.
Though both men and women can be classified individually as "froward" or "forward," men tend to be more "forward" than women.
This impression is confirmed at the Temple of Venus, where the
six companion virtues of Womanhood—Shamefastnesse, Modestie,
Silence, Obedience, Curtesie, and Cherefulnesse—are notably "froward" (IV.x.49–51).

For Spenser, then, the dispositions rooted in gender are surprisingly maleable, but their fashioning has limits. However much Artegall and Britomart may moderate the extremes of their dispositions,

they cannot entirely escape the natures that incline them to those extremes in the first place. This conclusion is borne out by other prominent pairs of idealized lovers in the poem, such as Florimell and Marinell, Amoret and Scudamour, and Belphoebe and Timias. Like Britomart, the ladies in each of these pairs tend to withdraw from the society and (at least initially) to react to sexuality in chilly or neurotic ways. Belphoebe and Florimell are isolated figures, the former dedicated to virginity and to the life of a solitary hunter and the latter compelled by timidity to flee from most males that she encounters. Even Amoret, the exemplary figure of fruitful married love, begins as a "nun of Venus" dedicated to a life of withdrawal from the temptations of the world (IV.x). Although, after some resistance, she allows Scudamour to lead her out of the Temple and marry her, she then has difficulties on her wedding night, withdrawing into herself and suffering nightmarish fantasies of sexual degradation.

The lovers matched with these ladies all suffer because they are too domineering and aggressive. Marinell attacks any knight who approaches the gold and jewels that he has amassed on the Rich Strond. Scudamour bears on his shield the image of the conquering Cupid, which also figures in his wife's nightmares (cf. III.xi.7 and 47–49), and he is prone to forget the third of the admonitions written above the doors in the House of Busirane: "Be not too bold!" Timias is also inclined to be too easily carried away by his passions, as he demonstrates when he happens on Amoret after her wounding by the giant Lust.

As these relationships develop, both partners are forced to the opposite extreme. Like Britomart, Florimell is forced to overcome her timidity and undertake a quest for the man she loves, in the course of which she is subjected to the advances of nearly every male that she meets. In the 1596 edition, Amoret, too, is denied an easy and ecstatic union with Scudamour after her release from bondage to Busirane. She is forced to take up with warlike Britomart and ultimately to travel with Prince Arthur to the Castle of Corflambo. Though this last site allegorizes the frustrated desires of Petrarchan love,[21] even it is a step forward for Amoret, for it allows her to experience the state to which she has condemned Scudamour and prepares her to consummate her marriage. Even Belphoebe cannot maintain her usual aloofness, being drawn into the turbulent world of eros by her love of Timias and by her jealousy of her more sexually active sister, Amoret.

Like Artegall, each of the men is forced to spend time in confinement. The excesses of Marinell are punished in Cymoent's cave, those of Scudamour in the Cave of Care, and those of Timias in a

forest hermitage. Though such isolation is brought about by their
own worst failings—arrogance in Marinell, jealousy in Scudamour,
and despair in Timias—it is also beneficial, since it humbles them
and helps them to discover their mistakes in dealing with women.
At the end of the period of isolation, Scudamour discovers that
Amoret has been faithful to him, Timias that Belphoebe loves him
and forgives his lapse with Amoret, and Marinell that he should
pay more attention to Florimell and less to his mother's fears of
Proteus's prophecy.

Spenser's procedure of drawing the sexes together by forcing them
to the opposite extreme is like that recommended by the English
humanist Sir Thomas Elyot. In the chapter on dancing in *The Boke
Named the Governour*, Elyot characterizes the genders in terms reminiscent of those employed by Spenser, stating that "A man in his
natural perfection is fierce, hardy, strong in opinion, covetous of
glory, desirous of knowledge, appetiting by generation to bring forth
his semblable. The good nature of a woman is to be mild, timorous,
tractable, benign, of sure remembrance, and shamefast." In dancing,
as in life, the sexes draw toward one another and so toward a common
mean. At the midpoint between the extremes of masculinity and
femininity lies a virtue that neither could attain without the other.
Elyot writes,

> Wherefore, when we behold a man and a woman dancing to-
> gether, let us suppose there to be a concord of all the said
> qualities, being joined together. . . . Fierceness joined with
> mildness maketh severity; audacity with timorosity maketh
> magnanimity; willful opinion and tractability . . . maketh con-
> stancy a virtue; covetousness of glory adorned with benignity
> causeth honour; desire of knowledge and sure remembrance
> procureth sapience; shamefastness joined to appetite of genera-
> tion maketh continence, which is a mean between chastity and
> inordinate lust. These qualities, in this wise being knit together
> and signified in the personages of man and woman dancing, do
> express or set out the figure of very nobility. . . .[22]

Though the sexes have different dispositions, they attract one another
to a common standard of nobility.

It would be a mistake, of course, to suppose that Spenser's views
of gender are as simple or reductive as those expressed in this passage
from *The Governour*. For one thing, the dispositions natural to the

genders in *The Faerie Queene* vary a good deal in intensity and complexion and are not always as neatly divided between the sexes as
they are in Elyot's image of the dance. The "frowardness" of Belphoebe, for instance, mixes virginal shamefastness with a number of
Elyot's masculine traits, including "audacity," "willful opinion," and
"covetousness of glory." For another, Elyot does not pay much attention to stages in personal development, and Spenser does. Although
Amoret is a figure for heterosexually and maternally inclined womanhood, she progresses from frigidity (on her wedding night) through
mild homoerotic attraction (when she shares a bed with Britomart)
to autoeroticism (when she is overcome by Lust as she goes into the
woods alone "for pleasure, or for need") and finally to heteroerotic
desire (in her encounter with Corflambo). For Spenser, disposition is
neither invariable nor irresistible. The tendencies inherent in gender
remain in constant, dynamic interplay with a person's own will and
with outside influences, particularly the influence of divine grace.
Britomart matures through her encounter with Malecasta and Artegall through his encounter with Radigund, but not in ways that either
of them sought—or even apprehended—at the time. Their "fashioning" is the outworking of divine providence. Still, Elyot's very un-
Aristotelian adaptation of Aristotle's theory of the Golden Mean
seems to me the best *entrée* we have into the treatment of gender in
The Faerie Queene, which owes a large debt to Renaissance Humanism.

V

Spenser's position on gender and ethics has not, I think, received
sufficient attention in recent discussions of cross-dressing in the early
modern period. Since scholars have focused most of their attention on
medical treatises, anti-theatrical polemics, and stage plays, narrative
works—such as prose romances and the heroic poems—have not
been examined with sufficient care.[23] This is unfortunate, since a
work such as *The Faerie Queene* provides a subtler and more complex
analysis of many of the issues that have interested recent cultural
historians than do many works that have been more closely examined.
What is particularly interesting about Spenser is that, though he seems
at first to confirm many of the general conclusions of such scholarship, on closer examination he proves exceptional.

Consider, for example, his apparent ambivalence about women's
role in the public sphere. The fact that he initially glorifies the armed

and independent Britomart but ultimately idealizes her submission to Artegall suggests that he is pursuing what Jean Howard terms a strategy of "recuperation." As Howard points out, most Elizabethan and Jacobean plays involving cross-dressed women find ways to restore the prevailing gender hierarchy late in the action (though, in the process, some implicitly support an enlargement in the prerogatives of women).[24] Spenser's procedure seems similar, but it is not really so recuperative as we might suppose. In the celebrated passages in Book III on the ancient glories of women, the narrator is responding to a different stage in Britomart's ethical development than he is after the defeat of Radigund in Book V. So long as Britomart's problem is "frowardness," he praises her every move in the opposite direction. When, however, she arrives at the opposite, manlike extreme in her violent triumph over the Amazons, he lauds her for drawing back to a more submissive stance. As the prophecy of Merlin suggests, however, traditional submission and domesticity are hardly the poet's final intention for her, for she and Artegall will continue to alternate in their dominance of one another far into the future. First his ferocity will take precedence as he frees her father's land from its enemies. Then her clemency will prevail, tempering his "cruell doomes" to the needs of peacetime governance. Finally, at his death she will rule their kingdom alone (III.iii.26–29).

The poet's opposition to the Amazons in Book V must be understood in terms of the same sort of ongoing dynamic between the genders. Angry at being mistreated by men, Radigund and her followers emulate the worst excesses of their enemies, making a virtue of manlike belligerence and cruelty. Since Spenser is opposed to such excesses in either gender, his condemnation of the Amazons need not be interpreted as a reversal of his earlier call for women to recover their Golden-Age prominence in the public arena. Although he clearly thinks women less well suited to rule a state than men, at least in the world's current stage of degeneration (see V.v.25),[25] his statements in favor of women's active participation in arms, the arts, and public "pollicy" are pretty much what his theory of cross-gendered ethical development would lead us to expect. In light of that theory, Louis Montrose's suggestion that Britomart is simply out to "justify her authority by putting other women in their places" seems needlessly reductive. Mary Bowman captures more of the complexity of the situation when she interprets Britomart's suppression of the Amazons as a rejection of their "isolation, self-reliance, self-centeredness," and "vengeful cruelty."[26]

Another matter in which Spenser reminds us of certain other writers of his age but actually sets himself apart involves the inherent

instability of gender roles. Thomas Lacqueur, Laura Levine, and others have noted in the early modern period a persistent sense of unease
that arises from the notion that gender can be readily altered. Lacqueur finds the source of this unease in medical treatises, which were
dominated by Galenic theories that minimized the anatomical and
physiological differences between male and female.[27] Levine refers
the phenomenon to beliefs among Puritan polemicists that men can
become inwardly "womanish" and women inwardly "manly" simply
by adopting the outward clothing and comportment of the opposite
sex.[28] In a 1579 polemic, for instance, Stephen Gosson warns that
actors who play women's roles risk becoming "effeminate,"[29] and in
a 1583, Phillip Stubbs goes a step further to contend that such actors
not only become "Monsters of both kinds, half women, half men,"
but also contribute to a breakdown of gender distinctions in those
who watch them.[30] Though I do not think that Spenser ultimately
agrees with the anti-theatrical writers on this point, there are certain
affinities between his position and theirs.

For one thing, the poet of *The Mutabilite Cantos* seems to think
that the way one dresses and behaves has power to "fashion" the
inward self. Britomart, after all, needs only the armaments of the
warlike Angela and "practize small" to transform herself from a love-
sick princess into an altogether convincing and formidable knight
(III.iii.53–59). The malleability of gender in her case is suggested by
her chosen weapon, the lance "Which *Bladud* made by Magick art
of yore" (60). As Michael Leslie has pointed out, her spear has phallic
associations throughout the poem,[31] and by wielding it she gains the
power to master her male opponents as they master others, both
erotically and socially. In Spenser's poem, as in the Puritan anti-
theatrical tracts, to dress and act as a member of the opposite sex has
transforming power of a sort that we, who know something of the
difficulty of retraining people after sex-change operations, find curious. Yet ultimately, Spenser is not like the Puritan polemicists in
this matter, for he believes in an inherent "frowardness" in women
and "forwardness" in men that cannot be altered by clothing or
conduct. The maleability in personal dispositions that we see in his
allegorical characters has more to do with an extreme interpretation
of Aristotle's view that *ethos* comes by action and habituation than
it does with the more extreme and moralistic forms of Puritanism.

Finally, Spenser leaves many readers with the sense that he shares
a double standard regarding the genders that is evident in other writers of his age. Throughout the poem, he adopts a strategy that one
might call "poetic inoculation," first exposing his readers to enticing

images of male characters who violate traditional boundaries of gender, then eliciting feelings of disapproval and revulsion toward these same figures. As Stephen Greenblatt and others have noted, the image of Verdant's "effeminate" life in the transforming embrace of the witch Acrasia seems designed to be attractive and repellant at the same time.[32] Like some of the womanish men that Levine cites in the work of Gosson and others, Acrasia's knight has become little more than a succubus, a passive extension of her will and desires. Others emasculated by Acrasia have gone another common route identified by Levine, becoming beasts and "monsters." Even Artegall's less selfish subjection to Radigund is rendered enticing and repellant in the same way. On the one hand, his decision to spare her once he has her at his mercy appeals to the audience's sense of chivalry. On the other, his refusal to strike brings disgrace and emasculation. The emotional reaction that serves to inoculate the reader against such conduct is exemplified in his rescuer, Britomart, who feels deep revulsion at the "lothly uncouth sight" of her beloved knight "disguiz'd in womanishe attire" (V.vii.37). As in other works involving cross-dressing in this period, Britomart's transvestism seems far more acceptable, both to her and to the poet.[33]

Clearly, however, Spenser is not, at the deepest level, like Gosson or Stubbs in this matter either. For one thing, he is not as content as they are with the norms for the genders prevalent in his own day. As he makes clear in Book III, he admires the women of antiquity for their achievements in areas that have since been dominated almost entirely by men, and he blames the "envy" of men for the suppression of such abilities (III.ii.2). For just this reason, I believe, he may regard a man who becomes womanish as more shocking than a woman who becomes manlike. The men, after all, start with all the advantages on their side. It is the women who must be freed from unjust constraints to raise themselves to a higher standard.

Spenser's position on gender is, in short, unusually rich and complex. Although he seeks to inoculate his readers against the notion that traditional definitions of gender are arbitrary, he also calls into question crucial elements of those definitions, such as the exclusion of women from matters involving arms, the arts, or public policy. Though he believes that ethical dispositions can be readily "fashioned" through choice and habit, he also maintains that the natural dispositions of the sexes are different. Though such dispositions cannot be completely changed, they can be moderated, and under ideal circumstances such moderation draws the natural inclinations of one sex closer to those of the other. Although he regards it as ennobling for a woman to dress as a man, and not the other way around, his position is based on the belief that men have long used their superior strength and aggressiveness to demean women, not that women are inherently inferior in their ethical, political, or intellectual capacities. Behind the apparently fortuitous episodes of cross-dressing in the story of Britomart and Artegall, he depicts a grand providential design. At least in "gentlemen" or "noble persons," nature and the God of nature incline the genders toward a single standard of "vertuous and noble discipline."

Saint Louis University

NOTES

1. My warmest thanks to Carol Kaske, Mary Ellen Lamb, and Lauren Silberman for their helpful comments on earlier drafts of this paper.

2. See Kathleen Williams, *Spenser's "Faerie Queene": The World of Glass* (London: Routledge & Kegan Paul, 1966), pp. 91–93, 168–76; Richard A. Lanham, "The Literal Britomart," *MLQ* 28 (1967):426–45; Sheila Cavanagh, *Wanton Eyes and Chaste Desires: Female Sexuality in "The Faerie Queene"* (Bloomington: Indiana University Press, 1994), pp. 139–53, 171–72; Lauren Silberman, *Transforming Desire: Erotic Knowledge in Books III and IV of "The Faerie Queene"* (Berkeley: University of California Press, 1995), pp. 29–30, 49–51. 75; Mary R. Bowman, "'She there as Princess rained': Spenser's Figure of Elizabeth," *RenQ* 43 (1990):509–28.

3. See Susanne Woods, "Spenser and the Problem of Women's Rule," *HLQ* 48 (1985):141–58; Pamela Joseph Benson, "Rule, Virginia: Protestant Theories of Female Regiment in *The Faerie Queene*," *ELR* 15 (1985):277–92, reprinted with revisions in *The Invention of the Renaissance Woman* (University Park: Pennsylvania State University Press, 1992), pp. 251–303; and Josephine A. Roberts, "Radigund Revisited: Perspectives on Women Rulers in Lady Mary Wroth's *Urania*," in *The Renaissance Englishwoman in Print: Counterbalancing the Canon*, edited by Anne M. Haselkorn and Betty S. Travitsky (Amherst: University of Massachusetts Press, 1990), pp. 187–207; Lillian S. Robinson, *Monstrous Regiment: The Lady Knight in Sixteenth-Century Epic*. New York: Garland, 1985), pp. 286–386; Ann Ashworth, "Paradoxes of the Feminine in *The Faerie Queene*," *Essays in Renaissance Culture* 19 (1993):147–59.

4. See my article "The Two Deaths of Mary Stuart: Historical Allegory in Spenser's Book of Justice," *SSt* 9 (1992): 81–105; Maureen Quilligan, "The Comedy of Female Authority in *The Faerie Queene*," *ELR* 17 (1987):156–71; Louise Scleiner, *Cultural Semiotics, Spenser, and the Captive Woman* (Bethlehem, Penn.: Lehigh University Press; London and Toronto: Associated University Presses, 1995), pp. 130–35; and Bowman, pp. 518–27.

5. See Harry Berger, Jr., "*The Faerie Queene*, Book III: A General Description," *Criticism* 11 (1969):234–61, reprinted in *Revisionary Play: Studies in the Spenserian*

Dynamics (Berkeley: University of California Press, 1988), pp. 89–117; Linda Gregerson, "Protestant Erotics: Idolatry and Interpretation in Spenser's *Faerie Queene*," *ELH* 58 (1991):1–34, and Benjamin G. Lockerd, Jr., *The Scared Marriage: Psychic Integration in "The Faerie Queene"* (Lewisburg: Bucknell University Press; London: Associated University Presses, 1987), pp. 67–73, 141–51.

6. All quotations from *The Faerie Queene* follow the edition of A.C. Hamilton (London: Longman, 1977). Inversions of i and j, u and v, have been normalized.

7. Montrose, "Shaping Fantasies of Elizabethan Culture," in *Rewriting the Renaissance: The Discourses of Sexual Difference in Early Modern Europe*, edited by Margaret W. Ferguson, Maureen Quilligan, and Nancy J. Vickers (Chicago: University of Chicago Press, 1986), p. 79. For a detailed reading of Britomart's dealings with the Amazons based on Montrose's view, see Bowman, pp. 509–18.

8. Berger, *Revisionary Play*, pp. 105–107; Lockerd, p. 68.

9. Benson, *Invention*, pp. 261–62, 293–303.

10. See, for example, Robinson, pp. 286–386, and Ashworth, "Paradoxes of the Feminine."

11. See John Erskine Hankins, *Source and Meaning in Spenser's Allegory: A Study of "The Faerie Queene"* (Oxford: Clarendon Press, 1971), p. 146.

12. See T.K. Dunseath, *Spenser's Allegory of Justice in Book Five of "The Faerie Queene"* (Princeton: Princeton University Press, 1968), pp. 48–59.

13. See Thomas P. Roche, Jr., *The Kindly Flame: A Study of the Third and Fourth Books of Spenser's "Faerie Queene"* (Princeton: Princeton University Press, 1964), pp. 59–60.

14. For this reason, extensive travel was sometimes thought unsuitable for a vertuous woman in Spenser's day. See Cavanagh, p. 140.

15. III.i.65n.

16. Though the pronouns in the description of the joust are ambiguous, it seems most likely that both riders were unhorsed and their horses knocked down. Spenser writes, "with the terrour of their fierce affret,/They rudely drove to ground both man and horse,/That each awhile lay like a sencelesse corse" (ix.16).

17. See Dorothy Stephens, "Into Other Arms: Amoret's Evasion," *ELH* 58 (1991):523–44.

18. On the distinctions between legal justicy, equity, and mercy as they are represented respectively in Artegall, Britomart, and Mercilla, see my article "Isis Versus Mercilla" and Michael O'Connell, *Mirror and Veil: The Historical Dimension of Spenser's "Faerie Queene"* (Chapel Hill: University of North Carolina Press, 1977), pp. 142–47.

19. 1109b2–7, trans. Hippocrates G. Apostle (Boston: D. Reidel, 1975), p. 34.

20. See, for example, Benson, "Rule Virginia," and Margaret Olofson Thickston, *Fictions of the Feminine: Puritan Doctrine and the Representation of Women* (Ithaca: Cornell University Press, 1988), pp. 52–55, in which the case is made that the poet did not intend Britomart to be a pattern for all women but only for those blessed with extraordinary gifts and responsibilities, such as Queen Elizabeth and the heroic women of antiquity.

21. See Reed Way Dasenbrock, "Escaping the Squire's Double Bind in Books III and IV of *The Faerie Queene*," *SEL* 26 (1986):25–45.

22. *The Boke Named the Governour*, edited by S.E. Lehmberg (London: J.M. Dent; New York: E.P. Dutton, [1907]), Bk. I, Chapt. XXI. That Spenser knew Elyot's work is suggested by, among other things, his plan to compose *The Faerie Queene* in two volumes, one on ethical virtues and the other on political ones. On Elyot's similar conception of a two-part book to fashion gentlemen for public service, see A. Leigh DeNeef, "Ralegh, Letter to," in *The Spenser Encyclopedia*, edited by A.C. Hamilton, et al. (Toronto: University of Toronto Press, 1990), pp. 581–84.

23. For a useful introduction to recent scholarship on this topic, see *Erotic Politics: Desire on the Renaissance Stage*, edited by Susan Zimmerman (New York: Routledge, 1992), and *Crossing the Stage: Controversies on Cross-Dressing*, edited by Lesley Ferris (New York: Routledge, 1993).

24. Howard, "Sex and Social Conflict: The Erotics of *The Roaring Girl*,"in Zimmerman, pp. 170–90.

25. On Spenser's views of gender and his belief in the ultimate restoration of a pre-Fall state of equality between men and women, see my article "A Slow Return to Eden: Spenser on Women's Rule," *ELR* 29 (1999):401–21.

26. Bowman, pp. 510–11 and 517.

27. Thomas Laqueur, *Making Sex: Body and Gender from the Greeks to Freud* (Cambridge: Harvard University Press, 1990), pp. 125–42.

28. Levine, *Men in Women's Clothing: Anti-Theatricality and Effeminization, 1579–1642* (Cambridge: Cambridge University Press, 1994), pp. 14–25.

29. Stephen Gosson, *The School of Abuse* (London: Shakespeare Society, 1841), p. 19.

30. Phillip Stubbs, *The Anatomie of Abuses* (Netherlands: Da Capo Press, 1972), sigs. F5v and L8v.

31. Leslie, *Spenser's "Fierce Warres and Faithfull Loves: Martial and Chivalric Symbolism in "The Faerie Queene"* (Cambridge: D.S. Brewer; Totowa, N.J.: Barnes & Noble, 1983), pp. 75–84.

32. See Greenblatt, *Renaissance Self-Fashioning: From More to Shakespeare* (Chicago: University of Chicago Press, 1980), pp. 170–74.

33. On the tendency of writers of this period to show less disapproval for women who cross-dress than for men, see Levine, pp. 23–25, and Laqueur, pp. 140–42.

JOSEPH BLACK

"Pan is Hee": Commending *The Faerie Queene*

An unrecorded manuscript in the Edinburgh University Library reveals that the commendatory verses printed with the 1590 *Faerie Queene* may not have been the first poems written to praise Spenser's epic. Dated 1588, this manuscript commendation is intriguing for both its form, a Spenserian sonnet before any Spenserian sonnets were in print, and its content (its tropes of praise differ interestingly from those deployed by the printed commendations). The essay suggests reasons for thinking the poem the work of Thomas Watson, and explores the evidence it provides for the pre-publication circulation of *The Faerie Queene* and, more generally, for the culture of manuscript communication and commentary that linked Spenser and his circle of friends and patrons.

SEVEN COMMENDATORY VERSES accompanied the 1590 *Faerie Queene*, singing variations on the tropes of praise for Spenser and his achievement. Sir Walter Ralegh, Gabriel Harvey, "R. S.," "H. B.," "W. L.," and "Ignoto" collectively note Spenser's move from pastoral to epic, announce his triumph over Petrarch, point out the nationalist implications of Spenser's project by invoking comparisons with Homer and Virgil and by linking him with the national hero Sidney, and anticipate the reward awaiting the author should Elizabeth prove as grateful as Augustus for being celebrated at epic length.[1] Like all commendations and other paratextual apparatus in books of the period, these poems also served to remind readers of the social and patronage networks that underlay literary production. In these commendations, members of a coterie community linked by knowledge of *The Faerie Queene* before it reached print make their claims not only *about* but also *on* Spenser's work. Signaling their identity to other literary insiders through initials and pseudonyms, they in effect attach themselves to the text whose importance they praise, thereby participating vicariously in the addresses Spenser himself makes in his dedicatory sonnets to the most powerful dispensers of patronage in the Elizabethan court.

Ralegh begins the second of his two sonnets with the potentially self-deprecating observation that "The prayse of meaner wits this worke like profit brings,/As doth the Cuckoes song delight when *Philumena* sings"—which is to say, not much.[2] The only reader whose opinion *really* matters, he argues, is the queen. Since she embodies the virtues the poem describes, Elizabeth is not only the most authoritative critic but also the person best able to translate praise into "favour." Ralegh acknowledges that praise unsupported by the ability to offer reward is essentially parasitic: like the opportunistic Cuckoo laying its eggs in a nest built by another bird, commendatory poets take advantage of the work of genuinely creative singers. Ralegh implicitly asks readers to think about why people offer praise, and his invitation to enquire after motive extends beyond the poems that follow his within the printed text to the commendatory competition generally—to any poems of praise that were circulating independently as well as those written after Spenser's work was published.[3] Post-publication celebrations of *The Faerie Queene* did indeed soon appear: Thomas Watson proved the quickest off the block, incorporating a passage on Spenser's achievement in his 1590 eclogue on the death of Sir Francis Walsingham.[4] But the apparently unrecorded manuscript poem reproduced and transcribed here is the first piece of evidence we have that the commendations printed with the 1590 *Faerie Queene* were not the only texts written to praise Spenser's epic *before* it entered the public sphere.

This manuscript is held by the Edinburgh University Library (LA II 358, fol. 6), where it is located in a folder of loose-sheet manuscript poetry, primarily eighteenth-century ballads, collected by the Scottish editor and antiquary David Laing (1793–1878) and bequeathed to the university at his death. The poem is on a single, unfolded sheet, with the reverse left blank; the paper is without watermark (measuring approximately 18.5 by 27.5 cm, the page could have been cut from a larger sheet, perhaps one without a countermark). The manuscript is enthusiastically, if amateurishly, decorated. At first sight it seems unlikely to have been a presentation copy, though it might have been intended as a model from which a professional scribe could produce a finer version. As I will argue below, however, the decoration itself offers clues that may signal the identity of the writer; if the decorative elements are indeed interpretable, then the manuscript

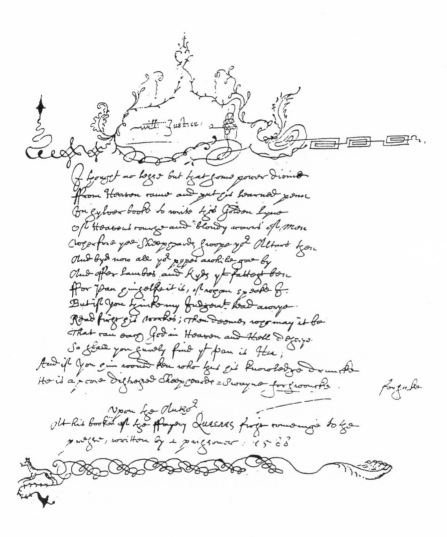

Figure 1: Edinburgh University Library, LA II 358, fol.6

might very well have been intended for coterie circulation as is. Of
particular interest is the date in the manuscript's final line: 1588, up
to two years before *The Faerie Queene* was printed. But the poem
itself is also intriguing for its form, a Spenserian sonnet before any
Spenserian sonnets were in print; for its riddling play with questions
of authorial identity; and finally for its content, for what *kind* of
accomplishment this poet thought *The Faerie Queene* represented.

> Will: Justice: [abbreviation tilde over "Will:"]
> I thought no lesse but that some power divine
> ffrom Heaven came and put his learned penn
> In sylver booke to write this Golden Lyne
> Of Heavens course and bloudy warrs of Men
> Wherfore yee Sheepheards swepe your Altars then
> And byd now all your pypes awhile goe by
> And offer Lambes and Kyds *that* fattest ben
> ffor Pan himselfe it is, of whom speake I.
> But if you thinke my Judgem*ent* lead awrye
> Read first his workes; Then deeme, who may it be
> That can each God in Heaven and Hell descrye
>   So shall you surely find *that* Pan is Hee;
> And if you him would ken who thus his knowledge druncke
> He is a poore distressed Sheepheards=Swayne *forswoncke*
>   forsaken

> Upon the Autho*ur*
> At his bookes of the ffayery Queenes first comeinge to the
>   presse, written by a prissoner:
>   1588.

While this sonnet, like six of the seven printed commendatory
verses, does not mention Spenser by name, there is little doubt that
his *Faerie Queene* is its subject. The poem is an accomplished homage,
skillfully and self-consciously appropriating Spenserian pastoralism
and language as well as sonnet form. Perhaps because he assumed that
The Faerie Queene, like *The Shepheardes Calender*, would be published
anonymously, the writer adopts as his central conceit a knowing play
on the question of authorship. Who could possibly have written this
mighty work, he asks. Why, none but Pan himself, and all the shep-
herd-poets should now lay aside their pipes (their own art) and honor

the achievement of their shepherd-poet god. The answer he provides to his own riddle links *The Faerie Queene* with *The Shepheardes Calender*, revealing the writer's knowledge that the two works were written by the same poet. The "Sheepheards=Swayne forswoncke" of the last line clearly echoes Hobbinol's praise of Elisa in the April Eclogue(ll. 98–99), and the marginal gloss (in the same hand) of "forswoncke" as "forsaken" gestures toward the commentary by E. K. With its borrowing of Spenserian subject, language, and form, this sonnet is in fact more explicit than most of the printed commendations in the way it signals Spenser as the absent presence at its center.

Was this poem written in the hopes of its being printed with the 1590 *Faerie Queene*? While there is no external evidence one way or the other, the poem's rhetorical and formal strategies imply that its author could very well have had such a thought in mind. The poem reads as if it were in the company of other commendatory texts—the (paratextual) offerings, presumably, that the writer suggests his fellow swains lay as sacrifices on Pan's (epic-sized) altar. The poet is addressing readers, not just writing to himself, and he assumes his audience might be in the dark about who wrote the book his poem praises. Furthermore, he also expects readers to wonder who *he* is: the identity of the poet doing the commending is as much part of the game as the identity of the poet whose work is being commended. Like the writers of the printed commendations, this poet addresses both a coterie audience, providing them with at least one clue about his identity, and a wider public, one that does not necessarily know the answers to either of the riddles he poses.

While the writer offers no clear evidence that he has actually read *The Faerie Queene* before it was printed, he does know that *The Faerie Queene* was organized into books, which might suggest that he has at least seen or heard report of the *Letter to Ralegh* (where Spenser mentions "these first twelve books"). Firmer evidence for this writer's participation in the coterie circulation of Spenser's texts is provided by his use of a characteristically Spenserian rhyme scheme. While no "Spenserian" sonnets were in print in 1588, Spenser had employed the form in a 1586 letter to Harvey that remained in manuscript until he included it in the *Foure Letters* of 1592; Harvey could have shown the letter around Cambridge. The only other known examples of Spenserian sonnets that might have been circulating in manuscript were several eventually collected in the *Complaints* volume of 1591: the dedicatory sonnet to the Earl of Leicester (who died in 1588) for *Virgils Gnat*; the sonnets in *Visions of the Worlds Vanitie*; and the final sonnet (no. 7) of *The Visions of Petrarch*.[5] While no other poet appears to have picked up on Spenser's use of the form before these texts were printed, somebody with access to a Spenser manuscript did recognize the possibilities it offered as a vehicle with which to praise *The Faerie Queene*. Intriguingly, the deployment here of alexandrines in the final couplet is not borrowed from any of the known possible models, though Spenser occasionally completes his sonnets with a couplet of eleven-syllable lines with feminine endings. Perhaps our poet had seen something of *The Faerie Queene* in manuscript after all, and integrated into his borrowed sonnet form the concluding alexandrine of the Spenserian stanza.

If this poem were written to be included among the other commendatory verses, the manuscript does suggest one potential reason for its exclusion: the author's status as a prisoner. Other than demonstrating his competence as a poet, however, the poem itself offers little that might help identify its writer. While the abbreviation tilde over the last few letters of "Will" implies "William," I have yet to find a "William Justice" in any of the usual archival sources, though the surname "Justice" does turn up in records in the period. But the appearance of these words at the head of the manuscript, rather than more conventionally at the bottom as a concluding signature, argues against this being the poet's real name. In addition, the more general objection could be made that including a name at all deprives the riddle in the last two lines of any point. A more plausible reading of the heading is as a pseudonym, prefacing the poem in a manner similar to the way eclogues in *The Shepheardes Calender* announce the names of their interlocutors. Another way of reading these words is as a reference of some kind to what would become Book Five, though Justice is not mentioned as a titular virtue in the *Letter to Ralegh*. A further possibility is that the heading could work in conjunction with the concluding lines, framing the poem with the implied question: Will Justice prevail for me, a prisoner?

The biographies of many well-known writers with connections of some sort to Spenser, let alone those of numerous lesser lights, are sketchy if not blank for the late 1580s. But this text does contain enough clues to permit a few general speculations about its writer. The somewhat arch tone of the poem's play with the mystery of Spenser's identity implies a literary insider, though Spenser's authorship of *The Shepheardes Calender* was a widely open secret by 1588. The manuscript's date, however, does suggest someone reasonably close to Spenser's circle of friends and acquaintances. *The Faerie Queene* was entered in the Stationers' Register in December 1589 and published some time in 1590, possibly early in the year. The date of 1588 could refer to a period up to 25 March 1589. If the date on the manuscript is to be trusted, then this text was written at least about a year before *The Faerie Queene* came to press, and possibly longer. It is consequently one of the very few pieces of evidence extant for the coterie circulation of Spenser's epic, either in manuscript or in report. We know that Harvey read an early version (he was less than impressed), and so presumably did Ralegh. In *A Discourse of Civill Life* (1606), Lodowick Bryskett frames his translation of Cintio with a narrative set in the early 1580s in which a group including Spenser meet for conversation in Bryskett's cottage outside Dublin; Spenser discusses *The Faerie Queene*, and Bryskett claims in passing that "parcels" of the poem "had bin by some of them seene" in manuscript.[6] There is also evidence that by 1588 parts of the poem in something close to its final form were circulating in England in manuscript. Marlowe appears to have scooped everyone by borrowing from *The Faerie Queene* (I.vii.32) in the second part of *Tamburlaine* (IV.iii.119–24), written in 1587 or perhaps 1588; and Abraham Fraunce quotes from *The Faerie Queene* (II.iv.35) in his *Arcadian Rhetoricke* of 1588, citing the proper book and canto number.[7] With so few people having left records of pre-publication acquaintance with *The Faerie Queene*, the writer of this sonnet probably had some connection to the literary networks in which these men participated. One possibility is the community at Cambridge (Harvey was a Fellow of Trinity Hall, Marlowe had been at Corpus Christi until 1587); another is the circle at Wilton patronized by Mary Sidney Herbert, the Countess of Pembroke (with which Fraunce was affiliated in the late 1580s). This writer is likely somebody we know other things about; if nothing else, he almost certainly wrote poetry in addition to this metrically accomplished sonnet.

Definitive identification of this writer might require the discovery of second manuscript in the same hand, or a verbal echo in another text. But I would like to suggest one candidate based on evidence, admittedly not conclusive, supplied by this manuscript alone: Thomas Watson (d. 1592), the first English poet to write an amatory sonnet sequence and, with friends that included Camden, Lyly, Peele, Greene, and Marlowe, very much a literary insider.[8] In addition to being the first person to praise *The Faerie Queene* in print, Watson enjoyed several other points of contact with Spenser and with people known to have had access to Spenser's texts in manuscript. Spenser at least knew of Watson and his work. His reference in *The Faerie Queene* to the "sweet Poets verse" that immortalized "*Amintas* wretched fate" (III.vi.45) is usually read as a compliment to Watson's *Amyntas* (1585), either in its original Latin version or in the English paraphrase by Abraham Fraunce (1587). After Watson returned the compliment in *Meliboeus*, Spenser responded in turn by noting his pleasure that Walsingham "hath a Poet got" to sing his praises (*The Ruines of Time*, line 436).[9] Although Watson attended Oxford, not Cambridge, his good friend Marlowe certainly had access to Spenser manuscripts. The evidence for this friendship is strong. Marlowe would fulfill Watson's dying wish by presenting his *Amintae Gaudiae* (1592) to the Countess of Pembroke; he also arranged for its posthumous publication. More tantalizingly, as far as the "Will: Justice:" manuscript is concerned, Watson was imprisoned for five months in late 1589 and early 1590 for killing a man while defending Marlowe in a street fight.[10] While he was eventually judged to have acted in self-defense and received the Queen's pardon, Watson's situation during those months in Newgate would account both for the claim that the poem was written by a prisoner and for the manuscript's concern to highlight the question of justice.

Of course, the dates do not quite work out: Watson was imprisoned in September 1589, at least six months too late for the manuscript's date of 1588. Since Watson's experience as a poet and his social connections make him the kind of person likely to have written this poem, and since he is the only potential candidate I have found so far who was a prisoner near the right period, it is tempting to think that a mistake of some kind has been made in the date of the manuscript. Strengthening this suspicion is the probability that *The Faerie Queene* was much more obviously "comeinge to the presse" during the period Watson was in Newgate (18 September to 10 February) than it would have been a year earlier. Spenser's poem was entered in early December, 1589; people in the know would be anticipating its publication. A commendatory poem written in these months would still signal membership in a relatively narrow social and literary circle, a membership that is in effect the *subject* of this sonnet. The writer assumes a place in the pastoral/poetic literary world and foregrounds his knowledge of Spenser's identity in order to draw attention in the concluding alexandrine and the framing texts to his current plight. Watson's situation—a literary insider in trouble, looking to remind people connected with a major publishing event of his difficulties—provides an explanatory context for an otherwise puzzling manuscript.

One further piece of evidence may connect Watson with this manuscript, though it does not, unfortunately, solve the problem of the date. My colleague Allen Carroll has pointed out the possibility of a signature rebus in the decoration along the bottom of the text. On the right, the ornamental swirls culminate in a realistic and not at all conventionally decorative set of toes; on the left is a creature that is, in my opinion, almost certainly meant to be a hare.[11] Since the homonymic equivalent "Thos" is an abbreviation for "Thomas," and since a hare was commonly known in the period as "Wat,"[12] the two images combine to signal "Thomas Watson" in a manner quite in keeping with Renaissance strategies of naming through images. The rebus may be even more complete: if the decorative flourishes in the manuscript are seen as comprising a series of mazes, the bottom line could be read as something like "Wat's in [a] Toe-maze," or, "Watson, Thomas." While this reading may push the patience of those who hesitate to acknowledge the language games that Renaissance texts often play, signature rebuses in the period did tend to work on such syllable-by-syllable identifications; I have reproduced John Harington's "hare-ring-tun" rebus for comparison.

It may prove impossible to ascribe this poem to Watson with certainty, or, even if the attribution seems likely, to account satisfactorily for the manuscript's date. But if the poem is not by Watson, it is by somebody with similar experience as a poet, similar access to the literary circles around Spenser, and in a similar predicament around the time *The Faerie Queene* was approaching publication. What did a poet in this position decide to *say* about *The Faerie Queene*? Unlike the printed commendations, this sonnet ignores the political and patronage implications of Spenser's praise of the Faery Queen and the nationalist dimensions of the epic project (no "Bryttane *Orpheus*" doing England proud). The comments it does offer about the poem are like those in the other commendatory verses only in that they are rather generalized. Here, Spenser's "sylver booke" treats of "Heavens course and bloudy warrs of Men" and descries "each God in Heaven and Hell." As descriptions of what happens in *The Faerie Queene,* these lines are, to say the least, unsatisfactory. Do they indicate that the writer had yet to read the text he was praising? Somebody without specific knowledge of Spenser's poem could very well have assumed that "bloudy warrs" would be included in the epic package. But while Spenser would have disappointed readers who bought epics because they liked descriptions of clashing armies, the assumption that the poem contained such moments does not necessarily push this writer outside the circle of people reasonably close to Spenser and his project. Spenser's own references to knightly adventures and to Tasso in his *Letter to Ralegh,* or his promise of "fierce warres" at the beginning of the poem (I.i.1), would do little to challenge that assumption, and even readers who knew the published text of the poem foregrounded its apparatus of battle. Lodowick Bryskett, for example, has his interlocutor "Spenser" summarize its action as consisting of "feates of armes and chivalry" (*A Discourse of Civill Life,* 27).

Figure 2. "Now riddle me what name is this": John Harrington's "hare-ring tun" rebus, from the *Metamorphosis of Ajex* (1596)

Figure 3. The hare, from Edward Topsell, *The Historie of Foure-Footid Beastes* (1607)

The poem's reference to traditional epic carnage, however, is almost token: Spenser's treatment of human struggle seems very much of secondary importance to this writer. What is perhaps most interesting about the reading (actual or anticipatory) offered here of *The Faerie Queene* is the focus on gods and heaven. While this sonnet retains the pastoral fiction deployed by other commendations, Spenser here is not Colin but Pan, the shepherd's greatest god. That is, the poem figures Spenser not only as a kind of divinity but also as somebody with access to divine knowledge: he descries the gods, he understands Heaven's course (the acts of God as providence). What this poem in fact praises Spenser for is writing a cosmology informed by a divine (encyclopedic) knowledge of all things in the universe. The implicit narrative here is Spenser's successful move upward from pastoral to epic: the human and particular Colin has taken up his pipe once more only to find himself, upon completing his song, translated into the divinely all-encompassing Pan. The identification of Spenser with Pan is unusual: the only other even potential example is in *Greenes Funeralls* (1594),[13] though Thomas Watson, also unusually, figures Spenser as Apollo in *Meliboeus*. But Spenser was, of course, very interested in the link between poetry and divine inspiration and in the capacity for poetry to shadow divine truths. These Platonizing ideas turn up early in his work (in the October eclogue, with its conception of poetry returning to its heavenly source), but also appear throughout Spenser's later poetry, in his admiration for Du Bartas, and in the testimony of his friend Harvey.[14] Whoever wrote this sonnet was aware that Spenser and his circle could have thought of Spenser's project as an extended effort to reach the divine (and/or as evidence of the divine reaching inspirationally down to him), and perhaps even shared this conception of the purpose of poetry.

Whether or not this poet proves to be Thomas Watson, this manuscript does appear to be the earliest extant poetic praise of *The Faerie Queene,* and, perhaps, the earliest attempt to exchange praise of this new epic for some sort of favor within the patronage system. After all, the claim that the sonnet was "written by a prissoner" is a fairly transparent plea for attention. In addition to being an unrecorded document connected with Spenser and the early history of *The Faerie Queene,* this poem also reminds us of the social and literary networks that helped shape literary production of the period. Spenser was more determined than most of his poetic contemporaries to make his vocation public through the possibilities offered by print. But, as this text and other references reveal, Spenser's work was still surrounded by a culture of manuscript communication and commentary, response and appropriation, that linked communities of writers, readers, and potential patrons. Finally, and more generally, the commendatory poem is in itself an understudied genre. Along with the funeral elegy, commendatory verse is an important site for the negotiation of influence, legacy, and poetic filiation in the period. Given the thousands of commendatory verses extant, this poem reminds us that we could do more with the evidence they provide about how Renaissance poets read the work of their contemporaries.

University of Tennessee

NOTES

I would like to thank the many people who have helped me with suggestions, particularly Gavin Alexander, James Carscallen, Allen Carroll, Lisa Celovsky, Anne Coldiron, Jay Dickson, Wayne Erickson, Heather Hirschfield, and David Hill Radcliffe; I would also like to thank the Edinburgh University Library for permission to reproduce the manuscript.

1. Ralegh contributed two poems; "R. S.," "H. B.," "W. L.," and "Ignoto" all remain unidentified. For discussions of the commendatory verses, see *Edmund Spenser: The Critical Heritage*, ed. R.M. Cummings (1971; rpt. London and New York: Routledge, 1995), 52–53, 63– 68; L.G. Black, "*The Faerie Queene*, commendatory verses and dedicatory sonnets," *The Spenser Encyclopedia* (Toronto: University of Toronto Press, 1990), 292; James P. Bednarz, "The Collaborator as Thief: Ralegh's (Re)Vision of *The Faerie Queene*," *ELH* 63 (1996), 279–307; David Hill Radcliffe, *Edmund Spenser: A Reception History* (Columbia, SC: Camden House, 1996), 6–7; and Wayne Erickson, "Spenser and His Friends Stage a Publishing Event: Praise, Play, and Warning in the Commendatory Verses to the 1590 *Faerie Queene*," *Renaissance Papers 1997*, ed. T. H. Howard-Hill and Philip Rollinson (Columbia, SC: Camden House, 1997), 1–22. Erickson, who offers the fullest consideration of the verses as a group, suggests that all seven were the product of a collaboration among Spenser, Ralegh, and Harvey, "perhaps along with others" (21), to frame the issues raised by the publication of an English epic.

2. All quotations from *The Faerie Queene* and its apparatus are from *The Faerie Queene*, ed. A.C. Hamilton (London and New York: Longman, 1977). The commendatory verses are found in Appendix 2 (pp. 739–40).

3. Ralegh does perhaps manage to distinguish his contributions from those by "meaner wits." Since his verses, signed "W. R.," follow immediately upon the Letter addressed to "To the Right Noble, and Valorous, Sir Walter Raleigh knight," his identity would not have been a mystery to most readers, and Spenser's praises of him authorize a reading of this sonnet as an exercise in polite humility. In addition, by the time readers reached these lines, they would have already admired the first of Ralegh's two poems, and would have been less likely to apply his caveat retroactively than to carry it forward to praises written by others.

4. Watson, *Meliboeus Thomae Watsoni, sive Ecloga in Obitum F. Walsinghami* (1590), sig. D; and in Watson's own, separately published English version, *An Eglogue Upon the Death of the Right Honorable Sir Francis Walsingham* (1590), sigs. C3v-C4. Responses to Spenser are collected in *Edmund Spenser: The Critical Heritage; Spenser Allusions in the Sixteenth and Seventeenth Centuries*, collected by Ray Heffner, Dorothy E. Mason, Frederick M. Padelford and edited by William Wells, Part I, *SP* 58:5 (1971) and Part II, *SP* 59:5 (1972); and R.M. Cummings, "Spenser Allusions before 1700: Addenda to Wells," *Spenser Newsletter* 26:2 (1995), 1–11.

5. Spenser's dedicatory sonnets to *The Faerie Queene* are also Spenserian in form, but these were not likely to have been circulating one to two years before the poem was printed. Even more remote is the possibility that this poet discovered the form in James VI's *Essayes of a Prentice* (1584) and employed it to praise Spenser, without knowing of Spenser's own sonnets.

6. Bryskett, *A Discourse of Civill Life* (1606), 28. Bryskett's frame narrative could be fictive, but there seems no particular reason to doubt that Spenser showed parts of his poem to his acquaintances in Ireland.

7. Full references for the allusions by Marlowe and Fraunce are provided in *Spenser Allusions*, Part I, 10, 15–19. In *Marlowe's Counterfeit Profession: Ovid, Spenser, Counter-Nationhood* (Toronto: University of Toronto Press, 1997), Patrick Cheney offers the most sustained discussion of Marlowe's response to Spenser, beginning with Marlowe's significant rewriting of this passage (15–17). Less widely accepted as a pre-publication reference is the similarity between *The Faerie Queene* III.vi.6 and a line from Robert Greene's 1589 *Menaphon*: "Our *Arcadian* Nimphs are faire & beautifull, though not begotten of the Suns bright rayes" (sig.Hv); see *Spenser Allusions*, Part I, 12.

8. Watson, *Hekatompathia: or passionate centurie of love* (1582). For biographical information on Watson, see Mark Eccles, *Christopher Marlowe in London*, Harvard Studies in English, vol. 10 (Cambridge, MA: Harvard University Press, 1934), 9–26; William Ringler, "Spenser and Thomas Watson" *MLN* 69 (1954), 484–87; S. K. Heninger, Jr., introd., *The Hekatompathia* (Gainesville: Scholars' Facsimiles & Reprints, 1964); Eccles, *Brief Lives: Tudor and Stuart Authors*, *SP* 79:4 (1982), 130; Wendy Phillips, "Thomas Watson's *Hekatompathia or Passionate Centurie of Love* (1582): A Facsimile Edition with Notes and Commentary," PhD diss., UCLA (1989), 2–12, 522–50; the article by Eccles on Watson in *The Spenser Encyclopedia*; and Carmel Gaffney, "Thomas Watson," *Dictionary of Literary Biography: Sixteenth-Century British Non-Dramatic Writers, First Series*, vol. 132, ed. David Richardson (Detroit: Gale Research, 1993), 322–28.

9. Since the eclogue to Walsingham was signed, there is no doubt that these lines refer to Watson. Both references emphasize that the verse being praised was written by a "poet"; the repeated compliment encourages a reading of the passage in *The Faerie Queene* as referring to Watson rather than Sidney. If Watson is indeed the "prissoner" who wrote this manuscript poem, Spenser's allusion to "*Amintas* wretched fate" could be read as signaling his awareness of Watson's predicament.

10. Mark Eccles was the first to identify the people involved in this incident as Marlowe and Watson; see his *Christopher Marlowe in London*, passim and *Brief Lives*, 130.

11.   Some might object that this creature is not a hare but a dog. However, running hares in Renaissance hunting paintings can be just as lean and lanky as the dogs that chase them; they seldom have the plumpness we might associate with rabbits. In addition, this creature has a long, rabbit-like face and what look like whiskers, as well as reasonably prominent ears. The line that looks as though it could be a long, curling tail seems to be part of the decoration: it appears in fact to loop behind the creature's rear legs, catching at them. Judging by the rest of the decoration, the person who drew this image was not an accomplished artist.

12.   For the hare as "Wat," see the *OED*. A well-known example, closely contemporary with this manuscript, is Shakespeare's description of the hunt in *Venus and Adonis* (1593): "By this, poor Wat, far off upon a hill,/Stands on his hinder-legs with list'ning ear,/To hearken if his foes pursue him still" (lines 697–99).

13.   In a passage defending Robert Greene, "R. B." (thought to be either Richard Barnfield or Nicholas Breton) denounces those who have attacked Greene; among the people invoked, "Pan" is thought to refer to Spenser. See D. Allen Carroll, "A Play on Spenser's Name?," *Spenser Newsletter* 25:3 (1994), 29–30.

14.   I thank James Carscallen for his discussions with me about the implications of this poem's focus on the cosmological as a target for praise and about Spenser's interest in "Uranian" (divine) poetry. Harvey's comments about Spenser's work, including his lists of other "sons of Urania" with whom he groups Spenser, are gathered in *Spenser Allusions*, Part I, 3–4; and *Edmund Spenser: The Critical Heritage*, 49–55.

JAMES FLEMING

A *View* from the Bridge: Ireland and Violence in Spenser's *Amoretti*

The apparently extremist sonnets of Spenser's *Amoretti* have often puzzled critics. Although the Petrarchan tradition provided
some writ for violent allegations against the beloved, Spenser
seems to expand this tendency beyond sonnet sequence decorum. A popular solution has been to read the violent poems as
intentionally hyperbolic, but this view is insecure and does not
explain why Spenser would want such an effect in an amatory
and marital sequence. Instead, this paper argues that the violent
sonnets should be read in the same Irish context of politics and
conquest that has proved so illuminating for Spenser's other
works. Specifically, the essay argues for structural similarities
between the war against the "unquiet thought" in *Amoretti*, and
that against kerns and rebels in *A View of the Present State of
Ireland*. An analysis of attitudes toward the slaughter of the
yielded in both texts indicates that the extremist poet of *Amoretti*
is unburdening himself of a long-held grudge.

A LTHOUGH ELIZABETHAN sonneteers in the Petrarchan tradition could draw on severe constructions of the cruel beloved—one
thinks of *Rime* twenty-three, in which the lady opens the lover's
chest and grasps his heart (72–73)[1]—it is generally accepted that the
sonnets of Spenser's *Amoretti* sequence contain unusually violent expressions and allegations. In some of these poems the beloved is a
predatory beast and/or murderer of prisoners; in others, the lover
addresses vicious and incorrigible affects of his own. The first kind
of übersonnet continues well past the middle of the sequence, while
the second marks both its beginning and its end. Apparently extremist
poetry, in short, is a major characteristic of the *Amoretti* sequence.

Critical responses to this poetry have followed two main strategies. The first is one of avoidance: a number of writers mount extensive discussions of *Amoretti* while treating its violent poems briefly or not at all.[2] Some of these critics scant Spenser's violence in the course of schematizing his sequence, fitting onto it a pedagogic narrative in which the lover climbs from a Petrarchan wasteland into a Christian or a specifically Protestant landscape of earthly or spiritual love.[3] Yet the first two-thirds of *Amoretti* are marked with images of captivity and enclosure, torture and death, in which no progress is easily discernible. When it comes, the change in the sequence is sudden, not gradual. And the undiluted return of extreme images in the sequence's last phase, while consistent with a probable liturgical framework,[4] is a problem for any progressive scheme.

The second strategy controls the extreme sonnets by explaining them as parodies or travesties of Petrarchan violence. Louis Martz, the originator of this theory, offers a general reading of Spenser's sequence as tinged with comedy and then reads the violent poems against this background (he refrains from identifying the most furious sonnets as parodic per se).[5] Elizabeth Bieman varies the theory by suggesting that the sequence's sexual undercurrents make it funny,[6] while William Johnson extends the Martzian analysis by claiming that Spenser's most savage images are directly posed against the "delicate mockery" of their presumptive tone.[7] Compelling textual evidence, however, would be necessary to prove that the sonnets are written against themselves in this way; and the fact is that no such evidence, other than the very language that we are trying to explain, is apparent. The parodic reading is therefore insecure. Recently, Kenneth J. Larsen has offered a sophisticated modulation of the parodic theory while fixing most of the *Amoretti* within a liturgical scheme. Larsen argues that the calendrical association of Spenser's sonnets with specific biblical passages tends to "unlock the private nature of a sonnet and enforce a new reading," and that Spenser's extremism "avoids becoming offensive or ridiculous through the further substance and interest it acquires from . . . semi-theological and scripturally based undertones."[8] Although Larsen's work is learned and compelling, on this question it succeeds only in deepening the insecurity of the Martzian view. In his discussion of *Amoretti* 10, for example, Larsen connects the lady's "licentious blisse" (x.3) to the "uncleane spirits" of the relevant Bible readings (Mark 1, 5) and asserts: "that Spenser is prepared to associate his bethrothed with the powers of darkness can only be construed as good-natured teasing."[9] Even if this were clearly true, the question would remain why Spenser should wish to write a poem teasing his lady in this rather hideous way; and in any case, how can we be sure that the intended effect of the poem is teasing? How can we be sure that terms like "offensive" and "ridiculous" are interpretatively appropriate to this poem and this group of poems, or that we are necessarily called upon to avoid taking Spenser's alleged hyperbole seriously? Is there really no context in which we as critics might be required to imagine Spenser literally associating the lady of *Amoretti*—a syncretic and problematic personage—with cruel and possessive forces?

I want to suggest that there is such a context, and it lies in the Ireland of Spenser's career. The Irish angle, quite ubiquitous in Spenser scholarship, has rarely been applied to *Amoretti*;[10] yet there are good circumstantial bases for such an application. The 1595 printed text of the sequence is dedicated, for whatever reason, to a man knighted for military service on the island.[11] Its sole friendship-sonnet (xxxiii) is to a colleague in the New English administration there. Its lover exclaims, at his lady's early obduracy, "let her a rebell be" (xix.14); and he ends his courtship of her with a self-conscious settlement on expropriated land. With his "Nymphes of Mulla" (*Epith* 56) and his squawking birds and frogs, the poet of *Amoretti and Epithalamion* situates himself in a pastoral Ireland as explicitly as does the poet of *Colin Clouts Come Home Again*, Spenser's other publication of 1595. The title of Spenser's sonnet sequence, moreover, seems to be offered as a bridge between the "sweete rauishment" of Amoret in the 1590 *Faerie Queene* (III.xii.45a), and the Amoret "thereof beguyled" in the 1596 version (III.xii.44).[12] The Amoret who follows *Amoretti*, then, must be sought in an increasingly recalcitrant Irish land: one that receives the impatient justice of Artegall/Talus in *FQ* V, and finally the sword and famine of Lord Grey in *A View of the Present State of Ireland* (1598).[13] Grey, Spenser's boss from the poet's earliest years in Ireland, looms large in both late works. He does not appear in *Amoretti*. His crime, however—the slaughter of the yielded—does.

In this essay, I hope to show that a comparison of *Amoretti* with the *View* yields a valuable new reading of the sequence's extreme sonnets. My use of the *View* may appear either predictable or exorbitant: predictable because the interpretative application of Spenser's tract has proliferated, as Willy Maley says, "to a worrying extent" in recent studies[14]; exorbitant because *Amoretti* is a sonnet sequence, not an epic or complaint, and to drag it all the way to the historicist Pale may seem a bridge (so to speak) too far. Yet the violent patterns of *Amoretti* are noticeably congruent to those of the *View*, characterized by eruption, imprisonment, insurgency, and slaughter. Moreover, *Amoretti and Epithalamion* and the *View* exhibit similar strategies in the treatment of their respective bad affects: moving from a hopeless series of reactions, to a singular escalation that annihilates the series.

These congruencies, to be sure, are of heuristic value only. Once established, however, they allow insight of some hermeneutic depth into *Amoretti*'s most troubling materials. My contention is that the violent poems of the sequence, far from being negligible or merely parodic, show Spenser exorcising a perennial frustration. The pretty rooms of sonnets, and the tradition that startling images might be found there, allow him both the freedom and the obscurity in which to be unburdened.

I

Spenser begins *Amoretti* by addressing its text.

Happy ye leaves when as those lilly hands,
    which hold my life in their dead doing might
  shall handle you and hold in loves soft bands,
    lyke captives trembling at the victors sight.
And happy lines, on which with starry light,
    those lamping eyes will deigne sometimes to look
  and read the sorrowes of my dying spright,
    written with teares in harts close bleeding book.
And happy rymes bath'd in the sacred brooke
    of *Helicon* whence she derived is,
  when ye behold that Angels blessed looke,
    my soules long lacked foode, my heavens blis.
Leaves, lines and rymes, seeke her to please alone,
  whom if ye please, I care for other none.

(i.1–14)

The book is "happy," according to this poem, because it is held captive by the lady. Possessed by her, it is held, observed, and treated to sacred pleasures, enacting a hoped-for intimacy with the beloved. Yet this schedule is also somewhat troubling. To be held in "loves soft bands" is obviously good, but to be held by hands with "dead doing might" is potentially bad. The fearsomeness of possession, it seems, varies directly with the materiality of the possessed subject:

the immaterial "rymes" of the sequence are pleasured by their bath
in the lady's mind (10–11), while the transitional "lines" make a
neutral submission to "lamping eyes" (5–6), and the material "leaves"
are directly compared to prisoners of war shaking with fear (4). In
other words, as the subject can be held more physically captive, its
situation is more frightening. This sonnet inaugurates a discourse of
love as captivity in which the poet's fears compete with his desires.

For the first two-thirds of the sequence, fear has the upper hand.
The lady is powerful, martial, violent and sadistic. The poet's best
hope is to be killed rather than tortured (xi, xxv, xlii, xlvii), or to be
only moderately tortured (xxiv, xli, lvii), or to get some eventual
reward for his torture (xxv, xxvi, li). At sonnet 11 he complains that
he would gladly yield his life "her wrath to pacify" (10): "but then
she seekes with torment and turmoyle, / to force me live and will not
let me dy"(11–12). At 42 he agrees to let the lady "yf please her, bynd
with adamant chayne" (10) his "poore captyved hart" (8), "Onely let
her abstaine from cruelty, / and doe me not before my time to dy"
(13–14). On the other hand, at 25 he wheedles,

> But yet if in your hardned brest ye hide,
>   a close intent at last to shew me grace:
>   then all the woes and wrecks which I abide,
>   as meanes of blisse I gladly wil embrace.
>
>   (9–13)

And at 47 he muses on the "mighty charm which makes men love
theyrbane, / and thinck they dy with pleasure, live with payne"
(13–14). On the one occasion when he considers love-captivity without these violent metaphors, the poet continues to reject it, telling
his eyes to avoid the "guilefull net" of the lady's dressed hair, "in
which if ever ye entrapped are, / out of her bands ye by no means
shall get": "Fondness it were for any being free, / to covet fetters,
though they golden bee" (xxxvii.10–12; 13–14). The "net" imagery
of this poem connects it and the issue of captivity with other poems,
discussed below, in which the lady appears as a bloodthirsty spider
or other entrapping creature.

All of this accords with a Petrarchan dynamic in which amorous
pursuit is reconfigured as flight and the active lover poses as the
passive, wronged party. Given that Spenser's suit in *Amoretti* is to
break the Petrarchan mold by actually being successful, it is reasonable

to expect a concomitant change in the poet's attitude toward captivity. And indeed after the "peace" concluded at sonnet 57, and apparent success of his courtship from 63 to 67, the poet seems to re-envision captivity in love as a "pleasant mew" (lxxx.9): "there fayth doth fearlesse dwell in brasen towre,/and spotlesse pleasure builds her sacred bowre" (lxv.13–14). At 76 he praises the "fayre bosome fraught with vertues richest treasure,/The neast of love, the lodging of delight:/the bowre of bliss, the paradise of pleasure,/the sacred harbour of that hevenly spright" (1–4). Similar sentiments are expressed at 72 and 73, and after sonnet 80 images of captivity do not reappear. We may therefore be tempted to suggest that, whatever its early manifestations, the rather conflicted captivity discourse of *Amoretti* is resolved by the success of the courtship.

There is, however, a related discourse (or "plot" as Roger Kuin might say[15]) which is not so resolved. This is a discourse of enclosure. As images of captivity originate from sonnet 1, those of enclosure originate from sonnet 2 — inside, so to speak, the captivity discourse. As at sonnet 1, at 2 Spenser makes an apostrophe to his text:

Unquiet thought, whom at the first I bred
  Of th'inward bale of my love pined hart:
  and sithens have with sighes and sorrowes fed,
  till greater than my womb thou woxen art:
Breake forth at length out of the inner part,
  in which thou lurkest lyke to vipers brood:
  and seeke some succour both to ease my smart
  and also to sustayne thy selfe with food.
But if in presence of that fayrest proud
  thou chance to come, fall lowly at her feet:
  and with meeke humblesse and afflicted mood,
  pardon for thee, and grace for me intreat.
Which if she graunt, then live and my love cherish,
  if not, die soone, and I with thee will perish.

The "unquiet thought" is identical with the "leaves, lines and rymes" of sonnet 1: both are effusions of love-longing, directed toward the lady and envisioned as submitting to her. Sonnet 2, in this sense, is an alternative beginning to the *Amoretti* sequence. More than that, it is a rival beginning. Sonnet 1 spoke to the materialization of the poet's longing in the sonnet sequence text; sonnet 2 addresses longing itself, pre-textual and inchoate. This is, first of all, a reversal of chronology: impulse to text should come before text, not after. What is worse, the placement of thought after text—within the limit, as it were, that has been set by and for text—is an indication of structural instability. The book cannot contain a thought that exists before the book. By invoking the concrete book at sonnet 1, and the unquiet thought at sonnet 2, Spenser makes his sequence enact just this instability: an attempt at impossible enclosure.[16]

This structural finding is semantically mirrored in sonnet 2. Like the matricidal baby snakes of medieval beast-lore,[17]the unquiet thought is explosive and rupturing. It originates from an enclosure marked by the poet's womb, just as, within the sequence, it originates from an enclosure marked by sonnet 1. Unfortunately the somatic arrangement is revolting and unstable: the thought generates in "bale," it is compared to "vipers brood," and waxes greater than the womb that holds it in (1–6). It must be alienated, even at the cost of a somatic breach (5). Once alienated, however, the thought is rapacious and must be re-enclosed in the lady's captivating love (9–12). At the end of sonnet 2, then, the unquiet thought is led back into the figure of captivity sketched in sonnet 1. As is initially implied by their respective placement in the first and second sonnets, captivity is re-established as primary, enclosure as subsidiary. However, part of the structural implication of sonnets 1 and 2 is of a subsidiary discourse erupting where it does not belong. And sonnet 2 ends with the question left open: either the unquiet thought will be tamed in captivity, or it and the poet will die.

It is important to stress that the life-cycle of the unquiet thought introduces to *Amoretti* a lose-lose dynamic in which volatile energies demand outlet, but once let out demand re-containment and re-control. On the one hand, the poet cannot abide hermetic enclosure. He is fascinated with gates: at sonnet 4, "New yeare forth looking out of Janus gate/doth seeme to promise hope of new delight"(1, 2); at 81, "the gate with pearles and rubyes richly dight:/throgh which her words so wise do make their way" (10, 11) is called "the worke of harts astonishment" (14), fairer than hair or cheeks or breasts. The danger of enclosure seems to be its lack of egress, causing an unbearable fullness: at sonnet 35 the poet's eyes are "so filled with the store of that faire sight, that nothing else they brooke,/but lothe the things which they did like before,/and can no more endure on them to looke" (9–12). "And if I speake, her wrath renew I shall," he complains at sonnet 43: "and if I silent be, my hart will breake,/ or choked be with overflowing gall"(2–4). Clearly, energies that swell inside must be allowed to escape.

On the other hand, if unenclosed energies range abroad they can themselves become enclosing:

So as I then disarmed did remaine
  a wicked ambush which lay hidden long
  in the close covert of her guileful eyen,
  thence breaking forth did thick about me throng.
Too feeble I t'abide the brunt so strong,
  was forst to yeeld my selfe into their hands:
  who me captiving streight with rigorous wrong,
  have ever since me kept in cruell bands.

                                                    (xii.5–12)

Much to be preferred is a pre-emptive enclosure in which the poet is the active party:

Retourne agayne my forces late dismayd
  Unto the siege by you abandon'd quite;
  . . . Gaynst such strong castles needeth greater might
  then those smal forts which ye were wont belay.

                                          (xiiii.1–2; 5–6)

To speak reductively, the enclosure dynamic that develops through the sequence may be understood as subjective horror vs. objective approval. The poet views enclosure of his own productive energies as unstable and appalling; but he views his own enclosure of alien and destructive energies as absolutely necessary. Attaining a bivalent control of enclosure, then, might be considered part of the psychic project of the *Amoretti*.

In the pleasant mew the project seems to have at least half-succeeded. Because it is so closely related to his fear of captivity, the poet's dread of self-enclosure is largely taken over by that larger discourse. When captivity is accepted late in the sequence, worries about enclosure seem also to be defused. The thoughts after the poet wins his lady are happy, amorous, and temperate. There is no discourse of containment here, or worry about being contained. The "fraile fancy" of sonnet 72 deconstructs the corrosive dynamics of enclosure in the same way that the lady deconstructs captivity at 67: by choosing enclosure willingly, thus putting an end to the push and pull of escape and recapture. The change is possible because in love settling down is much the wisest choice: "fed with full delight," the poet's thought "doth bath in blisse and mantleth most at ease:/ne thinks of other heaven, but how it might/her harts desire with most contentment please" (9–12). At 73 the poet's "hart" actually breaks from a distant captivity "in care" and flies "lyke as a bird" to the lady (1, 5). "Do you him take, and in your bosome bright/gently encage," she is asked, "that he may be your thrall" (9–10). Although the language resembles that used in the earlier poems of fearful captivity, here is no mention of torture or death but rather of "rare delight." We seem to see the truth of Leigh Deneef's assertion that for Spenser captivity "is neither destructive nor delimiting; it is instead a guarantee of safety and productivity if correctly viewed."[18] Indeed, the wages of love in sonnet 73 appear to be poetry, as the poet promises "to sing your name and prayses over all" (12). And all of these delights culminate in sonnet 82:

> Joy of my life, full oft for loving you
>   I blesse my lot, that was so lucky placed:
>   but then the more your own mishap I rew,
>   that are so much by so meane love embased.
> For had the equall hevens so much you graced
>   in this as in the rest, ye mote invent
>   som hevenly wit, whose verse could have enchased
>   your glorious name in golden moniment.
> But since ye deigned so goodly to relent
>   to me your thrall, in whom is little worth,
>   that little that I am, shall all be spent
>   in setting your immortal prayses forth.
> Whose lofty argument uplifting me,
>   shall lift you up unto an high degree.

If the sequence ended here it would make an effortless segue into the *Epithalamion*, conceived as a sort of glorious sequel.

That putative concord, however, is utterly confounded by sonnet 83; a reprint (with "seeing" for "having" at line 6) of 35.

> My hungry eyes, through greedy covetize
>   Still to behold the object of theyr payne:
>   with no contentment can themselves suffize,

but having pine, and having not complayne;
For lacking it, they cannot lyfe sustayne,
  and seeing it, they gaze on it the more:
  in theyr amazement lyke Narcissus vayne
  whose eyes him starv'd: so plenty makes me pore.
Yet are myne eyes so filled with the store
  of that fayre sight, that nothing else they brooke:
  but loath the things which they did like before,
  and can no more endure on them to looke.
All this worlds glory seemeth vayne to me,
  and all theyr shewes but shadowes saving she.

Although J. W. Lever was content to call this poem a printer's error, such an explanation is speculative and rendered very unlikely by the extensive numerological work that has been done on *Amoretti* as a sequence of eighty-nine sonnets.[19] Read as it stands, the poem returns the sequence to ravenous unsatisfaction (Loewenstein's "erotics of predation"[20]) after the apparently conclusive satisfactions, or plans for satisfactions, of the preceding sonnets. Its glutted, stopped eyes (8–12), moreover, reintroduce the poet's subjective horror of bloated enclosure to a text which seemed to have gotten over such things. As a repetition, the poem makes very explicit the re-appearance of a totally unprogressive enclosure discourse after and outside the apparent resolution of the apparently progressive captivity discourse. Given that sonnets 1 and 2 showed enclosure as subsidiary to and contained within captivity, the appearance here of unquiet thoughts in need of enclosure—after the amen chord of captivity—indicates that the ruptures foreseen at the sequence's outset have begun to occur.

Sonnet 84 widens the breach. In its opening lines the poet must suddenly and vituperatively exclaim: "Let not one sparke of filthy lustful fyre/breake out, that may her sacred peace molest" (1–2)—this after he has dwelt quite lustfully on the "sweet odour" of his lady's body at sonnet 64 (14), on the "sweet spoyle of beautie" at 76 (8), and on the rich table of his lady's breasts at 77. That banquet was laid in the context of the pleasant mew, "the bowre of blisse, the paradice of pleasure" (lxxvi.3), where the wings of fancy could sit "to rest themselves" (12). Now, it seems, the vigilant enclosure of an alienating thought has become the ruling imperative. The peace and protection of the pleasant mew, that positive resolution of the text's captivity discourse, has been lost—or is about to be lost, and

will be lost if the poet cannot keep the volatile "sparke" from breaking out. The rest of this sonnet shows the poet trying to keep a lid
on things:

> But pure affections bred in spotlesse brest,
>   and modest thoughts breathd from well tempred sprites
>   goe visit her in her chast bowre of rest,
>   accompanyde with angelick delightes.
> There fill your self with those most joyous sights,
>   the which my self could never yet attayne:
>   but speake no word to her of those sad plights,
>   which her too constant stiffenesse doth constrayn.
> Onely behold her rare perfection,
>   and blesse your fortunes fayre election.
>
>   (5–14)

Again, the poet's attempt to disallow the happily wanton thoughts
which were freely allowed in 76 and 77 suggests an ongoing dissolution of the pleasant mew that made those thoughts possible. The
thoughts at issue now are unquiet thoughts, and these must not be
allowed to reappear. But reappear they have; the poet's attempt to
control them shows that. Sonnet 83, then, shows the poet once more
fearing and loathing enclosure of his own energies; 84 shows him
harboring vicious energies that need to be enclosed, triggering precisely the nauseating dynamic feared in the previous poem. The late
discovery of *Amoretti* is that no matter how strongly one locks up
the brasen tower of love, unquiet thoughts may break out any time.
   Not only that: they may break *in* any time, violating any protected
space. Sonnet 86 finds the poet in a state of emotional apostasy:

> Venemous toung tipt with vile adders sting,
>   Of that self kynd with which the Furies fell
>   theyr snaky heads doe combe, from which a spring
>   of poysoned words and spitefull speeches well,
> Let all the plagues and horrid paines of hell,
>   upon thee fall for thine accursed hyre:
>   that with false forged lyes, which thou didst tel,
>   in my true love did stirre up coles of yre,

The sparkes whereof let kindle thine own fyre,
  and catching hold on thine own wicked hed
  consume thee quite, that didst with guile conspire
  in my sweet peace such breaches to have bred.
Shame be thy meed, and mischiefe thy reward,
  dew to thy selfe that it for me prepard.

This is one of Spenser's most vitriolic poems. The vipers exiled from
the poet in sonnet 2 have finally returned, to bore holes in his hard-
won peace. Whether or not it is the case, as Myron Turner suggests,
that here "poisonous thoughts and words . . . are outside the poet
and have no place in him,"[21] it is quite clear they have an ineradicable
place in his sonnet sequence. Imprecations against them shatter the
sequence's peace—as the limp to denouement then proves
(lxxxvii-lxxxix).

The poet's response to his late ruptures is sequential and reactive:
in a series of poems he tries to keep down the burgeoning problem.
What is so interesting about this attempt is that it actually seems to
make matters worse: in 83 the poet is sickened, but in 84 he is
desperate, and in 86 beside himself. The counterproductivity of normal, reactive work is expressed at various points in the *Amoretti*. In
several conventional but notable sonnets fire hardens ice (xxx) and
blows stiffen iron (xxxii). In sonnet 44 the poet complains that in
"this cruell civill warre,/the which my self against my selfe doe
make" (5–6),

    when in hand my tunelesse harp I take,
    then doe I more augment my foes despight:
    and griefe renews, and passions doe awake,
    to battaile fresh against my selfe to fight.

                                                            (9–12)

"Mongst whom the more I seeke to settle peace," he concludes, "the
more I fynd their malice to increace" (13–14). The reappearance of
the incorrigibly unquiet thought from sonnets 83 to 86 triggers the
same kind of attempt, with the same counterproductive result. Something like a better strategy is preferred at sonnet 50, when the lover
"long languishing in double malady/of my harts wound and of my
bodies griefe" (1) asks his doctor "is not the hart of all the body
chiefe?" (7) and requests:

Then with some cordialls seeke first to appease
the inward langour of my wounded hart,
and then my body shall have shortly ease.

$$(9-12)$$

This is matching the treatment to the task on a correct order of
power, rather than flailing away uselessly in an obviously incorrect
mode. But as the lover ruefully concludes, "such sweet cordialls passe
Physitions art" (12); and it passes the poet's art to bring ease to the
Amoretti sequence. The conundrum of egress and enclosure proves
intractable, because the energies that cause it are perennial. The poet's
reactive enclosures of these energies cannot control them, but succeed
only in augmenting them.

II

Here I wish to make my first connection to Spenser's *View*. This
tract constructs an incorrigible Irish problem that acts through explosive and mercurial alien energies. Every aspect of the culture, from
its bloodthirsty loves (*View* 81) to its wandering cattle-drives (65),
from its all-weather mantles (67) to its intemperate wailings (72),
counts in an indictment of Ireland's immeasurable savagery.[22] As presented by the New English spokesman Irenius, the Irish problem has
demanded and received correction through enclosure, but has proved
too deep and volatile to be met in ordinary reactive modes.

The discourse of continual enclosure runs throughout the *View*.
In Ireland it is necessary, says the weary Irenius, to "contayne the
unrulye people from a thousand evill occasions" (16). The volatility
of Irish life must be resolved by ruthless laws; the openness of the
island must be closed by towns and garrisons. "To haue the lande
thus inclosed and well fenced . . . is both a principall barr and ym-
peachment ynto theives . . . and also a gaule against all Rebells, and
outlawes that shall ryse vpp in any nombers against gouerment" (108).
The Irish kerne is "a flyinge Enymie hydinge him self in woodes
and bogges, from whence he will not draw forth, but into some
straight passage or perillous forde where he knowes the Army must
needes passe" (127). Indeed, though unenclosed himself, the kerne
knows all too well the advantage of coralling the English "like sheep
in a pynfold" (100): pursued by English forces, he "vseth commonlie
to draw him self into the straight passages thitherward and oftentimes

doth dangerouslie distresse them" (129). To avoid this kind of thing, it is necessary first of all to "bringe in all that rebellious rout of loose people which eyther doe now stand out in open Armes or in wandringe Companies" (124). At the present time "one Noble person"—possibly Essex—"beinge him self most stedfast to his soueraigne Quene stoppeth the ingate of all that evill which is loked for" (122).

Failed enclosures and exclusions also mark Irenius' history of the English presence in Ireland. When Henry the Second imposed laws on the island, most of the Irish

> fledd from his powre into the desertes, and Mountaines levinge the wyde Countrie to the Conqueror who in theire stead eftsones placed English men who possessed all the land and did quite shutt owte the Irish or the most parte of them.
>
> (19)

Similarly, the Duke of Clarence

> did shutt them vpp within those narrow corners and glennes vnder the mountaine foote, in which they lurked, by buildinge stronge holdes vpon everie border, and fortefyinge all passages and kepte them from breakinge any further.
>
> (20)

In the next rebellion, however,

> Morris of the ferne or wylde waste places . . . shortelye breakinge forth lyke a suddaine tempest he overran all Mounster, and Connaught, breakinge downe all the holdes and fortresses of the Englishe, defacinge and vtterlie subverting all corporate townes that were not stronglie walled . . . neyther in deed would he staye at all about them, but spedelie ran forward . . . yt was his pollicie to leaue noe houldes behind him, but to make all plaine and waist.
>
> (21)

It is clear from this account that the mercuriality and volatility of

Irish rebellion has prompted attempts at enclosure/exclusion, but that the reactive and incomplete nature of these attempts has rendered them useless. Useless, and counterproductive: Irenius speaks of "patchinge vpp one hole to make manye" (121). "What bootes yt," he asks his interlocutor Eudoxus, "to breake a Colt and to let him streight rvn Loose at random: So were this people at first well handled and wiselye brought to acknowledge alleigance to the kinges of England,"

> but beinge streight left vnto them selues and there owne inordynate lyfe and manners, they eftsones forgott what before they were taught, and so soone as they were out of sight by them selues shooke of theire brydles and begann to Colte anewe, more licensiouslye than before.
>
> (9)

The image of the rebounding colt, which appears several times in the *View*, might be cribbed directly from *Amoretti*'s vision of creative breakout: "then as a steed refreshed after toyle,/Out of my prison I will breake anew" (lxxx.5–6). Eamon Grennan argues that the metaphor serves Irenius as "a rhetorical argument in favor of the right of one people to deprive another of its freedom" (105).[23] It seems to work rather better as an image of the inefficacy of English attempts to cage and control the Irish people while leaving them essentially as they are.

But if reactive enclosure of the Irish vitriol will not conclude the Tudor reconquest, what will? Irenius' answer is very clear: the English strategy must advance in magnitude, moving from sequential and hopeless enclosures, to a complete and final resolution. After all the wasted work of the never-ending reconquest, it is necessary now to reform by "new framinge as yt were in the forge all that, is worne out of fashion, for all other means will be but lost labour" (121). Irenius' new frame consists, first, in "such an Armie as should tread downe all that standeth before them on foote, and lay on the ground all the stiffe-necked people of that land" (124). This move, perhaps, is a change more of degree than of kind, increasing a military presence that already exists. However, it is presented by Irenius as a paradigmatic change, and is accompanied by such counter-intuitive and inversionary measures as a plan to campaign in winter rather than summer (130–31). The second part of the new frame, moreover, is an unmistakable methodological advance. This is the harnessing of famine. It will be employed first of all by effecting a clear boundary between those Irish who are part of the problem, and those who are not: "those which [will] afterwardes, remaine without are stout and obstynate Rebells, such as will never bee made duetifull and obedyent, nor brought to labor, or civill . . . conversacion and therefore needfull to be cutt of" (134). Although this move continues to employ the dynamics of enclosure and exclusion, it is a once and final deployment powered by a terrible expedient. Excluded from English mercy, and enclosed in their own areas, the rebels will perish not by the sword but by "being kepte from manvrance, and their cattle from runninge abroad by this hard restrainte." The starvation of Munster in the early 1580s—"the verie Carcases they spared not to scrape out of theire graues"—becomes the type for application to the whole island, leaving "a most populous and plentifull Countrye suddenlie left voyde of man and beast." Irenius is at pains to emphasize that as a general strategy this is an irresistible escalation: "the end I assure mee will bee verie shorte and much soner then can bee in so great trouble (as yt semeth) hoped for," although "there should none of them fall by the sworde, nor bee slaine by the soldyer" (135).

In sum, the *View* recommends a large strategic shift, from a sequential and imperfect life of containment, to a final extirpation that extinguishes the sequence. And this is the second connection between Spenser's tract and *Amoretti and Epithalamion*. For as Larsen puts it, the final result of *Amoretti* "is not internal to itself, but lies outside the sequence in *Epithalamion* . . . *Amoretti* is, therefore, unique among Renaissance artifacts, because any rhetorical *concordia* ultimately remains foreign to it, to be sealed later from beyond its bounds."[24] The "viper thoughts" that Joseph Loewenstein identifies in *Amoretti* are finally defeated only by the leap the poet makes to *Epithalamion*. This is a leap to higher ground: a strategic advance from the sequentiality and reactivity of the sonnet sequence, to the singularity and productivity of the marriage song. There, it is hoped, no unquiet thoughts can follow: "let this day let this one day be myne," begs the poet (*Epithalamion* 125), abandoning the rest of the calendar to the depredations of mind. The bad affects of the lover's courtship are carefully anathematized in *Epithalamion* 19, where "hidden feares" (336) must not appear "within nor yet without" (334–35). (The programmatic significance of song 19 for the relationship to *Amoretti* can be proved as follows: it contains a "Quyre of Frogs" (349); this echoes and inverts the "quyre of Birds" of the *Amoretti* sonnet of the same number, 19; from that sonnet the marriage poem's "echoing woods" refrain also derives.) Although we might offer a poststructuralist quibble to the poet here, pointing out that he must include his unquiet thoughts in order to exclude them (as Freud says, "the thing which is meant to be warded off invariably finds its way into the very means which is being used for warding it off"[25]), his effort nonetheless appears conclusive: no snaky evils interfere with his wedding night. The point, in any case, is that only through this advance and escalation from sequence to song can *Amoretti*'s enclosures find quietus. The sequence of sonnets tries and fails to control the unquiet thought; the marriage song shows a conclusion of the project under a larger magnitude, deployed in a single round. This pattern is congruent to that offered by the *View*.

III

The denial of resolution to unquiet thoughts in *Amoretti* leads us to re-examine the sonnets' discourse of captivity. Is this really resolved within the sequence? While it is quite true that in sonnets 72 through 80 the poet looks with pleasure on the mew of love, it is equally true that his presence there is abstract, and that he envisions himself "breaking out" of this prison (lxxx). The change in his attitude to captivity, moreover, is achieved only through an initial reversal of its subjectivity. The first positive mention of captivity in the sequence is at sonnet 65—but here it is the lady who is captive and the poet who is captor, reassuring her of her security.

> The doubt which ye misdeeme, fayre love, is vaine,
>   That fondly fear to loose your liberty;
> . . . Sweet be the bands, the which true love doth tye,
>   without constraynt or dread of any ill:
>   the gentle birde feeles no captivity
>   within her cage, but singes and feeds her fill.
>
> (1–8)

This after dozens of sonnets in which captivity was discussed as it affected the poet, not the lady, and was consistently rejected by him as hideous. Similarly, at sonnet 67 the poet whose "hart" has been captured and tormented throughout the sequence suddenly appears as the hunter, and the lady as a "gentle deare" (7) "with her owne goodwill . . . firmly tyde" (12). (That the syntax of this poem also makes the "gentle deare" [7] "lyke as a huntsman" [1] shows only

that Spenser is firmly in control of these wish-fulfillment contents.[26])
Role-reversal through animal metaphor continues at 71:

> I joy to see how in your drawen work
>   Your selfe unto the Bee ye doe compare;
>   and me unto the Spyder that doth lurke
>   in close awayt to catch her unaware.
> Right so your self were caught in cunning snare
>   of a deare foe, and thralled to his love:
>   in whose streight bands ye now captived are
>   so firmely, that ye never may remove.
>
>   (1–8)

This poem contrasts directly with the poet's fruitless attempt, "broken with least wind," to cast himself as the spider at sonnet 23; as
well as with his horror, in numerous mid-stage poems, at the lady's
ability to lure and trap him. At no time in the *Amoretti* does the poet
actually accept his own captivity on the lady's terms; he rather makes
the lady captive on the lady's terms, and claims her role of captor for
himself. The whole subject is then elided rather than addressed in
the poems of abstract self and mutual love.

But if captivity is evaded in the later *Amoretti*, this is surely because
its earlier construction is too severe to allow any other solution.
From sonnet one onwards, Spenser's language of captivity is simpy
too brutal ever to be featured on the walls of the marriage cage.
Deneef's attempt to cast this language within a Christian symbology
of mutual help is sound but, for much of the sequence, implausible:
unless they have a very strange marriage indeed, spouses simply cannot greet "lyke captives trembling at the victors sight "(i.4). Language
of this kind proliferates through the sequence:

> Dayly when I doe seek and sue for peace,
>   And hostages doe offer for my truth:
>   she cruell warriour doth her self addresse
>   to battell, and the weary war renew'th.
>
>   (xi.1–4)

> Too feeble I t'abide the brunt so strong,
>   was forst to yeeld my selfe into their hands:

who me captiving streight with rigorous wrong
have ever since me kept in cruell bands.

(xii.9–12)

So oft as homeward I from her depart,
   I goe lyke one that having lost the field:
is prisoner led away with heavy hart,
   despoyled of warlike armes and knowen shield.
So doe I now my selfe a prisoner yeeld,
   to sorrow and to solitary paine.

(lii.1–6)

The reference to "solitary paine" indicates what happens once the captives are within the mistress's power. She has a tendency to massacre them. "See how the Tyranesse doth joy to see," cries the poet,

the huge massacres which her eyes do make:
and humbled harts brings captives unto thee,
that thou of them mayst mightie vengeance take.

(x.5–8)

Is it her nature or is it her will
   to be so cruel to an humbled foe?

(xli.1–2)

It is in this context that the lady is compared to various unmagnanimous predatory beasts:

The Panther knowing that his spotted hyde
   Doth please all beasts but that his looks them fray:
within a bush his dreadfull head doth hide,
   to let them gaze whylest he on them may pray
Right so my cruell fayre with me doth play.

(liii.1–5)

Fayre be ye sure, but cruell and unkind,
   As is a Tygre that with greedinesse

hunts after bloud, when he by chance doth find
a feeble beast, doth felly him oppresse.

(lvi.1–4)

The great problem with this behavior is not only how consistently
the lady engages in it but how much she enjoys it, using her beauty
for procurement and anaesthesia. Thus at 31 the lover complains that
while nature has given most predators predatory appearances, that
"warne to shun the danger of theyr wrath,"

my proud one doth worke the greater scath,
through sweet allurement of her lovely hew:
that she the better may in bloody bath
of such poore thralls her cruell hands embrew.

(8–12)

Similarly at 41:

And that same glorious beauties ydle boast,
is but a bayt such wretches to beguile
as, being long in her loves tempest tost,
she meanes at last to make her piteous spoyle.

(9–12)

And at 47:

So she with flattring smyles weake harts doth guyde
unto her love and tempte to theyr decay,
whome being caught she kills with cruel pryde,
and feeds at pleasure on the wretched pray.

(5–8)

It is not accidental that some critics have been puzzled and offended
by these poems. For Donna Gibbs the imagery is "ridiculously extravagant and not to be entertained"[27]; Reed Way Dasenbrock suggests
that "it is almost as if Spenser had difficulty writing these poems
naturally but felt he needed them."[28] Yet it is hard to understand on
what basis we can scold Spenser's taste, or what we learn by doing

so. Even if, as seems unlikely, the effect of these poems can securely be called parodic—even if we can be quite sure that Spenser has written intentional travesties—the question still remains, why? The answer "to parody the Petrarchan tradition" simply reposes the question, while completely ignoring the issue of who or what provides content for the alleged parody. We have still to understand the reason and the purpose, straight-faced or smiling, for these troublesome, violent poems.

Our understanding may begin from sonnet 20. Here, the lady is unfavorably compared to magnanimous and merciful power, and is impugned with the peculiar guilt of murdering those who have submitted to her.

> In vaine I seeke and sew to her for grace,
>   and doe myne humbled hart before her poure:
>   the whiles her foot she in my neck doth place,
>   and tread my life downe in the lowly floure.
> And yet the Lion that is lord of power,
>   and reigneth over every beast in field:
>   in his most pride disdeigneth to devoure
>   the silly lambe that to his might doth yield.
> But she more cruell and more salvage wylde,
>   then either Lyon or the Lyonesse
>   shames not to be with guiltlesse bloud defylde,
>   but taketh glory in her cruelnesse.
>
> (xx.1–12)

This stunning poem yields the following admonition:

> Fayrer then fayrest let none ever say,
>   that ye were blooded in a yeelded pray.
>
> (13–14)

That prescription becomes basic to the sequence.

> But by his death which some perhaps will mone,
>   ye shall condemned be of many a one.
>
> (xxxvi.13–14)

Chose rather to be praysed for dooing good,
   then to be blam'd for spilling guiltlesse blood.

                        (xxxviii.13–14)

Ó fayrest fayre let never it be named,
   that so fayre beauty was so fowly shamed.

                        (xli.13–14)

know, that mercy is the mighties jewell,
   and greater glory thinke to save, then spill.

                        (xlix.3–4)

Great shame it is, thing so divine in view,
   made for to be the world's ornament:
to make the bayte her gazers to embrew,
   good shames to be so ill an instrument.
But mercy doth with beautie best agree,
   as in theyr maker ye them best may see.

                        (liii.9–14)

Then sith to heaven ye lykened are the best,
   be lyke in mercy as in all the rest.

                        (lv.13–14)

These injunctions disappear with the end of the fearful captivity discourse at sonnet 57. But as I have shown, that discourse is elided, not resolved, when the poet finds his wishes of love so suddenly fulfilled. The point of the captivity discourse is not in fact directed at the poet; it does not tell him how to combine earthly and spiritual love, or how to accept enclosure in the sacred space of marriage, or how to socialize and control his own unquiet thoughts. These ideas are in the sequence (where they are ultimately frustrated), but not in this aspect of it. The captivity discourse is directed at the lady, and its point may be paraphrased as follows: never let it be said that you murdered those who had laid down their arms before you.

IV

Now, this is very curious. For the ghost that haunts the *View* is Spenser's onetime boss Lord Grey, a man who was recalled and disgraced, Irenius tells us, partly because he murdered prisoners.[29] Grey enters the text just after Irenius outlines his plan to starve Ireland into submission. Eudoxus asks what will happen when the country has been reduced in this manner and the Queen hears the reports: "Then shee perhapps for verie compassion of such Calamities, will not onelie stopp the streame of such vyolence . . . but also con them lyttle thanks which haue bene the aucthors and Counsellors of such bloody platformes."

> So I remember that in the late gouerment of that good Lord, Graye . . . lyke complainte was made against him, that he was a bloodye man: and regarded not the lyfe of her subiectes, noe more than dogges, but had wasted and consumed all . . . Eare, was soone lente therevnto, all suddenlie turned topsye turvye, He noble Lord eftesoones was blamed . . . and not onelie all that greate and long charge which shee had before bene at quite lost and cancelled, but also all that hope of good which was even at the dore put back and frustrate . . .
>
> (138)

As we know, it was to attend the Lord Lieutenant Grey as personal secretary that Spenser first came to Ireland in (probably) 1580. The young poet and bureaucrat seems, on the evidence of all his written comments, to have admired his boss immensely. The two setpieces of Grey's tenure were the starvation of Munster and the slaughter of 600 Spanish mercenaries after they had surrendered at the "golden fort" of Smerwick. The policy in Munster led, it seems, to Grey's recall by Elizabeth; the Smerwick incident, as Irenius complains, left him "blotted with the name of a bloodye man, whom who that well knewe, knewe to bee most gentle, affable lovinge and temeperate."

That Eudoxus has touched a sore spot with his mention of Grey is shown by Irenius' immediate account of "that sharpe execution of the Spanyards at the forte of Senawicke . . . some saye that he promised them lyfe, others that at least he did putt them in hope thereof":

> Both the one and the other is most vntrue, for this I can assure you, my self beinge as neare then as anye, that he was so far from [either] promisinge or puttinge in hope, that when first theire secretarie called . . . he was flatlye refused, and afterwards their Coronell . . . came forth to entreate that they might parte with their armors lyke soldyers at least with theire lyves, according to the Custome of warr and lawe of nacions, yt was

strongelie denyed him, and told him by the Lord Deputie him self, that they could not iustlie plead eyther Custome of warr or lawe of nations, for that they were not any lawfull Enemies . . . the Irish them selues, as the Earle and Iohn of Desmond with the rest were noe lawfull Enemies, but rebells and trators, and therefore they that came to succor them noe better than roges and Runnagates . . . so as yt should be dishonorable for him in the name of his Quene to Condycion or make any tearmes with such raskalls: but lefte them to theire choyce to yeild and submitte them selues or noe, wherevpon the said Coronell did absolutelie yeild him self, and the forte with all therein, and Craued onelye mercye, which yt beinge thought good not to showe them . . . theire was no other waye but to make that shorte ende of them that was made. . .

"Therefore" he concludes, "most vntrewlie and malyciouslie doe those evill tonges backbyte and slander the sacred ashes" of Grey, "whose least vertue . . . they were never able to aspyre vnto"(138–41).

We have, apparently, a contradiction of attitude between the two texts under consideration. In *Amoretti* Spenser constructs a lady whose crime is to slaughter those who have yielded to her power. This crime is presented as ugly and irredeemable, and the lady is persistently urged against it. In the *View*, Spenser remembers a leader whose crime was to have slaughtered those who had yielded to his power. This crime is presented as necessary and honorable, and the leader is vigorously defended against those who would say otherwise. If, in fact, Elizabeth and her advisors fell into the category of naysayers, it seems impossible that Spenser is saying what he thinks they want to hear (an inference that the possible suppression of the *View* would support[30]). In any case, the *View* proves that Spenser could look on the slaughter of the yielded with considerable equanimity. Yet in *Amoretti* he constructs it with considerable horror. The generic barrier between the tract and the sonnet sequence cannot fully explain this contradiction, especially given the symbolic and structural links I have tried to show between them. Why, then, does Spenser make slaughter of the yielded so central to *Amoretti*, and associate this crime in particular with his beloved?

A partial answer to this question must be that the poet of *Amoretti* does not actually urge his lady not to kill her captives. He assumes that she tortures and kills them as a matter of course. The admonitory couplets of the sequence speak not to behavior but to blame: "Let none ever *say* that ye were blooded in a yeelded pray," etc. (my emphasis; see p. 155 above). This clarification makes the sequence's relationship with the *View* less problematic. In neither text does Spenser express concern with the moral valence of slaughtering prisoners. He expresses, rather, concern with the public opprobrium that can be successfully attached to such conduct.

Yet this turn around the problem merely leads us to re-encounter it. For however carefully Spenser may frame his depictions of cruel slaughter in *Amoretti*—however nicely he may separate a normative concern with reputation from a descriptive concern with action—the innate egregiousness of the actions color the sequence and impugn its object, the beloved. Furthermore, it is precisely Spenser's separation of the normative from the descriptive that raises the question of the normative in the first place. One could almost believe that the author of the *Faerie Queene*, when he came to write a sonnet sequence, might create a cruel fair much crueller than any that had gone before. No moral issue would be raised by such a representation; everyone would know that it was just hyperbolic love-language. But by producing a normative register in counterposition to his metaphors—and then by suggesting that if she does not change her metaphorical behavior, the lady will be morally smeared—Spenser, in fact, morally smears her. *Amoretti* is in this sense like an open letter defending someone's reputation that publicizes bad reports under cover of denying them; or like those tabloid stories that publish offensive photographs with the pretense of expressing shock at them. Even as the text urges the lady to avoid the moral stain of cruel slaughter, it in fact fixes on her that very stain. This is especially true given the allegation that the lady enjoys and delights in her bloody deeds—unlike Grey, who, we are told in the *View*, would never have cuffed a kerne if he had not been so extremely provoked. The question of why cruel slaughter is in the *Amoretti*, then, admits of a simple answer: it is there to slander the lady.

Unless the poet and his beloved are to have an unusually unhappy marriage, this particular agenda cannot be directed at any young Miss Boyle. And in fact Spenser's object can only be the queen. The presence of Elizabeth Tudor in the Elizabeth of the sequence has long been recognized: she is implicit in all the sonnets that treat a powerful lady, and explicit in Spenser's praise of "three Elizabeths" at sonnet 74: "the second is my sovereigne Queene most kind/that honour and large richesse to me lent" (7–8). Although R. Headlam Wells reads the sequence as Spenser "continuing his supplications for preferment" after the frustrations openly expressed in *Colin Clouts*

Come Home Again, this assessment does not square with the poet's rather conflicted attitude to his martial lady.[31] Closer to the mark are Catherine Bates, who finds *Amoretti* "designedly ambiguous" in its feelings about the queen, and Donald Cheney, who feels that the poet is striking dangerously close to "the irascible Belphoebe."[32] If, as I am suggesting, the sequence purposely impugns its "soverayne beauty" (iii.1) as a slaughterer of prisoners, Cheney's insight is shown to be apt.

Indeed, we must question the prudence of involving this inaccessibly Petrarchan and permanently unwed queen in the compound lady of a sonnet sequence that ultimately abandons her for the "mayden Queene" (*Epithalamion* 158) of a marriage song. When the old Elizabeth through her motif of Cynthia is made to witness the newlyweds' conjugal happiness at *Epithalamion* 21 (377)—is urged not to "envy" the pair (376), and is then asked to bless them and "goodly enlarge" the young wife's womb (384)—Spenser's audacity is at a peak. Can we imagine Raleigh writing such a poem after 1592, when he required enlargement from the prison to which he had been committed for enlarging another young Elizabeth? Bates suggests that "the structural ambivalence of the *Amoretti* and *Epithalamion* . . . seems to enact Spenser's sense of the complexity of his position as a poet on the margins of Elizabeth I's court." It seems to me that in *Epithalamion* at least, Spenser's distance from court is a distinct advantage. Surely, as Cheney puts it, he is asking for trouble.[33]

In the sonnet sequence itself Spenser's deniability is more secure. The Petrarchan tradition already involved a certain amount of violence and strong language, and the Petrarchan lady was one of the templates of Elizabeth's cult. Eyebrows need not be raised, therefore, over Spenser's articulation of these tendencies. But I hope I have prepared the ground in this paper for an allegation that is both more specific and more obscure. I have suggested heuristic links between the *View* and the *Amoretti*, and that Spenser brings the crime of Grey into the sonnet sequence. I have shown in addition that he visits on the lady the fate that fell to Grey: to be slandered and villified for this crime. Since the queen forms part of the lady's profile, I conclude that one purpose of *Amoretti* is to allow Spenser rhetorical revenge on the queen, by fixing Grey's unique disgrace on her. Through the peculiar voodoo of poetry, Spenser transfers this ancient chafe. He brings the queen into his sonnets' pretty rooms, and there maligns her in the way I have described.

This is not to deny that the sequence is addressed to Elizabeth Boyle. It is not to deny that the sequence is about love, or that it develops a model of mutual over individual desire, or that it elevates the Protestant marriage bed. I believe all of these things to be true. I mean only to show other work that the sequence does, in the context of Spenser's Irish career. The tendency I have identified can coexist with others in *Amoretti*, as Spenser's mother, sovereign, and wife coexist in the person of his Elizabeth. I do feel, however, that when *Amoretti*'s discourse of slaughter and blame slanders the lady, it slanders the queen. It does so with reference to the crime, and in the country, that led to Grey's destruction through slander a decade and a half before. It is possible that Spenser could have written the crime of Grey into his sonnets, made blame the moral issue of his sequence, and aligned his queen with the figure of his blameworthy lady, all without meaning anything by it. But it does not seem very plausible. At the very least, the conjunctions I have identified must have satisfied Spenser in a way not entirely clear to himself. The *View* shows, as does *Faerie Queene* V, that Grey's fate still rankled with Spenser in the 1590s. *Amoretti* shows evidence of the same abiding animus.

Columbia University

NOTES

1. *Petrarch's Lyric Poems: The* Rime Sparse *and Other Lyrics,* trans. and ed. Robert M. Durling (Cambridge: Harvard University Press, 1976), p.63.

2. See Patrick Cheney, *Spenser's Famous Flight: A Renaissance Idea of a Literary Career* (Toronto: University of Toronto Press, 1993); Donna Gibbs, *Spenser's* Amoretti: *A Critical Study* (Aldershot, England: Scolar Press, 1990); Myron Turner, "The Imagery of Spenser's *Amoretti*," *Neophilologus* 72 (1988), pp. 284–99; and R. Headlam Wells, "Poetic Decorum in Spenser's *Amoretti*," *Cahiers Élisabethains* 25 (1984): 9–22.

3. See Alexander Dunlop, "The Drama of *Amoretti*," *Spenser Studies* 1 (1980), pp. 107–20; and Lisa M. Klein, "'Let us love, deare love, lyke as we ought': Protestant Marriage and the Revision of Petrarchan Loving in Spenser's *Amoretti*," *Spenser Studies* 10 (1989): 109–37.

4. As reconstructed by Kenneth J. Larsen in *Edmund Spenser's Amoretti and Epithalamion: A Critical Edition* (Tempe, AZ: Medieval and Renaissance Texts and Studies, 1997), pp. 54–59 and 218–22. Anne Lake Prescott suggests, meanwhile, that Spenser may have borrowed the structure of *Amoretti*, with its "bilateral symmetry and calendrical curves" from du Bellay's "abjectly Petrarchist but gracious" *Olive* sequence (1550). See "Spenser (Re) Reading du Bellay: Chronology and Literary Response," in Judith H. Anderson, Donald Cheney and David A. Richardson eds., *Spenser's Life and the Subject of Biography* (Amherst: University of Massachusets Press, 1996), p. 139.

5. "Spenser's *Amoretti:* 'Most Goodly Temperature'," in Louis Lohr Martz, *From Renaissance to Baroque: Essays on Literature and Art* (Columbia: University of Missouri Press, 1991), pp. 100–13.

6. Elizabeth Bieman, "'Sometimes I mask in mirth lyke to a Comedy': Spenser's *Amoretti*," *Spenser Studies* 4 (1983): 131–41.

7. William C. Johnson, *Spenser's* Amoretti: *Analogies of Love* (London and Toronto: Associated University Press, 1990), p. 166. A recent discussion of indeterminacy in the sequence also accepts the ironic or hyperbolic reading of its violence: see Roger Kuin, *Chamber Music: Elizabethan Sonnet-Sequences and the Pleasure of Criticism* (Toronto: University of Toronto Press, 1998), pp. 202–06.

8. Larsen, pp. 30–31.

9. Larsen, p. 32

10. I am aware, in fact, of only one published instance other than my own: that of Scott Wilson in his *Cultural Materialism: Theory and Practice* (Oxford: Blackwell, 1995). Wilson discusses the Irish and royal Elizabeths of *Amoretti* during a critique of Greenblatt's reading of the Bowre of Bliss. He accepts a version of the Martzian parodic theory, in which Spenser's "ludicrous hyperbole" produces the requisite inaccessibility of a sonnet sequence mistress (p.78). He also connects the "absence and non-place" of Spenser's wife with the space occupied by rebels in *A View of the Present State of Ireland;* without, however, articulating this connection (p. 79). (I am grateful to Andrew Hadfield for pointing out this essay.)

There may of course be other Irish *Amoretti* readings, and in time there inevitably will be. The 1999 Millenium Spenser Conference in Doneraile, Ireland featured papers on Ireland and Amoretti by Christopher Warler and Elliott M. Hill.

11. All citations of *Amoretti and Epithalamion* are from *The Yale Edition of the Shorter Poems of Edmund Spenser,* eds. William A. Oram et al. (New Haven and London: Yale University Press, 1989).

12. All citations of *The Faerie Queene* are from the edition of Thomas P. Roche (Harmondsworth, Middlesex: Penguin, 1987).

13. I follow consensus in taking the *View* as Spenser's. Doubts about his authorship, and about whether or not the *View* was suppressed, have been expressed by Jean Brink in "Constructing the *View of the Present State of Ireland*," *Spenser Studies* 11 (1994): 203–30. Responses have been given by Willy Maley in his *Salvaging Spenser: Colonialism, Culture and Identity* (London: Macmillan Press, 1997), pp. 163–94, and by Andrew Hadfield in "Was Spenser's *View of the Present State of Ireland* Censored? A Review of the Evidence," *Notes and Queries* 41.4 (1994), pp. 459–63, and "Certainties and Uncertainties: By Way of Response to Jean Brink," *Spenser Studies* 12 (1998): 197–202.

14. See Maley, p. 167.

15. Kuin, p. 202

16. All of my comments on *Amoretti,* but none more than these, assume that the original numbering of its sonnets is an integral aspect of the text. The numerological and calendrical work that has been done on *Amoretti and Epithalamion* supports this view. See p. 12, n. 19.

17. See Joseph Loewenstein, "A Note on the Structure of Spenser's *Amoretti*: Viper Thoughts," *Spenser Studies* 8 (1987): 320.

18. *Spenser and the Motives of Metaphor* (Durham: Duke University Press, 1982), p. 70.

19. See, for example, Alexander Dunlop, "The Unity of Spenser's *Amoretti*" in Alastair Fowler ed., *Silent Poetry* (London: Routledge and Kegan Paul, 1970); Shokachi Fukuda, "The Numerological Patterning of *Amoretti* and *Epithalamion*," *Spenser Studies* 9 (1988): 33–48; Carol V. Kaske, "Spenser's *Amoretti and Epithalamion* of 1595: Structure, Genre, and Numerology," *English Literary Renaissance* 8 (1978): 271–95; Charlotte Thompson, "Love in an Orderly Universe: A Unification of Spenser's *Amoretti*, Anacreontics," and *Epithalamion*," *Viator* 16 (1985): 277–336 (a particularly ambitious essay in this mode); along with Kent A. Hieatt's pioneering study *Short Time's Endless Monument* (New York: Columbia University Press, 1960). J.W. Lever's comments on *Amoretti*, which deal with the violent poems of the sequence by the tidy expedient of ejecting them, are in his *The Elizabethan Love Sonnet* (London: Methuen, 1956); see especially p. 101.

20. Loewenstein, p. 315.

21. Turner, p. 287.

22. Although I have consulted the recent edition of the *View* by Andrew Hadfield and Willy Maley, *A View of the State of Ireland, from the First Printed Edition (1633)* (Oxford: Blackwell, 1997), all my citations of the *View* are from the edition of W.L. Renwick (London: Eric Partridge Ltd at the Scholartis Press, 1934). Renwick seems to me a particularly valuable custodian of this text because he is committed enough to the tail end of the English expansionist enterprise to approve much of Spenser's inaugural perspective. Speculating on Spenser's motive for writing the tract, Renwick notes its dialogue form and suggests that "in plain fact people were asking questions of this official on leave—as it might be, nowadays, one from India—and he wrote his answers down to satisfy them" (p. 239). Later, Renwick defends Grey's decision to massacre the Spaniards as follows: "Five hundred prisoners. . . could not be brought off in the face of a strong enemy, through 100 miles of difficult country, in a wet November, by a force whose reliable strength was eight hundred" (p. 245). The analysis is clinical and briskly realist, and claims a real affinity with the mindset of New English officials.

23. "Language and Politics: A Note on Some Metaphors in Spenser's *A View of the Present State of Ireland*," *Spenser Studies* 3 (1982): 105.

24. Larsen, p. 56. John Mulryan suggests in "'Is My Team Ploughing?': The Struggle for Closure in the Faerie Queene 1590," *Ben Jonson Journal* 3 (1996), that even the apparently full-stop conclusion and resolution of the 1590 Book III is necessarily "to be continued." The struggle for closure in *Amoretti*, then, might be considered less remarkable than Larsen and I claim. The point, though, is that *Amoretti* enacts, in the transition to *Epithalamion*, an abandonment of the struggle rather than its continuation.

25. *Notes Upon a Case of Obsessional Neurosis*, in *The Standard Edition of the Complete Psychological Works of Sigmund Freud* v. 10, trans. James Strachey (London: Hogarth Press, 1955), p. 225.

26. See Loewenstein, p. 314.

27. Gibbs, p. 39.

28. "The Petrarchan Context of Spenser's *Amoretti*," *PMLA* 100 (1988): 46.

29.   In "Reconstructing Grey's Reputation: A New View of the *View,*" *The Sixteenth Century Journal* 29.1 (1998): 3–18, Catherine G. Canino argues from an examination of State Papers and other documents that Grey's actions in Ireland were not particularly brutal by contemporary standards, that they were not regarded as such by most observers, and that Grey was recalled simply because he spent too much money. Canino's evidence is inconclusive and squares badly with Spenser's account in the *View* and in *FQ* V. Her suggestion that Spenser may have made up the stories about Grey's brutality is adventurous and does not accord with the reverential tone of the Legend of Justice, or with the dedicatory sonnet to Grey in the 1590 *Faerie Queene.* The *View* is substantial surviving evidence that Grey was "blotted with the name of a bloody man." In any case, I am exclusively interested in what Spenser *says* in the texts about Grey and about slaughter of the yielded. This assumes, of course, that Spenser wrote the *View*; but as I have already said, this is the consensus view, and also mine. See n. 13.

30.   See n. 13.

31.   Wells, p. 51.

32.   Catherine Bates, "The Politics of Spenser's *Amoretti,*" *Criticism* 33 (Winter 1991), p. 83; Donald Cheney, "Spenser's Fortieth Birthday and Related Fictions," *Spenser Studies* 4 (1983): 8.

33.   Bates, p. 85; D. Cheney, p. 8.

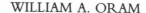

WILLIAM A. ORAM

What Did Spenser Really Think of Sir Walter Ralegh When He Published the First Installment of *The Faerie Queene*?

The dedicatory sonnet to Sir Walter Ralegh in the 1590 *Faerie Queene* suggests how independent Spenser was of his patron in the early 1590s, and how willing to criticize him. The independence probably has roots in their early acquaintance in the 1580s, when they would have been closer in rank than they were later, and it appears in 1590 when Spenser steers clear of Ralegh's rivalry with Essex. In the sonnet Spenser seems to set the sophisticated, melodious art of the courtier above his own rustic verse, but the poem's language suggests something quite different: that Ralegh's amorous verse limits his naturally lofty talents to the merely pleasurable. In Helgerson's terms, a determinedly "laureate" poet insists on his place by critizing a greatly gifted "amateur."

*A*BOUT TEN YEARS AGO I published an account of Spenser's relation to Sir Walter Ralegh in which I argued that Spenser's attitude toward him was friendly but critical, and that he felt that Ralegh's poetic wooing of his queen in order to further his court career misused his talents.[1] One poem in which I found this criticism was the dedicatory sonnet to Ralegh appended to *The Faerie Queene*. Here I'd like to contextualize the argument more thoroughly, taking advantage of the work on the dedicatory sonnets done meanwhile by Wayne Erickson and others.[2] I'll argue that we tend mistakenly to project the conditions of Spenser's relation to Ralegh in 1590 onto his first acquaintance with him in the early eighties and to underestimate Spenser's quiet independence of his patron. In reading the dedicatory sonnet which Spenser appended to the 1590 *Faerie Queene*, I'll focus on how, for all its praise, it sets Spenser against Ralegh and criticizes the latter as a poet.

I

We don't know if Spenser was present when Lord Grey's troops, Ralegh among them, slaughtered the disarmed, papally-funded garrison of Smerwick. In the *View*, years after, Spenser has Irenius defend Grey's actions, claiming to have first-hand knowledge.[3] But whether or not Spenser met Ralegh here, the great likelihood is that they knew one another during the year Ralegh was in Ireland.[4] They were both the same age, both intellectuals, both English Protestant nationalists. The upper ranks of the New English campaigning with Lord Grey would have had knowledge of one another and Ralegh was the kind of man who makes a strong impression on others. Grey himself knew Ralegh and disliked him. He complained about him to Cecil in 1582 when it was thought that Ralegh, back at the English court, would soon return to Ireland: "I like neither his carriage nor his company; and therefore other than by direction and command-ment, and what his right can require, he is not to expect at my hands."[5] Ralegh had been speaking against Grey's belief that the Irish rebels must be subdued by the sword, in favor of a less expensive policy of recruiting some Irish to join the English cause. As Grey's secretary, Spenser would have known his views, though he may not have shared them.

In imagining this first acquaintance, we have tended to project onto their early meetings the great difference of rank which charac-terized their relations in 1599. But in their earliest relationship the distance would have been significantly less. Ralegh was, indeed, the younger son of a Devonshire gentry family. but he was not an aristo-crat: indeed, later he would be reviled at court as an arriviste who had risen more rapidly than his birth merited. In Lord Grey's army he was a captain, responsible for his own troop of soldiers, but no more. On the other hand as Lord Grey's secretary, Spenser was close to the supreme authority in Ireland, and in position to become part of the English administration.[6] While we know nothing of his birth (he later claimed to be related to the rich gentry family of Spencer in Althorp), his B.A. and M.A. from Cambridge had enabled others to make a career in government or at court. Here, when they first knew one another, Spenser and Ralegh were not radically different in rank.

Ralegh left Ireland in 1582, to make his fortune at court, while Spenser remained in Ireland. Both did well, but by 1589 Ralegh had done much better. In 1582 he was thirty, dashing, bold, intelligent, charismatic, and his queen was fifty. He charmed and impressed

Elizabeth who made him captain of her Guard, which gave him access to her person, Lieutenant of the County of Cornwall, and Lord Warden of the Cornish Tin-Mines. Later she gave him a farm or tax of wines, which was worth 2,000 pounds per annum, and awarded him (among other Irish grants) twelve thousand acres of the earl of Desmond's confiscated lands. Spenser, meanwhile, had made himself a place in the English administration of Ireland, and acquired the small castle of Kilcolman in Munster and three thousand acres, an estate a quarter the size of Ralegh's, which he was to "plant" with Englishmen. When the two men met again in 1589 there was much greater distance between their stations. Spenser's achievements were considerable, but Ralegh was a great man at court with the queen's ear.

It's remarkable how little this social inequality appears in *Colin Clouts Come Home Againe*, Spenser's pastoralized account of the meeting. Indeed when Colin describes how he meets a "strange shepherd" and the two sing together, Spenser stresses their likeness.

> He pip'd, I sung; and when he sung, I piped,
> By chaunge of turnes, each making other mery,
> Neither envying other, nor envied,
> So piped we, untill we both were weary.
>
> (lines 76–79)[7]

The lines stress the similarity—almost the interchangeability—of the two poets. As usual pastoral disguising represents its shepherds as equal, joined by a common humanity and a common art. The "strange shepherd" is distinct from Colin only because he is *Cynthia's* shepherd with knowledge of court, not for any other reason. Spenser minimizes present differences between the two in favor of the equality characterizing their earlier relationship. The equality stands out especially in the light of Spenser's dedication of *Colin Clout* to Ralegh where (as in the dedicatory sonnets to *The Faerie Queen*) he plays a simple pastoral figure for whom Ralegh is so immeasurably his superior that his poem is "*unworthie of [his] higher conceipt for the meanesse of the stile.* . . . "[8] If the dedication thus playfully exaggerates the distance between Spenser and Ralegh in the present of the 1590s, the poem exaggerates their relation in the early 1580s, when they were near equals.

In all likelihood, then, Spenser would not have seen Ralegh simply as a patron come over to help him to the presence of the queen, nor simply as fellow poet engaged on a common literary enterprise. Rather, he was a former companion and equal who had *made himself* a great courtier. (Spenser would have been able to say "I knew him when. . . . ") Ralegh had taken a particular path, using his wit to woo his sovereign, while Spenser had taken another and had written the first three books of *The Faerie Queene*.

II

In 1589 Ralegh's relation with the queen was under strain. Three years earlier Robert Devereux, the young earl of Essex, had come seriously to Elizabeth's attention, becoming her last important favorite. He was pleasing, charismatic, better educated and far better born than Ralegh, the eldest son of an aristocratic family: he was, as Spenser addressed him for *his* dedicatory sonnet, *"the most honourable and excellent Lo. the Earl of Essex*. Great Maister of the Horse to her Highnesse, and knight of the Noble order of the Garter, &tc." In 1589 he was 24 to Ralegh's 37. There was immediate rivalry between the two proud, ambitious courtiers: Essex resented and scorned the older man. When in 1589 Ralegh left for Ireland, one court gossip suggested that Essex had "chased" him there.[9] Whether or not the statement was true, it suggests the rivalry was common knowledge at court. When Ralegh returned from Ireland in the fall of 1589 he brought Spenser with him, and while he may have wished to see talent rewarded, it would have been at the same time a feather in his cap to introduce to Elizabeth the author of the often-reprinted *Shepherds Calender*, who had written an epic in her praise.

Ralegh's sonnets commending the epic suggest that in introducing Spenser, Ralegh also has his own stock in mind. Both poems are intended primarily for the queen. Indeed, they don't make much sense as rhetorical praises without the queen as audience, since they focus so little on Spenser and so much on Elizabeth. "Uppon this conceipt of the *Faerie Queene*" envisions the graces abandoning the tomb of Petrarch's Laura to follow the Faerie Queene, "at whose approach the soule of Petrarke wept."[10] Here the conquest of Petrarch by Spenser (one line) receives less attention than the conquest of Laura by Elizabeth, the Faerie Queene (nine lines). Ralegh envisions Spenser as a love-poet, Petrarch's rival, concerned primarily with praise of his royal mistress, and only in the couplet does he mention that in the heavens *"Homer's* sprite did tremble all for griefe/And curst th'accesse of that celestiall thiefe" (lines 13–14) Here Homer as epic poet is overgone by Spenser—or is he? Is the "celestiall thiefe" Spenser or Elizabeth, the Faerie Queene herself, who has stolen Laura's graces? I think that the sonnet leaves it unclear: if the the queen didn't like the compliment, Ralegh could always say the thief is not his queen but his friend the poet.

The second poem of compliment is even more obviously concerned with Elizabeth. It argues, speaking to Spenser, that "if thou hast formed right true virtues face herein:/Virtue herself can best descerne, to whom they written been" (lines 3–4). Virtue herself is of course the queen, and the poem continues to develop an account of how she is both the model and the judge of all Spenser's virtues. It may be, as Wayne Erickson has argued, that there is an implicit challenge here to the queen to live up to the idealized portrait in Spenser's poem.[11] But it seems the primary thrust of the compliment is to delight the queen by celebrating her, and the event of the publication of this epic in her honor gave Ralegh another opportunity to do so.

III

What was Spenser's part in all this? We know little for sure. He had come from Ireland with Ralegh as his patron—at least he suggests as much in the dedication to *Colin Clouts Come Home Againe* as well as in the text—and had probably presented his poem to the queen—or would soon do so. It seems likely that he knew Ralegh's agenda. But it's striking how clearly Spenser keeps his independence, remaining neutral in the Raleigh-Essex conflict. Spenser's dedicatory sonnet to the earl is one of the original eight written for the book, not added hastily afterward. It addresses Essex's "virtues excellent" which "merit a most famous Poets wit", and suggests that when his muse moves on to "the last praises of this Faery Queene/Then shall it make more famous memory/Of thy heroic parts, such as they beene." (lines 10–12) None of the other dedications offer to include the subject (as Spenser had Ralegh) into later installments of the epic. (The poem to Walsingham suggests that Spenser may someday write his praises as well, but not in *The Faerie Queene*.) Perhaps Spenser already saw Essex as a potential Protestant hero, ready for resolute action in Ireland. He was certainly not going to move into an anti-Essex camp.

Spenser's poem to Ralegh sets itself off from the other dedicatory poems in several ways. It's considerably richer in its density of image and affect, and it's also a much *trickier* poem, a work in which tone and intention are harder to determine. Its trickiness comes partly from the ambiguity of its central images, and partly from its syntax. After four lines of seemingly rhetorical questions, the poem launches into an eight-line sentence, much of which consists of floating clauses that complicate, limit, and even undercut what the primary clause seems to say.

The poem is built around the opposition of Spenser and Ralegh. On one reading the opposition is simply an extreme instance of the humility *topos* that occurs in so many of the dedicatory sonnets: it claims that with his greater talents Ralegh should have written *The Faerie Queene* or a similar poem of praise, but that until he does so Spenser's poem will have to do. But it also insists, I think, that it's better to write *The Faerie Queene* than to write Ralegh's kind of poetry.

The sonnet begins with the difference between the two poets:

> To thee that art the sommers Nightingale,
>   Thy soveraine Goddesses most deare delight,
>   Why doe I send this rusticke Madrigale,
>   That may thy tunefull eare unseason quite?

(lines 1–4)

Spenser stresses Ralegh's sophisticated melodiousness, linking it with his position as his "sovereigne Goddessess most deare delight." Ralegh is *her* nightingale. Spenser, by contrast offers this sophisticated courtly singer an uncourtly "rusticke Madrigale" whose unfashionable, wintry harshness might unseason Ralegh's tuneful summer ear. Yet this is hyperbole meant to be seen through. On the one hand the art of the passage belies its explicit humility: the language with its pattern of long vowels is self-consciously melodious and decorative. If this is a simple madrigal, what's a sophisticated one? On the other, the opposition of rustic and courtly brings with it the common opposition of country virtue and courtly elegance that is a staple of Renaissance satire.

The next three lines give Ralegh his highest compliment and simultaneously suggest the limitations of his superiority.

> Thou only fit this Argument to write,
>   In whose high thoughts Pleasure hath built her bowre,
>   And dainty love learnd sweetly to endite.

(lines 5–7)

The style of the poem abruptly rises as Spenser apostrophizes Ralegh, who is "only fit" to write Spenser's poem. But in showing Ralegh's fitness, the lines develop a paradox: Ralegh, Spenser says, possesses "high thoughts" in which "Pleasure has built her bowre." High thoughts suggest aspiration but pleasure's bower suggests the comfort of a valley, even a Bower of Bliss. Not all Spenserian bowers are lowly, of course. When I first read these lines I thought them a reference to the "lofty love" Piers advocates in *The Shepheardes Calender*. While pleasure often seduces in Spenser, it can also be a good: in the Garden of Adonis Pleasure appears as the child of Cupid and Psyche. There's even a comparable line in the *Amoretti*. Imagining the relation between the lovers as a place, Spenser adds: "There faith doth fearelesse dwell in brasen towre,/And spotlesse pleasure builds her sacred bowre" (*Am* 65 lines 13–14). Once more pleasure resides in a high place. Yet the contexts of these two images, and hence their meaning, differ greatly. The passage from the *Amoretti* images a relationship set off from the everyday world, differing from it in faith as well as pleasure. By contrast the account of Ralegh is concerned not to sanctify a relationship but to characterize a kind of poetry. The tension between the ideas of height and pleasure is, I believe now, deliberate. Ralegh possesses a naturally lofty mind, but has allowed easy pleasure (associated with the lowly, the enjoyable, the sensuous) to make it her bower. While he may not be dwelling with Acrasia, he's not using his gifts as they might be used.

After this apostrophe, Spenser reintroduces the opposition of the harsh, tuneless countryman and the melodious court singer:

> *My rimes I know unsavory and sowre,*
> *To tast the streames, that like a golden showre*
> *Flow from thy fruitfull head, of thy loves praise.*

> (lines 8–10)

Spenser's poetry is "unsavery and sowre," unable to taste like the water that Ralegh's imagination produces or (perhaps) unworthy to drink at the same fountain. But in stressing Ralegh's subject—"thy loves praise"—he also insists on the political object of his verse: the line reminds us that the love he sings is the source of his court career. The fruitfulness of Ralegh's imagination is important, but so are the ends to which he puts it. While Spenser the rustic may seem to say "I can't write your kind of poetry," he may mean, like Wyatt addressing his friend John Poins, "I won't."

One can, of course, argue that *The Faerie Queene* is also a poem praising Elizabeth—even a love poem to her.[12] I think that this idea lies beneath the next lines which further distance themselves from Ralegh by focussing on what he has not done.

> *Fitter perhaps to thonder Martiall stowre,*
> *When so thee list thy lofty Muse to raise:*
> *Yet till that thou thy Poeme wilt make knowne,*
> *Let thy faire Cinthias praise bee thus rudely showne.*
>
> (lines 11–14)

As I have argued elsewhere, I think that the first two lines suggest that Ralegh's real fitness is for "Martial stowre" the fierce wars as well as the faithful loves that animate Spenser's song.[13] "When so thee list thy lofty muse to raise" returns us to the stress on Ralegh's high thoughts. But Ralegh's height here is in the future: he still needs to raise his muse, and when he does he will not be writing court love poetry. He will be writing epic. The final couplet, however, reminds the reader that Ralegh has *not* written an epic or, for that matter, any major poem. Until he does so, Spenser's praise of Cynthia in *The Faerie Queene* will have to do. It turns out that this complex praise dwells at length on Ralegh's talents only to foreground the fact that Ralegh hasn't yet written the poem that would justify them.

In this context one needs to consider Spenser's attitude toward love-poetry of the kind Ralegh actually wrote, poems that functioned as a Petrarchan game for himself and the queen. Although Spenser treats love in every book he wrote except for the *Complaints*, his attitude toward this politicized flirtation is at best mixed. By and large the characters in Spenser's work engaged in love complaint—Colin Clout in *The Shepheardes Calender*, Ralegh's double Timeas in *The Faerie Queene*, Alcyon in *Daphnaida*, even the poet himself in the first half of the *Amoretti*—are treated with distancing comedy. True high thoughts don't vent themselves in complaint, or in Petrarchan games. When in *Colin Clouts Come Home Againe*, Colin describes the various court poets he comes eventually to Ralegh, the Shepheard of the Ocean. Unlike his extended and enthusiastic praise of poets like Alabaster and Daniel, he says of the strange shepherd only that the "spends his wit in loves consuming smart", adding "Full sweetly temperd is that Muse of his/That can empierce a princes mightie hart" (*CCCHA* lines 429–31). To spend one's wit is potentially to use it up, and the following lines reemphasize the peculiar temper of a muse created to move a sovereign mistress.

IV

In his seminal book on Renaissance "laureate" poets who, like Spenser, Jonson, and Milton model themselves on the great classical figures, asserting that their art has a national dignity and purpose, Richard Helgerson distinguishes such laureates from poets he calls "amateurs."[14] The latter don't concern themselves with publishing, and see their poetry as part of and subsidiary to their court careers, an advertisement of wit and ability. Ralegh is the most pointed example of such an amateur. For Spenser it was necessary to insist on the importance of poetry—on the vocation that he had chosen—and so the mild censure of Ralegh here has behind it an attempt to clear a place in the world for his own view of art. Amateur status was, after all, familiar to everyone in 1590; it was the idea that poetry was a serious business that looked strange. It led Spenser to insist, quietly in this case, more shrilly elsewhere in poems like *The Teares of the Muses*, that poetry was more than the amateurs were willing to admit.

Spenser's insistence here on keeping his distance from Ralegh, refusing to engage in elaborate adulation, is consistent with the other portraits of Ralegh he would draw in the later *Faerie Queene* and in *Colin Clouts Come Home Againe*. It's of a piece, too, with Spenser's refusal when Ralegh had incurred the Queene's anger, to abandon his former patron. Spenser could simply have struck Timeas from the second half of *The Faerie Queene*. Instead he chose to stage the episode of the queen's anger in his poem, and to suggest that it was misguided. These various acts share a common stubbornness which is one of Spenser's most enduring characteristics, a refusal to abandon a position he feels is right. In a recent essay on his court career, F. J. Levy comments that Spenser "never understood the political system at court well enough to manipulate it."[15] It may have been a matter of temperament rather than one of understanding: Spenser insists stubbornly on the rightness of his own way, and often enough on the wrongness of the alternatives. Morally, as aesthetically, this stubbornness marks his poetry.

Smith College

NOTES

1. "Spenser's Raleghs" *Studies in Philology* 87 (1990): 341–62.
2. See Wayne Erickson, "Spenser's Letter to Ralegh and the Literary Politics of *The Faerie Queene's* 1590 Publication," *Spenser Studies* 10 (1989): 139–74; "Spenser

and His Friends Stage a Publishing Event: Praise, Play and Warning in the Commendatory Verses to the 1590 *Faerie Queene*," *Renaissance Papers 1997* ed. T. H. Howard-Hill and Philip Rollinson (Published for the Southeastern Renaissance Conference by Camden House, 1997), 13–22; and Jeffrey B. Morris, "Poetic Counsels: the Poet-Patron Relationship of Spenser and Ralegh," Diss. Penn. State, 1993.

3. *Spenser's Prose Works* ed. Rudolf Gottfried, vol 9 of *The Works of Edmund Spenser: A Variorum Edition* ed. Edwin Greenlaw et al. (Baltimore. Johns Hopkins University Press, 1932–49), p.161.

4. In "Spenser and Ralegh", *ELH* 1 (1934): 37–60, still the best biographical account of the relationship, Katherine Koller comes to this conclusion.

5. Quoted in J. H. Adamson and H. F. Folland, *The Shepheard of the Ocean* (Boston: Gambet, 1969), p.75.

6. On the position of secretary, see Richard Rambuss, *Spenser's Secret Career* (Cambridge, England: Cambridge University Press, 1993), esp. 31–48; for what it would have meant for Spenser to obtain this appointment see "Factions and Fictions: Spenser's Reflections of and on Elizabethan Politics" in Judith Anderson et al., eds, *Spenser and the Subject of Biography* (Amherst: University of Massachusetts Press, 1996), pp.31–44.

7. Quotations from Spenser's Shorter Poems are taken from *The Yale Edition of the Shorter Poems of Edmund Spenser* ed. William A. Oram et al. (New Haven: Yale University Press, 1989).

8. *Shorter Poems*, p.525.

9. Adamson and Folland, p. 169.

10. Line 7. Quotations from Ralegh's commendatory and Spenser's dedicatory sonnets are taken from Edmund Spenser, *The Faerie Queene* ed. Thomas P. Roche, Jr. (Harmondsworth: Penguin Books, 1978).

11. See Erickson, "Spenser's Letter to Ralegh . . . . "

12. See Thomas Cain, Praise in *The Faerie Queene* (Lincoln: University of Nebraska Press, 1978).

13. "Fitter" may of course look back to "thou only fit" and reemphasize that Ralegh is fitter than Spenser to write his epic. But then the "perhaps" would be unnecessary: it would, indeed, weaken Spenser's earlier compliment.

14. *Self-Crowned Laureates: Spenser, Jonson, Milton and the Literary System* (Berkeley: University of California Press, 1983), pp. 4–11.

15. "Spenser and Court Humanism" in *Spenser and the Subject of Biography*, p. 75.

WAYNE ERICKSON

Spenser Reads Ralegh's Poetry in(to) the 1590 *Faerie Queene*

In his dedicatory sonnet to Walter Ralegh and in the Proem to Book 3, Edmund Spenser characterizes Ralegh's poetry, situates it within a discussion of genre, and asserts Ralegh's preeminence as the appropriate singer of Cynthia's praise, the only person truly capable of writing Spenser's "Argument." Spenser flatters his friend and patron and even offers some advice, but he also engages Ralegh in intellectual play, as Ralegh engages Spenser in his two commendatory verses. These men, culturally visible personalities at crucial moments in their careers, seize the opportunity of Spenser's momentous publishing event to have some mildly dangerous fun, partly at the expense of the queen who apparently inspires their poetry and controls their lives. The tone of Spenser's passages is, at best, ambiguous: the sensuous language describing Ralegh's poetry and the potentially controversial evocations of genre and the queen demonstrate the kind of sophisticated ironic play so much a part of the proems and appended texts of the 1590 *Faerie Queene* and so obviously a part of Spenser's ongoing literary-cultural dialogue with Ralegh.

*E*DMUND SPENSER REFERS explicitly to Walter Ralegh's poetry—in particular his poetic representations of Queen Elizabeth—at least three times in the 1590 *Faerie Queene* volume. In his letter to his friend and patron, Spenser acknowledges Ralegh's "excellent conceipt of Cynthia" as the source from which he "fashion[s]" Belphoebe's "name," suggesting that Ralegh's Cynthia, like Spenser's Belphoebe, "expresse[s]" Elizabeth the "vertuous and beautifull Lady" rather than the "royall Queene."[1] In his dedicatory sonnet to Ralegh and in the Proem to Book 3, Spenser claims for Ralegh

175

certain poetic powers surpassing his own while taking upon himself some of the responsibilities of the public poet that Ralegh eschews. In these passages, Spenser characterizes Ralegh's poetry, situates it within a discussion of genre, and asserts the preeminence of Ralegh's poetic voice as the appropriate singer of Cynthia's mortal self—that is, the ablest praiser of the queen's natural beauty. Spenser stages various versions of decorum—epic, personal, and otherwise—while keeping the tone of the passages suggestively ambiguous. Some of what goes on here is dead serious literary-cultural work, but I'll focus in what follows on some readings that reflect a familiar Spenserian inclination toward serious fun. Specifically, the sensuous language describing Ralegh's poetry and the potentially problematical evocations of genre and the queen demonstrate the kind of sophisticated ironic play so much a part of the Proems and appended texts of the 1590 *Faerie Queene* and so central to Spenser's ongoing literary dialogue with Ralegh.

Recent critics who mention these passages almost invariably take it all very seriously: noting the delicious sensuousness of the imagery describing Ralegh's poetry, they satisfy their narrow assumptions about Spenser's Virgilian epic project by proposing that Spenser subtly or not so subtly chides Ralegh for writing erotic, courtly, amateur poetry rather than heroic national epic. Patrick Cheney argues that "Ralegh's verse inverts the *honourable* end of Spenser's own civic verse" (emphasis in original), and Jeffrey Morris agrees: "Spenser has seized upon the gaps and weaknesses in his patron's poetic efforts and has used them to forward his own identity as the right poet for the English nation."[2] William Oram, noting Spenser's suggestion in the dedicatory sonnet that Ralegh's poetic powers are "Fitter perhaps to thonder Martiall stowre," asserts absolutely: "Where Ralegh might in Helgerson's terms be a laureate poet he has settled for amateur status, and the decision is a mistake." Furthermore, reading the poem in the context of conventional historicist assumptions about Elizabethan social status and the culture of patronage, Oram argues that Spenser does not reprimand Ralegh "directly" because "Ralegh is a great man and his patron, and to stress the criticism would risk that necessary support."[3] I find it hard to imagine that Ralegh would miss the criticism if it is there. But James Bednarz, in his analysis of Ralegh's commendatory verse "A Vision vpon this conceipt of the *Faery Queene*," makes a similar assumption about Spenser's daunted or naive attitude toward his friend. In the course of interpreting Ralegh's Petrarchan spin on Spenser's epic, Bednarz sets up Spenser, "an outsider, a low-level colonial administrator," as the passive foil to Ralegh's assertion of originary power: "Ralegh usurps Arthur's central position in the epic," apparently without Spenser's knowledge or complicity.[4]

Spenser and Ralegh are probably teasing each other and perhaps engaging in some serious play concerning competitive analyses of their careers; indeed, Spenser may even be giving Ralegh some advice about the practical limitations of amateur, amatory lyric. As if Ralegh didn't already know, better than Spenser! Whatever the case, nothing Spenser writes about Ralegh in the 1590 *Faerie Queene* seems to have strained relations between them, considering the friendly playfulness of Spenser's dedication to Ralegh of *Colin Clouts Come Home Again* (dated 27 December 1591): "Sir, that you may see that I am not alwaies ydle as ye thinke, though not greatly well occupied, nor altogither undutiful, though not precisely officious, I make you present of this simple pastorall."[5] Of their careers, Spenser may be conceding, half-seriously, that he idles away his time writing pastoral poetry in Ireland while Ralegh does the queen's work in England. But here and in the 1590 *Faerie Queene*, both men know well the various possibilities of tone and emphasis in their literary dialogue with each other. They're culturally visible personalities at crucial moments in their careers, and they seize the opportunity of Spenser's momentous publishing event to, among other things, have some mildly dangerous fun with representations of genre and the queen in a poem officially advertised—in the Commendatory Verses, among other places—as an epic celebration of a divinely ordained monarch.

Concerning the genre issue, Spenser may be both serious and playfully ambiguous when, in the dedicatory sonnet, he suggests at least three different things about Ralegh's poetic powers: that Ralegh is "onely fit [Spenser's] Argument to write"; that Ralegh's verse and muse are "Fitter perhaps [than Spenser's] to thonder Martiall stowre"; and that Ralegh himself as well as his verse and muse is "Fitter perhaps to thonder Martiall stowre" than to allow his "high thoughts" to languish with "dainty loue" in "Pleasure['s] . . . bowre." But until Ralegh is willing either to "raise" his "lofty Muse" and write epic or "make knowne" his (Cynthia?) "Poeme," Spenser asks that Ralegh "Let thy faire Cinthias praises bee thus rudely showne"—in *The Faerie Queene*. The fact remains, however, that Spenser's dedicatory sonnet calls Ralegh more "fit" than Spenser to "write" Spenser's "Argument," whether in heroic or erotic form.

Ralegh may not be the only one unwilling or unable to "thonder Martiall stowre." In the Proem to Book 1, Spenser concedes that he is "far vnfitter" to play "trumpets sterne" than "Oaten reeds." And although he goes on to announce that "Fierce warres and faithfull loues shall moralize my song" (1), the wars, at least the imperial wars of heroic epic, do not materialize in the 1590 *Faerie Queene*. Indeed, at the one moment in the poem (including, perhaps, Book 5) when "bloudy *Mars*" might take the field—that is, just before Redcrosse fights the dragon—Spenser explicitly defers this kind of epic action to a part of the poem that he never writes, specifically, the second twelve books of *The Faerie Queene*. The poet invokes Clio (or Calliope) to "Come gently, but not with that mighty rage" that her "dreadfull trompe" announces: "Faire Goddesse lay that furious fit aside,/Till I of warres and bloudy *Mars* do sing,/And Briton fields with Sarazin bloud bedyde,/Twixt that great faery Queene and Paynim king" (I.xi.6–7). Similarly, in his dedicatory sonnet to Essex, which naturally points to Ralegh, Spenser again defers his writing heroic epic to the same indefinite future, when his muse "dare alofte to sty/To the last praises of this Faery Queene."

The point is that neither Spenser nor Ralegh engages his "lofty Muse" to "thonder Martiall stowre." This absence of heroic epic might be part of the reason why Spenser half-seriously tells Ralegh that he "send[s]" him *The Faerie Queene* as "this rusticke Madrigale," a short lyrical song about love written "rudely" in "vnsauory and sowre" "rimes."[6] In contrast, Ralegh sings "sweetly" in a "golden showre" of verse, which apparently makes him more "fit" than Spenser to "write" Spenser's—that is, *The Faerie Queene*'s—"Argument." Of course, one might legitimately dismiss Spenser's apparent disparagement of his poetic powers as a fairly radical instance of the humility *topos*, perhaps a corrective to the heightened praise he and his poem receive in the Commendatory Verses. Then again, Spenser may be speaking accurately about one version of stylistic and generic decorum. Elsewhere in the Dedicatory Sonnets, he calls *The Faerie Queene* "vnripe" and "wilde fruit, which saluage soyl hath bred"; a "rude rime" and "base Poeme" full of "verses base" inspired by a "lowly Muse"; and "Rude rymes, the which a rustick Muse did weaue/In sauadge soyle, far from Parnasso mount,/And roughly wrought in an vulearned Loome."[7] Spenser seems to be characterizing his poem as rough pastoral (collapsed into georgic?) conceived and written in Ireland, far from the source of his "Argument" and inspiration. Ralegh, on the other hand, writes "golden" amatory verse "of [his] loues praise" because he resides in intimate proximity to the source of his (and Spenser's) "Argument" and because, for better and worse, he remains for the time being his "soueraine Goddesses most deare delight." From the perspective of Spenser's dedicatory sonnet—and of Ralegh's first commendatory verse—the "Argument" of *The Faerie Queene* has little to do with "Martiall stowre" or even Gloriana and much to do with romance and with the beautiful mortal bodies of Belphoebe and Cynthia. In other words, pastoral complaint plus amatory celebration ("louers deare debate" [IV.Proem.1]) or, more specifically, Spenser's and Ralegh's erotic representations of the queen fill the void left by deferred heroic epic.

Spenser confronts his own struggle to represent the queen at the very beginning of *The Faerie Queene*, where his "argument" dominates the final stanza of the Proem to Book 1. After invoking Clio and Calliope and a "mother milde" Venus linked with disarmed Cupid and Mars (2–3), Spenser invokes Queen Elizabeth, the "true glorious type" of whom he names his "argument," which (according to the sonnet) only Ralegh is "fit . . . to write." Spenser is unfit to write his argument because he has an "afflicted stile": no doubt the "rusticke," "lowly," and "rude" style referred to in the Dedicatory Sonnets. But his "stile" is also his stylus, which attempts, relatively unsuccessfully, to write the words that properly and successfully pen the queen. Of course, these words, for whatever they're worth, do appear in "true glorious type" in the book the reader is holding. But the "stile," unlike the type, is "afflicted"; the pen has something wrong with it: it's daunted, blinded by the light of the queen's "faire beames," broken, impotent, haunted by the persistently unresolved thematic tensions between erotic and poetic production. The "afflicted stile" recalls the pipe Colin Clout breaks in January of the *Shepheardes Calender*, the refusal to write that paradoxically generates the poetry. But even before readers meet Colin, they view the woodcut with the damaged bagpipe. In short, Spenser implicitly coordinates poetry, pipe, pen, post, phallus; we are dealing with some kind of staged anxiety concerning impotence or castration, an inability to perform or produce.[8] Spenser can't pen Elizabeth, cannot generate the conceit he conceives, but Ralegh can conceive, perform, and produce.

In the dedicatory sonnet to Ralegh, Spenser—producer of unripe and wild fruit bred in savage and barren soil and issuing in unsavory and sour rhymes—celebrates the "golden showre" that "Flow[s] from [Ralegh's] fruitfull head." Ralegh's head, many of his contemporaries contend, was a big one. In Spenser's sonnet, it is the seat of Ralegh's "high thoughts," in which "Pleasure hath built her bowre," the source of the conceit of Cynthia. Its generative power allows Ralegh to shower the queen with dreams and gifts of gold and "fruitfullest *Virginia*" (II.Proem.2). The golden shower evokes Zeus as Phoebus' beams impregnating Danae, the same seminal conduit that pierces Chrysogone's womb to conceive Belphoebe and Amoret (III.vi.5–9). Ralegh's "fruitfull head," in contrast to Spenser's "afflicted stile," becomes the fountain from which flows the potent stream of Ocean's golden verse, poetry capable of accurately depicting the queen.[9]

In the Proem to Book 3, Spenser describes what Ralegh produces. He spends three stanzas convincing himself and his readers that no "liuing art" can "figure plaine" the "glorious portraict" of his "dred Soueraine." He therefore asks the queen's pardon "That I in coloured showes may shadow it,/And antique praises vnto present persons fit" (2–3). Finally, Spenser recommends that if Elizabeth would "couet" to see herself "pictured" in "liuing colours, and right hew" instead of "shadow[ed]" in "colourd showes," she should study the "sweet verse, with *Nectar* sprinckeled" of her "gracious seruant" Ralegh, whose depiction of "his heauens fairest light" sends Spenser, sounding pretty much like Colin Clout,[10] over the edge: "That with his melting sweetnesse rauished,/And with the wonder of her beames bright,/My senses lulled are in slomber of delight" (4). Ralegh's poetry, particularly his picture of Cynthia, creates in Spenser a ravished slumber by depicting a version of the same "faire beames" (I.Proem.4) that inspire—indeed, induce—Spenser's "afflicted stile," the beams that could, but don't, "raise [Spenser's] thoughts" (and his "stile") to the level of Ralegh's "high thoughts." Spenser's language here evokes Belphoebe's bower, the Garden of Adonis, Arthur's "dream or vision" of the Faery Queene (the source of Ralegh's commendatory verse), and various other places where Spenser uses the words *ravished, slumber, Nectar*, and *delicious*. Of course, readers of Spenser's poem—who, at this point, know nothing of the Garden of Adonis—remember the ravished slumbering of Redcrosse (I.vii.2–7) and of Arthur (I.ix.12–15) and, especially, having just left the Bower of Bliss, the picture of Verdant slumbering in Acrasia's lap (II.xii.72–73), reenacted in the various forms of Venus and Adonis in Book 3.

Faced with his own impotence and fear, Spenser lets the "delitious Poet" Ralegh, who can "picture" Cynthia "more liuely" and "more trew" than he, sexualize the queen's mortal body (III.Proem.4–5). Implicitly, tongue lightly in cheek, Spenser makes Ralegh the nominal source of any potentially subversive portraits of the queen. At the beginning of Book 3, these portraits include, among others, Arthur's faery queen, Belphoebe, and Acrasia. In his *Letter to Ralegh*, Spenser says that Arthur was "rauished" by the "excellent beauty" of the Faery Queen. In the poem, Arthur, like Spenser in the Proem to Book 3, is "rauished with delight" when the "Queene of Faeries" seduces him with "Most goodly glee and louely blandishment" (I.ix.14).[11] Aroused by this projection of his desire, this eroticized version of Gloriana, Arthur enters Faeryland to seek her out. In the first of his commendatory verses, taking his cue from Arthur's "dream or vision," Ralegh describes his own "Vision vpon this conceipt of the *Faery Queene*." Ralegh's poem posits a Petrarchan version of Spenser's (and Arthur's) faery queen that suggests Cynthia and, by extension, Belphoebe, the source of Timias's unremitting frustration.[12] Spenser's language describing Ralegh's poetry also evokes Belphoebe, whose "Sweet words, like dropping honny she did shed" (II.iii.24), as well as Braggadocchio's reaction to her: the "foolish man" is "fild with delight/Of her sweet words, that all his sence dismaid,/And with her wondrous beautie rauisht quight" (II.iii.42). The same sweet speech that ravishes Braggadocchio also ravishes Arthur and Timias and, in the form of Ralegh's poetry, ravishes Spenser as well. Ralegh, of course, has long since been ravished by Cynthia/ Belphoebe, who inspires his "sweet verse" and initiates Timias's obsession.[13] Spenser appears to adopt Ralegh's courtly language of erotic lyric to flesh out some of his representations of the queen.

At the end of the Proem to Book 3, just before he announces his intention to represent "[Ralegh's] fairest *Cynthia* . . . In mirrours more then one," Spenser asks Ralegh's leave to do so: "But let that same delitious Poet lend/A little leaue vnto a rusticke Muse/To sing his mistresse prayse, and let him mend,/If ought amis her liking may abuse" (5). Ralegh answers directly the second part of this request in his second commendatory verse, deferring all judging and mending to, respectively, Elizabeth and Spenser: "If thou hast beautie praysed, let her sole lookes diuine/Iudge if ought therein be amis, and mend it by her eine." Entering Spenser's game of serious play, Ralegh wryly instructs Spenser to attempt what he himself has no doubt often attempted: to figure out what Elizabeth is thinking by reading her eyes. Perhaps such a feat is possible, if Elizabeth wants them read, in which case Spenser might have a taste of Ralegh's experience: ecstatic joy if the eyes be pleased and crushing reprobation and disdain if they are not. In the latter case, of course—if there's something wrong with Spenser's poem—it's too late: neither Ralegh nor Spenser can mend an already published book. Furthermore, Ralegh commands Spenser to look directly into the living eyes that daunt his poetic powers, "beames bright" that he must "enfold/In couert vele, and wrap in shadowes light"; otherwise, "feeble eyes . . . could not endure" them "But would be dazled with exceeding light" (II.-Proem.5). Those eyes blind. If Spenser looked into those eyes, which is apparently what affected and afflicted his "stile" in the first place, he could not see to write; and if his readers had to look at a clear, naked, and direct image rather than a clouded, veiled, and mirrored one, they couldn't see to read. In fact, readers would probably be ravished, as Spenser is when he reads (or hears) Ralegh's depiction of Cynthia in "liuing colours" (III.Proem.4).

In his second commendatory verse, an oddly old-fashioned sonnet, Ralegh might be teasing Spenser because of Spenser's over-wrought—whether overly sensual or overly Neo-Platonic—charac-terization of his poetry and because Spenser calls him "that . . . delitious Poet." The word connotes sensual pleasure and, in its etymological relation to *delight*, something very alluring that entices one away from something else, with possible suggestions of wandering and delay. According to the OED, the word *delicious*, when applied to persons, suggests one "addicted to sensual indul-gence; voluptuous, luxurious, dainty." A "delitious harmony" intro-duces the Masque of Cupid (III.xii.6), and the "figures hideous" that Acrasia "hath transformed," says the Palmer, embody the "mournef-ull meed of ioyes delicious" (II.xii.85). Ravished by Ralegh's deli-cious representations of the queen and daunted by any attempt to paint Elizabeth the way she really is, Spenser leaves Gloriana offstage and concentrates on the erotic and romantic dynamics of his plot, though he creates a setting and larger plot structure capable of accom-modating heroic epic. But neither Spenser nor Ralegh seems ready to "thonder Martiall stowre" any time soon. Have they both, like Verdant, hung up their arms? And if Ralegh is already slumbering in Acrasia's lap, could his poetry, which lulls Spenser's senses into a slumber, pull Spenser into the Bower of Bliss as well?

I have tried to tease some interpretations out of passages in which I detect a subtly ironic tone of intellectual play, so, like Spenser and Ralegh, I am almost half joking about some of this. But I do think there is plenty of mildly subversive play going on between Spenser and Ralegh. I also think that Spenserians who have convinced them-selves that Spenser is always awed and intimidated by royal power or by the social status of someone like Ralegh and always absolutely committed to an imperial, Virgilian epic project should lighten up a bit (as Spenser often does) and notice how *The Faerie Queene* is at least as Ovidian and Ariostan as it is Virgilian. For much of its bulk, *The Faerie Queene* is about the problem of how to accommodate desire. Just as Redcrosse's vain murder of Errour lets error loose on the poem, so Guyon's vain and desperate annihilation of the Bower of Bliss lets the erotic allure of the Bower loose on the poem, making error a much more complicated matter, perhaps, than in the first two books.

Speaking of the Proem to Book 3, Jeffrey Morris contrasts Spens-er's "epic poetry of 'colored shows' and 'antique praises' with Ra-legh's poetry of 'living colors, and right hew,'" suggesting that

Spenser's poetry is serious, nation-building epic while Ralegh's is self-absorbed and courtly versifying.[14] But Spenser is not always quite so serious, even about his method of poetic composition: in the *Letter to Ralegh*, he says that he "colour[s]" his history with fiction to make his story "pleasing" and to provide the "variety of matter" that "the most part of men delight to read"; and he says that he serves up his "good discipline" "clowdily enwrapped in Allegoricall deuices" in order to "satisf[y]" the "vse of these dayes, [when] all things [are] accounted by their showes, and nothing esteemed of, that is not delightful and pleasing to commune sence."[15] According to this justification of his allegorical method, Spenser says he writes what most people enjoy reading, something beautiful, diverting, and pleasurable: the same kind of poetry—sweet, sensual, pictorial, even naturalistic—that he claims Ralegh writes better than he does.

Georgia State University

Notes

1.   All citations of Spenser's *Letter to Ralegh*, the Commendatory Verses, the Dedicatory Sonnets, and *The Faerie Queene* are to A. C. Hamilton, ed., *The Faerie Queene* (London: Longman, 1977). I do not cite page numbers for the *Letter*, the Verses, or the Sonnets; they are, respectively, 737–38, 739–40, and 741–43.

2.   Patrick Cheney, *Spenser's Famous Flight: A Renaissance Idea of a Literary Career* (Toronto: University of Toronto Press, 1993), 134. Jeffrey Morris, "Poetic Counsels: The Poet-Patron Relationship of Spenser and Ralegh" (PhD diss., Pennsylvania State University, 1993), 283.

3.   William A. Oram, "Spenser's Raleghs," *Studies in Philology* 87 (1990): 346. Oram has not, I think, substantially changed his mind about this since he wrote it.

4.   James P. Bednarz, "The Collaborator as Thief: Ralegh's (Re)Vision of *The Faerie Queene*, *ELH* 63 (1996): 285, 283; cf. Cheney 134. For a critique of Bednarz's treading of Spenser's and Ralegh's relationship, see Wayne Erickson, "Spenser and His Friends Stage a Publishing Event: Praise, Play, and Warning in the Commendatory Verses to the 1590 *Faerie Queene*." *Renaissance Papers* (1997): 15–17.

5.   *The Yale Edition of the Shorter Poems of Edmund Spenser*, ed. William Oram et al. (New Haven: Yale University Press, 1989), 525. Cf. Oram, "Spenser's Raleghs," 344–45.

6.   I assume, consistent with the convention, that when Spenser "sends" his poem to his dedicatees he offers them *The Faerie Queene*, though Bill Oram treats Spenser's sonnet to Ralegh as if the poem he sends is the sonnet itself. I can almost see a possible double meaning here, but in most of the dedicatory sonnets the poem Spenser sends, with hopes that his dedicatees will protect it, is clearly his epic.

7. Citations from sonnets to, respectively, Oxford, Ormond, Buckhurst, Essex, Carew, Walsingham, and Grey. Other sonnets play on genre and humility in various ways, from calling *The Faerie Queene* "ydle rimes" (both Hatton and Burghley) to calling it a "Pageaunt" of "lasting verse" (Howard, Hunsdon). Spenser advertises his poem, for the most part, as lowly matter while telling several of his dedicatees that they will live forever in his verse.

8. While I admit that the sexual connotation of *stile* is secondary to other meanings, I cannot help thinking of Amoret bound to a "brasen pillour" in the House of Busirane (III.xii.30). As a fearful and submissive version of the obedient wife who has been "cruelly pend" (III.xi.11) by a lustful man, her life has been written for her, and part of that life includes being shackled to her husband's penis.

One more possibility here: since a stile is also a set of steps for crossing a wall or fence, perhaps an "afflicted stile" inhibits Spenser's attempt to scale the wall from pastoral to epic. But maybe that is too much of a stretch.

9. I would not want to insist upon the bawdy connotation of *head*, but a few minutes with a historical dictionary of slang makes the suggestion hard to resist. Furthermore, as a fountain or source, *head* suggests generative power not unlike the "storme of raine" that "angry *Ioue* . . . Did poure into his Lemans lap," the event that initiates and generates the narrative of *The Faerie Queene* (I.i.6). As a counter example of sorts, there is the "fountaine" that simultaneously debilitates and arouses Redcrosse just before he is "Pourd out in loosenesse on the grassy grownd," expended and therefore allegorically ready for the timely entrance of Orgoglio (I.vii.3–7).

10. I find myself becoming more and more convinced that Colin Clout might legitimately be named the narrator of *The Faerie Queene.* There seem to be three levels of narration in the 1590 volume: various voices of Spenser the poet predominate in the appended matter; Colin just barely infiltrates the proems; and some version of a grown-up Colin comes to dominate the narration of the poem itself, which eventually causes a problem on Mount Acidale that I have not worked out. For the most part, Spenser's narrator sounds like some original take on Chaucer and Ariosto.

11. Of course, ravishment does include spiritual ecstacy, but Arthur is asleep, and Ralegh's poetry lulls Spenser into a slumber. Compare other instances of ravishment at I.i.41, I.xii.39, II.x.69, IV.v.14, VI.Proem.1, VI.ix.26, VI.x.30, VII.vii.12, and VII.vii.34.

12. See Bednarz, 281–90.

13. Morris suggests that "a sweet voice . . . can indicate deceptive speech," a quality he attributes to both Ralegh and Elizabeth (98). It's the kind of talk Colin thears at court.

14. Morris, 278.

15. See Wayne Erickson, "Spenser's Letter to Ralegh and the Literary Politics of *The Faerie Queene*'s 1590 Publication," *Spenser Studies* 10 (1992): 147–61.

JEROME S. DEES

Colin Clout and The Shepherd of the Ocean

Despite increased critical interest in the political and literary relations between Spenser and Ralegh, surprisingly little close attention has been paid, first, to Ralegh's side of the picture and, second, to the vexed question of the precise intertextual relations between *Colin Clout* and *The 11th: and last booke of the Ocean to Scinthia*. While readers have long recognized that Colin's brief account of the "lamentable lay" sung to him by the "straunge shepherd" in lines 163–71 of *Colin Clout* may well refer to *Ocean to Scinthia*, the uncertain dating of the two poems has led most recent critics and editors to be cautious. I argue that in fact Colin does refer to Ralegh's poem, that Ralegh's poem in turn engages Spenser's, and that both should be read as embodying a "dialogue" carried out over a period of time. In particular, the two poems echo each other in their handling of the Neoplatonic idea of love, and especially in the way Ocean repeatedly scrutinizes Colin's too-easy reliance on Neoplatonic idealism. His critique is based on Ralegh's own lived courtly experience and hinges on the two poets' epistemological differences. My aim in part is to adjust a critical tendency to privilege Spenser as a morally superior teacher of Ralegh.

SPENSER SCHOLARS have in the last decade or so become increasingly interested in the political and literary relations between Spenser and Sir Walter Ralegh. The impetus of the New Historicism has led in particular to a reexamination of ground covered by older historians in the first three decades of the century, and recent studies by William Oram, Patrick Cheney, James P. Bednarz, and Jeffrey B. Morris, among others, have greatly refined our understanding of the two

men's relationship.[1] Oram's comprehensive 1990 survey is typical of
the way most of this work has concentrated on Spenser's several
representations of his patron and friend in *Colin Clouts Come Home
Againe* and, more prominently, in *The Faerie Queene*. Given this flurry
of interest, it remains surprising how little close attention has been
paid, first, to Ralegh's side of the picture and, second, to the still-
muddy question of the precise intertextual relations between *Colin
Clout* and *The 11th: and last booke of the Ocean to Cynthia*. Recently,
in a review of Patrick Cheney's *Spenser's Famous Flight* I took Cheney
mildly to task for rightly claiming that Ralegh and Spenser "participate in a sustained and complex process of intertextual relation that
they uniquely forge out of the Elizabethan system of patronage," by
noting that he does less than justice to that complexity by concentrating too one-sidedly on Spenser, reducing Ralegh almost to a "background source." A similar one-sidedness obtains in Jeffrey Morris's
full-scale examination of the poet-patron relationship in his 1993
dissertation, to date our most throughgoing and nuanced study of
the subject.[2] Here I want to follow through on my claim by paying
closer attention to Ralegh's side of the relation, concentrating primarily on the evidence that *Ocean* itself directly engages the central
issues raised in Spenser's poem.

To make this argument, I'm going to assert the following scenario,
none of which can be proved, all of which is entirely plausible.
Some time before his visit to Kilcolman in 1589, Ralegh wrote a
"lamentable lay" (based in all likelihood on his being out of favor
with the queen in 1588–89), a poem that he read to Spenser and
that later became, or was assimilated into, *Ocean's Love to Cynthia*.[3]
Sometime between his visit to London to oversee the publication
of the 1590 *Faerie Queene* and late 1591, Spenser composed most,
but not quite all, of *Colin Clout*, a copy of which he sent to Ralegh
some time after his Dedication, dated 27 December 1591, though
he did not publish it at that time, probably because of the fallout
from Ralegh's 1592 marriage to Elizabeth Throckmorton.[4] In prison
following that marriage, Ralegh composed a fragment of a purported
twelve-book epic poem—the *Ocean* that we now have—making use
of earlier work alluded to in Spenser's poem.[5] His revision consisted
in part of giving the poem a pastoral frame, which was not originally
a part of his conception, though consistent with it, and which was
suggested to him largely by Spenser's poem. Ralegh sent or gave this
later fragment to his friend.[6] At some time before the publication of
Colin Clout in 1595, Spenser added two substantial passages that allude
to issues brought on by Ralegh's disgrace: the Mole-Mulla- Bregog
myth at 104–55 and the Neoplatonic cosmology at 835–94 (Ellrodt

19–23, 222). Ralegh's and Spenser's poems thus maintain a dialogue carried out over a period of three or more years.

Ralegh's poem engages Spenser's most immediately at the generic level. Although readers of *Ocean* have not agreed as to whether it should be called a "pastoral," it seems unassailable that its first 36 and last 26 lines constitute a pastoral frame.[7] Here it may be helpful to keep in mind, as Jeffrey Morris has reminded us, that pastoral is a genre preeminently suited to rivalry, providing "both a site of poetic competition and a space to argue safely on serious social questions" ("Poetic Counsels" 285). I suggest that the frame has been added to an earlier poem largely in response to Spenser's *Colin Clout*, with the purpose of calling attention to some of those "serious" political and poetic issues about which the two men disagree, especially as these center on a Neoplatonic "reading" of the meaning and social effects of love.

What mainly convinces me of this is the way Ralegh's "Thus home I draw, as deaths longe night draws onn" (509) engages not only Spenser's title, but the concluding stress that Colin also places on "the languours of my too long dying" (948).[8] Critics have not, I think, paid close enough attention to the similarities, both of substance and tone, between the way Colin speaks of Rosalind here and the way Ocean speaks of Cynthia throughout. But even without such conspicuous echoes, the pastoral images in Ralegh's two frame sections ask to be read as evoking the "waste" or "desert" landscape that, according to Hobbinol, Colin's departure created:

> Whilst thou was hence, all dead in dole did lie:
> The woods were heard to waile full many a sythe,
> And all their birds with silence did complaine:
> The fields with faded flowers did seeme to mourne,
> And all their flocks from feeding to refraine:
> The running waters wept for thy returne . . . .
>
> (22–27)

All of these conditions are intensified in Ocean's description of "The blossumes fallen, the sapp gon from the tree," and of being "Lost in the mudd of thos hygh flowing stremes/Which through more fayere feilds their courses bend"; his world is a wasteland in which "All in the shade yeven in the faire soon dayes/Vnder thos healthless trees I sytt alone,/Wher joyfull byrdds singe neither lovely layes/Nor Philomen recounts her direful mones" (13, 17–18, 25–28). It is impossible for me not to feel that, as his poem approaches its end, Ralegh's

"Vnfolde thy flockes, and leve them to the feilds/To feede on hylls, or dales, where likes them best" (497–98) deliberately *counter* Spenser's last line, in which "glooming skies" have "warnd" the assembled shepherds "to draw their bleating flocks to rest." As I see it, Ralegh's language here evokes Spenser's sense of subdued, sober resolution precisely so as to intensify the irresolution, the disorder, of his own Sisyphean state, where "Constraynt mee guides as old age drawes a stonn/Agaynst the hill, which over wayghty lyes/For feeble armes" (511–13).

The normal approach of scholars to Spenser's relationship with Ralegh is to privilege a morally superior Spenser, who is intent at every turn *either* on "correcting" by means of his humanist and "public" poetics the wrongheadedness of his patron's "private" politics of love, *or* on controlling the damage brought on by his friend's rash misguided application of them. This is a view that—while I think it fundamentally "correct"—does less than justice to Ralegh. He *is* rash, intemperate, arrogant; he repeatedly makes bad choices; and he does too often wallow in self-pity. But still there is something to be said for his side. And I want to do that here by teasing out what amounts to Ralegh's analysis and critique, from inside his own lived experience, of Spenser's habitual reliance on a Neoplatonic view of love.

Is it purely coincidental that both poems contain three sustained passages in which their personae are preoccupied with finding, unsuccessfully, a heightened, elevated language, capable of conveying adequately their sense of the meaning that "Cynthia" has for them? In *Ocean* these come at 344–55, at 390–415, and at 426–45; in *Colin Clout* at 336–47, at 596–615, and at 620–43. As will be obvious, I'm fudging a bit here, since the last two passages might well be considered a single one, merely interrupted for a moment, and also since Spenser's poem has a fourth passage, similarly elevated in tone (464–79) which, though it is really about Rosalind, is written in a way that can apply ambiguously to Cynthia as well. *Ocean* also contains a fourth passage (173–200) that, while not quite matching the others in its elevated rhetorical style and apparently serving a different purpose, bears on the discussion because of the subject matter it shares with them.

What all of these passages have in common is a reliance, in varying ways, upon Neoplatonic ideas of love and beauty, in Spenser's case affirming those ideas with straightforward ease, even aplomb, but in Ralegh's case subjecting them to a skeptical, at times tortured, scrutiny. It is in that tortured scrutiny that Ralegh engages Spenser's poem most deeply.

In the first of Spenser's passages, Colin tries to convey to his auditors something of the unexplainable nature of Cynthia's *glorie*. After rehearsing a series of emblematic analogues, all of which suggest the perfection of the circle ("crowne of lillies . . . circlet of a turtle true . . . faire Phebes garlond"), Colin admits that "vaine it is by paragone/Of earthly things, to judge of things divine"; rather than seek to *explain*, as he has been asked to do, the better response is "t'adore with humble *mind*,/The image of the heavens in shape humane" (344–45, 350–51; emphasis mine). There is a tinge of smugness here in the rather gratuitous way Colin has interjected an issue that he's unfitted to carry through on, and a sharp-witted Alexis catches him out, wryly suggesting that he seems more concerned to "upraise" himself than to address the more immediate desires of his auditors to be told, as Corylas has requested, "the rest of thine adventures"; in effect, Alexis is telling him, "Do not as some ungracious pastors do . . . ."[9]

The passage in Ralegh's poem that *answers* this one most directly is the one at the end of his poem beginning "But in my minde so is her love inclosde/And is thereof not only the best parte/But into it the essence is disposde . . . /Oh love (the more my wo) . . . " (426–29). Here he siezes on Spenser's word *mind* (after all, we might well have expected *heart*) in such a way as to indicate the difficulty, if not impossibility, of following that easy injunction "t'adore." Like Spenser, Ralegh also is seeking a series of "earthly" analogues for Cynthia. But with a crucial difference: whereas Spenser seeks to express something of the essence of Cynthia herself, Ralegh's focus is on "her love"—an ambiguous phrase in which we lose sight of both origin and direction. And in sharp contrast to Spenser's iconic images, his are resolutely "naturalistic": "Yeven as the moysture in each plant that growes,/Yeven as the soon vnto the frosen ground,/Yeven as the sweetness, to th' incarnate rose . . . ," Cynthia is "the sowle of that vnhappy minde/Which *being by nature made an Idell thought/* Begon yeven then to take immortall kynde/When first her vertues in thy spirrights wrought" (430–32, 438–41; my emphasis). It's as though Ralegh is saying "Eddie, my friend, let's take a different, less idealistic viewpoint. Suppose the divinity of which you speak is the wholly natural product in the human mind of 'an Idell thought'?" In fact, Cynthia is *in* Ralegh's mind in a way that is radically different from the way she may be said to be *in* Colin's mind. In discussing the Walsingham Ballad, Greenblatt notes that while the ballad employs a language expressing the "very heart" of the Neoplatonic system, "the *amor divinus* which 'possesses itself of the highest faculty in man, that is, the mind or intellect, and impels it to contemplate the intelligible

splendour of divine beauty,'" for Ralegh, "the essential content of
that system—the religious vision—has disappeared" (73–74). For
Ocean I would push this claim to its implied next level—that, in
effect, Relegh's and Spenser's poems operate according to different
epistemologies.

Before proceeding with my general aim of looking at examples
of where a commonly held language of Neoplatonism informs an
intertextual dynamic between the two poets, I'd like to put some
pressure on what I am claiming to be an epistemological difference,
by looking more closely at the way the two poems employ a complex
of closely related terms, including *mind, thoughts hink, conceit, speak,*
and *write.* In the second of Spenser's passages that I referred to, Colin
answers Aglaura's request to "finish [his] storie" of Cynthia's
"goodnesse and high grace" with another series of carefully balanced
iconic equivalences, devoting a quatrain each to her *words,* her *deeds,*
her *looks,* and her *thoughts,* the last of which are "like the fume of
Franckincence," rising

> In rolling globes up to the vauted skies.
> There she beholds with high aspiring thought,
> The cradle of her owne creation:
> Emongst the seats of Angels heavenly wrought,
> Much like an Angell in all forme and fashion.
>
> (608–15)

To Cuddie's quick objection that Colin is now flouting "decorum"
(he intends the word both socially and aesthetically) by making himself "mount so hie," Colin rejoins in a rhetoric even more "yrapt":

> For when I think of her as oft I ought,
> Then want I words to speake it fitly forth:
> And when I speake of her what I have thought,
> I cannot thinke according to her worth.
> Yet will I thinke of her, yet will I speake,
> So long as life my limbs doth hold together,
> And when as death these vitall bands shall breake,
> Her name recorded I will leave for ever.
>
> (624–31)

This exchange draws attention to a global effect that Cynthia has on

Colin: from her comes not only what capacity he has to "think" and to "speak" (feeble though he might profess those to be), but also both the *will* to speak and the *confidence* that his message will be efficacious: "And long while after I am dead and rotten . . . My layes made of her shall not be forgotten" (640–42).

Although Ralegh nowhere "answers" this passage directly, it is fair to say that it reverberates throughout his poem. He insists from the beginning that the problem he is concerned with is radically "mental," in fact solipsistic: there is no question of his speaking to the "living"; nor is it even the case that his "minde" can now "inhold" Cynthia's "spirrit" (though by implication it once could). What he now must deal with is merely "The Idea but restinge, of a wasted minde" (5–12). Even when Ralegh can write most positively of Cynthia, as in the following lines, she has no reality apart from his mental "invention" of her:

> O hopefull loue my object, and invention,
> Oh, trew desire the spurr of my consayte,
> Oh worthiest spirrit, my minds impulsion, . . .
> Oh, eyes transpersant, my affections bayte,
> Oh, princely forme, my fancies adamande,
> Devine consayte, my paynes acceptance. . . .

> (37–42)

These lines, of course, contain nothing that is incompatible with an assumed Neoplatonic reality—except that Ralegh makes it clear time and again that he has no certain grasp on whatever such an imagined reality might be. What he seems to be saying is that when reality is so radically mental, as the Neoplatonists claim, when the "eyes" of the "minde" are entrusted to "hold her beames / In every part trans-ferd by love's swift thought," obliterating the distinction between "Farr off or nire," between "in waking or in dreames," then what remains when the mind loses grip on that realilty, withers (85), drowns in "deapts of missery" (142), goes mad in an effort to "scourge mine owne consayte" (146)? Ralegh is here wrestling with a problem remarkably similar to that of Coleridge in the "Dejection" Ode.[10] My point is that by concentrating too closely on Ralegh's external biographical and political situation, to the exclusion of that strain of rationalistic "skeptical" thought by which an earlier genera-tion of readers knew him, we may blind ourselves to real intertextual connections.[11]

I want to look more closely now at what may be the most resonant moment in the two poems' intertextual dynamic, at *Colin Clout* 464–79 and *Ocean* 173–200, where Ralegh first and most self-consciously deploys the Neoplatonic theory of beauty. In Spenser's passage Colin is praising Rosalind in a way that, as many have noted, ambiguously evokes Cynthia as well. A major effect of this ambiguity is to suggest that one can successfully negotiate the boundaries between a public and a private devotion—boundaries that, by implication, Ralegh has failed to negotiate. This is not a happenstance ambiguity, but runs throughout the poem, and is nowhere more prominent than at poem's end, when Colin uses his crucial term for Cynthia in affirming Rosalind's "bright glorie."[12] Here at its midpoint, Colin avows that he is

> Vassal to one, whom all my dayes I serve;
> The beame of beautie sparkled from above,
> The floure of vertue and pure chastitee,
> The blossome of sweet joy and perfect love,
> The pearl of peerlesse grace and modestie:
> To her my thoughts I daily dedicate,
> To her my heart I nightly martyrize:
> To her my love I lowly do prostrate,
> To her my life I wholly sacrifice:
> My thought, my heart, my love, my life is shee
> And I hers ever onely, ever one
> One ever I all vowed hers to be. . . .

These lines resonate again and again throughout *Ocean*, though most explicitly in the lines cited, where Ralegh confesses that, while reason holds before his eyes ideal "images and forms," which teach him that

>   thos flames that rize
> From formes externall, cann no longer last,
> Than that thos seeming beauties hold in pryme
> Loves ground, his essence, and his emperye,

nevertheless, "his hearts desire," confined in time, cannot make the easy leap that Spenser advocates. It *"could not conceve/. . . A beawtie which tyme ripeth not/. . . A sweetness which woes wronges outwipeth not,/A vestall fire that burnes, but never wasteth,/. . . Blosumes*

of pride that cann nor vade nor fall" (181–92; my emphasis). Paradoxically, he goes on, these "perfections" were rather "the parents of
my sorrow and my envy," and, far from liberating, they are "Tirants
that in fetters tye/Their wounded vassalls, yet nor kill nor cure,/But
glory in their lasting missery" (196–98). The spiritual sublimation
that Spenser avows in *dedicate, martyrize, prostrate*, and *sacrifice*, are to
Ralegh merely the untenable "effects of pourfull emperye" (200).
Once again, Greenblatt has caught the essence of the problem: as
long as Ralegh was in favor, an "imaginative synthesis of public and
private" was possible, but only so long as Elizabeth deigned to be both
mistress and ruler (74). Both as lover and servant he was always—as he
now so painfully realizes—sat the mercy of her tyranny. Colin's poem
describes a situation in which the private and public, mistress and
ruler, since they remain discrete need never bring about the dilemma
that tears Ocean apart. Of course, we could say that Ralegh merely
gives vent here to a love-sickness, the "disease" that results from the
false, physical following of beauty that Bembo condemns near the
beginning of his Neoplatonic disquistion in Book IV of *The Courtier*.
But that would be too easy a reading. After all, the misery expressed
here is not physical. His pain resides precisely in a *mind* cut off from
the healing and revivifying spiritual currents in which his friend places
so much faith.

Spenser's central moment returns (whether repressed or not) in
Colin's paean to "loves perfection" at lines 775–822. The way to
that passage has been paved by an extended critique of corrupt court
life that concludes with an account of the falseness of love there. In
an enigmatic passage near his own poem's end, Ocean takes on
Spenser's view of love at court in a particularly powerful way. He says

My love was falce; my labors weare desayte.
Nor less then such they ar esteemde to bee,
A fraude bought att the prize of many woes,
A guile, whereof the profitts vnto mee—
Could it be thought premeditate for thos?

                                        (465–69)

The first line (Oakeshott says that its first four words are underlined
in original ink) seems to indict the queen and admit that all his
efforts were merely self-deceiving. But the next four lines unsettle
that reading by taking us outside Ocean's perspective to look at the
situation through the critical and envious eyes of other members of

the court—at which point we realize that line 465 is already implicitly a concession to their view that his love for Cynthia was merely a pretence in the service of those "profitts" that the heavily commercial vocabulary of the stanza (*esteemde, bought, prize*) underline. His picture of court is quite close to that painted in *Colin Clout*, where pervasive habits of "malice and . . . strife," and of "slaundring his well deeemed name,/Through leasings lewd" drive an analogous profit motive:

> So they themselves for praise of fools do sell,
> And all their wealth for painting on a wall;
> With price whereof, they buy a golden bell,
> And purchace highest rowmes in bowre and hall.
>
> (690, 695, 723–26)

As we recall, this extended piece of rhetorical blame provokes Corylas to wonder whether courtiers "love," thereby enabling Colin to posit a sharp distinction between the falseness of what they do and the truth of shepherds' love. It's the possibility of this distinction that is the real focus of Ralegh's attack, first in the passage discussed, then, more dramatically, in the lines that follow, both in the inverted Neoplatonic imagery that colors the last lines of the poem proper ("Thow lookest for light in vayne . . ./Strive then no more, bow down thy weery eyes,/Eyes, which to all thes woes thy hart have guided") and in the absolute psychological stasis of "She is gonn, Shee is lost! Shee is fovnd, she is ever faire" (489–93)!

The point has to do, finally, not with a difference in philosophical outlook, but with Neoplatonism's effect on the way the two men perceive themselves as existing within a "reality" that is its central concern. As Marion Campbell has shown, for Ralegh "identity" is conferred by the social system (237). That he has none apart from it is a condition consistent with the naturalistic epistemology that I've been examining. Colin may suffer from Rosalind's rejection of his love, but an idealism that permits him to discriminate the true from the false prevents him from being destroyed by it. Not so Ocean. Throughout his poem, and nowhere more forcefully than here at its end, one of Ralegh's determined aims has been to show his friend that the comforts of a distancing and consoling idealism are not for all.

In closing, I'd like to speculate briefly on what might have happened at the next stage of the dialogue, between Ralegh's composition of *Ocean* and Spenser's final, published version of *Colin Clout*. The standard interpretation of Colin's myth of Bregog and Mulla is that it allegorizes the effects of Ralegh's disastrous 1592 marriage, with an important piece of the evidence being the way the "merry tale" plays on the idea of water, Elizabeth's pet name for him. But I wonder whether the details of Bregog/Ralegh being a stream, and of old father Mole rolling down upon him "mightie stones" that "scatter" him "all to naught" and destroy his very name do not glance more pointedly at the dried-up and muddy streams that are so prominent in Ralegh's own poem. Similarly, I suspect strongly that the details of the Neoplatonic cosmology in *Colin Clout* likewise glance *specifically* at the way Ralegh has dealt with what he has seen to be Spenser's too easy assumptions about the ideal nature of reality. I think the passage does so in three ways. First, in opposition to Ralegh's emphasis on the dessicating and withering effects of love, Spenser reaffirms its fruitful and revivifying nature. Second, Spenser reaffirms his belief that in man, the highest of Love's creations, Love works its creative and healing effects through reason and the mind. Finally, Spenser calls pointed attention to the fact that to deny this basic principle of cosmic concord is to doom oneself to outlawry: "Ne mongst true lovers they shall *place* inherit,/But as *exuls* out of his court be thrust" (893–94; my emphasis). Not only does this couplet circle back to Bregog's loss of place and name, it also, in a sense, ratifies Ralegh's self-presentation and closes the circle of debate that the two friends have carried forth in these remarkable poems.

Kansas State University

NOTES

1.   William A. Oram, "Spenser's Raleghs," *SP* 87 (1990): 341–62; Patrick Cheney, *Spenser's Famous Flight: A Renaissance Idea of a Literary Career* (Toronto: University of Toronto Press, 1993): 112–48; James P. Bednarz, "Ralegh in Spenser's Historical Allegory," *Spenser Studies: A Renaissance Poetry Annual* 4 (1984): 49–70, and "The Collaborator as Thief: Ralegh's (Re)Vision of *The Faerie Queene, ELH* 63 (1996): 297–307; Jeffrey B. Morris, "To (Re)Fashion a Gentleman: Ralegh's Disgrace in Spenser's Legend of Courtesy," *SP* 94 (Winter 1997): 38–58. The seminal article on Ralegh's and Spenser's relationship is that of Katherine Koller, "Spenser and Ralegh," *ELH* 1 (1934): 37–60. Also valuable, particularly from the perspective of Ralegh, is Marion Campbell, "Inscribing Imperfection: Sir Walter Ralegh and the Elizabethan Court," *ELR* 20 (1990): 233–53. See also Donald Cheney, "Spenser's Fortieth Birthday and Related Fictions," *Spenser Studies: A Renaissance Poetry Annual* 4 (1984): 3–31; Walter Oakeshott, *The Queen and the Poet* (London: Faber and Faber, 1960: 81–99; and J. Christopher Warner, "Poetry and Praise in *Colin Clouts Come Home Againe* (1595), *SP* 94 (197): 368–81.

2.   See Dees, *JEGP* 96 (1997): 126; Morris, "Poetic Counsels: The Poet-Patron Relationship of Spenser and Ralegh" (Pennsylvania State University, 1993), especially chapter 5, "Orphic Counsels: Friendship, Patronage, and Poetic Rivalry" passim.

3.   For arguments concerning this point and relevant bibliography, see Oram, "Spenser's Raleghs," 342–43, note 3 and 346–49; see also his notes to lines 164–71 of the poem in *The Yale Edition of the Shorter Poems of Edmund Spenser* (New Haven: Yale University Press, 1989), 532–33.

4.   The evidence that Spenser revised *Colin Clout* shortly before its publication, first suggested by Koller, is developed in detail by Robert Ellrodt in *Neoplatonism in the Poetry of Spenser* (Geneva: Librarie E. Droz, 1960).

5.   Oakeshott (131–38) provides a detailed summary of evidence regarding the dating of the fragment contained in the Hatfield MS, concluding that "there is no doubt that this poem was written, in the tower, in the late summer of 1592."

6.   Spenser was "absent" from Cork in August and September 1592 and, according to Willy Maley, was "possibly in England," which would have put him there at about the time of Ralegh's release from prison; see *A Spenser Chronology* (Lanham: Barnes & Noble, 1994), 58.

7.   For Stephen Greenblatt the poem is essentially "anti-pastoral," continuing a "theme that concerned Ralegh before *Ocean to Cynthia*"; see *Sir Walter Ralegh: The Renaissance Man and His Roles* (New Haven: Yale University Press, 1973), 80–85.

8.   All citations are to *The Poems of Sir Walter Ralegh*, ed. Agnes Latham (Cambridge: Harvard University Press, 1962) and to *The Yale Edition* cited in note 3.

9.   Throughout I use Spenser/Colin and Ralegh/Ocean interchangeably because for my purposes the distinction does not finally matter. Even if, as Bill Oram insisted at the Toronto conference, the poem's Neoplatonism is Colin's and not Spenser's, who stands at some ironic distance from it (by implication reducing *my* Ralegh to an uncharacteristically imperceptive reader), we can still say that Ocean, from whom Ralegh stands at some ironic distance, works within the rules of the serio-playful game that Wayne Erickson proposes. However many layers of irony we may need to peel away, the philosophical point at issue remains constant.

10.   It seems important that while Colin's customary pose is that of "speaking," Ocean's is that of "writing," but just how is not yet clear to me.

11.   The notion of Ralegh's intellectual skepticism, first advanced by Arthur Acheson, *Shakespeare and the Rival Poet* (London: John Lane, 1903) is developed at length by Muriel Bradbrook, *The School of Night: A Study in the Literary Relations of Sir Walter Ralegh* (Cambridge: Cambridge University Press, 1936); rpt New York: Russell & Russell, 1965), and by Frances A. Yates, *A Study of* Love's Labors Lost (Cambridge: Cambridge University Press, 1936).

12.   For the opposed idea that Spenser's audience would not have seen ambiguity because they would have recognized his different rhetorical strategies for presenting Cynthia and Rosalind, see Warner (note 1).

MICHAEL RUDICK

Three Views on Ralegh and Spenser: A Comment

This comment proposes some adjustments to the views on Spenser and Ralegh argued by Dees, Erickson, and Oram. In general, the comment urges that the differences in their poetic projects not be perceived as categorically opposed. Ralegh's antiplatonism in the twenty-first book of "Cynthia" is not a consistent stance, and the contrast of Ralegh the poet of pleasure against Spenser the poet of morality can be drawn too sharply. Any difference of intent is much diminished by both poets' agreement on the nature of their putative audience, Queen Elizabeth. The agreement is evident in both poets' commendations of each other.

ALL THREE WRITERS explore what similarities and differences there may be between the two poets' understandings of their respective projects. Most valuable is the approach implicit in all three contributions: in different degrees and with different emphases, all imagine Ralegh and Spenser in a kind of conversation, giving voice, to themselves and their readers, to what they have observed in each other's work and—the point I wish to emphasize—testing what they have found against the fiction (close enough to fact) maintained by both, that is, that their poems' inspiration is Queen Elizabeth, that, moreover, she is their subject and their audience.

Jerome Dees's contribution asks us to consider the two poets' differing intellectual positions. He fruitfully proposes that the twenty-first book of "Cynthia" and *Colin Clouts Come Home Againe* be read as a dialogue of opposed stances toward neoplatonic love: Spenser as its faithful partisan, Ralegh as the sceptic. The passages from both poems that Dees juxtaposes reward consideration, and do support the claim that the two poems "operate according to different epistemologies" of Ralegh's poem is less settled and less than the absolute contrary of Spenser's. The adjustment to Dees's thesis that I wish to suggest is based on a perception of movement in the poem, the meditation of one who wavers between the Platonic and antiplatonic poles, the former being what devotion to Cynthia should and did promote, the latter being what experience has taught.

One example: In the twenty-first book of "Cynthia," vv. 438–41, Ocean addresses Love,

> Thow art the sowle of that unhappy minde
> which beinge by nature made an Idell thought
> begann yeven then to take immortall kynde
> when first her vertues in thy spirrights wrought, . . .[1]

Dees appears to read this as Ocean's statement that the presence of Cynthia in his mind is an adventitious notion rather than a divine reality that prompts immortal longings. Could we paraphrase differently, recognizing the tincture of an Aristotelean, rather than a Platonic, concept behind the thought? "Love became my soul (identity, formal cause), my soul which, in its natural state, was merely idle (non-intellective); but from that moment, my immortal potential became evident through the effects of Cynthia's immortal virtues." Allow this to reflect not scepticism, but a once-powerful, perhaps Spenserian, faith in transcendence, even if ripe for disillusion under the circumstance of loss.

Dees argues the source of the disillusion to be the condition "of a wasted [i.e., destroyed or annihilated] minde" (26.12). He finds Ralegh to be confessing sceptically the limitation of his own intellectual power, and hence finds that the prominent evocations of Platonism (e.g., 173–200) are framed such to undercut their own claims to describe and credit a transcendent reality. The argument cannot be made at length here, but I suggest that the appeal of Spenserian Platonism had not altogether lost its shine for Ralegh, however elusive it may have been to him in the moment represented by this poem. He reminds himself at the opening of "an Idea but restinge [i.e., remaining]" (26.12) and later of "Th'Idea remayninge of thos golden ages" (26.348).[2] The twenty-first book of "Cynthia" is a paramount source of Dees's recognition of Ralegh's penchant to "wallow in self-pity." One symptom of that in the poem is the repeated complaint against how cruel a master Platonism is to the poet. The characteristic sequence (26.436–73 is an example) is to show how, in the poet's mind, the timeless ideas of Beauty, Virtue, and so forth, struggle with the personified Sorrow working to efface or replace them.

Both Spenser and Ralegh show their awareness of having to deal with the mortal and immortal parts of their queen. Dees finds Spenser comfortable with his Platonic synthesis of mortal and immortal, mistress and sovereign, but it might be worth asking if Spenser does not sometimes betray a hint of Ralegh's problem. Would it be un-Spenserian to think of the Rosalind who calls for martyrdom, prostration, and sacrifice (*CCCHA*, 473ff.) as a figure for the costs exacted by platonizing the object of love?

The differences between William Oram and Wayne Erickson are ones of degree. Oram argues a clean separation of the poets' ways, while Erickson prefers to see a more loosely defined and perhaps ambiguous relation of difference. Observing the external conditions of each man in 1590, Oram points to their social inequality and infers this as one of Spenser's cues to articulate their poetic differences and to counter Ralegh's social superiority with his own poetic superiority. I find this problematic because I do not find in the poetry under scrutiny the same stress on difference of social status that Oram does. In his commendations of *The Faerie Queene,* Ralegh does not write as Spenser's superior. Thus Spenser would have no cause to write as Ralegh's inferior, though he could do so when his address, like Ralegh's, was governed by poetic roles rather than social positions, the former calling for humility. We should notice that, of the sixteen persons to whom Spenser wrote dedicatory sonnets, Ralegh stands near or at the bottom in power and rank—he has precedence of play only over the women—and is the only one addressed for poetry, not for nobility or office or patronage.

Both Oram and Erickson foreground the tensions between erotic poetry and heroic poetry, which Spenser's sonnet and proem to Book III obliquely express. But Erickson sees a certain "ironic play" as characteristic of the *parerga* to the 1590 *Faerie Queene* and the comments written into the poem. Against Oram's reading them as seriously-intended critique of Ralegh's poetry, he reminds us of Spenser's more immediate project: to place himself in the company of those who celebrate the queen and thereby to control (or at least to influence) the reception of his epic.

Ralegh, too, engages the issue of heroic and erotic poetry; his commendatory sonnet asserts Spenser's preeminence in both, as *The Faerie Queene* steals precedence from both Petrarch and Homer. The sonnet's stress on Spenser as Petrarch's supplantor indicates that Ralegh would not have readers take seriously Spenser's self-deprecation in the poetry of amorous pleasure. If Spenser thought "Pleasure hath built her bowre" in Ralegh's poetry, Ralegh may have accepted this, but he is unlikely to have thought Spenser lagged in this department—whether or not he appreciated, as Oram does, Spenser's plural understandings of pleasure in the The Faerie Queene. I do not see much irony either in Ralegh's sonnet or in his commendation in poulter's measure that follows it, and so I cannot quite credit Erickson's belief that the two poets were "teasing each other," unless affecting modesty or professing admiration self-consciously in a public arena is teasing. The exchange of compliments before a readership entails a certain amount of serious business, and this puts limits on how much that readership may itself be teased.

None of this makes Oram wrong; with respect to what might affect his historical status, Spenser surely believed that writing a national epic on the Vergilian model was a worthier use of poetic talent than writing poetry "to feede youthes fancie and the flocking fry" (SC, Oct. 14).[3] But we should ask Oram's question—if Ralegh is the poet of pleasure, did Spenser think his kind of achievement inimical to heroic poetry?—as it was circumstanced. In the Letter to Ralegh, Spenser justifies the allegorical rendition of "good discipline" as an accommodation to "the use of these dayes" which esteem nothing "that is not delightfull and pleasing to commune sense." We may read the phrase in at least two ways: "commune sense" as the normal sensory apparatus of all persons (sensus communis, or "commune sense" as the "vulgar" or "ordinary" reception of mimetic stimuli like poetry. Let me isolate two places in Ralegh's poetry to the queen where he refers to the recipient's pleasure as his effect.

In the earlier lyric, "Now we have present made," the poet complains that praising the queen's immutable nature is impossible work for a mutable being; her praise must be left to "Love, nature, and perfection"; further, that if Love could write with an angel's quill or if the Muses could sing as Love would have them do, then

> perchance he could endyte
> to pleas all other sence
> butt loves and woes expens
> Sorrow cann only write

> (23.25–28)[4]

The phrase "all other sence" seems, in the context, to mean "all senses other than hers," that is, the queen's. Therefore, the queen as audience requires a more exalted verse than Love, even assisted, can muster, however much ordinary beings might find themselves pleased by it; on the other hand, the poet has Sorrow to help him quite adequately record his love and woe as he experiences them. In the later passage, from the twenty-first Book of "Cynthia," Ocean describes Cynthia as she was to him before his loss ("the seat of joyes, and loves abundance"), and speaks of the verse this produced:

> Out of that mass of mirakells, my Muse,
> gathered thos floures, to her pure sences pleasinge
> out of her eyes (the store of joyes) did chuse
> equall delights, my sorrowes counterpoysinge
>
> (26.45–58)

If the earlier passage expresses futility, the effect here is more successful; his Muse pleased his listener's "pure sences" and composed verse delightful to Cynthia because answerable to the joy and illumination of gazing at her eyes. Common to both passages is the assertion that Queen Elizabeth is a unique audience, that poetry addressed to her had to meet an unconventional standard if it was to give pleasure.

Whatever Spenser meant by "commune sence," it was, to Ralegh, not a factor in the queen's reception of poetry. Her senses were neither normal nor vulgar, and so it required a special talent (or supernatural assistance) to please her in the representation of her own surpassing excellence, that is, to get beyond mere flattery (see 23.21–24). If Spenser wished to commend Ralegh as the poet of pleasure par excellence because he could delight "commune sense," he is likely to have missed Ralegh's stated notion of a poetic project (at least as far as poetry to the queen was concerned). If, on the other hand, Spenser recognized Ralegh's talent, or even just the ideal poetic required by his estimate of the queen as audience, why would he wish to distinguish this achievement from his own project? Do "liuing colours, and right hew" (FQ, III.proem.4) necessarily denote a sensuousness directed at the pleasure of an ordinary audience?

In the poulter's measure commendation, Ralegh refers directly to the distinction between audiences, the ordinary ("meaner wits") versus Spenser's object of representation and his ultimate addressee: "If thou hast formed right true vertues face herein: / Vertue herself can best discerne, to whom they writen bin" (3.3–4). The only judge of Spenser's success, then, and the only corrector of what faults he may have committed, is the queen herself, in whose "Princely mind" virtue, temperance, and chastity are comprehended.[5] Ralegh acknowledges the difficulty; much as in the earlier lyric quoted above, the queen's "vertue can not be exprest, but by an Angels quill" (3.12). Spenser says much the same about inexpressibility in III.proem. 3. The poulter's measure commendation is surely Ralegh's answer to Spenser's offer (III. proem.5) to have him, Ralegh, "mend / If ought amis her liking may abuse." He reserves his own opinion of Spenser's accomplishment to the poem's concluding couplet.

Both Erickson and Oram acknowledge Spenser's power of ravishingly attractive poetry, at least insofar as "commune sense" may judge poetry to be ravishing in the way suggested by the vocabulary Spenser uses to describe Ralegh's. On either account, there is a reservation. Oram argues that not all that Spenser names "pleasure" is good pleasure; Erickson suggests that Spenser may warn himself against letting his own poetry tend too far in the direction of Ralegh's. Either may be the case, as long as Spenser addresses the "commune sense" of that audience—but the queen is a different case. I think both critics may be overstressing the language that suggests Ralegh's voluptuousness, thereby obscuring Spenser's effort to commend him for having gotten the queen "right."

I suggest that Spenser not only appreciated this, but wished as well to signal Ralegh's unique position with respect to the queen as audience. Interpret minimally the content of his commendations of Ralegh in III.proem.4–5 and in the dedicatory sonnet; let them be no more than good offices extended to his friend and sympathetic patron. Still, they are the only commendations of a contemporary's poetry found in and with *The Faerie Queene*,[6] and, as pointed out above, the dedicatory sonnet is altogether in contrast to its surrounding company. In *Colin Clouts Come Home Againe,* Spenser uses Marin's comment on the Shepherd of the Ocean's "lamentable lay" to marvel that it succeeded in assuaging Cynthia's displeasure and caused her "to take him to her grace againe" (173–75). Later, in the descriptive catalogue of contemporary poets, only Ralegh is explicitly said to have affected the queen with his verse; his is a *"Muse . . . That can empierce a Princes mightie hart"* (430–31). These several versions of praise may describe what was hoped rather than what was (or would be) fact, but Spenser works within a fiction that he and Ralegh had agreed to share. Their audience and their subject were their queen. Her essence might be inexpressible and her satisfaction uncertain of attainment; nevertheless, her inspiration guaranteed good faith on the poets' part, and, as Ralegh put it, "thereby will [she] excuse and favour thy good will" (3.11). Thus might each claim the deserts so earned.[7]

University of Utah

NOTES

1.   Citations of Ralegh's poetry are to *The Poems of Sir Walter Ralegh: A Historical Edition,* ed. Michael Rudick (Tempe, AZ: Renaissance English Text Soc., 1999), by poem and line number, in this case, 26.438–41.

2.   See A. D. Cousins, "The Coming of Mannerism: The Later Ralegh and the Early Donne," *ELR* 9 (1979): 86–107 at 93–94; also Robert E. Stillman, " Words cannot knytt": Language and Desire in Ralegh's *The Ocean to Cynthia*," *SEL* 27 (1987): 35–51, and Marion Campbell, "Inscribing Imperfection: Sir Walter Ralegh and the Elizabethan Court," *ELR* 20 (1990): 233–53 at 241–48. The latter two articles stress the unstable (even incoherent) movement of positions clung to in the speaker's despair. A little closer to Dees's reading is Michael L. Johnson, "Some Problems of Unity in Sir Walter Ralegh's *The Ocean's Love to Cynthia*," *SEL* 14 (1974): 17–30.

3.   Still, in this connection, one must credit Erickson's plea that those who see *The Faerie Queene* and its poet as monolithic should "lighten up": Spenser's poem is not invariably Vergilian epic, neither does it, as fiction, preclude pleasure as an effect. Citations of Spenser are to *The Faerie Queene*, ed. A. C. Hamilton (London: Longman, 1977) and to *The Shorter Poems of Edmund Spenser*, ed. William A. Oram et al. (New Haven: Yale University Press, 1989).

4.   Most scholars have, since its discovery, dated this poem after the twenty-first book of "Cynthia"; for its earlier dating, see my edition, pp. xlvii–xlviii.

5.   Pointed out by Erickson in "Spenser's Letter to Ralegh and the Literary Politics of *The Faerie Queene*," *Spenser Studies* 10 (1992): 139–74 at 144–46, but I do not agree with him that the preceding sonnet substitutes Ralegh for the queen as the authoritative critic; its having mediated the poet's judgment through its "Vision" shows, at least, Ralegh's care to depersonalize the commendation.

6.   Though Sidney's is referred to in the octave of the sonnet to the countess of Pembroke.

7.   Campbell, cited in note 2, argues that the confused movement of the twenty-first book of "Cynthia" is due to Ralegh's having lost the queen who is his audience (p. 248).

CHRISTOPHER WARLEY

"An Englishe box": Calvinism and Commodities in Anne Lok's *A Meditation of a Penitent Sinner*

Anne Lok's *A Meditation of a Penitent Sinner* (1560), the first sonnet sequence in English, articulates changing conceptions of social authority in early Elizabethan England through the formal tension of the sonnet sequence—the strain between sonnet and sequence, lyric and narrative. This strain is apparent in the complex relation between the individual sonnets of the sequence and the text of Psalm 51 which appears in the margin. The psalm provides a model for the speaker's lyric authority, but it also provides a narrative of the founding of the New Jerusalem which tacitly celebrates England's return to Protestantism under Queen Elizabeth. By creating a lyric authority out of the logic of commodity circulation and Calvinism, however, the speaker tacitly challenges Elizabeth's assertion of absolute monarchical power. The authority of Lok's speaker consequently points to the need to reimagine the class dynamics embodied in the English sonnet.

I. Lok and the Sonnet Sequence

THE FIRST SONNET sequence in English appeared in print in 1560 at the end of a translation of four sermons by Calvin. *Sermons of John Calvin, upon the Songe that Ezechias made . . .* [1] was entered into the Stationer's Register on 15 January 1560, a little over a year after Elizabeth's coronation. The translator of the sermons is named "A.L." at the end of the dedicatory epistle and since at least the nineteenth-century has been identified as Anne Lok, a Marian exile

and prominent member of the London merchant community.[2] Lok
is generally known to literary scholars as the mother of Henry Lok,
a writer of religious sonnets and occasional courtier, though she herself is garnering increasing attention.[3] Appended to the end of the
sermons is *A Meditation of a Penitent Sinner: Written in Maner of a
Paraphrase upon the 51. Psalme of Dauid*, a collection of twenty-six
sonnets (five prefatory and twenty-one "meditations") which are
deeply Calvinist in tone and content but which employ the particular
form of the sonnet devised by Surrey a few decades earlier. A preface
to the sonnets by the translator claims this "meditation" "was deli-
uered me by my frend with whom I knew I might be so bolde to
vse & publishe it as pleased me," but no friend has been positively
identified. Patrick Collinson has suggested that this preface indicates
that Lok did not write the poems which follow (his candidate is
Knox).[4] Yet as Roland Greene notes, this is a "routine disclaimer of
authorship" by a female writer in this period in which "one recognizes this [preface] as a circumlocution that generates an understanding beyond what it actually says, an acknowledgment that 'I wrote
this book.'"[5] Because the writer conventionally protests too much,
the note strongly suggests that Lok is in fact the author of the sequence. Almost certainly, then, the first sonnet sequence in English,
over twenty years before sequences by Watson and Sidney, was written by Anne Lok.

The first thing anyone looking at Lok's sequence is likely to notice
is that these poems can be very hard to read—occasionally bordering
on inscrutable. If this is partially due to the undeniable fact that Lok
is not always the smoothest of poets, the main reason Lok's sonnet
sequence is so difficult is that it confounds many of the critical contexts we might deploy to try to make sense out of it. As Greene
suggests, "Lok's poem belies much of what we think we know about
the cross-cultural valences and eventual domestication of the sonnet
sequence—and that such a poet is a Calvinist, and a woman, complicates received literary history all the more."[6] Lok's work is in many
ways representative of other Protestant writing of the period, particularly writing by women. We owe much of our knowledge about
Lok to the on-going effort to catalogue writings of early modern
women,[7] and Lok's work, like the work of other Renaissance women
writers, uses translation to acquire literary authority otherwise not
much available.[8] *A Meditation* also clearly participates in what Rivkah
Zim calls "a stable tradition of attitudes to the Psalms" as a distinct
literary mode.[9] Lok's use of the sonnet, however, is not at all typical
of English Protestant verse. Although we see little of the sorts of

language and maneuvers generally associated with sonnets in imitation of Petrarch or in courtly circles, no other sonnets in this period express the fervent Calvinism of Lok's work. While there are many examples of women writing sonnet sequences on the continent before Lok, there are none in England. Likewise, though Lok's book is dedicated to an aristocratic patron, it noticeably lacks the fawning such dedications customarily employ, and Lok seems completely uninterested in acquiring a patron for social or political advancement. Indeed, as I will argue, in using the sonnet Lok seems to be drawing on an economic language that substantially complicates aristocratic rule.

Yet it is largely the difficulty of figuring out how to read Lok's sequence which makes her work so fascinating as a discrete exercise in interpretation and so compelling as a moment in literary history. The interpretive problems are both compounded and expressed in the really remarkable aspect of Lok's work: she writes the first sonnet sequence in English. In the formal tension of the sonnet sequence—the strain between sonnet and sequence, lyric and narrative—Lok's work articulates social strains and contradictions of a re-Protestantized England at the start of Elizabeth's reign. These strains are apparent in the complex relation between the individual sonnets of the sequence and the text of Psalm 51 which appears in the margin. Following the psalm, Lok's sequence gathers together the cultural strains of Calvinism, mercantilism, and absolutism to construct a narrative of the founding of the New Jerusalem which tacitly celebrates England's return to Protestantism. Yet the very forces Lok's speaker draws on to articulate this vision—Calvinism and mercantile commodity circulation—implicitly resist Elizabeth's assertion of absolute monarchical power, an assertion that facilitated England's re-Protestantization. For Lok, the languages of commodity circulation and biblical interpretation are inseparable; her speaker conceives of his declaration of sin as a commodity that embodies God's grace. Yet the speaker's lyric authority resists the political "narrative" that the sequence seeks to tell—the refounding of the New Jerusalem with Elizabeth's coronation—because it locates authority not in the monarchy or ecclesiastical institutions but in the individual interpreter of the Bible. This discrete interpretation circulates publicly, like a commodity, in published sonnets probably aimed at urban, non-aristocratic, Protestant buyers like Lok herself. Lok's work thus articulates a tension between the narrative authority of the queen's Protestant church and the individual acts of interpretation expressed by Lok's lyric speaker.

While Lok's work shares much in common with other women writers of the period, her class and her socio-economic existence generally still need to be investigated.[10] Attention to the particular relations between religion and class embedded in Lok's work is crucial to understanding the implications of the most distinctive feature of *A Meditation*—its use of the English sonnet. Though Lok's profile in the godly community ensured her considerable social power, she was not noble, and her work challenges "our still-lingering sense of Renaissance writing as somehow aristocratic."[11] Indeed, much of what makes her work so unrecognizable to literary scholars is its origins in social formations—Calvinism, mercantilism, women—whose literature and social power still remain at best partially mapped territory. Situated at the crossroads of Calvinist, courtly, and mercantile discourses, Lok's work presents the cultural faultlines that marked fundamental, long-term alterations in the means of producing social distinction in England. Much of what is interesting about Lok and her work, then, is that neither Renaissance writers or current criticism offers compelling terms to describe people like her. In terms of sonnet criticism, the issue is further complicated by a tradition of viewing sonnets as a privileged location for the creation of an aristocratic subject.[12] Indeed, we may need to reconsider the extent to which current critical orthodoxy about Elizabethan "court" culture depends upon representations of an idea of court created by non-nobles like Lok. Placing Lok in literary history thus demands that we write about people like her in this period without absorbing them into aristocratic court culture or implying a triumphant "rise" of a transcendent bourgeois subject.

Lok's life situates her in a nexus of Protestant merchants who, while not represented as a distinct party or class in 1560, nevertheless constituted a powerful voice in early Elizabethan England. Though Lok was not a member of court, her prominence in these circles meant that she was hardly as marginal as her nearly complete absence from literary history might suggest. Lok's father was, among other things, a Mercer and president of the Merchant Adventurers, Henry VIII's representative at the important Antwerp trade, Crown representative in the attempt to bring Tyndale back to England, an object of Sir Thomas More's attacks on suspected Tyndalians, and securer of a Crown loan from Antwerp merchants for £272,000. Her stepmother was a relative of Henry Brinkelow, whose *The Complaynt of Roderyck Mors* (?1542) and *Lamentacion of a Christian against the Citie of London* (1542) followed other apologists in arguing for further church reform and particularly criticized the distribution of recently claimed church property among aristocrats rather than the poor. Her father-in-law Sir William Lok was also a Mercer who had endeared himself to Henry VIII when, while on business in Dunkirk in 1533, he pulled down the papal bull excommunicating Henry; the king responded by allowing him £100 a year and making William a gentleman of the privy chamber (the king even dined at William's house once). Anne's brother-in-law Michael Lok was a prominent, polylingual merchant who traveled extensively throughout the world, and in 1576 he put up much of the money for Martin Frobisher's first attempt to find a Northwest Passage, a voyage in which the Sidneys also heavily invested. Michael Lok went bankrupt, however, and in 1582 dedicated a map of the world he had made to Sidney which was included in Hakluyt's *Divers voyages*, possibly in the hopes that Sidney would give him money. After her first husband died, Lok married the high profile Protestant preacher and brilliant scholar Edward Dering, who once, with shocking explicitness, criticized Elizabeth's handling of religion to her face in a public sermon. Most famously, Lok maintained a life-long friendship with the Presbyterian instigator John Knox, who stayed with her in London, persuaded her to travel to Geneva in 1556 (conspicuously without her husband, though nothing has been proven), and wrote to her to garner support and money for the Scottish Presbyterians. When in 1583 John Field sought to publish some of Knox's works, he seems to have acquired them from Anne. Her son Henry Lok carried on his mother's literary interests; in 1591 he contributed a sonnet to James VI's *His Maiesties Poeticall Exercises at vacant houres*, and he published two collections of sonnets dedicated to Queen Elizabeth: *The first Parte of Christian Passions, conteynyng a hundred Sonnets of Meditation, Humiliation, and Prayer* (1593) and *Ecclesiasticus, otherwise called the Preacher . . .* (1597). The later contains commendatory verse by, among others, John Lyly, as well as an appendix of sixty sonnets dedicated to such notable courtiers as John Whitgift, Lancelot Andrewes, Sir Walter Ralegh, Sir Edward Dyer, and Fulke Greville. Henry also seems to have managed to obtain a position in the 1590s working for the Cecils. Even Lok's last husband, Richard Prowse, a draper from Exeter, was an alderman, three times mayor, and Member of Parliament. Anne seems to have been important enough for the puritan Christopher Goodman to travel to Exeter to preach—a place Patrick Collinson suggests he normally would not go.[13]

Lok's social position and her translation of Calvin consequently situate her at the center of what Robert Weimann terms the fundamental alterations in the "conditions of discursive practice" and reconception of locations of authority which took place in England partially as a result of the Reformation. While much authority remained "external," located in traditional ecclesiastical and political institutions, the Reformation created a new "internal," self-directed authority. Weimann stresses that in England the Reformation was particularly vexed, since Tudor absolutism used Protestantism to create the idea of a Protestant nation even while this combination divided locations of authority. In England "secular power and religious reform become intertwined"[14] to create "an alliance between representation and the 'redemption of the world' through interpretation."[15] Protestant state authority simultaneously imposed Weimann's "external" institutional authority—an authority which exists, a priori, as a condition of its discursive utterance—as well as fostering the "internal" authority of Protestant subjects—an authority which emerged "in the perception of meaning as process."[16]

Recognizing this dynamic relation among politics, religion, and class in Elizabethan England helps to make sense of Lok's work because it begins to clarify one of the work's most distinctive features: the difficult and complex relation between the sonnets themselves and the text of the psalm which appears in the margin. Lok's work enacts the tension between these two modes of authorization in her appropriation and use of the form of the sonnet sequence. The tension between sonnet and sequence, between lyric and narrative, is expressed in Lok's work in the relation between sonnets and the psalm. This tension is particularly evident in the final two sonnets in the sequence, numbers 20 and 21. On one hand, the psalm facilitates a specifically religious lyric authority by providing both a model and a text for the speaker. On the other hand, the psalm provides a historical narrative of the founding of the "New Jerusalem" within which the speaker's lyricism occurs—England's return to Protestantism under Queen Elizabeth:

Shew fa-	Shew mercie, Lord, not unto me alone:
vour, o lord	But stretch thy favor and thy pleased will,
in thy good	To sprede thy bountie and thy grace upon
will unto	Sion, for Sion is thy holly hyll:
Sion, that	That thy Hierusalem with mighty wall
th [sic] *walles*	May be enclosed under thy defense,
of Hierusa	And bylded so that it may never fall
lem may be	By myning fraude or mighty violence.
bylded.	Defend thy chirch, Lord, and advaunce it soe,
	So in despite of tyrannie to stand,
	That trembling at thy power the world may know

It is upholden by thy mighty hand:
That Sion and Hierusalem may be
A safe abode for them that honor thee.

Then shalt	Then on thy hill, and in thy walled towne,
thou accept	Thou shalt receave the pleasing sacrifice,
the sacri-	The brute shall of thy praised name resoune
fice of righ	In thankfull mouthes, and then with gentle eyes
teousnesse,	Thou shalt behold upon thine alter lye
burnt of-	Many a yelden host of humbled hart,
fringes and	And round about then shall thy people crye:
oblations.	We praise thee, God our God: thou onely art
then shalt	The God of might, of mercie, and of grace.
they offre	That I then, Lorde, may also honor thee,
yonge bul-	Releve my sorow, and my sinnes deface:
lockes upon	Be, Lord of mercie, mercifull to me:
thine al-	Restore my feling of thy grace againe:
tare.	Assure my soule, I crave it not in vaine.

As lyrics, these sonnets derive their authority partially by ventrilo-quizing and ritualistically reenacting the voice of David, usually thought to be the author of the psalms. As Greene remarks, the psalms "require the reading voice to assume the identity of their represented speaker; in a certain sense a psalm scarcely represents a speaker at all, but is the script for sacred ritual cast in lyric discourse." In this sense Lok's work is a "prolonged incantation" which recreates in its performance the authority of a collective identity—here, quite specifically, the identity of an English Calvinist.[17] The individual son-nets eventually become, literally, the psalm itself, as the speaker's extension of David's voice through sonnets gradually unfolds and articulates the lines of the psalm. Following the tradition of seeing David as author and speaker of the psalms, I gender the speaker male, though Lok herself, by employing the first person, never specifies the gender of her speaker. Nevertheless, what Spiller calls, "the ap-propriation of supposedly male penitence and prayers by women's voices"[18] points to a disjuncture in the emergence of this lyric author-ity. As I will argue in the next section, the question of the gendered authority of the speaker is intimately linked to the question of the work's published existence.

However, the unanswerable question of the speaker's gender sug-gests that the ritualistic script provided by the Psalm is never seam-lessly enacted, for the lyric authority of these poems also emerges out

of a *reading* voice: Lok's sonnet "meditations" are as much interpretations of the psalm as they are reenactments of it. The product of
these interpretations is the New Jerusalem itself which consists of
the process of authoritative biblical interpretation, of the "people"
praising God much as the speaker himself does by reading and interpreting the psalm. As Norman Jones notes, for the godly in the 1560s
"the True Church [was] not built of stone and lime. Rather it [was]
a congregation of the faithful, where the pure and sincere word of
God [was] preached and the sacraments [were] duly ministered."[19]
The speaker's lyric authority emerges as God "[s]hew[s] mercie" to
him by assuring his soul that mercy has been attained and the New
Jerusalem has been created; conversely, the speaker knows mercy has
been attained when God decides, as sonnet 17 puts it, to "loose my
speche, and make me call to thee"—itself a paraphrase of the psalm's
request that the Lord "open thou my lippes, and my mouth shal
shewe thy praise." God's mercy is enacted as it "resource[s]" in
"thankfull mouthes." The realization of God's mercy through the
articulation of sin creates the New Jerusalem, the true church; authority emerges, in Weimann's terms, through "the perception of meaning as process." The creation of the New Jerusalem is thus in one
sense roughly equivalent to the emergence of the speaker's lyric authority; both stage the process by which God's mercy is realized.

The psalm provides the text upon which the speaker will meditate
to construct a distinctive lyric authority, but it also provides a *narrative*
of the founding of the New Jerusalem itself. Lok's sonnets coalesce
into a *sequence* by following the "plot" of the psalm and ending
with the foundation of the New Jerusalem. Thus while the sequence
narrates the emergence of the speaker's spiritual awareness, it also
tells a very specific historical story within which the speaker's lyric
authority emerges. Hannay notes that building the New Jerusalem,
line eighteen of Psalm 51, had effectively become code for Protestant
activities in pursuit of the true churcha connection Lok herself makes
quite clearly in the dedication to her other published work, the 1590
translation of Jean Taffin's *Of the markes of the children of God.*[20] More
than a theological abstraction, "church" also refers quite explicitly
to the activities of the godly attempting to create and reinforce Protestantism in England. Reciting and interpreting the psalm generates
the speaker's lyric authority, but that authority is also facilitated by
a "safe abode" "enclosed" under Queen Elizabeth's defense against
the "tyrannie" of the Inquisition and papal authority generally. As
the legal tag on the title page of the work suggests, Lok's poems
exist "*Cum Gratia & privilegio Regiæ majestatis*"; Elizabeth's protection
facilitates this "safe abode." Within this historical narrative, Elizabeth

herself becomes the "Lord" who spreads "bountie" and "grace" on "Sion," who defends the church against "tyrannie." And in this sense, the specifically narrative authority of the sequence lies in Elizabeth's princely power to protect the godly. Lok's rendition of the psalm consequently creates a narrative which acts, in Fredric Jameson's famous phrase, as an ideologeme—a symbolic resolution and response to real historical problems.[21] Yet for Lok's speaker, the "end" of the narrative is not merely symbolic; the return to Protestantism under Elizabeth promises that the New Jerusalem will exist as more than a theological abstraction.

Considered as a narrative, Lok's sequence expresses the conditions within which the speaker exists. The internal authority of the lyric speaker—a discursive authority derived from the process of interpretation—becomes possible as a result of Elizabeth's institutional authority. And it is here that the "strain" between lyric and narrative, sonnet and sequence, becomes evident. For the internal authority which Elizabeth's Protestantism facilitates potentially resists Elizabeth's institutionalized monarchical power. This contradiction produces what Norman Jones wryly terms "The Unsettled Settlement of Religion," the complex question of the relative authority of political, ecclesiastical, and social discourses which remained perhaps the central issue throughout Elizabeth's reign.[22] Lok herself was centrally involved in these issues through her own work, through her relationship with John Knox, and through her marriage to her second husband Edward Dering. Peter Lake has suggested Dering himself was effectively a Presbyterian. Called before the Star Chamber in 1573 to comment upon Thomas Cartwright's controversial book, Dering assured the interrogators that "princes have full authority over all ecclesiastical and civil persons and equally over both to punish the offenders or give praise to the well doers," but his firm belief in evangelical preaching became clear when he added that "in the church there is no lawgiver but Christ Jesus."[23] But the power available to women like Lok was not only dependent upon their connections to men. In 1565 during the controversy over clerical vestments (which the godly felt were merely papist robes), Jones reports that

[o]ne man, a Scot who had earlier provoked a riot with a sermon against the surplice, appeared wearing one early in June. Some of the women of the parish stoned him, then dragged him from his pulpit, ripping his surplice and scratching his face in what Bishop Grindal described as a "womanish brabble."[24]

While Lok's privileged connections and social standing distinguished her from any mere "brabble," these circumstances, what Lok herself, writing in 1590, called the "*Halcyon daies*" of the puritan movement, provided the discursive conditions of her existence: "I have according to my duetie, brought my poore basket of stones to the strengthning of the walles of that Iuresalem, whereof (by grace) wee are all both Citizens and members."[25] The tension of the sequence is a tension between the "Citizen" and the "member," between narrative and lyric, and finally, in a sense, between metaphoric and real stones.

II. Calvinism and Commodities

Nevertheless, viewed strictly in political-religious terms, Lok's work is compelling but certainly not distinctive. Instead, her use of the *sonnet* to formally embody this tension complicates the relation of lyric and narrative in the sequence further by introducing a form with distinct class and economic affiliations. Her choice of the sonnet in 1560 associates her specifically with an urban, non-aristocratic readership, and Lok's work articulates the forces which gradually, over the next hundred years, would more clearly map the murky terrain between "the better sort" and "the worser sort."[26] English Calvinists are a group which has notably resisted attempts to assign them to a particular class; the "culture of puritanism," as a recent collection of essays terms it, was a religious, not an economic, phenomenon that crossed over many and varied socio-economic groups.[27] But at the same time, Lok's religion does not occur in a vacuum, and the English context into which she brings Calvin's thought is articulated in the specific language and form of the sonnet. English Protestant poetry itself emerged out of native traditions of verse that were generally non-aristocratic; early Reformers, and especially Edwardians, took over native, medieval traditions of plain, didactic verse and applied Protestant messages to them. And while Protestant verse enjoyed prestige at the Edwardian court, much of its purpose was to educate and inculcate the lower classes.[28]

In 1560 the "sonnet" as a form was, at best, loosely defined in English, but Lok quite specifically chooses the form devised by Henry Howard, earl of Surrey. Where precisely she encountered and copied Surrey's form is a question open to historical speculation. Spiller suggests that Lok probably found the form in Surrey's sonnet "The great Macedon that out of Perse chasyd/Darius," a preface to Wyatt's *Psalmes*. Spiller argues that "[t]his is a eulogistic and pious sonnet, and Locke would not even have had to know what a sonnet was to realize that here was a stanza form she might herself use for prefatory or translating purposes." He goes on to note that "this is actually one of the very few sonnets by Surrey to obliterate the octave break," the form of the Surrey sonnet Lok employs.[29] The choice of Wyatt as Lok's main model is further supported by Alexandra Halasz's persuasive situating of Wyatt's *Psalmes* in relation to Henry VIII's control of church and state. Halasz argues that "Wyatt creates a perspective in his poem from which 'the values of a system that has an absolute monarch as head of both church and state' can be judged, the power of the monarch notwithstanding." Wyatt effects this critique by distinguishing "between himself, the narrator, and David . . . [Wyatt] can call the king to account, but he cannot do so from a position of innocence or spiritual purity." [30] Indeed, Wyatt's historicizing of David bears considerable resemblance to the paradoxical position of Lok's speaker between lyric and narrative senses of Psalm 51.

Yet the high praise Spiller gives Lok for her technical poetic skill seems at odds with his description of her as "a completely innocent poet" who was "not even aware that she was looking at a sonnet."[31] Given that Spiller persuasively demonstrates Lok's familiarity with Wyatt's *Psalmes*, it seems much more likely that, were she "innocent" of the sonnet, she would employ Wyatt's quatrains. Instead, Lok seems quite familiar not only with "The great Macedon" but with the sonnet generally, and she probably found Surrey's sonnets (as well as poems by Wyatt, Grimald, and others) from the great source of the sonnet form in English, *Songes and Sonettes, written by the ryght honorable Lorde Henry Howard late Earle of Surrey, and others*, the landmark publication of 1557 usually known as Tottel's *Miscellany*. It is exceedingly likely, though probably not provable, that Lok was familiar with Tottel's. Even assuming, as Spiller does, that Lok could not have seen Tottel's while she was in exile on the continent (which does not necessarily seem like a likely assumption, since she was in Frankfurt, a center of the book trade, by late March 1559), she was back in England in June 1559, giving her six months to read Tottel's before her work was published in January 1560.

The probability that Tottel's was Lok's source suggests, even more strongly than Wyatt's *Psalmes*, the particular socio-economic and class conditions tied up with Lok's use of the sonnet in 1560. As a source, Tottel's, like the form of the sonnet itself, removes Lok from an anachronistic religious vacuum and places her and her book in English society broadly conceived. What Lok and other non-aristocratic readers found in Tottel's was a representation of aristocratic England meant to reinforce specifically the values of an urban Protestant. As Mary Thomas Crane suggests, Tottel's shows evidence of a "middle-class," "humanist" emphasis on "aphoristic matter that tended to confirm the superiority of the middle-class's own unambitious way of life and frugal values."[32] Crane reads Tottel's famous preface to his book ("It resteth now, [gentle reader], that thou thinke it not evill done, to publish, to the honor of the English tong, and for profit of the studious of English eloquence, those workes which the ungentle horders up of such treasure have heretofore envied thee"[33]) as emphasizing not the superiority of such aristocratic "treasures" but the power of those acquiring them:

> To a readership including members of the urban merchant class, the social credentials of the authors of such poems were important not just because those readers were interested in the life-styles of the rich and famous, but because the effect of the poems is to judge the rich and famous by middle-class standards and to find them wanting.[34]

Crane also points out that

> [a]lthough the title page stresses the prestige and social rank of the poets whose "treasure" Tottel has gathered for public consumption, his preface describes them as "ungentle"—an explicit denigration of their social status—in hoarding these poems as a private, courtly luxury.

In opposition to "social status" and "private, courtly luxury," Tottel presents, according to Crane, "a gathering designed to share among common people a textual commodity that is rightfully theirs."[35] As a commodity, the stylistic matter in Tottel's attains value and authority not only through what Marx calls its "use value"—the tropes and stylistic matter one copies, for instance—but through its "exchange value" and circulation through the purchase and ownership of such tropes.[36]

What Crane calls "middle-class values" points less at a specific group (the "rising" bourgeoisie[37]) than at a distinct process of creating social value. These discursive conditions make possible the very idea of a "middle class" as a social group defined by process rather than by an existing social institution. The social authority of Tottel's commodified stylistic material consequently rests not in the social institution of the aristocracy but rather in the possession and circulation of that commodity through ownership. This argument inverts what has become a critical commonplace about sonnets: rather than descending from the aristocracy (or at least court), the sonnet appears post-Tottel as a commodified form employed by often non-aristocratic writers to erect representations of the national social order from a non-aristocratic perspective. Rather than centralizing the authority of court and celebrating Tudor absolutism, Tottel's demonstrates a *dislocation* of authority out of state institutions and into individuals—or as Weimann puts it, out of institutions and into process. In the circulation of the book market, Tottel's published sonnets become the active embodiment of an authority based upon the possession of a commodity; "prestige" itself becomes objectified in the rhetorical phrases Tottel sells to his readers. By adopting a form of the sonnet found in Tottel, Lok is thus participating in the relocation of authority out of social institutions and into commodity ownership, and, more generally, the reconceptualization of what constitutes social authority itself.

This objectification of aristocratic "luxury" also had a distinctly moralistic ambition to impose both the tastes of those who acquire social authority through circulation as well as the very processes which produce those morals and tastes.[38] The possession of courtly elegance enables readers, as Crane notes, to "judge the rich and famous by middle-class standards and to find them wanting." For Lok, this moral judgment takes the form of an unapologetically Calvinist vision of England that locates authority in the interpretation of scripture and the objective, textual declaration of sin. While Tottel's provides the language of class and commodity possession in which Lok functions, that logic is constantly filtered through and intertwined with the theology expressed in Calvin's four sermons on Hezekiah, King of Judah (2 Kings 18–21) which precede the sonnet sequence.

Lok herself outlines much of what she seeks to stress about the sermons in her dedicatory epistle. She is concerned with an inward sense of depravity in the face of God's law; but she is even more occupied with the need for a public display of this inwardness. On the one hand, Lok emphasizes that "the greues of the body and calamities of fortune do so farre onely extende, to afflict, or make a man miserable, as they approch to touch the mind, & assaile the soule" (A3ᵛ). The only sickness which really matters is an inward sickness, and one who has a "defense of inward understandyng" is safe from all outward, physical harm: "some men beynge pressed with pouertie, tossed with worldlye adversitye, tourmented with payne, sorenes, & sicknes of body . . . Yet hauing theyr myndes armed & fournished with prepared patience, and defense of inward understandyng, all these calamities can not so farre preuaile, as to make them fall" (A2ʳ). The cure for this sickness of the soul ultimately lies only with God, but the existence of that cure is marked by a sign, an external indication of a "defense of inward understandyng."

It is this material and outward indication of God's cure, her book itself, which Lok presents in the dedication to the duchess of Suffolk: "this receipte God the heauenly Physitian hath taught, his most excellent Apothecarie master Iohn Caluine hath compounded, & I your graces most bounden & humble haue put into an Englishe box, & do present vnto you" (A3ʳ). Lok describes her relation to Calvin and to the duchess as a transaction, the delivering of a textual commodity Lok has packaged—"put into an Englishe box." The book itself becomes the objective embodiment of Calvin's cure, a public enunciation and response to an intense sense of inward sin—to possess the book is to possess the cure. But the published book, Lok's "Englishe box," not only provides the cure; it also acts as a model for the public declaration of sin. In this sense the physical embodiment of Calvin's sermons in the book have an explicitly didactic function. They are meant to provide individuals with "prepared patience, and defense of inward understandyng" by providing an *outward* and public display of sickness. The title of the book stresses "the *Songe* that Ezechias made after he had bene sicke" (my italics). The interest of Calvin and Lok lies not simply in the inward sickness of sin but, as the order of the wording of the title implies, the public response and articulation of Hezekiah to his sickness—his song.

In the most general sense, then, what Weber famously termed the "Protestant ethic" becomes "part of a larger culture of early modern appropriation in which the possession of objects could reward the spirituality of subjects."[39] The social implications of such a relocation of authority are strikingly apparent in the dedicatory epistle. While dedicatory epistles customarily seek to honor the book with the prestige of the (would-be) patron, Lok's epistles reads more like a lecture than flattery—telling the (admittedly very willing) duchess of Suffolk, known as the mother of English puritanism,[40] what she ought to know. Instead of seeking to authorize the book with the prestige of the duchess, Lok's epistle presents and embodies a mode of authorized interpretation itself—Calvin's interpretation of Hezekiah's interpretation of sin, placed in an English box. Moreover, Lok's "Englishing" of Calvin, the process of presenting him to the duchess, becomes a transaction of commodified authority which undermines noble class distinction. In her book's title, Lok plays down Hezekiah's own nobility. The title of the French edition is "Sermons de Jehan Calvin sur le cantique que feit le bon roy Ezechias apres qu'il eut ete malade et afflige de la main de Dieu." In the English version, Lok cuts out "le bon roy," the good king, though it is a phrase which she translates frequently in Calvin's sermons. Rather than seeking simply to praise the duchess, Lok's dedication *presents* the possibility of authority to her.

But at the same time, Lok's presentation of her book is not simply a circulation of commodities. This transaction occurs within a strenuously hierarchical society ruled by the government of an absolute monarch. If the metaphor of Calvin as apothecary rings of a shifting world of trade and exchange, it also evokes a strict social hierarchy: God first, Calvin second, and finally Lok herself, "most bounden & humble." In this sense, Lok's "Englishe box" is presented to a duchess in a familiar act of patronage, and it seems likely that Lok hopes the duchess of Suffolk will use her social standing to help to disseminate the work. Even as Lok presents an individualized, commodified authority and "cure" of inward sickness, that transaction takes place within the aristocratic institution of patronage in which authority is located as an external social condition, not as an act of interpretation. If Calvin's name on the title page ensures that the book will possess a distinctively individual, commodified, and Protestant authority, the dedication to the duchess (despite, rather than because of, her endorsement of Calvinism) simultaneously invokes an authority which is based in social institutions rather than a discrete act of interpretation. In Lok's "Englishe box," in other words, two radically different modes of authorizing discourse coexist—a coexistence with important ramifications, as we will see, for the end of the narrative sequence.

Nevertheless, the title page of Lok's book provides no hint that besides Calvin's sermons the book contains a verse meditation, never mind *sonnets*; what is advertised and stressed—the biggest words on the page—is *John Calvin*. The book is a religious work meant to reinforce and reintroduce Calvin's interpretive methods into a specifically English context. It was published by John Day, who was responsible for a wide variety of godly books, including John Foxe's *Actes and Monuments* (1563) and the French and Dutch versions of *A Theatre for Worldlings* (1568). Lok's book itself is a tiny, pocket-sized octavo volume probably meant to facilitate daily, individual contemplation of the sort stressed in Calvin's sermons. These sermons constitute the bulk of the book and provide a detailed interpretive context,

a process of authorization, within which the sonnet sequence is constructed.[41]

In his discussion of Hezekiah, Calvin is specifically interested not
only in the significance of sin and suffering, but more importantly in
the reasons for *recording* one's suffering; that is, he is concerned with
the significance and procedure of the commodified declaration of
sin. He begins in the first sermon by asserting that while God is
immortal, his "trueth" in the world is not assured and requires constant attention: "our care should extende it selfe to the time to come,
to the end we may have in store some continuing seede of religion,
in such sort as the trueth of God may never be abolished" (B1ʳ).
The example of Hezekiah shows, Calvin argues, the importance of
recording one's penitence as a sign to others:

> Behold now wherefore Ezechias was not contented to make
> this protestation whiche we read here with his mouth, but wold
> also wryte it, that to the end of the worlde men might knowe
> how he had ben vexed in hys affliction, and that the same myght
> serve for doctrine to all the worlde: so as at this day we may
> take profyt thereof.
>
> (B1ᵛ)

By recording his affliction *in writing*, Hezekiah provides an example
and a means to maintain God's presence. Hezekiah is thus a typologi-
cal symbol, an example, by which Calvin himself understands contemporary sins—Calvin takes "profyt" from Hezekiah's example
because it establishes "doctrine": "let us not thynke it straunge that
god sendeth us afflictions whiche seme grevous and sharpe unto us,
seeing we see that Ezechias hathe walked before us to shewe us the
waye" (B7ᵛ). Such a recorded example is necessary as a sign because
while God is apparent in Nature ("For all the world is as a liuely
image, wherein God setteth fourth vnto vs his vertue and highnes"
C1ᵛ), the existence of God's presence in the world remains always a
fuzzy matter:

> So nowe the good kyng Ezechias sheweth us, that it were better
> for us all to have died before we had been borne, and that the
> earth should have gaped whan we came out of our mothers
> wombe, to swallow us, than to live here by lowe, if it were
> not for thys, that we do here alreadie see oure God: not that

we have a perfecte sighte. But first he showeth himselfe unto
us by his worde, which is the trew lokyng glass.

(C1ʳ)

While God may exist in nature, in "so manye signes of his presence,"
Calvin stresses, using the "glasse" conceit common in the period,
that the primary locale is scripture, "his worde, which is the trew
lokyng glass." The written Bible is the truth, for Calvin, to which
one looks to see oneself.

And yet one looks not "with a perfecte sighte." The way to gain
a more perfect sight for Calvin is not to attempt to clear up the
picture—not to attempt to contemplate or understand God's perfection. Instead, Calvin emphasizes the imperfection of the self we see
in the mirror, the gap—sin—between a self and God's presence in
the world. Hezekiah "did not here set fourthe his owne vertues to
be praised of the world, for he might have kept in silence that which
he hath declared of his owne waywardnesse" (B2ʳ). Instead of hiding
his sin, his "waywardnesse," Hezekiah displays it: "we see a poore
man tormented even to the extremitye, and so striken downe, that
he wiste not what myghte become of hym. We se a man astonished
with feare of the wrath of God, lokyng on nothyng but his own
affliction" (B2ʳ). Calvin closes the first sermon, as he does all four of
the sermons that Lok translates, not with an attempt to see unadorned
Truth itself in Hezekiah, but rather to use Hezekiah as a means better
to see sin:

Nowe let us throwe oure selves downe before the majestie of
our good God, in the acknowledgeynge of oure synnes, besech-
ynge hym, that more and more, he wyll make us to feele them,
and that he wyll in suche sort cleanse us from all oure fylthynesse, that we beynge perfectly awaked from oure dull drowsinesse, may grone and sobbe.

(C4ʳ)

The way to make God present in the world is always negative: not
through a contemplation of truth, but through a contemplation of
"our fylthynesse." Rather than asking God for forgiveness, Calvin
asks to feel sin more.

Because God's presence becomes manifest in man's contemplation
of sin, expressing sin becomes a complicated matter, for it necessarily

implies God's presence and the possibility of salvation for the person doing the articulating. Consequently, the sign of a man who truly feels his sins, suggests Calvin, is that he can barely articulate them:

> But whan that [Hezekiah] woulde frame anye request unto God, he was as it were dombe, and that on the one syde the sicknesse troubled hym, and yet he coulde not plainelye expresse what he ayled: so that he was in two extremities. Th[ ]one that he was in such sort locked up within, that with great payne could he fetch out any complaint. The[ ]other that he was oppressed with so vehement passyons, that he wyste no wheare too begynne to make his Prayer.
>
> (C8^r)

What marks the truly penitent sinner, Calvin suggests, is a pain so intense that a person cannot speak, and yet does; and an anguish so intense, a person does not know why he keeps silent: "And to be short, they that knowe in deede what the wrathe of God is, wyll speake and crye, and yet they know not on whiche side to begin: and again when they holde their peace they wote note why they doe it: but they are always in anguish. And we se a notable example of al these things in the good king Ezechias" (D1^{r-v}). True knowledge of God's wrath means true knowledge of sin, but this knowledge makes speaking of it difficult. The importance of Hezekiah lies thus in his capacity as both a sign of God's mercy and a model by which the "penitent sinner" knows where to begin.

The declaration of weakness consequently becomes the source of *authority*—a sign of God's presence. But it is simultaneously the precondition for writing and speaking, for a public display. Recording one's sins discursively becomes a sign of fallenness itself. Conversely, sin becomes the necessary precondition of all *authorized* discursive practice; if one were not fallen, a sign—a written sermon or poem—would hardly be necessary. In this sense Calvin's sermon itself, with its constant harping on man's filth and utter dependence upon God's good will, becomes a sign like Hezekiah. It is a public examination and exposure of inward sin that repeatedly emphasizes man's faults. At the same time, this emphasis is meant as a negative sign of God's presence which also depends upon the continual representation and objectification in discourse of sin. Calvin's sermon enacts a circulation of authorized representations of sin that acquire their authority through that very circulation. At least in Lok's translation, the logic of Calvin's authorized interpretation follows the logic of the valuation of commodities. It is the process of interpreting Hezekiah's sign, or of reading Calvin's sermon, or of reading Lok's sequence, which establishes, via its own negation, the authority embodied in the written sign; that is, only through the negation of the true does truth emerge.[42]

III. The Presuming Eye

At the start of her sonnet sequence, Lok adds a note which explicitly connects her work to the logic of Calvin's sermons. In so doing, the note simultaneously backs off from the claim of authorship and authority generally:

> I have added this meditation folowyng unto the ende of this boke, not as parcell of maister Calvines worke, but for that it well agreeth with the same argument, and was delivered me by my frend with whom I knew I might be so bolde to use and publishe it as pleased me.

While as we have already seen the prefatory note partially complicates questions of the identification of the author, it more crucially points directly at questions of *authority*, at the discursive practices by which the work understands itself to be true and convincing. For Greene, this preface resembles what Patricia Parker calls "a poetics of dilation and delay" characteristically gendered female. Like Parker's "literary fat ladies," Greene suggests that the gender of Lok's speaker "is implied by the symbolic association with a postmedieval context of feminine copiousness and dilation."[43] One effect of this sense of the speaker's gender is to reiterate the gap between the speaker and the appropriation of David's voice. Not only does the speaker interpret David's text, but that interpretation is performed within a context conventionally labeled female. The question "what is the gender of the speaker" thus rearticulates the more general question of the speaker's discursive authority.

Likewise, this poetic of dilation builds upon and expands the logic of Calvin's sermons; the preface insists it "well agreeth" with Calvin's argument. Within Calvin's world of circulating commodified sins, authorship and authority generally can only be ventriloquized and deferred. Because sin remains the precondition of all authorized discourse, only a speaker who defers authority—who acknowledges sin—can acquire any authority at all. In Lok's work, the conventional deflection of authorship by women becomes less a sign of the author's gender (though it may remain that) than a general model for all authoritative discursive practice. Consequently, though the preface defers authorship, it simultaneously insists that "I knew I might be so bolde to use and publishe it as pleased me." The boldness emerges specifically as the work is made public, *published*, because, as Calvin insists, it is only as sins are textually recorded that authority emerges. Publishing becomes the means whereby the work acquires authority without, as it were, an author; as it circulates publicly these poems propound the "same argument" as "maister Calvines work" because their authority emerges as they are exchanged and owned.

This "dilation" is specifically at issue in the question of the lyric authority of the speaker of the sonnets. Again and again, the speaker defers the question of God's mercy by focusing on sin; but, as in the preface, this declaration of sin tacitly emphasizes the speaker's salvation and, consequently, lyric authority. Moreover, as the speaker textually records this sin, his text itself becomes—like the texts of Hezekiah and Calvin—a model of the authority available to the penitent sinner. *A Meditation of a Penitent Sinner* is divided into two sections: "The preface, expressing the passioned minde of the penitent sinner," and "A Meditation of a penitent sinner, upon the 51. psalme." In the preface, the speaker is scared, passive, and tentative, and his lack of authority is expressed in the rambling and difficult syntax. In the Meditation itself, however, the lyric voice changes dramatically. This change is largely attributable to the inclusion of the text of Psalm 51 in the margin of the sequence. While the preface expresses "the passioned minde of the penitent sinner," a condition in which the speaker gropes about searching for authorization and hope for salvation, that authorization emerges quite forcefully in the meditation as the speaker interprets the fragments of scripture included in the margin. Interpretation of scripture—or rather, the declaration of sin that interpretation entails—becomes the basis for the authoritative voice of the sequence.

The drama of the preface, or "the passioned minde of the penitent sinner," as Lok titles it, is a desperate, almost hysterical, search for comfort and the assurance of salvation. But Lok's "penitent sinner" hardly knows where to begin to look as he blurts out a series of syntactically awkward assertions that articulate his "passioned minde." The first two sonnets, for instance, consist of one long sentence that expresses the speaker's inability to "find the way wherin to walke aright." Initially, the speaker tries to maintain a distinction between himself and his sin. As the opening sonnet puts it, "The

hainous gylt of my forsaken ghost/So threates, alas, unto my febled
sprite." But the distinction between his "hainous gylt" and his "febled sprite," between sin and self, collapses when, in the third sonnet,
the speaker finally encounters "despair":

> But mercy while I sound with shreking crye
> For grant of grace and pardon while I pray,
> Even then despeir before my ruthefull eye
> Spredes forth my sinne and shame, & semes to saye
> In vaine thou brayest forth thy bootlesse noyse
> To him for mercy, O refused wight,
> That heares not the forsaken sinners voice.
> Thy reprobate and foreordeined sprite,
> For damned vessel of his heavie wrath,
> (As selfe witnes of they beknowying hart,
> And secrete gilt of thine owne conscience saith)
> Of his swete promises can claime no part:
> But thee, caytif, deserved curse doeth draw
> To hell, by justice, for offended law.

Despair tells him what his "beknowyng hart,/And secrete gilt of
thine owne conscience saith": that his curse is "deserved," and he
goes to hell "by justice, for offended law." His guilt, God's wrath,
and his "febled sprite" are all his own fault: he is a "[f]or damned
vessel of his heavie wrath."

This knowledge of his own complicity in his suffering, of the fact
that it is his very existence which offends God, conversely provides
the authority by which he will begin to "try for mercy to releve [his]
woes." In sonnet four, though his "conscience wanteth to replye"
that he is not at fault, his "remorse" enforces his "offence" and "doth
argue vaine" his attempts at mercy:

> This horror when my trembling soule doth heare,
> When markes and tokens of the reprobate,
> My growing sinnes, of grace my senslesse cheare,
> Enforce the profe of everlasting hate,
> That I conceive the heavens king to beare
> Against my sinfull and forsaken ghost:
> As in the throte of hell, I quake for feare,

And then in present perill to be lost
(Although by conscience wanteth to replye,
But with remorse enforcing myne offence,
Doth argue vaine my not availing crye)
With woefull sighes and bitter penitence
To him from whom the endlesse mercy flowes
I try for mercy to releve my woes.

The speaker's despairing recognition of the "markes and tokens of the reprobate," becomes, implicitly, a mark that he is *not* one of the reprobate. According to Calvin, Hezekiah's ability both to articulate his sin and to recognize it *as* sin becomes a sign of God's grace. Likewise, the speaker's ability to recognize the signs of the reprobate simultaneously becomes a sign of his elect status. In line three, "[m]y growing sinnes" are transformed into "of grace my senslesse cheare," a "senslesse" expression of grace. As his awareness of his sins grows, so, implicitly, does his "senslesse cheare" of grace. The speaker's emerging authority is constituted by his recognition of his sin—of his lack of authority—because he begins to identity and express himself as deservedly forsaken from the start.

But he cannot explicitly articulate this nascent sense of his election, for his "conscience" argues that his "not availing crye" is "vaine." Instead, his "cheare," his expression, must always be "senslesse." To consider himself elect would necessarily force him to stop recognizing his own sin because it would mean not emphasizing that the violation of God's law is the fundamental condition of his existence. He would be "vaine," one of the reprobate who don't feel their sins. Consequently, in the fifth and final prefatory sonnet, he determines to ask for grace by

> not darying with presumming eye
> Once to beholde the angry havens face,
> From troubled sprite I send confused crye,
> To crave the crummes of all sufficing grace.

In 1560, "presume" pointed in many different, often contradictory directions. The speaker does not "presume" to look at God in the sense that he does not, as the *Oxford English Dictionary* puts it, "act or proceed on the assumption of right or permission." The speaker's position is one of abject humbleness, for he asserts that the grace he seeks is not his right, and that he does not have permission, as it were, to look upon God's angry face. To say that he does *not* dare "with presumming eye" underscores, however, his recognition that, though he does not dare look upon God and ask for mercy, he can conceive of doing so. Such protestation leads us to another, and quite contradictory, sense of "presume": "To take possession of without right; to usurp, seize." In claiming *not* to dare look upon God with a "presumming eye," the speaker simultaneously *stresses* his presuming eye. He has "taken possession of without right" in the sense that he *is* beholding here "the angry heavens face" even as he articulates the idea of a God he has offended, of a law he has violated. If the speaker "presumes" without right, he also presumes without authority. A third, equally current definition of "presume" is "To take upon oneself, undertake without adequate authority or permission." Indeed, in his articulation of his lack of authority (the recognition that God's wrath is completely justified) the speaker *acquires* authority. This fact of the speaker's condition leads us to yet another definition of "presume": "To assume or take for granted; to presuppose." The speaker's "presumming eye" must always be *presumed*, presupposed, for the speaker to be capable of articulating his lack of presumption at all. As in Calvin, sin becomes the necessary precondition of discursive practice—here, of presuming.

This presumptuously active contemplation in pursuit of a largely passive relation to God recalls Calvin's declaration that not knowing where to begin itself marks a truly penitent sinner. Calvin himself points to Psalm 51 as a means out of the sinner's dilemma: "when God sheweth hym selfe mercyfull towarde us, and uttereth some signe of hys favor toward us, he openeth oure mouthes, as it is sayde in the li. Psalme" (F6ʳ). Not accidentally, then, it is precisely to Psalm 51 that the speaker (and Lok herself) turns to open his mouth and express his moan. As the headnote to the Geneva Bible argues, "[w]hen David was rebuked by the Prophet Nathan for his great offences, he did not only acknowledge the same to God with protestation of his natural corruption and iniquitie, but also *left a memorial thereof* to his posteritie" (my emphasis).[44] Lok's sequence, in one sense, is a reading of the psalm much like the marginal notes of the Geneva Bible. Lok literally places the complete text of the psalm in the margin next to her sonnets, and by and large each sonnet is a meditation upon a verse of the psalm.[45] But unlike the biblical glosses, the sequence is also an enactment of the authority of the psalm itself as the speaker becomes a contemporary David, a speaker of the psalm. Thus the sequence emphasizes the truth of the psalm while redeploying its authority to become a sign of God's mercy. Lok's speaker and the sonnets themselves stand as both an embodiment of scriptural truth and authority as well as an active example of the textual performance of that authority.

While in the preface the speaker sends "confused crye" and is "tost with panges and passions of despeir," in the first sonnet of the meditation the tone is authoritative and optimistic. The authority of the speaker derives from his ability to recognize and articulate his sin by interpreting scripture. In sonnet one, for instance, the biblical text asks for mercy "after thy great merci," but the sonnet additionally stresses the speaker's own desire to "sound againe":

Have mer-	Have mercy, God, for they great mercies sake,
cie upon	O God: my God, unto my shame I say,
me (o God)	Beynge fled from thee, so as I dred to take
after thy	Thy name in wretched mouth, and feare to pray
great merci	Or aske the mercy that I have abusde.
	But, God of mercy, let me come to thee:
	Not for justice, that justly am accusde:
	Which selfe word Justice so amaseth me,
	That scarce I dare thy mercy sound againe.
	But mercie, Lord, yet suffer me to crave.
	Mercie is thine: Let me not crye in vaine,
	Thy great mercie for my great fault to have.
	Have mercie, God, pitie my penitence
	With greater mercie than my great offence.

What the speaker says, "unto [his] shame," is that he dreads to utter God's name "in wretched mouth." His voice is enabled by his ability to ask for mercy "that I have abusde"—that is, by his ability to ask to come to God even though he recognizes himself as "justly" accused. The imperative "Have mercy" which opens the sonnet repeats the opening of the psalm. The authority needed to use such a tense, to be able to ask for mercy, and to be able to speak at all, derives, quite literally in this instance, from the biblical text. While in the preface the speaker can only "crave mercy," in the first sonnet of the meditation he is able to say "mercy" *ten times* in fourteen lines. Likewise, in sonnet two he declares that "My many sinnes in nomber are encreast," and in sonnet three he assures us that

So foule with sinne I see my selfe to be,
That till from sinne I may be washed white,
So foule I dare not, lord, approche to thee.
                    (lines 2–4)

Like his "presumming eye," the speaker here claims he does not dare approach God, even as he does just that by announcing his foulness. By sonnet four the speaker insists that "I fele my sinne," and in sonnet five he puts it more colorfully:

> My cruell conscience with sharpned knife
> Doth splat my ripped hert, and layes abrode
> The lothesome secretes of my filthy life,
> And spredes them forth before the face of God.

Like both David and Hezekiah, Lok's speaker is not content merely to declare his sins; he also wants publicly to announce them, to spread "them forth before the face of God" and make a memorial.

It is not just before God that these "lothesome secretes" are spread. In sonnet six the speaker makes the claim implicit in the published existence of Lok's work itself. In expressing his sin, he wants to become a sign and example for others, a textual embodiment and declaration of sin:

That thou
mightest be
founded just
in thy say-
inges, and
maiest over
come when
thou art
judged.

But mercy Lord, O Lord some pitie take,
Withdraw my soule from the deserved hell,
O Lord of glory, for thy glories sake:
That I may saved of thy mercy tell,
And shew how thou, which mercy hast behight
To sighyng sinners, that have broke thy lawes,
Performest mercy: so as in the light
Of them that judge the justice of thy cause
Thou onely just be demed, and no moe,
The worldes unjustice wholy to confound:
That damning me to depth of during woe
Just in thy judgement shouldest thou be
    found:
And from deserved flames relevying me
Just in thy mercy mayst thou also be.

The text of the psalm stresses that God's "sayings" will be found just, but in the sonnet it is the speaker who desires to "tell" of God's mercy. God will be found "[j]ust in thy judgement" and "[just] in thy mercy," but that mercy is manifested in the voice of the speaker. He himself wishes to effectively *become* God's "sayings,"

That I may saved of thy mercy tell,
And shew how thou, which mercy hast behight
To sighyng sinners, that have broke thy lawes
Performest mercy[.]

As the speaker becomes increasingly concerned with his status as
a sign, he moves gradually away from introspection toward public
outbursts of optimism quite unlike anything we see in Calvin's sermons, which characteristically end by emphasizing the strictly negative articulation of God's mercy. At the close of sermon one, for
instance, Calvin envisions a time when he and his followers will
be "perfectly awaked from oure dull drowsinesse," but rather than
imagining this as a joyful time, he hopes that then they will be able
to "grone and sobbe." At the end of the third sermon he similarly
hopes that God "geve us suche tast of his goodnesse that we maye
not cesse to runne unto hym although our consciences doe reprove
and condempne [sic] us" (F3ʳ). In other words, in the sermons Lok
chooses to translate, Calvin adamantly refuses to impose a redemptive
narrative onto his description of suffering: redemption remains abstract, and suffering remains immediate.

In Lok's work, conversely, the ability to "tell" of God's mercy
produces a pervasive, if implicit, optimism derived from the narrative
provided by Psalm 51. The continual emphasis by the speaker of
Lok's sequence on sin and filth gives rise to a glimpse, if not an actual
manifestation, of cheer and joy. In sonnet ten, for instance, an initial
emphasis on sin gives way to a vision of hope:

Thou shale	Long have I heard, & yet I heare the soundes
make me	Of dredfull threates and thonders of the law,
heare ioye	Wich Eccho of my gylty minde resoundes,
and glad-	And with redoubled horror doth so draw
nesse, a[n]d	My listening soule from mercies gentle voice,
the bones	That louder, Lorde, I am constraynde to call:
which thou	Lorde, pearce myne eares, & make me to rejoyse,
hast broken	When I shall heare, and when thy mercy shall
shal rejoyse	Sounde in my hart the gospell of thy grace.
	Then shalt thou geve my hearing joy againe,
	The joy that onely may releve my case.

The speaker uses the possibility of joy in the psalm ("Thou shale
make me heare ioye and gladnesse, a[n]d the bones which thou hast
broken shal rejoyse") to construct an entire history. "Long have I

heard, & yet I heare" situates him amidst a history of God's "dredfull threates." But this history of guilty echoes resounding in his mind seems at an imminent end. In line seven the speaker uses the present imperative to rejoice *now*: "Lorde, pearce myne eares, & make me to rejoyse." Only with the enjambed line "[w]hen I shall heare" is the present put off to the future. The language of the poem strongly suggests, however, that the future is now:

> And then my broosed bones, that thou with paine
> Hast made to weake my febled corps to beare,
> Shall leape for joy, to shew myne inward chere.

"And then" refers to a time when relief is realized, when mercy is actualized, and when the speaker "Shall leape for joy, to shewe myne inward chere." But of course the sonnet itself is a demonstration of that "inward chere," a realization of his interior countenance, and a manifestation of God's mercy as the speaker's mouth is opened, "constraynde to call" *louder*. We see in this sonnet not a syntactically confused, anxiety-ridden voice but rather a confident manifestation of God's mercy, of *authority*, in the speaker's ability to demonstrate his "inward chere." Likewise, in sonnet 16 the speaker actively imagines an act of praise that is not negative, is not simply a reiteration of sin:

> So, Lorde, my joying tong shall talke thy praise,
> Thy name my mouth shall utter in delight,
> My voice shall sounde thy justice, and thy waies,
> Thy waies to justifie thy sinfull wight.
> God of my health, from bloud I saved so
> Shall spred thy prayse for all the world to know.
>
> (lines 9–14)

Though he is careful to place everything in the future tense, the energy of the speaker's syntax ("thy waies,/Thy waies" begins to sound like fervent sermonizing) embodies a sense that salvation is at hand. In line thirteen he declares "I saved so" but catches himself at the start of line fourteen and places his salvation in the future ("Shall spred thy prayse") even as he imagines publicly spreading praise. Though sonnet 17 begins with the return of despair ("Lo straining crampe of colde despeir againe/In feble brest doth pinche my pinying hart") it ends, characteristically, with zealous optimism:

Lord loose my lippes, I may expresse my mone,
And findyng grace with open mouth I may
Thy mercies praise, and holy name display.

(lines 12–14)

In displaying God's "holy name," the speaker also displays his own lyric authority, an authority made materially manifest by the declarations of sin the book makes possible.

IV. THE NEW JERUSALEM

The lyric authority of Lok's speaker emerges as he is able to "expresse" his "mone," to become a sign of God's mercy "and holy name display." In its capacity as a material sign, this authority is created (as in Hezekiah's desire for a sign or Calvin's desire to feel his sins more) as it is circulated, read, and interpreted. Commodity circulation becomes the source of the speaker's authority, the process whereby he is able to speak. When we consider the location of this authority within the narrative of Lok's sequence, however, the strain emerges between this lyric authority and the narrative in which it is embedded. Because the speaker desires to become a sign of God's mercy, the realization of that desire in the New Jerusalem means, paradoxically, the *elimination* of the very structures which provide the speaker with authority in the first place.

This contradiction emerges most dramatically in the final sonnets of the sequence, the two sonnets I initially looked at, where the hopes of the speaker become manifest in the New Jerusalem. While the lyric authority of Lok's speaker emerges in what Greene describes as a "dilated" space, waiting for God's judgment, the optimism of these two sonnets suggests that such judgment has, at least partially, arrived. This optimism appears as the work subtly shifts from a predominantly lyric mode to a narrative mode. The speaker begins to imagine himself as a character in a narrative, a participant, rather than an isolated subject groping about for grace. In sonnet 20, the speaker asks "Shew mercie, Lord, not unto me alone" and hopes that God's "favor" be stretched to "Sion," "thy Hierusalem," and "thy chirch." Likewise, the first nine lines of sonnet 21 imagine "thankfull mouthes," "a yelden host of humbled hart," and the cry of "thy people." As the speaker imagines the realization of his desire, he effectively ceases to be a lyric speaker and is transformed into a character in a narrative. The "I" of the poems becomes just one of a "yelden host of humbled hart." As a narrative realization of lyric desire, the New Jerusalem emerges as a paradise where the realization of the speaker's desires simultaneously means the end of commodity circulationthe very source of the speaker's authority in the first place. When all the "people crye:/We praise thee," a textual sign of God's mercy—a sermon, a book, a poem—is no longer necessary. Situated amidst communal praise, "God" becomes the figure who embodies and makes possible the realization of desire, a figure of "might," "mercy," and "grace" in which sins are "defaced."

The optimism of the sequence emerges (in contrast to Calvin's perennial anxiety) as a result of Lok's inhabiting a specifically English context, an "Englishe box," within which Protestantism rules; the time when God "releves" sorrow seems at hand. In an initial sense, Elizabethan England and the New Jerusalem become effectively synonymous terms. Absolute monarchy, like "God," both embodies and enables the realization of commodified, Calvinist desires; the queen's authoritative social position objectifies and resolves the dilemmas faced by people like Anne Lok. Much like Lok's presentation of her "Englishe box" to the duchess of Suffolk, the authority of the monarchy acts to protect the "most bounden and humble," be they Lok as she depicted herself in the dedicatory epistle or the "yelden host" of sonnet 21. And like Lok's appropriation of the sonnet from Tottel's *Miscellany*, the speaker of the sequence utilizes the position of the monarchy to foster and articulate desires based in a social authority derived from class—a true church where commodity circulation is both facilitated and, paradoxically, made unnecessary.

Nevertheless, the sequence ends not with narrative closure that erasures the speaker's lyric authority but with a contradictory reaffirmation of that lyric "I":

That I then, Lorde, may also honor thee,
Releve my sorow, and my sinnes deface:
Be, Lord of mercie, mercifull to me:
Restore my feling of thy grace againe:
Assure my soule, I crave it not in vaine.

The speaker's desire to "honor" his "Lord" reaffirms his desire for lyric authority, for a material, commodified sign so that he "may also honor" God; but this desire rearticulates the very fallenness and sin which *separates* him from relief. He must always "crave it . . . in vaine." The ability to record textually his sin suggests that a sense of mercy is emerging, but since a sign of mercy still remains necessary, it also means that mercy is not forthcoming. The rhyme "againe/in vaine" embodies both the hope and the fear of the penitent Calvinist: any hope is always again "vaine" and "in vaine." Reasserting the lyric "I" at the end of the sequence captures the contradiction between the "I" and the narrative of the foundation of the New Jerusalem which promises to relieve the desire of the lyric speaker. The speaker's resists that narrative because it undermines, even as it makes possible, his ability to speak at all.

The speaker's reassertion of his lyric authority consequently emphasizes that there remains an unbridgeable gap between the "New Jerusalem" as a Protestant apocalypse—the end of historical time—and the historical England which Lok seeks to transform and describe with her use of the term "New Jerusalem." From the vantage point of the speaker's authority, Elizabethan England and the New Jerusalem are certainly not synonyms, and the assertion of authority at the close of the sequence borders on open hostility. "Againe/in vaine," coupled with the imperatives "Restore" and "Assure," sounds less like resignation than anger; the speaker *tells* God or Elizabeth what to do, much as Lok herself told the duchess of Suffolk where to find mercy in the dedicatory epistle. While the narrative of the foundation of the New Jerusalem initially provokes the speaker's desire for mercy, his lyric authority comes to *resist* that very narrative when it paradoxically ends up endorses a monarchical power which threatens the authority of the speaker—a "tyrannie" of "myning fraude" and "mighty violence." The lord from whom the speaker seeks to acquire mercy is also the noble "lord" whose authority the speaker's commodified interpretation resists. Equating Elizabeth with God, or even making her head of the church, was, after all, largely what the godly resisted so insistently throughout her reign. Were she not to support the godly (as indeed she largely did not), Elizabeth potentially enacts the very "tyrannie" against which she is supposed to protect Calvinists like Lok. As early as November 1559, John Jewel, also a Marian exile who eventually made the difficult decision to become a bishop, complained to the Reformation figure Peter Martyr back in Geneva, "That little silver cross, of ill-omened origin, still maintains its place in the queen's chapel. Wretched me! This thing will soon be drawn into a precedent."[46] The paradox of the speaker's subjection occurs as he himself must assert his "presuming eye" and stand "in despite of tyrannie" against Elizabeth—against, in other words, the very historical narrative which facilitates his utterance in the first place. In the absence of the apocalypse, he himself must finally act as "lord" and occupy the position—of God and the monarch—which promises to foster the circulation of commodities that is the basis of his authority.

In the resistance of the lyric "I" to the very narrative which provokes it, then, we should see not only a powerful expression of a typically Calvinist speaker but the articulation of an emergent sense of authority both enabled by and resistant to monarchical authority. Rather than the New Jerusalem referring to a place and an institution—England and its church, both overseen by Elizabeth—it refers to a process, an internalized authority dialectically defined in relation to monarchical absolutism. We should consequently think of Lok's work not only as a reaction to the cultural moment of the re-Protestantization of England under Elizabeth, but also as a *representation* of England from the distinct and influential perspective of a Calvinism, wealthy, mercantilist woman. *A Meditation* not only exists "in" the "Englishe box" of Elizabeth's protection; it *is* the box—a textual construction of England circa 1560. Early Elizabethan England from this perspective looks much like Lok's sonnet sequence—a world where authority is spread among both those who maintain Calvinist convictions and those who can enact those convictions in the form of textual commodities; but also a world where this procedural authority is enabled by and resistant to institutionalized conceptions of authority, particularly absolute monarchy.

In terms of literary history, *A Meditation of a Penitent Sinner* becomes important less because of its negligible influence on later writers than because it opens up largely unexplored critical territory—the expression in sonnets of trade, commodity circulation, and the desires of non-noble people. If writers like Lok depict the monarchy in the service of non-noble interests, conversely, to what degree was this possible because monarchical authority itself was in part modeled on the authority of interpretive process? When Queen Elizabeth decides to write sonnets, when King James styles himself a "prentice" sonnet writer, when Astrophil checks himself in "Reason's *audit*," when Daniel claims that his sighs and sonnets are an account book, when Spenser's speaker claims the *Amoretti* emerge from "trade," when Shakespeare's speaker complains that his beloved is a "profitless usurer," and, finally, when Drayton describes these tensions as "the English strain" in sharp opposition to the king he despised—all these moments point to the need to reconceptualize social relations in Renaissance England and to the ways those relations are manifest in the sonnet in this period. Only when we begin to address these questions will Lok find a secure location in the literary-historical landscape. To situate Lok means not only rethinking the relations

between secular and religious poetry; it means reconceiving the class
dynamics bound up in the English sonnet.

Oakland University

NOTES

For comments and assistance my sincere thanks to Jenny Andersen, Emily Bartels,
Ann Coiro, Anne Coldiron, Rosanne Currarino, Susan Felch, Thomas Freeman,
Roland Greene, Margaret Hannay, Jacqueline Miller, William Oram, Anne Lake
Prescott, and Gordon Schochet.

   1.   *Sermons of John Calvin, upon the Songe that Ezechias made after he had bene sicke,
and afflicted by the hand of God, conteyned in the 38. Chapiter of Esay. Translated out of
Frenche into Englishe* (London, 1560). All further citations refer to the microfilm of
the British Library copy. A note on spelling: there is no critical consensus on how
to spell Lok's name, and given the number of editions forthcoming, no consensus
seems likely to emerge. "Lock," "Locke," and "Lok" are the major variants. I
employ "Lok" because that is the spelling encountered most frequently with other
members of her family. Nevertheless, in quotations I have retained the spelling
employed by other scholars.
   2.   She is so identified in the *Dictionary of National Biography* entry for her son
Henry Lok.
   3.   In his overview of the state of "Lok studies," Michael R. G. Spiller notes that
there are four editions of Lok's work out or forthcoming. See Michael R. G. Spiller,
"A literary 'first': the Sonnet Sequence of Anne Locke (1560)," *Renaissance Studies*
11.1 (1997): 41–55.
   4.   See Patrick Collinson, "The Role of Women in the English Reformation
Illustrated by the Life and friendships of Anne Locke," *Studies in Church History
Volume II*, ed. G.J. Cuming (London, 1965), 258–72, reprinted in *Godly People:
Essays on English Protestantism and Puritanism* (London: The Hambledon Press,
1983), 273–87.
   5.   Roland Greene, "Ann Lock's *Meditation*: Invention Versus Dilation and the
Founding of Puritan Poetics," in *Form and Reform in Renaissance England: Essays in
Honor of Barbara Kiefer Lewalski*, ed. Amy Boesky and Mary Thomas Crane (Newark:
University of Delaware Press, 2000). My thanks to Professor Greene for allowing
me to see his article in manuscript.
   6.   Greene, "Ann Lock's *Meditation*."
   7.   Elaine V. Beilin briefly considers Lok in her wide-ranging *Redeeming Eve:
Women Writers of the English Renaissance* (Princeton: Princeton University Press,
1987), and Kathy Lynn Emerson includes an entry for Lok in *Wives and Daughters:
The Women of Sixteenth Century England* (Troy, NY: Whitston Publishing, 1984).
See also Susanne Woods, "Ann Lock and Aemilia Lanyer: A Tradition of Protestant
Women Speaking," in *The New Seventeenth Century*; Woods, "The Body Penitent:
a 1560 Calvinist Sonnet Sequence," *ANQ* 5 (1992): 137; T. P. Roche, *Petrarch and*

the English Sonnet Sequences (New York: AMS Press, 1989), 155–57; and Michael R. G. Spiller, *The Development of the Sonnet: An Introduction* (London: Routledge, 1992), 92–3.

8. On the traditions of women's writing in the English Renaissance, see Linda Woodbridge, *Women and the English Renaissance: Literature and the Nature of Womankind 1540–1620* (Urbana and Chicago: University of Illinois Press, 1984); *Silent But for the Word: Tudor Women as Patrons, Translators, and Writers of Religious Works*, ed. Margaret Hannay (Kent: Kent State University Press, 1985); Beilin, *Redeeming Eve*; Ann Rosalind Jones, *The Currency of Eros* (Bloomington: Indiana University Press, 1990); *Women, Texts and Histories 1575–1760*, ed. Clare Brant and Diane Purkiss (New York: Routledge, 1992); Barbara Kiefer Lewalski, *Writing Women in Jacobean England* (Cambridge: Harvard University Press, 1993); *Women and Literature in Britain 1500–1700*, ed. Helen Wilcox (Cambridge: Cambridge University Press, 1996); and Elizabeth Hanson, "Boredom and Whoredom: Reading Renaissance Women's Sonnet Sequences," *Yale Journal of Criticism* 10 (1997): 165–91.

9. Rivkah Zim, *English Metrical Psalms: Poetry as Praise and Prayer 1535–1601* (Cambridge: Cambridge University Press, 1987) 25. On Lok's relation to the psalm tradition, see also Roland Greene, "Sir Philip Sidney's *Psalms*, the Sixteenth-Century Psalter, and the Nature of Lyric," *SEL* 30 (1990): 19–40; and Margaret Hannay, "'Unlock my lipps': the *Miserere mei Deus* of Anne Vaughan Lok and Mary Sidney Herbert, Countess of Pembroke," in *Privileging Gender in Early Modern England*, ed. Jean R. Brink (Kirksville, MO: Sixteenth Century Journal Publishers, 1993), 19–36.

10. Ann Baynes Coiro notes that "current studies devoted to early modern women writers have emphasized an idealized sisterhood among them, even though these studies discuss highly varied configurations of women across several generations and even across continents." Instead, Coiro emphasizes that "[t]he crisscrossings of gender and class is particularly intricate and codependent in the Renaissance when writing venues themselves carry class and gender stigmas." Nevertheless, Coiro stresses that her argument would scarcely be possible without pioneering efforts that have rescued writing by women from scholarly oblivion. "Writing in Service: Sexual Politics and Class Position in the Poetry of Aemilia Lanyer and Ben Jonson," *Criticism* 35 (1993): 358. Jonathan Goldberg's *Desiring Women Writing* (Stanford: Stanford University Press, 1997) builds upon and expands Coiro's argument.

11. Coiro, 357.

12. The classic statement is by Arthur Marotti, "'Love is Not Love': Elizabethan Sonnet Sequences and the Social Order," *ELH* 49 (1982): 396–428.

13. The best biography of Lok remains Collinson's "The Role of Women in the English Reformation"; but see Spiller for a list of forthcoming editions of her work which synthesize biographical material. On Stephen Vaughan see W. C. Richardson, *Stephen Vaughan Financial Agent of Henry VIII*, Louisiana State University Studies, Social Science Series Number Three (Baton Rouge: Louisiana State University Press, 1953); David Daniell, *William Tyndale: A Biography* (New Haven and London: Yale University Press, 1994), 4, 155, 174–222, 372; J. F. Mozley, *William Tyndale* (London: Society for Promoting Christian Knowledge, 1937), 187–320 passim; Penry Williams, *The Tudor Regime* (Oxford: Clarendon Press, 1979), 62–70, 190; and G.D. Ramsey, *The City of London in International Politics at the Accession of Elizabeth Tudor*

(Manchester: Manchester University Press, 1975), 33–80, who details the role of the Merchant Adventurers and the responsibilities of Vaughan and his later successor Thomas Gresham. On the Mercers and Merchant Adventurers see D. C. Coleman, *The Economy of England 1450–1750* (Oxford: Oxford University Press, 1977), 48–68. On Henry Brinkelow and the Cromwellian apologists see John King, *English Reformation Literature: The Tudor Origins of the Protestant Tradition* (Princeton: Princeton University Press, 1982), 44–56. On Sir William Lok and Michael Lok, see the respective entries in *The Dictionary of National Biography*. Kenneth R. Andrews, *Trade, Plunder and Settlement: Maritime Enterprise and the Genesis of the British Empire, 1480–1630* (Cambridge: Cambridge University Press, 1984), passim details the involvement of Michael Lok and other Loks in maritime voyages, especially that of Frobisher; see also Katherine Duncan-Jones, *Sir Philip Sidney, Courtier Poet* (New Haven and London, Yale University Press, 1991), 223–29 passim on Michael Lok's relation to Sidney and Frobisher's voyages. On Edward Dering see Patrick Collinson, *The Elizabethan Puritan Movement* (Berkeley and Los Angeles: University of California Press, 1967), passim; Collinson, "A Mirror of Elizabethan Puritanism: The Life and Letters of 'Godly Master Dering,'" in *Godly People*, 289–324; Peter Lake, *Moderate Puritans and the Elizabethan Church* (Cambridge: Cambridge University Press, 1982), 16–24; and Peter C. Herman, *Squitter-wits and Muse-haters: Sidney, Spenser, Milton and Renaissance Antipoetic Sentiment* (Detroit: Wayne State University Press, 1996), 25–68. On Lok and Knox see Collinson, "The Role of Women"; Susan M. Felch, "'Deir Sister': The Letters of John Knox to Anne Vaughan Lok," *Renaissance & Reformation* 19 (1995): 47–68; and Felch, "The Rhetoric of Biblical Authority: John Knox and the Question of Women," *Sixteenth Century Journal* 26 (1995): 805–22. On Henry Lok see Roche. I am also indebted to Felch's introduction to *The Collected Works of Anne Vaughan Lock* (Tempe, AZ: Arizona Center for Medieval and Renaissance Studies, 1999). My sincere thanks to Professor Felch for allowing me to see her manuscript.

14.   Robert Weimann, *Authority and Representation in Early Modern Discourse*, ed. David Hillman (Baltimore and London: Johns Hopkins University Press, 1996), 53.

15.   Weimann, 29.

16.   Weimann, 67.

17.   Greene, "Sidney's *Psalms*," 23. On David and the psalms, see Barbara Lewalski, *Protestant Poetics and the Seventeenth-Century Religious Lyric* (Princeton: Princeton University Press, 1979); Anne Lake Prescott, "Evil tongues at the court of Saul: the Renaissance David as a slandered courtier," *JMRS* 12 (1991): 163–86; and Prescott, "King David as a 'Right Poet': Sidney and the Psalmist," *ELR* 19.3 (1989): 131–51.

18.   Spiller, "A literary 'first,'" 54–55, note 14.

19.   Jones, *The Birth of the Elizabethan Age*, 49.

20.   Margaret P. Hannay, "'Strengthning the walles of . . . Ierusalem': Anne Vaughan Lok's Dedication to the Countess of Warwick," *ANQ* 5.2–3 (1992): 72. Gary Waller notes that "for Protestants of the sixteenth century, poetry was not something that could be separated from the godly pursuit of a Protestant state." *English Poetry of the Sixteenth Century* (London and New York, 1986), 95. Similarly, Prescott argues that post-Reformation readers viewed David as "something like a Renaissance anti-court poet" ("Evil tongues at the court of Saul," 165). In the

introduction to her forthcoming edition of Lok's work, Felch notes that "Hezekiah provided Lock with the requisite model for a Protestant England newly emerging from the turmoil of Mary's reign into the, as yet unformed and unstable, Elizabethan age."

21. Fredric Jameson, *The Political Unconscious: Narrative as a Socially Symbolic Act* (Ithaca and London: Cornell University Press, 1981), 128.

22. Jones, *The Birth of the Elizabethan Age*, 17–47. See also his *Faith by Statute: Parliament and the Settlement of Religion 1559* (London: Royal Historical Society, 1982), which details the parliamentary and political maneuvering necessary for the "Anglican Settlement." Jones, like all historians of the period, builds upon Patrick Collinson's seminal works. See in particular *The Elizabethan Puritan Movement; Archbishop Grindal 1519–1583: The Struggle for a Reformed Church* (London: Jonathan Cape, 1979); *The Religion of Protestants: The Church in English Society 1559–1625* (Oxford: Clarendon Press, 1982); and *Godly People*.

23. Lake, 20.

24. Jones, *The Birth of the Elizabethan Age*, 61.

25. *Of the markes of the chil-dren of God, and of their comforts in afflictions. To the faithfull of the Low Countrie. By John Taffin. Overseene againe and augmented by the Author, and translated out of French by Anne Prowse* (London, 1590), A4–A5.

26. See Richard Helgerson's discussion of the difficulty of distinguishing "gentlemen" from "merchants" in *Forms of Nationhood: The Elizabethan Writing of England* (Chicago and London: University of Chicago Press, 1992), 151–91.

27. See the introduction to *The Culture of English Puritanism, 1560–1700*, ed. Christopher Durston and Jacqueline Eales (New York: St. Martin's Press, 1996), 1–31, especially 10. Max Weber famously attempted to forge an alliance between Calvinism and the "spirit of capitalism" in *The Protestant Ethic and the Spirit of Capitalism*, 1930 (London: Routledge, 1992). Both the strengths and weaknesses of this position are definitively articulated by R. H. Tawney's *Religion and the Rise of Capitalism: A Historical Study (Holland Memorial Lectures, 1922)* (New York: Harcourt, Brace and Company, 1926). A collection on seventeenth-century "religious" verse (*New Perspectives on the Seventeenth-Century English Religious Lyric*, ed. John R. Roberts [Columbia and London: University of Missouri Press, 1994]) constantly calls into question that label. For instance, in "The Poetry of Supplication: Toward a Cultural Poetics of the Religious Lyric" Michael C. Schoenfeldt begins by noting that "[i]t is ironic that readers have tended to interpret the seventeenth-century religious lyric in deliberate isolation from social and cultural forces, since the early seventeenth-century practitioners of the devotional lyric . . . were themselves so profoundly aware of the social dimensions of their work" (75). See also Prescott, "Evil tongues at the court of Saul."

28. See generally King, and David Norbrook, *Poetry and Politics in the English Renaissance* (London: Routledge & Kegan Paul, 1984), 32–90. On the "plain style" and its origins in medieval, didactic, non-aristocratic verse see Douglas L. Peterson, *The English Lyric from Wyatt to Donne: A History of the Plain and Eloquent Styles* (Princeton: Princeton University Press, 1967), 3–38; and Yvor Winters, "The 16th Century Lyric in England. A Critical and Historical Reinterpretation," in *Elizabethan Poetry: Modern Essays in Criticism*, ed. Paul J. Alpers, (Oxford: Oxford University Press, 1967), 93–125.

29. Spiller, "A literary 'first,'" 49.

30. Alexandra Halasz, "Wyatt's David," in *Rethinking the Henrician Era: Essays on Early Tudor Texts and Contexts*, ed. Peter C. Herman (Urbana and Chicago: University of Illinois Press, 1994), 198. Halasz is responding in particular to Stephen Greenblatt's influential rendering of "the circumstances that shape the psalmic voice" (197) and the fashioning of "inwardness" in Henry's court. See Greenblatt, "Power, Sexuality, and Inwardness in Wyatt's Poetry," in *Renaissance Self-Fashioning From More to Shakespeare* (Chicago and London: The University of Chicago Press, 1980), 115–56.

31. Spiller, 49.

32. Crane, *Framing Authority*, 170. Cf. Wendy Wall, *The Imprint of Gender: Authorship and Publication in the English Renaissance* (Ithaca and London: Cornell University Press, 1993), 23–30, who argues that Tottel's uses "an aristocratic value to criticize an aristocratic practice" (27); and Arthur Marotti, *Manuscript, Print, and the English Renaissance Lyric* (Ithaca: Cornell University Press, 1995), 212–28, who like Crane notes that Tottel "reverses received notions of gentle and ungentle."

33. Rollins, 2.

34. Crane, *Framing Authority*, 170.

35. Crane, *Framing Authority*, 168. Wall similarly notes that "[i]n labeling the 'horders' of such texts as 'ungentle,' Tottel reverses the class distinctions generated by coterie circulation, inscribing the act of publishing as the more noble, 'gentle' mode of exchange and the book reader as the truly 'gentle' kind of textual consumer" (26).

36. On commodities and the value they acquire through circulation, see Karl Marx, *Capital: A Critique of Political Economy*, ed. Frederick Engels, trans. Ernest Untermann (New York: Random House, 1906), 41–162, "Commodities and Money."

37. See Ellen Meiksins Wood, *The Pristine Culture of Capitalism: A Historical Essay on Old Regimes and Modern States* (London and New York: Verso, 1991), who sharply criticizes what she terms "the bourgeois paradigm": "[i]n England, there was capitalism, but it was not called into being by the bourgeoisie. In France, there was a (more or less) triumphant bourgeoisie, but its revolutionary project had little to do with capitalism ... The [bourgeois] model is, rather, a composite picture formed largely by a retrospective superimposition of the French revolutionary experience upon the example of English capitalism, and, conversely, an interpretation of the French political experience in the light of English economic development" (3–4).

38. Here and throughout I follow the work of Pierre Bourdieu, especially *Distinction: A Social Critique of the Judgement of Taste*, trans. Richard Nice (Cambridge: Harvard University Press, 1984).

39. Weimann, 2.

40. See the entry for Catherine Willoughby, the duchess of Suffolk, in Emerson, 245–46.

41. Lok translates four sermons Calvin delivered on 5, 6, 15, and 16 November 1557 at Geneva. She may well have heard them in person, but her copy text seems to be not the manuscript version of the text but rather an early copy of a revision published in French in 1562. See Felch, *The Collected Works of Anne Vaughan Lock*.

42. My reading of Calvin and use of the term "negation" here draws on Theodor Adorno's conception of "determined negation," an idea he describes (with uncharacteristic clarity) in a conversation with Ernst Bloch on the question of "utopia" as a philosophic (rather than a literary) concept: "[U]topia is essentially in determined negation, in the determined negation of that which merely is, and by concretizing itself as something false, it always point at the same time to what should be. Yesterday you [Bloch] quoted Spinoza in our discussion with the passage, 'Verum index sui et falsi' [The true is the sign of itself and the false]. I have varied this a little in the sense of the dialectical principle of the determined negation and have said, Falsum—the false thing—index sui et veri [The false is the sign of itself and the correct]. That means that the true thing determines itself via the false thing, or via that which makes itself falsely known. And insofar as we are not allowed to cast the picture of utopia, insofar as we do not know what the correct thing would be, we know exactly, to be sure, what the false thing is." Adorno puts this concept somewhat more succinctly earlier: "One may not cast a picture of utopia in a positive manner" (Ernst Bloch, *The Utopian Function of Art and Literature: Selected Essays*, trans. Jack Zipes and Frank Mecklenburg [Cambridge: MIT Press, 1988], 10–12).

43. Greene, "Ann Lok's *Meditation*." Greene draws on Patricia Parker, *Literary Fat Ladies: Rhetoric, Gender, Property* (London: Methuen, 1987).

44. *The Geneva Bible: A Facsimile of the 1560 Edition*, introduction by Lloyd E. Berry (Madison: The University of Wisconsin Press, 1969).

45. Spiller, "A literary 'first,'" notes that there are two exceptions. Lok splits verses one and four into two sonnets, and Spiller sees this as evidence that Lok had read Wyatt's translation published in 1549/50. Spiller points out that Wyatt "writes in continuous *terza rime* verse, but allots between two and five lines to each psalm verseexcept for verse 1, which was nine lines, verse 4, which has eleven, and verse 6, which has eight. Locke thus twice expanded just where Wyatt expanded" (46).

46. *Original Letters Relative to the English Reformation . . .* , Vol. 50 (Cambridge: The Parker Society, 1846), 55.

GLEANINGS

ANDREW HADFIELD

Spenser and Chaucer: The Knight's Tale and Artegall's Response to the Giant with the Scales (*Faerie Queene*, V, ii, 41–42)

*I*N A RECENT NOTE, Colin Fairweather has observed how Spenser appears to have made a point of granting Chaucer equal status as a poet with Virgil in *The Shepheardes Calender*.[1] *The Squire's Tale,* as has often been noted, was continued by Spenser in *The Faerie Queene,* Book IV, and elsewhere Spenser signals his considerable debt to his most important English precursor.[2] As J. W. Burrow has commented, "No Elizabethan writer, displays a closer relationship to Chaucer than does Spenser."[3]

Chaucer's works clearly formed an important source for passages in Spenser's poetry, most notably in *The Faerie Queene.* Commentators, in particular, Judith Anderson, have often noted examples.[4] However, one example seems to have been overlooked by scholars, perhaps because the parallels are thematic rather than verbal. Before Talus throws the Giant with the Scales off the cliffs into the sea to drown (*FQ,* V, ii), Artegall attempts to refute the Giant's argument that curbing the power of tyrants and a more equal distribution of wealth is a desirable goal. Artegall argues that inequality is enshrined within the natural order of the universe and that "All in the powre of their great Maker lie: / All creatures must obey the voice of the most hie":

> They liue, they die, like as he doth ordaine,
>   Ne euer any asketh reason why.
> The hils doe not the lowly dales disdaine,
> The dales doe not the lofty hils enuy.
> He maketh Kings to sit in souerainty;
> He maketh subjects to their powre obay;
> He pulleth downe, he setteth up on hy;

245

He giues to this, from that he takes away.
For all we haue is his: what he list doe, he may.

What euer thing is done, by him is donne,
    Ne any may his mighty will withstand;
    Ne any may his soueraine power shonne,
    Ne loose that he hath bound with stedfast band.
    In vaine therefore doest thou now take in hand,
    To call to count, or weigh his workes anew,
    Whose counsels depth thou canst not understand,
    Sith of things subject to thy daily vew
Thou doest not know the causes, nor their courses dew.

V, ii, 41–42

Artegall's words appear to echo significant passages in *The Knight's Tale;* principally Theseus's "Firste Moevere" speech at the end of the tale (lines 2987–3074), but also Saturn's description of the effects of his rule over the universe (lines 2453–78).[5] Theseus claims that "thilke Moevere stable is and eterne" (line 3004) and that experience shows that mankind should accept the order and and plan outlined by the Gods:

What maketh this but Juppiter, the kyng,
That is prince and cause of alle thyng,
Convertynge al unto his propre welle
From which it is derryved, sooth to telle?
And heer-agayns no creature on lyve,
Of no degree, availleth for to stryve.
Thanne is it wysdom, as it thynketh me,
To maken vertue of necesitiee,
And take it weel that we may nat eschue,
And namely that to us alle is due.
And whoso gruccheth ought, he dooth folye,
And rebel is to hym that al may gye.

Lines 3035–46

The parallels between the two passages, although not immediately apparent, are striking on closer inspection. Both argue almost identical cases. Just as Artegall alleges that the Giant should accept his lot and accept the world as it is given, so does Theseus urge Palamon and Emily to accept their lot and the hand fate has dealt them. Both speakers make a strong case against complaint or resistance to the will of the Gods (*FQ*, stanza 42; *KT*, lines 3045–46). Each speech contains a list of structurally paralleled sentences that stand out from the surrounding text (*FQ*, 41, lines 5–8, 42, 2–4; *KT*, lines 3043–46). There are verbal and syntactic parallels between sentences and phrases, notably

What euer thing is done, by him is donne,
Ne any may his mighty will withstand.

FQ 42, lines 1–2

What maketh this but Juppiter, the kyng,
That is prince, and cause of alle thyng[.]

KT, lines 3035–36

He giues to this, from that he takes away.
For all we haue is his: what he list doe, he may.

FQ, 41, lines 8–9

And take it weel that we may nat eschue,
And namely that to us alle is due.

KT, lines 303–04

Artegall speaks of the almighty having bound everything with a "steadfast band" (42, line 4), which may be compared to Theseus's image of the "First Moevere's" "faire cheyne of love" (line 2988). In addition one might compare *FQ*, V, ii, 41, lines 5–8 to Saturn's rather more grisly boast of his power:

Myn is the drenchyng in the see so wan;
Myn is the prison in the derke cote;
Myn is the stranglyng and hangyng by the throte[.]

KT, lines 2456–58

The parallels between the two texts, thematic, stylistic and lexical, seem clear enough to suggest that Spenser had *The Knight's Tale* in mind when he wrote Artegall's reply to the Giant. Given Spenser's keen interest in Chaucer and the close reading of his works demonstrated elsewhere in Spenser's writings, a coincidence seems highly unlikely. Indeed, Artegall's description of the order of the universe perhaps owes a wider debt to Chaucer's translation of Boethius' *Consolation of Philosophy*, available in the folio edition of Chaucer's *Works* published in 1561, associated with John Stow.[6] Philosophy's conclusions in the *Consolation* have long been seen as the source of Theuseus's "Firste Moevere" speech (*KT*, lines 2987–3089), and it is possible that Spenser wrote his lines after having referred back to Chaucer's own source.[7] Certainly Philosophy's concluding two speeches in Book V of the *Consolation* can be read alongside Artegall's argument against the Giant. The substance of Philosophy's argument is that "devyne prescience ne chaungeth nat the nature ne the proprete of thinges, but byholdeth swiche things present to hymward as thei shollen betyde to yow-ward in tyme to comen" [i.e., the future and the present are seen in the same way by God].[8] Philosophy argues that because freedom exists in the sub-lunary sphere, it is a mistake to think that man can know the mind of God.

These arguments are analogous to Artegall's arguments against the Giant in stanzas 39–40. Against the Giant's claim that he can level the inequalities on earth because he knows the mind and purpose of God, Artegall asserts that "the earth is not augmented more,/ By all that dying into it doe fade" (40). God's constancy precedes the transitoriness of earthly things. The Giant has foolishly believed that he can read the divinity from his creations: "Of things unseene how vanst thou deeme aright,/ . . . Sith thou misdeem'st so much of things in sight?" (39). Artegall warns the Giant in exactly the same way that Philosophy educates her pupil, Boethius.

The relevance of Chaucer's tale to Spenser's epic is easy to understand. Both Artegall and Theseus are trying to establish a sense of divine stability in the universe against threats to the established order (Theseus has to explain the significance of Arcite's tragic death and so cement his preeminent position; Artegall has to establish his right to distribute justice). Significantly enough, having been accepted as mouthpieces for their authors by most critics, both have been read in an ironic light recently.[9] Furthermore, given that the importance of the classical gods increases as *The Faerie Queene* progresses, it is also easy to understand why Chaucer's tale, which places the influence of Saturn and Jupiter at the center of the action, should have served Spenser's purposes. In different places in *The Knight's Tale*, Saturn and Jupiter are seen as the dominant deity (lines 2453–78; lines 3067–74), holding sway over human and divine affairs alike. The struggle between Saturn, Jupiter (Jove) and the Titans becomes the most important contest of the later books of *The Faerie Queene*. The opposition between Artegall and the Giant with the Scales is one manifestation of this contest, Artegall holding his power from Jove through his sword, Chrysaor (V, 1, 9), while the Giant is undoubtedly of the race of Titans.[10]

University of Wales, Aberystwyth

NOTES

1. " 'I suppose he meane Chaucer': The Comedy of Errors in Spenser's *Shepheardes Calender*," *Notes and Queries* 244 (1999): 193–95.

2. Jonathan Goldberg, *Endlesse Worke: Spenser and the Structures of Discourse* (Baltimore: Johns Hopkins University Press, 1981), ch. 3. See also G. R. Crampton, *The Condition of Creatures: Suffering and Action in Chaucer and Spenser* (New Haven: Yale University Press, 1974); Alice K. Miskimin, *The Renaissance Chaucer* (New Haven: Yale University Press, 1975), passim.

3. "*Chaucer, Geoffrey,*" in A. C. Hamilton, ed. *The Spenser Encyclopedia* (London and Toronto: Routledge and Toronto University Press, 1990), 144–48, at p. 144. Burrow provides an excellent and systematic account of Spenser's use of Chaucer, but does not mention Artegall or the Giant with the Scales.

4. See, for example, *Words that Matter: Linguistic Perception in Renaissance English* (Stanford: Stanford University Press, 1996).

5. All references to *The Riverside Chaucer*, ed. Larry D. Benson et al. (Oxford: Oxford University Press, 1987).

6. Burrow, "*Chaucer, Geoffrey,*" p. 145.

7. For details of Chaucer's use of Boethius, see *Riverside Chaucer*, 841.

8. *Boece,* Book V, metrum 5, lines 136–40.

9. Terry Jones, *Chaucer's Knight: The Portrait of a Medieval Mercenary* (London: Weidenfeld and Nicolson, 1980); Stephen Knight, *Geoffrey Chaucer* (Brighton: Harvester, 1986), 83–90; Annabel Patterson, "The Egalitarian Giant: Representations of Justice in History / Literature," *Journal of British Studies* 31 (1992): 97–132.

10. For commentary see Susanne Lindgren Wofford, "*Spenser's Giants,*" in Mihoko Suzuki, ed., *Critical Essays on Edmund Spenser* (New York: G. K. Hall, 1996), 199–220; Jacqueline T. Miller, "*Jove*", *Spenser Encyclopedia*, 412–13; Anne Lake Prescott, '*Titans,*' *Spenser Encyclopedia*, 1961.

RICHARD F. HARDIN

Spenser's Aesculapius Episode and the English Mummers' Play

*T*HE MUMMERS' (Saint George) Play, based in oral and folk tradition, probably existed in Spenser's time, although there is no direct evidence of performance until the early 1700s.[1] The play enacts a "hero combat": a hero, often St. George, boasts of his fighting skill to an enemy, often a Turkish Knight; one opponent kills the other; a doctor, sometimes urged by an old woman, raises the dead combatant in the "cure scene." The play ends with comic speeches by several unrelated characters, who then collect money from the audience. Evidence exists that this folk play influenced Tudor drama, and I think it shapes Book I, Canto v of *The Faerie Queene*, where Duessa tries to resurrect Sansjoy in the underworld (stanzas 28–44). Night in her iron chariot takes the Saracen below, to be healed by Aesculapius. A two-stanza digression then describes that ur- physician's healing and revival of Hippolytus. Discussion of this episode has usually focused on the pagan Aesculapius as a negative image of Christ, true doctor of souls.[2] The Mummers' Play can account for other circumstances of this episode, especially the duel between Redcrosse and Sansjoy, the similarity of Duessa to "the king of Egypt's daughter" sometimes rescued by St. George, and the presence of the ancient female Night. All such details cohere, though—combat, damsel, old woman, physician, and cure—if read in the context of the Mummers' Play. The significance of this similarity for Spenser's narrative depends on how the poet himself interpreted its meaning. It is entirely possible that he thought of it rather as some modern folklorists do, as a remnant of paganism. His godly contemporaries, after all, regarded maypoles and Christmas festivity as such. At the very least, Spenser's digression offers yet another tantalizing clue that, a century before the earliest known date, the Mummers' Play was well enough known to appear in a parody.

Spenser scholars seem to have neglected the Mummers' St. George. E. K. Chambers approached him as a subject of source study, claiming that Spenser influenced Richard Johnson's St. George story in his *Famous Historie of the Seaven Champions of Christendom* (1596–97), which in turn prompted dramatized versions of the story among the "folk" who had read it. He thus sees the pagan folk play as converted by Spenser's high-culture original. Chambers admits that Johnson's St. George story has no Doctor episode and lacks "the pervasive Woman, whose dramatic function is so obscure" (194). However, his theory seems less likely than that both Johnson and Spenser appealed partly to their readers' own experience of the St. George story in pageants, puppet shows, or Mummers' Plays. Spenser often works folk motifs into his poetry (Archimago's dream-making, Britomart's summoning up the image of her future husband, the adaptation of the Green Man figure in the Salvage Man of Book VI). He describes Redcrosse himself as a rustic in the *Letter to Ralegh*, inviting us to consider that the clownish knight was as much the product of the pageant and festival St. George as of the story in the Golden Legend. Until the last three cantos, in fact, the gullible rustic behaves more like a rude pageant actor than the authentic hero as imagined by chivalry. As William Nelson observed, "the buffoonery of village St. George plays must have rendered the story [of Redcrosse] ridiculous" to the educated Londoner.[3]

Considering this episode as an educated Londoner's allusion invites reading it in terms of the meaning of the folk play. Roger Renwick has interpreted the combat and cure as concerned with "the interdependence of Self and Other"; the action begins in difference that is subsequently diminished.[4] Thomas Pettit goes so far as to define the Self-Other battle socially, the play showing "the interdependent relationship between agrarian classes."[5] We often read Sansjoy (like Sansfoy and Orgoglio) as Redcrosse's double, a kind of alter ego with whom the hero must carry on a struggle.[6] Thus, in the context of Holiness, Spenser's episode would enact a Pauline drama of divided self. The dark Sansjoy partakes of the "old man" to be left behind. The pagan healer-of-bodies Aesculapius has been relegated to the underworld, so that try as she might the "old woman," Mother Night, cannot elicit a Cure. Aesculapius practices an obsolete science. If the Mummers' Play is "about" creating or restoring harmony in communities, Spenser adapts it to the theme of restoration in the self and soul ("Holiness" starts with whole individuals). St. George's Cure scene finally does come in two stages during the three-day battle with the dragon in Canto xi: on the first day from the well, on the second, from the tree. The tree (Christ on the cross) brings the Doctor's cure, its medicine the balm flowing from it that gives "Life and long health . . ./And deadly woundes could heale, and reare againe/ The senselesse corse appointed for the grave" (Book I, Canto xi, 48). Having seen folk plays with magical cures, Spenser transforms them from buffoonery to blessedness, while preserving their original meaning.

University of Kansas

Notes

1.   Scholarship on the Mummers' Play has traveled some since E. K. Chambers, *The English Folk-Play* (Oxford: Clarendon Press, 1933). Among scholars agreeing that the Mummers' Play existed before the seventeenth century are Alan Brody, *The English Mummers and Their Plays: Traces of Ancient Mystery* (Philadelphia: University of Pennsylvania Press, 1969); E. C. Cawte, *English Ritual Drama: A Geographic Index*, Publications of the Folklore Soc., 127 (London, 1967); Alex Helm, *The English Mummers' Play*. Folklore Society Mistletoe Series, 14 (Woodbridge, Suffolk: D. S. Brewer, 1981); Glynne Wickham, *The Medieval Stage*, 3rd ed. (Cambridge: Cambridge University Press, 1987). On the Web, see the site of the Traditional Drama Research Group, centered at the University of Sheffield, <www.shef.ac.uk/uni/projects/tdrg>, who appear somewhat skeptical about an early date.

2.   See James Nohrnberg, *The Analogy of* The Faerie Queene (Princeton: Princeton University Press, 1976), 172, 175; F. David Hoeniger, s. v. "Aesculapius," in *The Spenser Encyclopedia*, gen. ed. A. C. Hamilton (Toronto: University of Toronto Press, 1990).

3.   Nelson, *The Poetry of Edmund Spenser* (New York: Columbia University Press, 1963), 150.

4.   Roger deV. Renwick, "The Mummers' Play and *The Old Wives' Tale*," *JAF* 94 (1981): 433–55 (445).

5.   Thomas Pettitt, "Early English Traditional Drama: Approaches and Perspectives," *RORD* 25 (1982): 1–30 (p. 10). This remains a most valuable starting point for research on the English Mummers' Play.

6.   See A. C. Hamilton's note on "double" (Book I, Canto ii, 9.2) in his ed., *The Faerie Queene* (London: Longman, 1980), 45; Paul Alpers, *The Poetry of* The Faerie Queene (Princeton: Princeton University Press, 1967), 340–41.

FORUM

LYDIA M. McGREW

A Neglected Gauntlet: J.W. Bennett and the Date of Amoretti 62

Alexander Dunlop's Lenten interpretation of Spenser's *Amoretti* is widely accepted in Spenserian scholarship, even though there have been serious challenges to it. Most importantly, J. W. Bennett's historical arguments made in 1973 have never been adequately answered. Dunlop himself passes over her skepticism without addressing her arguments. But the evidence she provides for dating Sonnet 62 as January 1 rather than as March 25 is compelling, and must be destructive of the Lenten interpretation unless it can be answered on historical grounds. The dating of Sonnet 62 as March 25 is crucial to Dunlop's thesis, and any ad hoc attempt to explain away its apparent references to January 1 would be fatal to the strength of Dunlop's original argument. While Bennett's attack on the March 25 date for Sonnet 62 provides the most important anti-Lenten argument, Carol Kaske has also brought forward corroborative evidence against it from the perspective of the sequence's overall structure. Scholars must seriously reconsider the strength of the evidence for Dunlop's interpretation of the sequence.

ALEXANDER DUNLOP'S Lenten interpretation of the *Amoretti* is taken as an unassailable given in contemporary Spenserian scholarship. In his book, *Petrarch and the English Sonnet Sequences*, Thomas Roche cites Dunlop's numerological Lenten sequence as if there could be no question about its presence in the sonnets.[1] And even G. K. Hunter, while cautioning scholars about the dangers of excessive numerology, states that the basic Lenten sequence is "indeed very simple and [does] not seem to be in doubt."[2]

The best-known articulation of Dunlop's thesis appeared in 1970, in a collection edited by Alastair Fowler.[3] Dunlop argues there that at the center of Spenser's sequence is a calendrical unit which represents the period of time between Ash Wednesday and Easter in the year 1594. Sonnet 22 is an Ash Wednesday sonnet, and between it and Sonnet 68, the Easter sonnet, "Most glorious Lord of life," there are exactly forty-seven sonnets, a figure which corresponds to the number of days in the Lenten period between Ash Wednesday and Easter—forty days of Lenten privation plus seven Sundays. Evidence for Dunlop's thesis seemed to be found not only in the distance between Sonnets 22 and 68, but also and most strikingly in the fact that Sonnet 62 is about the new year, and that on Dunlop's scheme of matching sonnets with days, Sonnet 62 would fall exactly on March 25 in 1594 (the year when Spenser married Elizabeth Boyle and when *Amoretti and Epithalamion* was entered in the Stationers' Register). March 25, being Lady Day, was one of the days from which a new calendar year could be reckoned in Spenser's time, so this content seemed a perfect match for this sonnet if we accepted Dunlop's numerology.

Dunlop gives this Lenten interpretation in a brief form in his introduction to *Amoretti and Epithalamion* in the 1989 Yale edition of Spenser's shorter poems.[4] Even a careful reader of both his introduction and his notes to the sequence might gain the impression that the Lenten interpretation has never been seriously challenged. The Yale edition does cite one article in its notes for further reading which calls the Lenten interpretation into question, a 1978 article by Carol Kaske from *English Literary Renaissance*.[5] But an even more important challenge to Dunlop is not mentioned anywhere in the volume. For all the acknowledgement given it in this important edition, Josephine Waters Bennett's 1973 article in *Renaissance Quarterly*[6] attacking the Lenten interpretation might never have been written.

Since Alexander Dunlop is an editor of the Yale edition responsible for the notes surrounding *Amoretti and Epithalamion*, it is an interesting question as to why he does not give students the opportunity to study this challenge to his views. There can be no question that Dunlop is aware of Bennett's article, for he mentions it explicitly in his own follow-up piece on the Lenten reading, his 1980 article "The Drama of *Amoretti*."[7] Dunlop's summary treatment of Bennett's article is most interesting:

> Criticism of *Amoretti* seems to be caught in an impasse between numerologists and traditionalists. At one extreme the

late Josephine Waters Bennett, rejecting entirely the notion of calendar symbolism in *Amoretti*, saw the sequence in an historical, representational context. . . . I want to suggest that we may break the impasse by approaching the sequence from a different standpoint.

Professors Bennett, Hieatt, and Fowler have studied two different aspects of *Amoretti:* the narrative-historical aspect, which is the author's *donneé*, and the symbolic aspect, which embodies the author's evaluation of the conventional and historical materials with which he works.[8]

Only one other statement in the article may be taken as a reference to Bennett:

This approach to *Amoretti* is, I believe, a middle way, synthesizing the insights of those who see the sequence in a representational, historical context [Bennett] and those who sometimes convey the impression that it exists in a wholly abstract context of religious and calendrical symbolism [Hieatt and Fowler].[9]

Whatever Dunlop means by "synthesizing the insights" of traditionalists such as Bennett, it apparently does not include responding to their arguments. For nowhere in this article does Dunlop attempt to address any of Bennett's specific disagreements with and arguments against his calendrical scheme. He seems to consider it to be possible to "break the impasse" between numerologists and traditionalists without any dialectical exchange which will convince a traditionalist such as Bennett that the Lenten scheme is, in fact, supportable.

But Bennett's attack, if her historical facts are correct, should be taken very seriously indeed, for, as it stands, it appears to refute the Lenten interpretation decisively. Bennett provides evidence indicating that Sonnet 62, far from supporting Dunlop's Lenten chronology, actually contradicts it, because Sonnet 62 is referring to a January 1 New Year's Day, not to Lady Day.[10] Of course, if Sonnet 62 is to be correctly dated as corresponding to January 1, 1594, then Sonnet 22 certainly cannot be about Ash Wednesday of 1594, and, hence, there can be no "Lenten sequence" corresponding to Lent of 1594 in the center of the *Amoretti*.

It is inadequate as a response to Bennett merely to state that she "saw the sequence in a historical, representational context." For

Dunlop's thesis turns crucially around his *own* claims about Spenser's "historical, representational context," specifically, the claim that Sonnet 62 represents March 25 of 1594. In the introductory section of his 1980 article, Dunlop elaborates for several paragraphs upon the contrast between Spenser's *"donnée"*—the historical facts represented in the sequence—and the larger context of symbolism to which those facts are related. Among the personal, historical details of the sequence Dunlop lists are "the references to [Spenser's] work on *The Faerie Queene*, to his friend Lodowick Bryskett, and to his three Elizabeths" and "the calendar symbolism linking the work to 1594. . . . "[11] Dunlop then talks about how such specific details are given symbolic significance in the course of the sequence. But it is, of course, impossible to give universal significance to a detail which does not exist in the first place. That is to say, if there is no "calendar symbolism linking the work to 1594" in the *Amoretti*, no universal significance can be derived from such a pattern in our interpretation of the *Amoretti*. Yet throughout the article, Dunlop takes his own initial thesis about the calendar pattern in *Amoretti* as a *given*, and develops his entire "dramatic" reading using the Lenten interpretation as a basis, without any acknowledgement that the traditionalists whose "insights" he means to "synthesize" have presented specific challenges to this supposed bit of historical detail.

Dunlop implies that traditionalists are simply working from a different interpretive paradigm and that the truly balanced critic can stand above both the traditionalist paradigm and that of the "abstract" numerologists and combine the best ideas of both while avoiding their errors. But Dunlop has made a particular historical claim about the *Amoretti*; Bennett has taken him on his own terms and offered evidence intended to refute that claim. If her argument is not answered in detail, the Lenten interpreters, as represented by Dunlop, have merely performed a side-step maneuver.

Bennett does not, unfortunately, begin her article with the strongest argument in favor of her thesis. In the first paragraph, she sets up her disagreement with Dunlop by stating that Dunlop has confused the rotation of the twelve zodiacal signs with the change in the Year of our Lord, *Anno Domini*. The former, she argues, was usually reckoned from January 1 in the Renaissance, while the latter could also be reckoned from March 25. It is true that Sonnet 62 probably refers to the rotation of the zodiacal signs in lines 1–2: "The weary yeare his race now having run,/The new begins his compast course anew." Bennett may well be right that "his compast course" means the rotation of the twelve signs. But she herself admits that Spenser begins the "course" of the twelve signs with the month of March in the *Mutabilitie Cantos*, so the distinction between the rotation of the twelve signs and the reckoning of *Anno Domini* is not really what Bennett needs to prove that Sonnet 62 is about January 1.

But in spite of this rhetorical flaw of emphasis, Bennett goes on to provide increasingly powerful evidence for a January 1 date for the poem. She points out that the phrase "New Year's Day" was always only used to describe January 1 (a fact which is acknowledged by Dunlop himself[12]). Several times in Sonnet 62, the speaker contrasts "the old year" with "the new": in lines 1–2, we find the "weary year" ending as "the new begins." In lines 7–10, "old yeares sinnes" are contrasted with "new yeares joy":

> the old yeares sinnes forepast let us eschew,
> and fly the faults with which we did offend.
> Then shall the new yeares joy forth freshly send
> into the glooming world his gladsome ray.

And in line 14, the lover tells his lady to "change old yeares annoy to new delight." In view of the reservation of the phrase "New Year's Day" for January 1, Bennett argues that phrases like these in Sonnet 62 make it more probable that the poem refers to a January 1 New Year's Day than to Lady Day.[13] Strangely enough, Dunlop makes a very similar argument in his 1970 article about Sonnet 4. There he says that the phrase "New yeare" in Sonnet 4 provides evidence that this is a January New Year's,[14] but he does not apply the same criterion to Sonnet 62.

Bennett's strongest arguments of all turn around the references in Sonnet 62 to specific customs which were associated with January 1 in the Renaissance. When most students of English literature are told confidently by Dunlop and others that Lady Day was also a day from which the new year could be reckoned, they are likely to disregard the fact that Sonnet 62 refers to customs we currently use for January 1—such as the making of New Year's resolutions. They may assume that, if the new year could be reckoned from two different days in the Renaissance, these customs must have been used equally with reference to either day, and so their presence in Sonnet 62 does not count against the Lenten interpretation. But according to Bennett, this is not true.

The first custom to which Bennett draws attention is the joyful welcome to the New Year, alluded to throughout the poem. Lines 9–14 read

Then shall the new yeares joy forth freshly send
  into the glooming world his gladsome ray:
  and all these stormes which now his beauty blend,
  shall turn to caulmes and tymely cleare away.
So likewise love cheare you your heavy spright,
  and chaunge old yeares annoy to new delight.

Bennett points out that New Year's Day, January 1, was a day of joy
because it was one of the twelve days of Christmas; it was also customary in the Renaissance, as now, to rejoice in and celebrate the
coming of the New Year on that day.

Here again, Bennett probably errs in emphasizing so strongly the
fact that Lady Day fell in Lent. From this fact she argues that Lady
Day, unlike January 1, would be unlikely to be celebrated with joy.
Such an argument makes it appear that Bennett is merely using the
Church Year in a rigidly deductive fashion—"January 1 was in the
Christmas season; therefore joy would be all right. Lady Day was in
Lent; therefore joy would be inappropriate." But her most important
point, which does not depend on such a use of the Church Year, is
that joyful New Year's celebrations were customarily associated in
the Renaissance with January 1 and were not similarly customary for
Lady Day. Therefore, a Renaissance reader encountering a sonnet
about joy in the coming of the new year (without any indication
that the joy had a specifically religious cause) would have been no
more likely to think of Lady Day than would a twentieth-century
man who heard someone cry, "Happy New Year!"[15, 16]

Bennett also cites evidence to show that New Year's resolutions
to "turn over a new leaf" were connected with the January New
Year's Day during the Renaissance, as they are now.[17] This custom
is clearly present in Sonnet 62, lines 5–8.

So let us, which this chaunge of weather vew,
  chaunge eeke our mynds and former lives amend;
the old yeares sinnes forepast let us eschew,
and fly the faults with which we did offend.

Bennett's clear implication is that New Year's resolutions of "amendment" were not customary on Lady Day.

The "chaunge of weather" in Sonnet 62, line 5, is also related to
the new year's theme. The sonnet's concern with the weather is, as

Bennett explains, a reference to a custom which we do not currently use but which *was* used in Spenser's time with particular reference to January 1—the practice of predicting the fortunes of the year to come by noticing the weather on New Year's Day.[18] Spenser actually begins Sonnet 62 with this bit of lore:

> The weary yeare his race now having run,
>   The new begins his compass course anew:
>   with shew of morning mylde he hath begun,
>   betokening peace and plenty to ensew.
>
> (Lines 1–4)

Since this custom is no longer common, it comes as a surprise to the modern reader; there can be no question here of anachronistic bias on the part of the interpreter. This unexpected confirmation provides particularly strong evidence for the January 1 interpretation.

All of these textual-historical points (except for the argument about the zodiacal signs) require an answer.[19] It would be particularly useful to Lenten interpreters if they could find instances in the Renaissance of a joyful welcome to a Lady Day new year, *in the absence of* any mention of the Incarnation. It would be one thing to be joyful, even in Lent, because of the conception of Christ celebrated on Lady Day, but this sonnet indicates only general joy in the fact of the new year—"new yeares joy." Dunlop and his followers also need to bring forward evidence showing that the customs of New Year "amendment" and of reckoning the fortunes of the coming year by the weather *were* used in the English Renaissance not only in connection with January 1, but also with Lady Day.

For the Lenten interpretation cannot stand if Bennett is correct about these customs. It would be *ad hoc* simply to say that Spenser arbitrarily shifted customs from January 1 to Lady Day. How would he have expected his original audience ever to know that he had made such a shift, when their ordinary assumption, given the customs to which he makes reference, would understandably be that the sonnet was about January 1? Why should he make the calendrical reference confusing and obscure by using the wrong set of customs if, indeed, he had a particular day he wished to commemorate and use for numerological purposes? It would not have been difficult for Spenser to make his meaning clearer, if he wished to write a Lady Day sonnet. He could so easily have alluded to the Annunciation or given thanks for God's mercy to mankind in sending his Son. In the two undisputed liturgical sonnets—Sonnet 22 and Sonnet 68–the religious significance of the day is clearly indicated. But whether or not Spenser might be expected to give such explicit evidence for a Lady Day allusion in Sonnet 62, he at least would have been unlikely to include details which would definitely mislead the reader about the sonnet's meaning.

Let us remember that the placement of Sonnet 62 was originally meant to be strong evidence *for* the Lenten interpretation. In fact, in his original article Dunlop begins by arguing for re-dating this sonnet and then outlines his calendrical scheme working outward from Sonnet 62.[20] The apparent strength of his argument lies in the striking fact that, using his Lenten pattern, this sonnet which speaks of a new year falls exactly on a day from which the new calendar year could be reckoned. As Dunlop points out, this exact number of days connecting Ash Wednesday, March 25, and Easter did not occur every year, as did the forty-seven days between Ash Wednesday and Easter; in fact, there is only one other year besides 1594 during Spenser's lifetime in which this pattern occurs—1583. But Dunlop is very likely right that 1583 is too early a date for the composition of *Amoretti and Epithalamion.*[21] Sonnet 62, then, apparently provides a third point of contact between the proposed numerology and the text of the sonnets themselves which relates the numbers not just to any year, as would the Ash Wednesday and Easter sonnets, but to a specific year which is known independently to be significant to the sequence. That a pattern of sonnets should occur which matches so exactly this particular year has seemed to critics too much for coincidence, causing them to take the Lenten interpretation to be established beyond doubt.

So we see how crucial the dating of Sonnet 62 as March 25 is as evidence in favor of the Lenten scheme. The virtue of Dunlop's thesis, a virtue which makes it attractive even to scholars usually skeptical about numerology, is that it seems so solidly tied to textual content. If the Lenten interpreters retreat to implausible explanations of the actual content of Sonnet 62, they have turned what was originally an important argumentative asset into an embarrassment which must be explained away.

The single numerological coincidence of Sonnets 22 and 68 being forty-seven sonnets apart is insufficient to carry the Dunlopian interpretation against solid historical evidence that Sonnet 62 is a January 1 poem. If Bennett is correct about the historical counter-evidence, the Lenten interpretation flies in the face of the text itself and must be abandoned. Arguments for numerological schemes in literary texts, if they are to be decisive, depend upon piling up so many connections between the proposed numerology and the textual content that the explanation of coincidence becomes highly improbable as compared with the hypothesis of authorial design. Furthermore, such interpretations are highly falsifiable, because they commit themselves to definite parallels between the proposed calendrical or numerological pattern and the content of certain parts of the text. (The Lenten interpretation, for example, commits itself to saying that March rather than January must be represented in Sonnet 62.) If the textual content is shown to be incompatible with the proposed pattern, the numerological scheme is untenable. Without Sonnet 62 working *for* the Dunlopian scheme, that interpretation can boast only one noticeable coincidence to support it—the number of poems between Sonnets 22 and 68. With Sonnet 62 working decisively *against* that scheme, the Lenten interpretation is not only under-determined but refuted.

In terms of the sonnet sequence as a whole, there are several details which serve to corroborate Bennett's interpretation rather than Dunlop's, although they would not be enough to establish that interpretation without her argument about Sonnet 62. Two of these points are elaborated by Carol Kaske, who attempts to re-establish what she calls "the traditional chronology."[22] According to this chronology, the sequence represents a period of about a year and a half.[23] Sonnet 22 is indeed an Ash Wednesday sonnet, and 68 an Easter sonnet, but they are Ash Wednesday and Easter of two different years, with Sonnet 62 marking January 1 of 1594 and falling in between. Kaske makes the interesting suggestion that Spenser eliminates reference to the Easter following the 1593 Ash Wednesday in order to portray the entire earlier part of the courtship (before the lady returns his love) as one long Lent.[24]

Kaske and Bennett both use Sonnet 60 in support of this chronology,[25] but Kaske emphasizes it more in her argument, claiming that Sonnet 60 is "contradict[ed]" by the Lenten interpretation and so must either be ignored by Lenten interpreters or explained implausibly, as, she says, A. Kent Hieatt does.[26] In Sonnet 60, lines 5–8, the speaker says,

So since the winged God his planet cleare
    began in me to move, one yeare is spent:
    the which doth longer unto me appeare,
    then al those fourty which my life outwent.

This chronological statement would indeed refute the Lenten interpretation *if* it were assumed that the courtship begins within the sequence. For according to the Lenten interpretation, the speaker is saying on approximately March 23, 1594 that "one yeare is spent" since he has been in love. But the sequence begins just before a New Year's Day sonnet (number 4) which must refer to January 1 because it is addressed to "New Yeare forth looking out of Janus gate."[27] If Sonnet 4 represents New Year's Day, 1594, it has been less than a year by March 23, 1594; on the other hand, if it represents New Year's Day of 1593, it has been more than one year by the time we get to Sonnet 60.

There is, however, another way of interpreting the sequence which saves the appearances for the Lenten interpretation while dealing with Sonnet 60. Dunlop gives this solution in his notes to Sonnet 60 in the Yale edition. "As he [the speaker] is already in love with Elizabeth at the beginning of *Amor*, we can make no inference from this line about time values in the sequence."[28] In other words, Dunlop is taking the statement that "one yeare is spent" to refer to some entirely unspecified point in time before the beginning of the sequence. Apparently, then, he is also taking it that Sonnet 4 is about January 1 of 1594, making it less than a year between the beginning of the sequence and Sonnet 60 (only, in fact, a little under three months); this causes no contradiction if the speaker is imagined to have been in love for some time—close to ten months—before the beginning of the sequence.[29]

Although this reasoning does deal with the problem after a fashion, and so refutes Kaske's initial claim that Sonnet 60 cannot be made compatible with the Lenten interpretation, Dunlop's reading is not so obviously correct as it might appear. While it is true, in a sense, that the speaker is apparently "already in love" with Elizabeth at the beginning of the sequence, he nevertheless refers in Sonnet 2 to the beginning of his love:

> Unquiet thought, whom at the first I bred
>   Of th'inward bale of my love pined hart
>   and sithens have with sighes and sorrowes fed,
>   till greater then my wombe thou woxen art . . .
>
> (Lines 1–4)

In so speaking of the beginning of his love near the beginning of his sequence, Spenser had precedent in Petrarch, who speaks of his first sight of Laura in Sonnet 3 of the *Canzoniere*. Sidney does the same thing in *Astrophil and Stella*, telling at length how Love first "gave the wound, which while I breathe will bleed" in Sonnet 2. And if the speaker is going to go to the trouble to tell us that "one yeare is spent" in Sonnet 60, it is at least a little more likely that this reference serves some structural purpose for the sequence itself than that it merely refers to some unspecified point before the beginning of the sequence. Even though he is "already in love" in Sonnet 1, the sequence may be meant to represent the entire period of his *self-conscious* service to the "winged God," as defined by the time from which his "unquiet thought" began to "breake forth" in poetry (Sonnet 2, line 5).

Or, more plausibly still, he may be speaking only approximately. We do not know for how long he has "already been in love" with the lady at the beginning of the sequence. The beginning of the sequence may correspond *roughly* with the beginning of his love, so that, although he is reflecting on a love which has already begun by the time the sequence begins, we cannot entirely discount Sonnet 60 when dealing with time values within the sequence (particularly not to the extent of nearly a ten-months' gap, as the Lenten interpretation requires us to do).

Indeed, it is some support for the traditional chronology that the sequence begins shortly before a reference to the coming of the New Year, and that we are told that "one yeare is spent" since he has been in love shortly before another poem about a new year, Sonnet 62. As Kaske emphasizes, the traditional chronology at least allows Spenser a full twelve months between his two new year sonnets.[30] Since the traditional dating is a chronology but not, per se, a numerology, it does not depend upon highly specific numbers of sonnets coming between or before certain other sonnets. Hence, there is no problem for the traditional chronology in the inexactness of the parallels—the fact that the first New Year's sonnet is four sonnets after the beginning of the sequence whereas the second one comes two sonnets after the reference to "one yeare."[31]

Another aspect of the sequence which Kaske stresses concerns the two parallel spring sonnets, or *reverdies*—Sonnets 19 and 70. These sonnets are so widely spaced as to throw doubt upon the thesis that they both refer to the same spring.[32] And they must refer to the same spring according to the Lenten interpretation because of the constraints placed upon the Lenten chronology by Sonnet 60. As we have seen, Sonnet 60 forces the Lenten chronologer to take Sonnet 4 as referring to January 1, 1594. Hence, both Sonnets 19 and 70 must be about the spring of 1594.

Kaske is right to indicate that the content of the poems fits better with their being so widely spaced if we imagine a longer courtship

in between than a little over forty days.[33] In Sonnet 19 the lady is a
rebel against Love:

> But mongst them all, which did loves honor rayse,
>   no word was heard of her that most it ought,
>   but she his precept proudly disobayes,
>   and doth his [the cuckoo's] ydle message set at nought.
> Therefore O love, unless she turne to thee
>   ere Cuckow end, let her a rebell be.
>
> (Lines 9–14)

But in Sonnet 70 she is a potential servant, who is merely drowsy
and must be roused with a *carpe diem* in order to join Love's train:

> Goe to my love, where she is careless layd,
>   yet in her winters bowre not well awake:
>   tell her the joyous time wil not be staid
>   unless she doe him by the forelock take.
> Bid her therefore her selfe soone ready make
>   to wayt on love amongst his lovely crew:
>   where every one that misseth then her make
>   shall be by him amearst with penance dew.
> Make hast therefore sweet love, whilest it is prime,
>   for none can call againe the passed time.
>
> (Lines 5–14)

Taking the two poems to be welcomes to two different springs is
therefore a good explanation of the lady's contrasting attitudes to
Love as well as of their spacing.[34]

But it must be emphasized that these two points—the "one yeare"
reference in Sonnet 60 and the spacing of the two spring sonnets—are
of secondary importance for the argument against the Lenten interpretation. The evidence for dating Sonnet 62 as January 1 is much
more crucial. Kaske, apparently unaware of Bennett's article when
writing her own (she states that the Lenten interpretation has been
accepted by critics "with only Lever dissenting"[35]), discusses these
lesser points but makes only a brief reference to the dating of Sonnet
62. She says that taking Sonnet 62 to refer to March 25 would "contradict the text," but does not elaborate on this claim, and mentions

in argument only the non-textual fact that E.K. endorses a January 1 beginning for the year.[36] Kaske is even willing to say that an interpretation which takes *both* Sonnet 4 and Sonnet 62 to be March New Year's is "almost as valid as the traditional chronology I am defending,"[37] although she does indicate that such an interpretation of Sonnet 4 is not really "credible."[38]

But Bennett's argument about Sonnet 62, unless it can be refuted directly on historical grounds, actually leaves the traditional chronology as the only tenable option. It is something of a scholarly disgrace that Bennett's gauntlet has remained so long neglected by those she challenged. Dunlop's brief mention of her hardly counts as a response, since he presents no contrary evidence regarding the customs surrounding New Years' Day in the 1590s. Perhaps this is because there is no contrary evidence he could provide.

In any event, it is fairly obvious that Dunlop, at least, has made no effort to search for such evidence and to refute Bennett's claim directly. Perhaps he believes that the forty-seven sonnet difference between the Ash Wednesday and New Year's sonnets is in itself so strong an argument for his thesis that he would be justified in any amount of ad hoc finessing required to explain away the text of Sonnet 62, without loss of evidential weight in favor of the Lenten chronology. As we have seen, this is not true. Is it possible that such a willingness to disregard or reinterpret the text whenever necessary is what Dunlop means by contrasting himself with Bennett on the grounds that she illustrates an extreme of the "historical, representational" approach to interpretation? Will historical facts be displayed triumphantly when they seem to support a numerological thesis (as the fact that the new year *could* be dated from March 25 seemed to support Dunlop's thesis), while contradictory facts are ignored on the grounds that we must not be overly historical?

Whatever the reason for the twenty-seven years' delay between Bennett's original article and the attempt in this essay to revive it, it is time for numerological interpreters of the *Amoretti* to return to the textual and historical basis which gave their claim its apparent force in the first place. We must see whether that basis can bear the weight they wish to put on it, whether, indeed, such a basis exists at all. Thomas Roche is prepared to claim that Dunlop's Lenten interpretation "was a major breakthrough in our reading of sonnet sequences."[39] Roche's entire approach in his book is, to some extent, based upon the insights he believes we have gained because of Dunlop's "breakthrough." It is important, then, to Renaissance scholarship, beyond the study of Spenser, that we re-examine the question of whether there has been any such breakthrough. Dunlop's interpretation must be established against serious criticisms of it before we use it to draw large-scale generalizations about the Renaissance sonnet sequence. If critics are not willing thus to reconsider and possibly to revise earlier opinions, they will be guilty of ignoring the canons of evidence in literary scholarship for the sake of retaining what is simply too important to them to give up. And that way lies critical dishonesty and chaos.

NOTES

1. Thomas Roche, *Petrarch and the English Sonnet Sequences* (New York: AMS Press, 1989), pp. xii-xiii. Roche speaks of Dunlop's "pointing out" the Lenten sequence, and refers to his "brilliant detection of a submerged Lenten subtext" which "was a major break-through in our reading of sonnet sequences" (p. xiii).

2. G. K. Hunter, "Unity and Numbers in Spenser's *Amoretti*," *Yearbook of English Studies* 5 (1975): 39.

3. Alexander Dunlop, "The Unity of Spenser's Amoretti," in *Silent Poetry*, ed. Alastair Fowler (London: Routledge and Kegan Paul, 1970), 153–69.

4. William A. Oram, et al., eds., *The Yale Edition of the Shorter Poems of Edmund Spenser* (New Haven, CT: Yale University Press, 1989), hereafter cited as *Yale*, 595.

5. Carol V. Kaske, "Spenser's *Amoretti and Epithalamion* of 1595: Structure, Genre, and Numerology," *English Literary Renaissance* 8 (1978): 271–95.

6. Josephine Waters Bennett, "Spenser's *Amoretti* LXII and the Date of the New Year," *Renaissance Quarterly* 26 (1973): 433–36.

7. Alexander Dunlop, "The Drama of *Amoretti*," *Spenser Studies* 1 (1980): 107–20.

8. Ibid.: 107.

9. Ibid.: 119.

10. Bennett, 433.

11. Dunlop, "Drama," 108.

12. Dunlop, "Unity," 154.

13. Bennett, 433–34.

14. Dunlop, "Unity," 154. But see below, note 27.

15. Bennett, 435.

16. Further textual evidence for a January 1 date which Bennett does not mention is also provided by lines 9–12. Although "the glooming world" and "these stormes which now his beauty blend" might refer to some specific bad weather in March of 1594, it is at least somewhat more probable that the reference is to the general fact that it is winter in January but that there is hope of the coming spring and improvement in the "glooming" weather. It is after the winter solstice that the days begin to lengthen, becoming less "gloomy." The new year is portrayed here as being like the sun, sending forth a "gladsome ray." Again, the poet is probably speaking of the absence of sunlight in January and the hope of more sunlight to

come as the year goes on. (Spenser makes a similar reference to the darkness of winter in the January New Year's poem, Sonnet 4, saying that the New Year is "calling forth out of sad Winters night,/fresh love, that long hath slept in cheerless bower" [lines 5–6].)

17. Bennett, 435.

18. Ibid.

19. It might be possible, if somewhat tendentious, for the Dunlopians to dispense with the problem of the term "new year" by arguing that the entire phrase, "New Year's Day", never occurs in Sonnet 62. To do so would be to contradict Dunlop's earlier use of the phrase "New year" as evidence of a January 1 dating for Sonnet 4, but since he is apparently no longer so confident even of the January 1 date for Sonnet 4 (see below, note 27), he might not mind abandoning this earlier evaluation of the evidence for that date.

20. Dunlop, "Unity," 154–55.

21. Ibid., 155.

22. Kaske, 293.

23. Not "a few years" as Dunlop states ("Unity," 155). See Bennett, 436.

24. Kaske, 294.

25. Bennett, 436.

26. Kaske, 293–94.

27. As mentioned above, Dunlop used to take the extremely obvious evidence of the phrase "Janus gate" (and the other textual evidence in the poem) at face value; in his earlier article, he says that Sonnet 4 is "unambiguous," ("Unity," 154). By 1989 Dunlop had, for some reason, abandoned this sensible confidence to say instead that the imminence of spring mentioned in lines 9–10 "may indicate a March new year" (*Yale*, 602). But he seems to have no particular numerological motive for this change of position.

28. *Yale*, 636, footnote to Sonnet LX, line 6.

29. I wish here to forestall accusations of "biographical interpretation" which may be leveled against this part of my discussion. The reader should notice my careful use of such phrases as "the speaker" and "is imagined to have been in love." Even if one is scrupulously "New Critical" and refrains from assuming that Spenser himself was actually in love for a certain amount of time when he wrote Sonnet 60, we can just as easily talk about "the speaker" and discuss the chronology of the sequence as a fictional entity. The same problems remain, for the fictional speaker's year-long love, mentioned in Sonnet 60, must then be made consistent with the date which we assign, in this fictional chronology, to Sonnet 4.

30. Kaske, 294.

31. Kaske is aware that the "one yeare" problem can be logically solved by beginning the love outside of the sequence. In response, she re-emphasizes the importance of the gap between the two new year's sonnets and between the two spring sonnets. Carol V. Kaske, "Rethinking Loewenstein's 'Viper Thoughts,' " *Spenser Studies* 8 (1987): 328–29, note 1.

32. Kaske, "Spenser's *Amoretti and Epithalamion*," 294.

33. Ibid.

34. It is interesting to note here that, near the beginning of his 1970 article, Dunlop lists six sonnets which are "clearly associated with calendar events." Although Sonnet

4 and the two spring poems, Sonnets 19 and 70, are part of the list he gives, the thesis he goes on to develop does nothing with these references to calendar events, only with those sonnets which serve directly to support his argument. (Hunter [40] makes a similar point to mine.)

35. Kaske, "Spenser's *Amoretti and Epithalamion*," 293.

36. Ibid., 294.

37. Ibid., 295

38. Ibid., 295, n.37. Joseph Loewenstein ("A Note on the Structure of Spenser's *Amoretti:* Viper Thoughts," *Spenser Studies* 8 [1987]) makes a much worse error in evaluating the relative importance of different arguments against the Lenten interpretation. While he does make some attempt to respond to Kaske's objection regarding the "one yeare" reference in Sonnet 60 (318), he actually seems to consider it a *defect* of her traditional chronology that it involves a rejection of the Lady Day interpretation of Sonnet 62: "But in order to defend this appealing reading Kaske is *obliged* to reject Alexander Dunlop's association of . . . Sonnet 62 with Lady Day . . ." (316–17, italics mine).

39. Roche, p. xiii.

ALEXANDER DUNLOP

Sonnet LXII and Beyond

*L*YDIA McGREW'S interest in the reading of *Amoretti* which I developed three decades ago is gratifying. Her perception that that reading "is taken as an unassailable given in contemporary Spenserian scholarship" is, fortunately, not entirely accurate; since then we have seen numerous insightful and valuable readings, some related to mine, others divergent. Seeing criticism as a continually revisionary communal discourse, I have welcomed work that rejects or disputes mine, such as that of Bennett, Hunter, Kaske, or McGrew, as well as work that extends or revises mine, such as that of Hieatt, Gibbs, Johnson, Prescott, Larsen, Loewenstein, Roche, or Thompson.[1] I hope my neglect of the Bennett piece has not been due to a desire to suppress it or to "critical dishonesty." After it appeared in 1973 I prepared a correction for *Renaissance Quarterly*, but, as the editors felt that the arguments on both sides were already "available to the scholarly world for evaluation"and as Bennett died in 1975, I dropped it. As no one had published work expressing interest in Bennett's claim between then and the *Shorter Poems* edition in 1989, I saw no justification for devoting space to it there.

The particulars of Bennett's argument have always seemed to me unessential quibbles, but McGrew, Roche, and I having arrived by our three separate ways at this meeting place, I shall undertake to put an end to the "scholarly scandal" by responding succinctly to those points McGrew finds most salient. Bennett's "most important point," McGrew believes, "is that joyful New Year's celebrations were customarily associated in the Renaissance with January 1 and were not similarly customary for Lady Day." McGrew, following Bennett, skews the issue from the outset by capitalizing "new" and "year" to lend specious plausibility to the claim that the allusions of LXII can only be to New Year's Day. But "the weary yeare his race now having run,/The new begins his compast course anew" seems to me to refer not to a *day*, but to the *process of change* from one year to the next, a process more strongly associated with March 25 than January 1.[2]

As for the "joyous New Year's celebrations," we know from *Epi-thalamion* that Spenser could throw a good party, but that does not appear to be what happens in LXII; Gibbs finds that "the mood of IIII is light and carefree, whilst that of LXII is relatively serious and contemplative."[3] Indeed LXII records a moral and spiritual rededication in response to or in accord with the comforting news of the Annunciation. The other three references to the year—"the old yeares sinnes" (line 7), "the new yeares joy" (line 9), and "old yeares annoy (line 14)—are even less to a specific day, describing rather the poet's emotional and, I think, spiritual experiences and expectations. The other customs Bennett adduces, those of New Year's resolutions and of prognostication of the fortunes of the coming year according to the weather on New Year's Day, are corollary to the idea of annual renewal and in various forms are associated in most cultures with the new year on whatever date it is celebrated. Neither Bennett nor McGrew offers evidence that these notions were exclusively linked with January 1.[4] That association is not made elsewhere in Spenser, and whatever the calendrical associations of these customs, it is not hard to imagine that Spenser may have wished to draw on them by analogy in a sonnet dealing with change.

Louis Martz in his brilliant 1961 *Amoretti* article, untainted by the notions of calendar symbolism in question here, identified LXII as a point of change in the sequence.[5] I suggest that even without reference to the ecclesiastically-derived "Year of the Incarnation"[6] we can recognize in the change signaled at LXII a spiritual dimension in keeping with the context established by XXII and LXVIII. The lover speaks of the "old yeares sinnes" and of "the faults with which we did offend."[7] He now resolves to amend his life, change his mind, eschew sins, and flee faults. The word "then" in line nine suggests that the act of penitence described in the second quatrain must precede the "new yeares joy" described in the third quatrain. Repentance is made a specific condition of the "new delight" which is to come. The concept, the diction, the tone seem to me perfectly appropriate to the system of calendar symbolism I identified in 1967. However self-qualifying or even self-subversive his systems may be, Spenser was clearly a militantly and contemplatively Christian poet with a lifelong interest in calendar symbolism; the assumptions and methods of *Amoretti* as I have described them are entirely in keeping with his work generally. Given the nature of the poem and of Spenser's general poetic practice, given the fact that LXII is the beginning of the second half of *Amoretti and Epithalamion* when we count stanzas of the anacreontics and the *Epithalamion* as units, and given that LXII announces a new year and a new attitude on the part of the lover, does it make sense to deny that, through the elaborate intricacy of the placement of LXII in relation to IIII and LXVIII and to the calendar of 1594, it announces also, in marking the beginning of the process of Christian revelation and of Holy Week, the New Evangel?

On the other hand, the observation of New Year's Day on January 1 was understood to be pagan in origin.[8] We would expect the custom most prominently and unambiguously associated in Elizabethan England with January 1, that of New Year's gifts, to figure in an argument concerning customs related to New Year's Day, yet the absence of any allusion to this custom in LXII is not noted by Bennett or McGrew. Bennett's claim demands an explanation of why Spenser, to suggest New Year's Day, should have relied on doubtful and ambiguous allusions rather than more obvious ones. Most important, Bennett does not sufficiently develop her alternative reading to suggest why Spenser should have alluded to New Year's Day at all.

It may be useful to ask what is at stake in all of this. Bennett appears to proceed from a strong sense of personal decorum; she gathers and arranges her evidence chiefly to verify her feeling that "a courtship during Lent would be both very short and rather improper." She reasserts this claim from her opening paragraph in her concluding sentence.[9] Bennett's notion of propriety rests comfortably and unselfconsciously on a base of what some would now label old historicism. She wants to show that we are dealing with sincere love poems by an individual who lives in what we recognize as normal linear time according to what E.K., in his elaborate justification for beginning *The Shepheardes Calender* with January ("which beginneth not the yeare"), calls "the simplicitie of commen understanding."[10] McGrew shows no interest in the propriety issue—it is, after all, the new millennium—but otherwise is committed to the comfortable commonsensical positivism she finds in Bennett. Despite the medievalism of her title, McGrew's inspiration appears to be the courtroom trial, so prominent in our culture in recent years. Her insistent references to "evidence," "facts," even "historical facts" lead inexorably to the directive "guilty" in her penultimate sentence. McGrew evaluates Bennett, but undertakes no research to verify Bennett's assertions, perhaps on the supposition that facts are facts. Doctrinally, Bennett and McGrew appear to share a commitment to writing as interior or exterior speech and a corollary resistance, in the Protestant tradition, to spatial and figurative interpretation.

My 1980 effort to propose a model of layered structuring for reading *Amoretti* appears to have left McGrew and others unconvinced. That model, influenced by Ingarden's notions of the literary work as a stratified formation, seemed to me then to have the advantages of resembling structurally the allegorical character of Spenser's vision and of encompassing multiple modern viewpoints in a larger structure. I still think it had those advantages, but the perspectives of my own work of 1969 and 1980 as well as of McGrew's essay in this volume seem to me needlessly narrow now in the context of a critisim that has learned to encompass the forces of a broader material, social, and intellectual history, a development that I think well befits the poet of arguably the most grandly comprehensive vision in literature. I hope that in the new delights of such criticism we will neither abandon the study of numbers and structures, for there is much to be done in that way, nor cease to question each other's readings.

NOTES

1.   Josephine Waters Bennett, "Spenser's *Amoretti* LXII and the Date of the New Year," *RenQ* 26 (1973):433–36; A. Kent Hieatt, "A Numerical Key for Spenser's *Amoretti* and Guyon in the House of Mammon," *YES* 3 (1973): 14–27; G.K. Hunter, "Spenser's *Amoretti* and the English Sonnet Tradition," in *A Theatre for Spenserians*, ed. Judith M. Kennedy and James A. Reither (Toronto: University of Toronto Press, 1973), 124–44 and "Unity and Numbers in Spenser's *Amoretti*," *YES* 5 (1975): 39–45; Donna Gibbs, *Spenser's Amoretti: A Critical Study* (Brookfield VT: Scholar, 1990); William C. Johnson, *Spenser's Amoretti: Analogies of Love*, (Lewisburg, PA: Bucknell University Press, 1990); Carol V. Kaske, "Spenser's *Amoretti and Epithalamion* of 1595: Structure, Genre, and Numerology," *ELR* 8 (1978): 271–95 and "Rethinking Loewenstein's 'Viper Thoughts'," *SSt* 8: 325–29; Kenneth J. Larsen, *Edmund Spenser's Amoretti and Epithalamion: A Critical Edition*, (Tempe, AZ: Medieval & Renaissance Texts & Studies, 1997); Joseph Loewenstein, "A Note on the Structure of Spenser's *Amoretti*: Viper Thoughts," *SSt* 8 (1987): 311–23; Anne Lake Prescott, "The Thirsty Deer and the Lord of Life: Some Contexts for *Amoretti* 67–70," *SSt* 6 (1985): 33–76; Thomas P. Roche, Jr., *Petrarch and the English Sonnet Sequences* (New York: AMS, 1989); Charlotte Thompson, "Love in an Orderly Universe: A Unification of Spenser's *Amoretti*, 'Anacreontics,' and *Epithalamion*," *Viator* 16 (1985): 277– 335. The list is meant to suggest, rather than exhaust, the range of interests.

2.   Dating from January 1 occurred in popular use and in printed works of popular appeal, such as almanacs, but popular dating practices were very erratic. Henslowe, for example, at times changed the annual date as early as December, at other times not until April. See *Henslowe's Diary*, ed. R.A. Foakes and R.T. Richert (Cambridge: Cambridge University Press, 1961), xxvi and passim. Royal records and some public documents were dated by regnal year beginning November 17. Otherwise those sophisticated enough to date consistently normally did so from March 25. Donne dated his deathbed hymn March 23, 1630; his epitaph reads "EXUTUS MORTE ULTIMO DIE MARTII MDCXXXI." See Izaak Walton, *Life of Dr. John Donne*

in *Izaak Walton's Lives*, ed. Henry Morley (London: Routledge, 1888), 58, 71. So "new yeare" may designate a day, January 1; a regnal year beginning November 17; a year beginning January 1, the popular usage; or a year beginning March 25, the official custom. On Elizabethan calendrical practice in general, see C. R. Cheney, *Handbook of Dates for Students of English History* (London: Royal Historical Society, 1945); Reginald L. Poole, "The Beginnings of the Year in the Middle Ages," *Proceedings of the British Academy* 10 (1921): 113–37; A.F. Pollard, "New Year's Day and Leap Year in English History," *English Historical Review* 55 (April 1940): 177–93; W.W.Greg, "Old Style-New Style," in *Joseph Quincy Adams Memorial Studies*, ed. James G. MacManaway et al. (Washington, D.C.: Folger Shakespeare Library, 1948), 563–69; Theodor Gaster, *New Year: Its History, Customs, and Superstitions* (New York: Abelard-Schumann, 1955).

3. Gibbs, 18.

4. My colleague Ward S. Allen informs me that the belief that a day's weather presaged coming fortunes was at least as clearly associated with Candlemas Day, February 2, the precursor of our groundhog day. See W. Carew Hazlitt, *Faiths and Folklore of the British Isles* (1905; rpt. New York: Benjamin Blom, 1965), volume 1, 87; also Robert Chambers, *Chambers's Book of Days* (Philadelphia: Lippincott, n.d.), 214.

5. "The *Amoretti*: 'Most Goodly Temperature'" in *Form and Convention in the Poetry of Edmund Spenser*, ed. William Nelson (New York: Columbia UP, 1961), 166–67.

6. Greg, 568.

7. Ward S. Allen observes that reading "yeares" also as plural brings out another coincidence of the symbolic and narrative levels of the work: the new years become those of the Christian era and the universal story of salvation is recapitulated in the personal experience of the lover in the particular year 1594. I think that the title of the sequence functions also in just this way. I note also, concerning LXII and perhaps more pointedly concerning Bennett's and Kaske's claims about LX, that Spenser often uses "yeare" figuratively to indicate either a long time or a measured span of time, as, Martz has observed (164), in XXIII, which if read by Bennett's literalist principles might require a $2^1/2$- rather than a $1^1/2$-year sequence.

8. See Greg 566–68, also Gaster 91–92, who notes that four Catholic councils had denounced the practice of exchanging New Year's gifts on January 1 and who quotes from *Antiquitates Vulgares* the 1725 explanation of Henry Bourne that "tho' the ancient Fathers did vehemently inveigh against the observation of the Calends of January; yet it was not because of those Presents and Tokens of mutual affection and Love that passed; but because the Day itself was dedicated to Idols, and because of some prophane Rites and Ceremonies they observed in solemnizing it."

9. Bennett, 433, 436.

10. "The generall argument of the whole booke," *The Yale Edition of the Shorter Poems of Edmund Spenser*, ed. William A. Oram et al. (New Haven: Yale University Press, 1989), 23–25.

Index